Business Cultures in Europe

Business Cultures in Europe
Second edition

Collin Randlesome
and
William Brierley
Kevin Bruton
Colin Gordon
Peter King

BUTTERWORTH HEINEMANN

Butterworth-Heinemann Ltd
Linacre House, Jordan Hill, Oxford OX2 8DP

&. A member of the Reed Elsevier group

OXFORD   LONDON   BOSTON
MUNICH   NEW DELHI   SINGAPORE   SYDNEY
TOKYO   TORONTO   WELLINGTON

First published 1990
Reprinted 1991
Second edition 1993

British Library Cataloguing in Publication Data
Randlesome, Collin
   1. Business Cultures in Europe. – 2Rev. ed
   I. Title
   338.6094

ISBN 0 7506 0872 2

Typeset by Hope Services (Abingdon) Ltd
Printed and bound in Great Britain by Redwood Press, Melksham, Wiltshire

Contents

Contributors

Collin Randlesome is a Senior Lecturer in European Management at the Cranfield School of Management. He has been based at Cranfield since 1972, after holding academic posts at the universities of Erlangen and Basle. He contributed a major section on West Germany to the influential report, *The Making of Managers*, which was later expanded into a book in 1988. In addition, he has worked on an audio-visual German language teaching project aimed at business executives and is the author of articles on aspects of management in Germany.

William Brierley is Associate Head of the School of Languages and Area Studies at the University of Portsmouth, where he has taught Italian and European Studies since 1974. His special areas of interest have included left-wing political culture, the peace movement and trade unions in Italy. He is also interested in computer applications to language teaching and learning. His publications include *Trade Unions and the Economic Crisis of the 1980s* (1987) and *Computers as a Tool in Language Teaching* (1991) (with Ian Kemble).

Kevin Bruton was appointed to a new Chair in Spanish at the University of Stirling in 1990, after previously holding lecturing posts at the University of Salford, Heriot Watt University and Middlesex Polytechnic. He has considerable marketing management experience in industry, and has published widely on modern Spanish poetry, on politics and business culture in Spain and on language teaching methodology. He has held many appointments and sits on the National Council of the International Higher Education Standing Conference.

Colin Gordon is a Senior Lecturer at the Cranfield School of Management, where he is Deputy Director of the MBA Programme. He contributed the chapter on France to *The Making of Managers* and wrote the sections on doing business in France for a major audio-visual French language teaching project (BBC) aimed at business executives. He spends much of his time developing courses in French business schools and companies and lecturing widely on both French and general European business issues.

Peter King (Professor Emeritus) has retired as Professor of Modern Dutch Studies at Hull University, where he was based from 1976–88 following twenty-four years as a lecturer in Dutch at Cambridge University. He is the author or co-author of a number of publications concerning Dutch language and culture, including *Dawn Poetry in the Low Countries* (1971), *Multatuli* (1972) and *The Netherlands* (1988).

Preface

If a country's 'culture' can be defined as 'the state of intellectual development among a people', then 'business culture' might be held to be 'the state of commercial development in a country'. But the concept of business culture surely embraces this and much more: it also takes in the attitudes, values and norms which underpin commercial activities and help to shape the behaviour of companies in a given country. These companies, in their turn, develop their own individual 'corporate cultures' which, put simply, manifest 'the way we do things round here'.

Implicit in the definition of a country's business culture provided above is the fact that there is no such thing as a single, homogeneous European business culture. Europe contains as many business cultures as it does countries. Although the similarities between the business cultures in Europe are legion, so are the differences.

What are the determinants of the business cultures of European countries? What are the factors affecting the similarities and differences between countries? It is self-evident that the relationship between business and government, the shape and orientation of the economy, the financial institutions, and the trade unions all exert a profound effect on the business cultures of all European countries. But is, for example, the attitude of business to green issues equally significant for the business cultures everywhere in Europe? Is, say, the practice of élitism sufficiently widespread to count as a determinant of business cultures in all European countries? The answer in both cases is 'no'. In contrast, the response of business to the completion of the European Community's (EC's) single market is highly significant, since it demonstrates the way in which business hopes to come to terms with the free movement of goods, services, capital, and labour and all that such implies for the future.

In other words, the business culture in a particular country grows partly out of what could be called the 'current business environment' of that country. Yet business culture is a much broader concept because alongside the impulses which are derived from the present business environment figure the historical experiences of the business community, such as the periods of hyper-inflation in Germany in 1923 and again after the Second World War. Of equal significance for the business culture are the future hopes and aspirations, not only of business but also of society at large in a given country. How long, for example, should people work in any one week in the 1990s and beyond?

This books attempts to portray the six major business cultures in the EC as indicated by the size of Gross Domestic Product (GDP) at current prices and exchange rates. Thus the countries included are, in order of GDP size and appearance in the book, Germany, France, Italy, the United Kingdom, Spain and the Netherlands.

The individual chapters in the book concentrate on those determinants of business culture which are held to be significant for the country under review. Some determinants are common to all six countries; others are relevant for several of the six; others still for one or two only.

Each chapter focuses on the business culture of the country concerned in the late 1970s, throughout the 1980s, and into the early 1990s.

The authors have not hesitated to use foreign words and concepts in their chapters because such expressions contribute much to the depiction of the nuances in the business culture of any country. They have, however, been at pains to provide a translation of the term in the foreign language on its first appearance in the chapter.

A conscious attempt has been made to use the common statistical base provided by the Organization for Economic Cooperation and Development (OECD) wherever possible, and especially with regard to leading economic indicators such as growth rates and inflation, so that the reader can make meaningful comparisons between countries. Where common statistics are not available, reputable national sources have been used. Sources have been indicated for all tables.

At the end of each chapter a list of publications has been provided in the form of sources and suggestions for further reading. Here only publications or standard works have been included which might stimulate the reader to delve deeper into special aspects of the business culture in the country under review. These lists should not be regarded as exhaustive.

The authors trust that an understanding of the six major business cultures in the EC will lead to a better appreciation of the structures and strategies of industries, markets, and consumer preferences in the countries covered. While it may not constitute the most important element of a practitioner's knowledge, much that is in the book could make that vital difference between actually gaining a contract or merely coming close.

Preface to the second edition

A business culture does not change quickly, but the business environment from which it is derived, and with which it constantly interacts, is sometimes subject to radical and dramatic transformation.

This is perhaps best illustrated in the case of Germany which, since the writing deadline expired for the first edition at the end of 1989, has experienced economic and monetary union, political union, and the first pan-German elections. The repercussions for business in western Germany have been enormous, beginning with a re-orientation of investment policy for all major companies, and continuing with tax increases for individual Germans in the west to raise the unification levy.

Yet in no way could it be argued that business in western Germany has begun to eschew the attitudes, values and norms which make up the business culture there. In fact, it could be maintained that unification, with all the problems which it has entailed, has obliged business to 'stick to its knitting' and the winning formulae of old.

In stark contrast, the business culture in eastern Germany is at present in a state of transition, gradually moving away from the influences of a centrally, planned economy and towards those of the social market economy. But the pace of the transformation in the business culture there is not rapid, which accounts in part for some of the grave problems currently being experienced in the east of the country.

In effect, the business culture and the business environment in the two former Germanies present such a contrast that it has been decided to reflect this in the current edition with a chapter divided into two distinct parts.

Changes in business culture are, however, not restricted to Germany. All the other countries covered in this book – France, Italy, the United Kingdom, Spain and the Netherlands – have witnessed changes of business culture since the end of 1989, and these are faithfully recorded here.

Similarly, all the statistical tables for the major economic indicators have been updated to the end of 1992.

Finally, a brief Conclusion has been added to this second edition which attempts to bring together just some of the contrasts and comparisons in the rich diversity of business cultures portrayed in this book.

Collin Randlesome
Cranfield School of Management

Acknowledgements

The authors would like to thank the *Financial Times* for permission to quote and refer to the newspaper. They are also grateful to Professor Charles Handy and Pitman Publishing for allowing them to use some of the material from *Making Managers*. Equally, they extend their thanks to the editors of the Price Waterhouse *Guides to Doing Business* in various countries for permission to quote from these works, especially in the sections of the chapters on business and the law. Similarly, the authors are grateful to *The Economist* for permission to quote and to the Economist Intelligence Unit for allowing them to refer to their annual *Country Profiles* and quarterly *Country Reports*, which are available for all the countries covered in the book. Finally, they thank Times Newspapers Limited for permission to use material which originally appeared in *The Sunday Times* and *The Times*.

Permission to reproduce tables and statistics has kindly been given by *Acquisitions Monthly*, the Bundesanstalt für Arbeit, BSL Business Strategies, the Central Bureau voor de Statistiek, NV SDU, Datastream International, *Employment Gazette*, and the OECD, whose publications are available through HMSO.

KIEL •
SCHLESWIG-
HOLSTEIN

MECKLENBURG-
WEST POMERANIA

Schwerin •

Hamburg ■

Bremen ■

LOWER SAXONY

BRANDEN-
BURG

Hannover •

Berlin ■
Potsdam •

SAXONY-
ANHALT

NORTH RHINE-
WESTPHALIA

Düsseldorf •

Halle •

SAXONY

Bonn •

HESSE

Erfurt •

THURINGIA

Dresden •

RHINELAND
PALATINATE

Wiesbaden •
Mainz •

SAAR
LAND

Saarbrücken

Stuttgart •

BAVARIA

BADEN-
WÜRTTEMBERG

München •

1 The business culture in Germany

Collin Randlesome

Part I Western Germany

Introduction

Most companies in western Germany are not in business to make profits which will subsequently be distributed to shareholders as dividends: they are in business to generate surpluses in order to stay in business.

This aspect of business culture goes a long way towards explaining much that puzzles the foreign observer. Above all, it reflects the conservatism and strength which are such outstanding features of the business culture in this part of the country.

Conservatism and strength manifest themselves in:

- Some 40 per cent of GDP still being derived from manufacturing industry, including construction, in the third-largest economy of the OECD countries.
- DM 65 billion per annum, or approximately 2.9 per cent of GDP, spent on research and development (R & D).
- Private commercial bank commitment to non-financial companies in the form of company rescues and the long-term holding of large amounts of equity.
- The training of some 1,650,000 apprentices per annum, a significant percentage of whom may not be given a permanent position by the company training them.

By any measure of performance, business in western Germany has flourished in the past from adopting a conservative approach but has done so in what could be called conditions of continuous change. However, with shorter product life-cycles, more volatile markets, and increased competition on a global scale – conditions of discontinuous change – concern is being expressed in certain quarters as to whether companies in western Germany are best equipped to face the challenges of the 1990s and beyond.

Criticism has focused particularly on aspects of the business culture such as:

- A tendency of companies in western Germany to be product-led rather than market-oriented.
- Manufacturing companies 'making nails with heads on', i.e. overengineering their products.
- Risk-aversion by large companies, with their preference for straightforward bank funding rather than complex share capital from financial markets.
- Publicity-shyness, especially by small and medium-sized firms which still cling to a legal status that allows them to remain extremely discreet even when they expand.
- Lack of entrepreneurial spirit throughout business, one of the manifestations of which is that western Germany figures at the bottom of the European management buyout league, with only forty-six recorded by the end of 1991.

The Federal government and the governments of the individual Federal states have displayed an awareness of some of these criticisms of the business culture, and a number of policies have been introduced to change this culture. Equally, business is subject to the changes imposed by non-governmental institutions. Finally, the EC's single market and the accompanying welter of legislation are also influencing the ways in which business people in western Germany think and act.

Business and government

The business culture in western Germany is affected inter alia by the attitudes and policies adopted by the Federal government in Bonn, subsequently to be transferred in part to Berlin, and by the governments of the eleven individual Federal states. In general, the relationship between business and government in post-war western Germany has been a function of the political tenets of the party in power and the economic circumstances prevailing at the time. However, the fact that not a single year goes by without important elections being held at Federal or state level contributes to compromises and even inconsistencies between policy-making and implementation.

Federal government

The official policy which all post-war Federal governments in western Germany claim to have espoused, to a greater or lesser degree, is that of the

soziale Marktwirtschaft (social market economy). The policy was established by Ludwig Erhard, initially in his capacity as Allies-appointed Director of Economic Affairs and later as Minister of Economic Affairs in the first four Federal cabinets after the Second World War. Indeed, Konrad Adenauer, the first post-war Federal Chancellor, provided a significant definition of social market economy, which he called: 'A renunciation of planning and the direction of production, labour or sales, but within a comprehensive economic policy which also embraces social measure to ensure the welfare of the population as a whole, including provision for the needy.'

The Federal Chancellor for most of the 1980s has been Helmut Kohl. He came to power in Bonn in October 1982, in a centre-right coalition led by the Christian Democrats (CDU) and their Bavarian sister-party, the Christian Socialists (CSU), with the Free Democrats (FDP) as junior partners. His accession to government marked the end of a thirteen-year period dominated by the Social Democrats (SPD) in centre-left coalitions with the FDP.

The new government under Helmut Kohl promised the people of western Germany the **wirtschaftliche Wende** (economic turnaround). What the country and business needed, according to Chancellor Kohl, was less state intervention of the type which had become commonplace in the last thirteen years, and more market instead. From the very outset of his Chancellorship, he pledged to put the market back into the social market economy! In addition, he stated that business had to rediscover the spirit of entrepreneurship which had made possible the **Wirtschaftswunder** (economic miracle) of the 1950s and 1960s.

Indeed, the state of the economy facing Helmut Kohl's government at the end of 1982 was anything but miraculous, with the leading indicators showing:

- Economic growth at minus 1 per cent in real terms (only the third minus figure since 1950).
- Inflation above 5 per cent (a very high figure for western Germany).
- Current account in equilibrium.
- Unemployment at an annual average of 1.85 million per month, or 8.8 per cent of the working population.

In addition, investment was down by 5 per cent on the previous year and private consumption down by 2 per cent, both in real terms.

As the *1983–1984 OECD Economic Survey on West Germany* observed: 'the new Federal government faced the difficult task of pursuing its medium-term goal of reducing government expenditure and intervention in order to achieve a durable improvement of growth and investment conditions, while at the same time supporting activity in the short run, the economy being in deep recession. In shaping the budget for 1983, it relied mainly on the retrenchment measures already proposed by its predecessor. But it raised the cuts in social expenditure to a total of DM 12 billion and placed limits on wage and salary increases of civil servants. In addition . . . it proposed improved incentives for private investment which, however, were to be financed by tax increases.'

An upturn in business activity began early in 1983 after a recession which had lasted for approximately three years. This recovery was initially due to domestic demand but became increasingly sustained by external requirements for goods made in western Germany. The rise in consumer prices fell to about 3 per cent per annum; the current account stayed in surplus; and even unemployment began to fall slightly.

Despite the favourable economic developments in the course of 1983, the CDU party lost the state elections in Hesse that year. CDU delegates were criticized in their constituencies for the Federal government's rigorous cost-cutting policies; business people began to demand more positive policies to take advantage of the economic upswing; *Bild*, the daily newspaper with the largest circulation in western Germany, demanded in its largest banner headlines: 'Do something, please!'

Cuts in Federal government subsidies, a clampdown on excessive bureaucracy, and a total overhaul of the tax system had already been promised, but in the autumn of 1983 Helmut Kohl launched a further initiative. In what has become known as his Marshall Plan speech, he proclaimed to a meeting of the CDU/CSU parliamentary party the privatization of state holdings in certain companies. The sale of Federal assets was intended to reduce the Federal borrowing requirement and at the same time to release the venture capital with which to subsidize future-oriented technologies. Shortly afterwards, Federal Finance Minister Gerhard Stoltenberg announced the partial privatization of the Federal holding in Veba, a large conglomerate company. Veba was to be only the first of several companies to be privatized. Others mentioned at the time were Volkswagen, Lufthansa, the national carrier, and Schenker, the Bundesbahn's very profitable subsidiary specializing in freight forwarding.

The tone had been set and the policies put in place, but what were the results by the time of the next Federal elections in January 1987?

Despite four years of cyclical upswing, real growth had averaged only just over 2 per cent, and unemployment had risen to in excess of two million or almost 9 per cent of the workforce. However, the current account had shown healthy surpluses, and inflation had remained low, at an average of less than 2 per cent over the period.

But what of other Federal government policies? As *The Economist* commented on 7 May 1988: 'In most other OECD countries, governments – conservative and socialist alike – have been deregulating, privatizing and cutting taxes.' They had been keeping the state out of business's decisions and letting markets, not governments, steer economic developments. In this respect, 'Helmut Kohl's government has done very little. Many of its subsidies to farmers, steelworkers, shipbuilders, coalminers and the rest have increased.' The cash subsidies alone were estimated to cost the tax-payer the equivalent of 2.2 per cent of GDP in 1988.

The price for all this profligacy in the public sector was that rates of business and personal taxation were still extremely high. Despite the promised 'tax reform of the century', pandering to special interest groups had delayed the much-needed legislation. In 1987, western German companies were confronted with a total tax of 70 per cent on retained earnings, double the rate in the United Kingdom. An unmarried employee with an annual income equivalent to $20,000 sacrificed 40 per cent of it in tax and social security contributions – between 10 and 20 per cent more than in any other of the five largest OECD economies. The marginal rate for a citizen on a half-average income was 36 per cent, as against only 7 per cent in the United States of America. Reform of the taxation system was completed in 1990, but even then the top rate of income tax was 53 per cent and corporation tax 50 per cent – still some of the highest rates in any of the OECD countries.

Similarly, the Federal government's privatization programme was very much a stop-start affair up to 1987. A start was made in 1984 with the sale of part of the government's holding in Veba for DM 800 million, thus reducing ownership from 43.85 to 30 per cent. In March 1985, a concrete action plan for further sales of Federal-held assets in thirteen companies was tabled by the government. But a year later it was decided to proceed with the sale of part of its holdings in only five cases. In June 1986, VIAG, a chemicals, energy and aluminium company, offered 40 per cent of its shares to private shareholders and was partly privatized, thus raising DM 766 million. But the jewels remained in the crown: the Federal government retained 75 per cent of the Lufthansa shares and 20 per cent of Volkswagen.

As far as business interests are concerned, one of the most positive aspects of Helmut Kohl's Chancellorship up to 1987 was probably the redistribution of wealth which was achieved. Taking into consideration taxes, social security contributions and the rate of inflation, the incomes of employees actually fell in the period from 1982 to 1985 by DM 17.5 billion as calculated on the basis of 1985 figures. Over the same period, the incomes of entrepreneurs rose by DM 100 billion. In 1986, profits also rose much more steeply than wages. However, business failed to invest proportionately. Of the net increase in revenue enjoyed by business from 1982 to 1986, which amounted to DM 154 billion, only DM 22 billion was reinvested in capital goods and plant in western Germany. Outward investment flourished instead, especially towards the United States, and worries about **Industriestandort Deutschland** (western Germany as a location for industry) began to appear – themes to which future reference will be made (see pages 14–16).

Helmut Kohl enjoyed at least two strokes of good fortune in the period from October 1982 to the end of 1986. Only three months after he first came to power, the recession ended and business activity began to pick up again. Then, in 1985 oil prices decreased dramatically – an extremely favourable development for an economy such as that of western Germany which is so dependent on imported sources of energy. He perhaps enjoyed a third piece of good fortune over the same period in that the SPD, the main opposition party, was in massive disarray.

Nevertheless, in the Federal elections held in January 1987, Helmut Kohl's CDU and its sister-party, the CSU, recorded their worst performance since 1949, winning only 44.3 per cent of second votes cast. Fortunately for Chancellor Kohl, the SPD, with 37.0 per cent of second votes also performed badly – their worst results since 1961. His coalition partners, the FDP, did well, with 9 per cent, while **Die Grünen** (The Greens) enjoyed their best Federal election results ever, polling 8.3 per cent.

Despite the disappointing results, the centre-right coalition returned to power with the slogan **Weiter so** (more of the same). The policies remained as before, but so did many of the problems:

- An economy which, despite an impressive surge towards the end of the decade, tended to grow only slowly compared with other OECD countries.
- Unemployment at around two million.
- A state pensions scheme which was becoming increasingly hard to fund from current contributions on account of the rising dependency ratio.
- Disturbing demographic trends of an ageing and declining population, the influx of immigrants from eastern Europe and eastern Germany notwithstanding.

In April 1989, Helmut Kohl reshuffled his cabinet, changing three of the top four posts, together with five others. Gerhard Stoltenberg was removed as Finance Minister and replaced with Theo Waigel of the CSU; Hans Klein, also of the more conservative CSU, became minister spokesman responsible for the projection of the Chancellor's personal image. But neither changes in personalities, let alone refurbished images, were to provide the boost for the economy.

In the summer of 1989, the country looked back on too many years of economic underperformance (Table 1.1). Growth of about 2 per cent per annum was too poor a performance to solve the underlying economic difficulties but too good to engender the kind of crisis atmosphere of 1982, when major changes had suddenly become possible. The OECD suggested

Table 1.1 *Western German growth rates (1979–92)*

	(%)
1979	4.0
1980	1.5
1981	0.0
1982	−1.0
1983	1.9
1984	3.3
1985	1.9
1986	2.3
1987	1.8
1988	3.4
1989	3.3
1990	4.5
1991	3.2
1992	0.8

Source: OECD

that western Germany could be trapped in a vicious circle where slow growth today leads to slow growth tomorrow. Average growth of just over 2 per cent was depressing business confidence and discouraging investment. If the low rate of investment had persisted, fiscal injections even of the modest variety envisaged in the tax reform could have resulted in major inflationary impulses.

It was generally agreed that western Germany's shortcomings lay not so much in the macro-economic policies which had been pursued by Helmut Kohl's three governments but in their failure to overcome constraints on the supply side of the economy, such as the over-regulation of services and labour-market rigidities – themes to which subsequent reference will be made (see pages 17 and 33).

By September 1989 at the latest, business and government alike were occupied with matters even more weighty than the inadequacies of the economy. Much of eastern Europe, including eastern Germany, was in turmoil (see pages 62–63). On 28 November 1989, Chancellor Kohl wrong-footed the political opposition in the Federal parliament with his presentation of a ten-point plan for overcoming the division of Germany. Though he had stated publicly only one year earlier that he would probably not see unification in his lifetime, Kohl and his CDU/CSU alliance seized the unity initiative from the outset.

The steps leading to unity are indicated in a later section of the chapter (see page 62), but it is worth pausing here to consider the results of the pan-German elections, held in December 1990. Helmut Kohl's CDU, together with their CSU allies, won only 43.8 per cent of the votes, fewer than they would have gained in any Federal election in western Germany since 1949. The reluctance of Germans to vote overwhelmingly for the Unity Chancellor appeared initially to indicate a lack of gratitude. After all, Helmut Kohl had demonstrated deft handling of most of the difficult problems surrounding unification in late 1989 and throughout 1990. Moreover, the economy in western Germany was continuing the surge begun two years earlier. Yet Germans, particularly in the west of the country, did not trust his pledge not to raise taxes to pay the unification levy.

The FDP, the second largest party after the elections in the centre-right government, had pursued a shrewd campaign, emphasizing the risk of a lurch to the right if the CDU/CSU achieved an absolute majority. The result was their best showing in a Federal election since 1961, and more representation in the government coalition.

The SPD gained only 33.5 per cent of all votes cast, their worst outcome since 1957, mainly as a result of their initial lukewarm stance on German unity. Yet perhaps the biggest surprise of all was the demise of The Greens in the west, who fell below 5 per cent of the vote.

After the elections, the burning question in the relationship between government and business became the one relating to payment of the unity bill. Two months earlier, on German Unity Day, 3 October 1990, Helmut Schlesinger, deputy president of the Deutsche Bundesbank at the time (see also page 74), had proposed a radical solution to the cost of unity. He suggested a privatization programme far more comprehensive than the country had ever witnessed before, which would even include the Deutsche Bundesbahn (German Federal Railways). He calculated, for example, that privatizing Deutsche Bundespost Telekom, the telephone system in western Germany, would raise at least DM 20 billion, more than twice as much as the privatizations in Kohl's first three governments. However, in December 1990, the government ruled out even the partial privatization of Telekom on the grounds that it would be contrary to the **Grundgesetz** (Basic Law) since the entire company would have to be transferred from the civil service to become a private firm.

Instead, Chancellor Kohl was obliged to renege on his election promise not to raise taxes in order to fund unification. Amid continuing doubts concerning the real costs involved, measures were announced in February 1991 to raise over DM 22 billion, in roughly equal amounts, through higher unemployment contributions and the surcharge on income tax which came into effect on 1 July 1991, the first anniversary of Gemu (German economic and monetary union). Additional petrol taxes were expected to raise DM 6 billion, with some DM 2 billion arising from higher telephone charges and a tax on insurance premiums. According to the German Taxpayers' Association, the increases added at least DM 1000 to the amount which the average wage-earner hands over to the state every year. Moreover, it was announced that the standard rate of VAT would be raised from 14 to 15 per cent as from the beginning of 1993.

According to an Allensbach opinion poll held in August 1991, 64 per cent of business people, politicians and civil servants in western Germany were confident that the country as a whole would experience an 'economic miracle' in the next three years – before the Federal elections in December 1994. Some 55 per cent of their counterparts in eastern Germany held the same belief. Yet among ordinary Germans only 24 per cent of westerners and 25 per cent of easterners were confident of a dramatic recovery for the country by the end of 1994. Given the parlous state of the economy in the east (see pages 67–71) and the fact that the west had entered a recession by early 1992, the sagacity of ordinary Germans must be admired.

State governments

Western Germany's decentralized political organization means that individual state governments have more power than in comparable nations. Although the official Federal government policy is non-intervention in business, one administrative level lower, in the eleven Federal states, the regional politicians are enthusiastic interventionists on behalf of business interests in their particular domains.

The result is that often state policies clash openly with Federal policies. The sale of the Federal government's 20 per cent stake in Volkswagen was announced in 1983, confirmed in 1985, but did not finally take place until March 1988. One of the reasons for the delay was because the company is the largest employer in Lower Saxony, and the CDU state government was reluctant to entrust the carmaker's fortunes to the whims of private shareholders. Indeed, the State of Lower Saxony still retains approximately 20 per cent of the Volkswagen shares.

Equally, Franz Josef Strauss, the late Minister President of Bavaria, objected most vigorously to the planned sale of the Federal government stake in Lufthansa. He suspected that a lower Federal stake-holding might result in the company changing its aircraft-purchasing policy from Airbus to Boeing. This would have affected the fortunes of Deutsche Airbus GmbH, which is located just outside Munich.

Perhaps, however, the leading proponent of state interventionism was the former Minister President of Baden-Württemberg, Lothar Späth. He persuaded many high-technology businesses to settle in his state by estab-

lishing centres of excellence for research into biotechnology and information technology, such as those at the universities of Stuttgart and Ulm. In
addition, he inevitably came to prominence in the Daimler-Benz series of
takeovers (AEG, Dornier, MTU and MBB) since the car company has its
headquarters in the state capital of Stuttgart. Minister President Späth was
especially active during the Dornier takeover because the aerospace company is based at Friedrichshafen in the south of Baden-Württemberg. In the
course of protracted negotiations, Lothar Späth smoothed the way for the
Dornier family and Daimler-Benz to finalize the transaction, which duly
occurred when the car company bought 66 per cent of the shares. The State
of Baden-Württemberg itself secured 4 per cent.

In sharp contrast, SPD's Oskar Lafontaine is beset by low-technology
problems in the Saarland, where the Arbed-Saarstahl steel company has
made huge losses. The remedy which he has recommended for Arbed's
problems is nationalization. This has been turned down repeatedly by the
centre-right Federal coalition, not only on grounds of cost but also because
the proposal runs contrary to its own fledgeling privatization policy.
Increased Federal subsidies have thus proved necessary to keep Arbed in
business – much to the chagrin of the Federal government, with its avowed
preference for a hands-off approach in the relationship between government and business.

Business and the economy

The business culture in western Germany is dominated by considerations
of manufacturing and the wealth-creation associated with it. Indeed, the
Wohlstandsgesellschaft (affluent society) in present-day western Germany
depends to a very large extent on the high-quality output of its manufacturing industries. High-value-added products, high technology and technical innovation are fundamental to maintaining this affluence, and almost
all large companies devote a considerable amount of their resources to R &
D, in many cases as much as 10 per cent of turnover. Manufacturing,
including construction, accounts for some 40 per cent of GDP in the west –
significantly more than in any of the other large OECD economies.

Western Germany is not only successful at **Technik** (the art and science
of manufacturing useful artefacts), it is also most adept at selling these
manufactured items abroad. Products made in western Germany enjoy a
larger share of world trade than those of any other country. Nevertheless,
the country's manufacturing industries are not without their problems; nor
are they being supported by a dynamic services sector, on account of the
supply-side rigidities already noted.

Manufacturing

Even by the late 1960s, manufacturing was by far the most important sector of the economy in western Germany, the contribution of agriculture having diminished steadily since the war until by 1992 it was responsible for only some 1.4 per cent of GDP. The traditional smokestack industries were severely affected by the oil crises of 1973 and 1979, though many of them have since staged impressive recoveries. Before the first oil shock, western Germany had to import 55 per cent of its energy requirements, but nation-wide conservation measures cut energy consumption by roughly 6 per cent from 1973 to 1983. This part of Germany is fortunate to possess large coal deposits, so it also shifted away from oil-fired power stations towards coal-fired and nuclear ones, until The Greens came to prominence.

As *The Economist* of 26 November 1988, recalled, energy conservation policies could not fully protect the manufacturing sector of the economy from the two oil crises. In addition, western Germany's goods-producers had to discard energy-intensive capital equipment and dismiss workers. Manufacturers of chemicals, pharmaceuticals, cars and aircraft all emerged from the oil-exacerbated downturn by installing more energy-efficient plant and reducing their workforces.

Consequently manufacturing industry's investment in new machinery and plant increased as a proportion of GDP between 1974 and 1984. While GDP rose at an average rate of 2 per cent per annum, private industry's investment in new equipment increased by almost 3 per cent a year. As has already been noted, this level of private investment has not been sustained since 1984.

Western Germany's major manufacturing industries are:

Iron and steel

In conjunction with coalmining, the iron and steel industry was one of the largest in the country until the mid-1970s. Thereafter, it suffered a sales crisis on account of oversupply on the world market. The receipt of public subsidies has since helped to promote the modernization of the industry, but its future will depend to a large extent on the world demand for special steels.

Mechanical engineering

Despite the predominance of small businesses, mechanical engineering is one of the largest sectors of manufacturing industry. In 1986, it employed a million people and turned over DM 165 billion. At the end of 1990, the exports of this sector were worth $64 million per annum.

Vehicle building

This is the largest single sector of manufacturing industry in the country in terms of turnover. In 1986, turnover amounted to DM 195 billion, with a workforce of 845,000. After Japan and the United States, western Germany is the third-largest car-manufacturer in the world. In 1986, 4.3 million cars and 300,000 utility vehicles such as trucks and buses were made, as well as 66,000 motorcycles and 3.3 million bicycles. At the end of 1990, exports of road vehicles were accounting for some $72 million every year.

Electrical engineering

With a turnover of just under DM 162 billion in 1986 and more than a million employees, the electrical industry figures prominently in the group of major industries in terms of its importance to the national economy. Siemens is the flagship of this sector, Europe's largest and the world's fourth-largest company in electrical and electronic products. In 1987, Siemens had 41,000 R & D staff and a research budget of DM 6.2 billion. At the end of 1990, exports of electrical engineering products were responsible for $45 million a year.

Precision instruments and optical goods

The structure of the precision engineering and optical goods industry, as of the watch and clockmaking sector, is accounted for by medium-sized companies. With some 130,000 employees, they constitute together one of the smaller sectors, but in international terms are among the largest in the world. These industries invest between 6 per cent and 10 per cent of turnover per annum in R & D in an attempt to safeguard competitiveness.

Chemicals

The chemical industry is the most important sector of the basic materials and production-goods area of western German industry. Of its workforce of 586,000 in 1986, almost one-third were employed in the three largest chemical companies in the world, Hoechst, BASF and Bayer. In addition, there are large numbers of medium-sized companies. In 1986, the chemical industry in western Germany turned over DM 168 billion. At the end of 1990, exports of chemicals had risen to $51 million per annum.

All of these industries have achieved success on account of the western German fascination with Technik and painstaking attention to the detail of the product – to such a degree in fact that manufacturing companies have been widely criticized for being product-oriented, even systems-oriented, rather than market-led. Yet these industries could not have been so successful for so many years with so many products without heeding the message of the markets. Nor has success been confined to the domestic market or even Europe.

The contribution of exports to output is greater for western Germany than for any other large OECD member. It rose from roughly 22 per cent of GDP in 1967 to 35 per cent of GDP in 1990. As could be expected from a predominantly manufacturing economy, manufactured goods constitute the major element, 79 per cent in 1990, of total exports. Similarly, western Germany's proportion of world exports increased from 11 per cent in 1967 to 14 per cent in 1990. The record within the EC is even more impressive: it was responsible for 54 per cent of all intra-community exports in 1990, compared with 44 per cent in 1967.

It cannot be denied, however, that manufacturing industry in western Germany is experiencing its share of problems. While it is not possible to share the criticisms of one American commentator – that western Germany is only skilled at making last century's products, and could soon become the new Sick Man of Europe because it is deficient in information technology and biotechnology, the industries which, it is alleged, are about to dominate the next century – certain aspects of the manufacturing economy do give grounds for concern.

One problem which has come into sharper focus recently is that of the **Nord-Süd Gefälle** (north–south divide). During the time of the economic miracle, the states in the north and west were the boom areas, the base for the smokestack or heavy industries. The south was less economically developed. But even then, western Germany's north–south divide was small compared with Italy's or the United Kingdom's (see pages 165–166 and 214–216). As the *Financial Times* noted on 28 October 1987: 'Though it is true that the north contains the problem industries like steel and shipbuilding, while the south has a large share of the high-technology businesses, German industry is so regionally diversified that there is no shortage of examples to counter the cliché.' All the same, a glance at the state-by-state growth rate increases and unemployment statistics over a sufficiently large timescale, and working roughly from north to south, does reveal a disturbing trend (Table 1.2). The national average growth rate over the period 1973–91 was 46.2 per cent, and the national average unemployment rate 7.5 per cent.

The embryonic north–south divide has been promoted by the interventionist activities of politicians at the Federal state level in the south. As already noted, the policies of former Minister Presidents Lothar Späth in Baden-Württemberg and Franz Josef Strauss in Bavaria attracted new sunrise, or high-technology, companies to the southern states. Their efforts were undoubtedly aided by the proximity of such celebrated holiday areas

Table 1.2 *Regional growth and unemployment rates (1973 and 1991)*

	Growth rate (1973–91) (%)	Unemployment 1973 (%)	1991 (%)
Bremen	30	2.0	10.7
Hamburg	35	1.0	8.7
Schleswig-Holstein	49	2.0	7.3
Lower Saxony	55	2.0	8.1
North Rhine-Westphalia	35	2.0	7.9
West Berlin	36	2.0	9.4
Saarland	43	2.0	8.6
Rhineland-Palatinate	49	2.0	5.4
Hesse	56	2.0	5.1
Baden-Württemberg	55	1.0	3.7
Bavaria	66	2.0	4.4

Source: OECD/Bundesanstalt für Arbeit (Federal Labour Office)

as the Black Forest and the Alps, since ever more Germans in the west are beginning to favour the **Freizeitgesellschaft** (leisure society) for the erstwhile **Leistungsgesellschaft** (high-performance society) – further themes to which reference will be made (see pages 41–42).

Far more disturbing than the north–south divide are the worries being expressed in certain quarters on the topic of **Industriestandort Deutschland** (Germany as a location for industry). Critics have concentrated on the surge of western German investments abroad, a dearth of inward investment, and the failure of companies in western Germany to invest within their own borders.

Over the period from 1985 to 1987, outward investment by western German companies totalled DM 51 billion, almost double the DM 27 billion recorded for the three preceding years. Taking 1986 as an example, the following major acquisitions were made:

- Hoechst bought Celanese for DM 5.7 billion.
- Bertelsmann, the publishing company, purchased Doubleday and RCA for DM 1.2 billion.
- Volkswagen paid DM 1.1 billion for Seat.
- Allianz, the insurance company, spent DM 1 billion on Cornhill.

Indeed, by early 1992, the United Kingdom had become the most favoured location for western German outward investment in Europe, lying second worldwide only to the United States. Direct investment in the United

Kingdom totally DM 23.5 billion, most of it by manufacturing industry (see page 219).

The scale of these investments need not necessarily be interpreted as evidence of a deterioration in western Germany's attractiveness as an industrial site: it could also be regarded as proof of stronger integration into the world economy. It might be held that it is only natural for companies to secure their export-built market shares abroad by investing on the spot. A company whose sales in another country reach a certain level may find it advantageous to invest there in order to move closer to the foreign market by shifting production facilities. This would reduce transport and distribution costs or avoid existing and impending protectionist legislation.

But western Germany itself has lost some of its appeal as a target for direct foreign investments from abroad. Though GoldStar, the Korean electronics company and Alps, another electronics firm but from Japan, set up in western Germany in 1988, total inward investment from 1978 to 1988 was only DM 28.5 billion. Total Japanese investment in western Germany was approximately one-fifth of that in the United Kingdom. The reasons most frequently quoted for this lack of inward investment, and for the slowdown in investments in western Germany by domestic companies, are the high levels of corporate taxation, which have already been noted, and the burden of labour costs.

In 1991, overall labour costs in western Germany overtook Switzerland's as the highest in the world, averaging DM 36 per hour. Though this is not so much due to increases in gross hourly rates as to the sustained rise and relative weight of indirect labour costs, it does have a deterrent effect on companies considering western Germany as a location in which to invest. In 1987, for example, manufacturers had to provide an extra DM 83.10 for every DM 100 of salary.

However, wage costs around the world cannot be compared without taking into account the differences in productivity. During the 1980s, productivity growth in western Germany averaged 2.5 per cent per annum, compared with 4 per cent during the 1960s. It came down as the technical progress in the capital equipment lapsed. In the 1980s, unit labour costs increased in real terms, and profitability diminished as the rise in real wage costs was not fully matched by productivity improvements. The deceleration in investment growth is clearly linked with the decline in profitability, and western Germany remains a relatively high-cost economy.

The debate about Industriestandort Deutschland flared up again in 1992. The issues were, as ever, high wages and social costs, lower productivity, high taxes and curtailed working hours (see also pages 43–45). The anxieties reappeared after one of the longest booms in post-war western Germany, which was artificially extended and then suddenly halted by unification and its financial consequences. Companies throughout the west of the country began to downsize their workforces. Siemens announced several thousand redundancies in 1992, with more to follow in 1993. BMW said it would cut 3000 jobs, while Mercedes-Benz sprang the biggest surprise of all by stating that it would seek up to 20,000 redundancies between 1992 and 1996 and move production units outside western Germany.

A company's choice of business location is not influenced by rates of corporate taxation and real unit labour costs alone. The innovation potential of an economy, its degree of technological sophistication, and the know-how it produces are all determined to a large extent by the size of its R & D outlays. Here, western Germany occupies a top position internationally. Annual research spending totalled some DM 65 billion in 1988, of which some DM 17 billion was earmarked by the state or by institutions of higher learning for basic research.

Perhaps, however, western Germany's most important competitive advantage lies in its system of business education and vocational training, which is regarded as a model by many other industrialized countries, and as such deserves separate consideration later in the chapter (see pages 45–50).

Other factors working in favour of Industriestandort Deutschland are its position in the centre of Europe, and its modern infrastructure. Geographically, western Germany lies at the heart of the European Community, with ready access to a market of more than 320 million consumers. In addition, it also represents a gateway to the east, i.e. to the economies of the former COMECON countries which have become increasingly attractive in the light of *glasnost* and *perestroika* and the momentous changes in eastern Europe. Moreover, in many countries of central and eastern Europe, an area of erstwhile German economic influence, the German language has remained the *lingua franca* of business.

The all-embracing concept of the 'infrastructure' becomes clearer, in terms of its contribution to the smooth running of manufacturing industry, if one looks at the individual elements. Among other things, the western German infrastructure consists of a total of 173,000 kilometres of regional and national roads, including 8400 kilometres of motorways whose total length is due to be increased to more than 10,000 kilometres by the year 2000. Infrastructure also implies 30,000 kilometres of railway track, of which 11,000 have been electrified, together with a rolling stock consisting of some 10,000 locomotives, 14,000 passenger carriages and over 30,000 goods waggons. The centrepiece of the western German passenger service for the 1990s is its inter-city express (ICE), linking Hamburg in the north to Munich in the south, launched in June 1991. The service aims to be the hub of a pan-European high-speed train network twice as fast as cars and half as fast as aircraft. Part of the infrastructure is accounted for by 4400 kilometres of navigable waterways, 1400 kilometres of the total being made up of canals. The Rhine–Main–Danube Canal now provides a link between the North Sea and the Black Sea. Infrastructure includes 1700 kilometres of pipeline through which 60 million tonnes of crude oil are pumped each year, and eleven international airports of which Frankfurt-am-Main is one of the busiest in the world.

References to the infrastructure imply references to services, and current concern about Industriestandort Deutschland could linger in the minds of potential foreign investors and domestic businesses alike, unless substantial progress is forthcoming in this sector.

Services

The services sector in western Germany is much more regulated than manufacturing industry, and growth in the economy as a whole could be higher if regulations and red tape did not cramp entrepreneurial verve in services. Alfred Herrhausen, the late Chairman of the management board at the Deutsche Bank and regarded by many as the most powerful man in western German business until he was killed by a terrorist bomb in November 1989, stated in *The Wall Street Journal* of 6 July 1988: 'Deregulation and open markets are a must: they would promote competition and stimulate demand.'

Against this background, it is interesting to note that growth in private services has increasingly exceeded growth in manufacturing. At two percentage points, the differential over the period from 1979 to 1985 was larger than in most other OECD countries. At the same time, however, the rise in service employment was small by international comparison.

Growth in service employment has been held back by a whole series of market regulations. Of these, restrictive practices in insurance, road haulage, telecommunications and the guild-based crafts system, as well as limitations on shop-opening hours, are prime examples. Insufficient access to venture capital may also have prevented the creation of small firms, which are particularly important for the provision of services.

Typical of the restrictions in this sector of the economy are the regulations on the retail trade, western Germany's third largest 'industry' employing 2.4 million people in some 380,000 outlets. As the *Financial Times* of 28 October 1987, pointed out, ever since the **Ladenschlußgesetz** (Shop Opening Hours Act) became law in 1956, retail establishments were obliged to follow a strict business routine. Shops could open anytime after 7 a.m., though some only began business much later, but all had to close by 6.30 p.m. during the week and by 2 p.m. on all but one Saturday per month. However, the Act was full of loopholes. Petrol stations, for example, could remain open later as long as they did not sell any goods beyond motorists' immediate needs – a proviso which was subjected to the most liberal of interpretations by almost every petrol station in the land. Newspaper kiosks were also allowed to remain open at different hours. Yet, there were even stranger exceptions with special rules for retailers in spa towns or shops in rural areas, which could sell certain items on Sundays.

In September 1989, the Federal government reformed the Act to let shops stay open until 9 p.m. on Thursday evening every week, but opposition built up to even this short weekly extension. The trade unions objected on social grounds. They argued that especially their women members would suffer through longer working hours and spend less free time with their families. Similarly, the opposition to the change included some of the largest retailers. Wulf Ridder, spokesman for Kaufhof, did not believe that there was any pressing need to stay open longer. Other retailers pointed to the large number of shops outside city centres which close early even on the once-per-month Long Saturdays, when they could stay open longer if they wanted.

Progress in the liberalization of the whole services sector looks like being slow. The Federal government set up a deregulation commission but it did not report until 1991. The commission's findings attracted considerable criticism not just from trade unions but also from the CDU, the dominant partner in the ruling coalition. Perhaps the main hope for deregulation lies with the further development of the EC's single market, which should enforce liberalization on a grand scale, even in western Germany's almost sclerotic services sector.

Business and the law

Society in western Germany is ordered and orderly. The concept of the **Rechtstaat** (rule of law) is constantly emphasized, and there are regulations and decrees governing most aspects of life. Indeed, it has often been maintained that the Germans in the west assume that anything not specifically permitted by the law is **verboten** (forbidden)!

The business culture takes the law equally seriously. Business activities are carried out, in general, within a clearly-defined framework, the **Handelsgesetzbuch** (Commercial Code). In addition, western German companies employ large numbers of law graduates to make sure that neither they nor their business partners break any of the rules. While it is not true that 'business by litigation' is the order of the day, firms in western Germany can be characterized as litigious by persuasion, and legalistic in many of their dealings.

To give an impression of the legal framework within which firms operate, and thus how the law affects the business culture, it will suffice to describe in brief the most important corporate entities found in a business context. A more comprehensive account can be found in the Price Waterhouse *Guide to Doing Business in Germany*, but the essential points are as follows:

1. Aktiengesellschaft – AG (corporation)

This is the most advanced form of company in western Germany and the only one whose shares can be traded on a stock exchange. There are approximately 2000 AGs in the country. The AG is regulated by the **Aktiengesetz** (Corporations Act) of 1965. At least five founder shareholders must sign the statutes before a notary public. These persons then appoint the **Aufsichtsrat** (supervisory board) and the **Vorstand** (management board), which together file the formation documents with the trade register at the local court in the district where the company is to have its main seat. The minimum share capital for an AG is DM 100,000, of which at least 25 per cent must be paid in. All shares have a specified par value, the legal minimum of which is, in most cases, DM 50.

Basic to the concept of an AG is the transferability of its shares. Thus bearer shares predominate. Some AGs also issue registered shares with limitations on transferability. Others have inserted clauses in their company statutes to the effect that no single shareholder may at any time exercise more than a certain percentage of total voting rights. A typical example of this is one of the large banks in western Germany whose statutes restrict such to 5 per cent. Others still have adjusted their statutes to ensure that non-voting shares are also issued. Provisions such as these limit the transferability of shares and make it virtually impossible for investors to buy up large quantities of an AG's shares on the stock market. They cannot in effect purchase a controlling interest and then take over the management of the company.

The management organs of an AG are the management board, the supervisory board and the Annual General Meeting (AGM) of shareholders. Although company statutes define the relationship between these three bodies to a certain extent, the Corporations Act and other legal provisions do set a general framework. The management board is responsible for the daily management of the company. The other two bodies have certain rights to information on management activities but have little power to restrict the management board in its dealings with third parties. The management board must consist of at least one member. If the total number of employees in the company exceeds 2000, one member of the management board must take prime responsibility for personnel matters. This **Arbeitsdirektor** (personnel manager) is required to devote him/herself full-time to employee matters, which means that all companies requiring a personnel manager need a management board of at least two.

The main responsibilities of the supervisory board are to monitor, guide and advise management on behalf of the shareholders. The supervisory board can consist of between three and twenty members, depending on share capital and the number of employees. In companies with fewer than 500 employees, all the members of the supervisory board are appointed by the shareholders. If the company employs between 500 and 2000 persons, one-third of the supervisory board members are appointed by employees. In larger companies, employee representation rises to one-half. This aspect of the business culture will be discussed more fully later in the chapter (see pages 40–41).

The responsibilities of the shareholders at the AGM are limited in scope. They decide by majority vote on: appointment of their representatives on the supervisory board; appropriation of profits; dismissal of members of the supervisory and management boards; appointment of auditors; changes in statutes; and liquidation of the company.

2. Gesellschaft mit beschränkter Haftung – GmbH (private company)

This form of corporate entity, which has a limited number of shareholders, is generally selected for family businesses and similar firms where the owners wish to exercise close personal control. The legal formalities, particularly at the formation stage, are less complex than for an AG. Moreover, prior to 1 January 1987, the GmbH was not subject to statutory audits. For all financial years beginning on or after this date, companies' audit requirements depend on size criteria only, and not on legal form.

Private limited companies are formed under the **GmbH-Gesetz** (Limited Liability Companies Act) of 1892 as amended. Many of the provisions regulating the actual operation of a GmbH are, however, based on other laws. The result is that most of the differences between a GmbH and an AG have effectively disappeared.

The formation of a GmbH is simpler than for an AG, but statutes must still be presented to a notary public. A GmbH may be formed by a single shareholder. The minimum share capital required is DM 50,000, of which one-quarter, but at least DM 25,000, must be paid up. A GmbH does not usually issue share certificates, but when it does these must be registered and cannot be made freely transferable.

The management bodies of a large GmbH and their duties are similar to those of an AG. The management board of the AG is, however, replaced by one or more directors, generally called **Geschäftsführer** (managing director(s)). But this is more a distinction in title than in function. A supervisory board is not usually required for a GmbH unless it regularly employs more than 2000 people, but if one is formed, its duties and functions are similar to those of the supervisory board in an AG.

3. **Offene Handelsgesellschaft – OHG (general partnership)**
   The OHG is a partnership formed on the basis of a partnership agreement. The members may be natural persons or legal entities but they may not exclude themselves from the liabilities of the partnership. Profits or losses are ascribed to the partners as agreed.

4. **Kommanditgesellschaft – KG (limited partnership)**
   This form of partnership is similar to an OHG except that the **Kommanditist** (limited partner(s)) can limit their liability in the partnership's debts to the amounts of their capital contributions. But at least one partner must assume unlimited liability, i.e. the **Komplementär** (general partner(s)). The management of the KG is the sole right and responsibility of the general partner(s). The limited partner(s) are excluded from the conduct of the company's affairs but may object to actions by the general partner(s) if these lie outside the firm's normal business activities.

   In a KG, the general partner may be a limited liability company. If so, the legal designation is amended to **GmbH & Co KG**. This is quite a common device in order to obtain the benefits of a partnership but without incurring legal liability. Thus, the limited partners subscribe for the entire partnership capital and form a GmbH to hold the general partnership share as well as to exercise management control. The GmbH acts here at the direction of its own shareholders and its unlimited legal liability is effectively worthless to an unsatisfied creditor because its only asset is its stake in the partnership's capital. This can, however, be as low as zero.

5. **Gesellschaft des bürgerlichen Rechts – GbR (civil law partnership)**
   In this entity, members agree to share in specified aspects of their own separate businesses. Law firms are a typical example where each partner shares in office costs but otherwise keeps his income as personal earnings.

6. **Einzelkaufmann (sole trader)**
   In such a construction, an individual conducts business as a single owner. His or her liability for the settlement of debts is unlimited. The

trade name must be registered, and a sole proprietor must use his or her full name but may add to it a description of the business.

No contribution on the law and the business culture in western Germany would be complete without mention of the **Prokurist**. He or she – it usually is he – is an employee of an AG or GmbH to whom the power of procuration has been granted by member of the management board in an AG or managing director(s) in a GmbH. This means that he is legally entitled to act for the company in business matters and to bind the firm vis-à-vis third parties. On letters received from AGs or GmbHs, two signatures will be found. The one at bottom left usually belongs to the Prokurist. Without his signature or that of a member of the management board or one of the managing directors, the letter would not be legally binding on the company.

Business and finance

Conservatism and overall strength, which are such outstanding features of the whole of the business culture in western Germany, are nowhere more in evidence than in the major financial institutions. This should not imply, however, that the Bundesbank, the Big Three private commercial banks and the financial markets are without their critics. Nor does it mean that long-delayed reforms of the financial institutions can be postponed much longer. In fact, all the financial service providers are currently under scrutiny from one quarter or another, and radical changes can be anticipated.

The Bundesbank

Even by the late 1950s, the Germans in the west had concluded that money was far too important a commodity to be left to politicians! Established in Frankfurt-am-Main in 1957 by the **Bundesbank Act**, the country's central bank is: '. . . required to support the general economic policy of the Federal government. (But) in exercising the powers conferred on it by this Act it shall be independent of instructions from the Federal government.' This high degree of autonomy has been zealously guarded ever since. Moreover, the Bundesbank has seldom shirked from imposing the policies which it has deemed to be appropriate, even at the risk of incurring the wrath of the political party or parties forming the Federal government at the time.

The Act is also quite specific as to the central bank's duties: 'The Deutsche Bundesbank shall regulate the volume of money in circulation

and of credit supplied to the economy, using the monetary powers conferred on it by this act, with the aim of safeguarding the currency . . .' Both
the independence of the Bundesbank and the stated goal of 'safeguarding
the currency' are a reflection of deep-seated German fears of inflation.

Twice in less than half a century, in 1923 and again after the Second
World War, the Germans suffered from periods of total inflation when,
quite clearly, the currency had not been safeguarded. Memories of these
bouts of hyperinflation are still etched on the popular consciousness. In the
first, workers were being paid their wages twice a day, taking them home
in wheelbarrows, then rushing out to spend their virtually worthless
money before the prices in the shops rose even higher. In the second, the
Reichsmark (RM) had been virtually ousted as the medium of exchange by
the cigarette and the nylon stocking! This bout of hyperinflation was not
terminated until the Currency Reform was introduced in 1948, when the
Deutsche Mark (DM) replaced the RM.

Given these experiences, it is small wonder that the western Germans
should want to leave monetary policy to the professionals, i.e. the central
bankers, and then specifically charge them with the task of 'safeguarding
the currency'. Moreover, the Deutsche Bundesbank's record in controlling
inflation has been extremely good.

Over the period from 1969 to 1992, the rate of inflation in western
Germany exceeded the average rate for all OECD countries in two years
only, 1972 and 1973. In the other years, it has been significantly below the
average (Table 1.3).

The Bundesbank's success in keeping inflation in check has found favour
in a whole succession of OECD reports, which constantly praise the central
bank's skill and pragmatism. Perhaps the most resounding testimony to its
efforts is contained in the *1987–1988 OECD Economic Survey*, which states:
'The sensitivity of the average citizen to inflationary developments and the
negative impact of inflation on the real side of the economy would seem to
be much greater in West Germany than in most other OECD countries. Not
surprisingly, therefore, price stability objectives have always figured at the
top of the policy priorities of German monetary authorities, and the
Bundesbank as the "inflation watchdog" has been constitutionally
entrusted with a high degree of independence. Given both the strong commitment to the maintenance of price stability and the wherewithal to fight
inflation effectively, the German price record has traditionally been better
than generally elsewhere.'

But the Bundesbank has no grounds for complacency. In 1988, a Joint
Finance and Economics Council was set up by the French and West
German governments. The Council is composed of the economics
and finance ministers and central bank presidents of the two countries. It
meets four times a year to coordinate policy, and was established under a

Business Cultures in Europe

Table 1.3 *Western German inflation rates (1969–92)*

Year	(%)	Year	(%)
1969	1.9	1981	6.3
1970	3.4	1982	5.6
1971	5.3	1983	3.7
1972	5.5	1984	2.8
1973	6.9	1985	2.6
1974	7.0	1986	−0.3
1975	6.0	1987	0.3
1976	4.3	1988	1.4
1977	3.7	1989	3.0
1978	2.7	1990	3.4
1979	3.8	1991	4.4
1980	5.1	1992	4.0

Source: OECD

supplementary protocol to the Franco-German friendship treaty. As such, its provisions would have prevailed over those of the 1957 Bundesbank Act which guarantee the western German central bank a degree of autonomy enjoyed by no other. After furious objections from the Bundesbank, and particularly its President at the time, Karl Otto Pöhl, the Federal government inserted a memorandum in the treaty to the effect that the Joint Council is consultative and not decision-taking.

As *The Economist* observed on 13 February 1988, behind this anger lie significant differences between the Bundesbank and the French. The latter complain that the western German central bank does little to support their Franc in the European Monetary System (EMS). Indeed, the French have maintained for a long time that the EMS is in reality a DM-dominated zone in which all the other countries have to bow to the Bundesbank's severe monetary policies. Initially, this strict discipline was appreciated by the French, but with inflation apparently under control in France, it is being interpreted as an obstacle to growth.

The Bundesbank was apprehensive that the Joint Council would be usurped by the French to press their demands for a European Central Bank, a development which was in fact sanctioned by the EC's Maastricht summit in 1991. Karl Otto Pöhl maintained that he would like a European Central Bank some time in the future, but only if it had as much freedom from political interference as the Bundesbank enjoys. He contended that inflation in western Germany had been among the lowest in the world because the central bank had not been obliged to finance deficits incurred by the Federal government or to trim monetary policy to satisfy short-term political expedients. The establishment of a politically-dependent European Central Bank, he concluded, would promote inflation and jeopardize the limited progress which the EMS had made to date.

Among the Bundesbank's major preoccupations in the early 1990s was one with its own structure. The seventeen-strong Bundesbank council, which sets monetary policy, had hitherto included a representative from each of the western German states' eleven individual central banks. In view of unification, the five new eastern states could have each sent a representative, thus swelling the council to twenty-two, and since there could be parity between permanent directors and regional representatives, the size of the council could have increased to thirty-two. Karl Otto Pöhl believed that such would be a recipe for confusion and wanted to see regional representation cut to eight, with a full council up to sixteen.

The matter was unresolved by the time of President Pöhl's resignation in July 1991. For further detail on this event and the Bundesbank's contribution to the Gemu debate, see pages 73–74.

The Big Three

Standard & Poor's, the US credit-rating agency, regularly awards AAA status to only fourteen banks in the world. The Deutsche Bank, the Dresdner Bank and the Commerzbank, western Germany's Big Three private commercial banks, are prominent members of the exclusive AAA Club. Although the west of the country is vastly over-banked, with one branch per every 1370 head of the population and one bank employee for every 100 the Big Three dominate because of their close links with big business.

The ties between the Big Three and large western German manufacturing companies were investigated in the 1970s by the Gessler Commission. It ascertained that the power of these banks lay in the combination of the proxy votes cast by banks on behalf of other shareholders at company AGMs; the tradition of the 'house bank' which keeps a firm linked to one principal lender; the sheer size of the banks' equity holdings; and the many seats on company supervisory boards to which these shareholdings give entitlement.

Concern lingers about the Big Three's influence on non-financial companies. Wolfgang Kartte, President of the **Bundeskartellamt** (Federal Cartel Office), recently affirmed much of the criticism of the Gessler Commission. In 1986, the Deutsche Bank had a direct equity holding of 35 per cent in Phillip Holzmann (construction); over 25 per cent in Daimler-Benz (vehicles); over 25 per cent in Hapag-Lloyd (shipping); over 25 per cent in Karstadt (department store chain); 18 per cent in Horten (another department store chain); and 6 per cent in Allianz (insurance). In the same year, the Dresdner Bank owned direct stakes of 25 per cent or more in Hapag-Lloyd (shipping), Flender Werft (shipbuilding), Gold-Pfeil (leather), Dortmunder Union (brewing) and Heidelberg Zement (cement). Also in 1986, the Commerzbank held more than 25 per cent of Karstadt and further substantial direct stakes in Sachs (ball bearings) and Hannoversche Papierfabriken (paper).

In addition, the Big Three's indirect involvement is sometimes masked by holding companies. The Deutsche Bank had a 75 per cent share of a Frankfurt holding company which owned 25 per cent of Horten; the other 25 per cent of the same holding company belonged to the Commerzbank. Similarly, the Commerzbank held a twice-removed interest in Daimler-Benz through its 25 per cent share in a Munich firm which owned 25 per cent of a holding company, which in its turn held 25 per cent of Daimler-Benz.

The large equity holdings by the Big Three entitle members of their management boards to sit on the supervisory boards of non-financial companies. In the 1960s, Hermann Abs, a former Chairman of the management board at the Deutsche Bank, sat on the supervisory boards of over thirty firms! A law has since been introduced to restrict to ten the number of supervisory board seats which can be held simultaneously by any one natural person. Nevertheless, in the early 1990s members of the management board of the Deutsche Bank had seats on the supervisory boards of BASF and Bayer (chemicals); Siemens, SEL, and AEG-Telefunken (electricals); Volkswagen and Daimler-Benz (vehicles); Thyssen, Klöckner, Rheinmetall and Arbed Saarstahl (steel); Karstadt, Kaufhof and Horten (department store chains); Bertelsmann and Gruner + Jahr (publishing); and many more.

At first glance, it would appear that there is a clear case of conflict of interest for a representative of the Deutsche Bank to sit on the supervisory board of, say, BASF and Bayer, two companies in the same sector of industry. But where is the conflict? The Deutsche Bank has a vested interest in the well-being of both companies: it has put its money into the two companies and wishes to see a return on that investment from both, so it will not be inclined to favour one more than the other. In fact, it could be argued that the presence of the man from the Deutsche Bank actually avoids conflicts of interest.

The supervisory board of a western German company has two sets of clearly-defined duties. It hires and fires the management board, and it gives or withholds approval for major financial decisions. In the example above, let us assume that BASF decides, with the assent of its supervisory board, to make a major investment in plant in Country X. Let us further assume that Bayer has been thinking along similar lines. Once the decision has been taken at BASF, the person from the Deutsche Bank would advise against such action by Bayer, and since he/she is the representative of a major shareholder they would be listened to. Conflict, in the sense of 'needless' competition between two domestic companies, would thus have been avoided.

The presence on large western German companies' supervisory boards of representatives of the Deutsche Bank, Dresdner Bank and Commerzbank is also advantageous in terms of consortium formation and consortium management. Each of the Big Three has shareholdings in a whole range of companies, so consortium formation from within that circle of companies is relatively straightforward. Moreover, in the unlikely event that the companies forming the consortium fail to cooperate satisfactorily, the bank could apply the ultimate sanction.

Approximately 400 large western German companies have banks' representatives on their supervisory boards, and the management boards of these companies welcome their presence. They bring to the manufacturing companies a high degree of financial expertise and, what is more, a high degree of financial security. A predatory takeover bid for one of these large companies is virtually out of the question, though attempts at hostile takeovers are becoming more frequent in the 1990s, because the banks' equity holdings are tantamount to corporate poison pills. In conditions such as these, manufacturing companies can operate, plan, invest and train for the long term, without worrying about the effects of a bad set of figures on their share price.

When subjected to criticisms of excessive power, the Big Three defend themselves in the following terms: as for proxy votes, the banks state that shareholders are at liberty to cast their votes as they see fit, and not to follow the recommendations made by the bank in question. They claim further that many of their large shareholdings in manufacturing companies arose from company rescues, when debt was turned into equity. The bailout of Klöckner & Co in 1988 by the Deutsche Bank was a case in point; the rescue of AEG-Telefunken at the beginning of the 1980s, when a banking consortium stepped in to stop the country's second-largest electricals group going to the wall, was yet another. Finally, the banks maintain that seats on supervisory boards given them better radar with which to detect companies' problems.

Each of the Big Three is already a so-called universal bank, i.e. heavily involved in virtually all aspects of banking, from company financing, personal lending and deposit-taking, to foreign exchange dealing and stockbroking. But one of the latest trends for the private commercial banks has been to diversify even further. Led by the Deutsche Bank, they have entered the fields of mortgage finance, property broking, management consultancy, venture capital, and insurance, with the aim of offering their clients **Allfinanz** (all-inclusive financial services).

At the end of 1988, the Deutsche Bank decided to establish its own life insurance company. Although this move inevitably resulted in a clash with Allianz, Europe's largest insurance company in which it had a major share-holding, the leading member of the Big Three felt it had little choice. In 1987, western Germans invested 30 per cent of their savings in insurance policies, up from less than 20 per cent in 1977, with premium income totalling approximately DM 120 billion. Life insurance made up the largest segment of this premium total, which does not include reinsurance. In March 1989, the Dresdner Bank announced that it was also diversifying into the insurance market through a cooperation with Allianz, which had 14 per cent of the life and 16 per cent of the non-life market.

Diversification at home and expansion abroad, with the Deutsche Bank buying Banca d'America e d'Italia, an Italian commercial bank in 1986, and Morgan Grenfell, the British merchant bank, in 1989, and Commerzbank taking a 10 per cent holding in Banco Hispanoamericano of Spain in 1988, are the hallmarks of the Big Three as they face up to the European Community's single market. They wish to secure their home market against ever-increasing penetration by foreign banks, especially from Switzerland, and to position themselves in expanding markets abroad. There is very little to stop them – certainly not a lack of financial clout.

For information on the 'bank grab' in eastern Germany by the Deutsche Bank and the Dresdner Bank, see page 70.

Stock markets

In sharp contrast to the private commercial banks, the equity markets in western Germany are tiny. Attempts to foster 'equity-mindedness' among business people and investors alike have met with only limited success. Nevertheless, change is in the air, and this is an aspect of business culture which could embrace significant developments in the near future. There is certainly plenty of scope for innovation and reform.

The minor role played by share financing, and the relatively heavy dependence on bank finance, have been typical of industry in western Germany. Broadly speaking, debt-to-equity ratios have traditionally been about twice as high as in the USA or comparable European countries. Of the two million or so companies in western Germany, approximately 2000 are AGs, or public limited companies, with a joint stock capital structure. At the end of 1987, only 574 domestic companies were actually listed on the markets of the stock exchanges, and companies themselves owned about half of the country's equity, often through complicated cross-holdings. The market's capitalization represented only about 20 per cent of GDP, compared to around 85 per cent in the United Kingdom.

The structure of the market reflects the dominance of manufacturing industry, with services underrepresented. According to the *Investor's Chronicle* of April 7 1988, chemicals, including the world's three biggest firms, Hoechst, Bayer and BASF, were responsible for 25 per cent of the market's capitalization. Banks and insurance accounted for another 16 per cent. The vehicles and engines sector (another 16 per cent) was dominated by Volkswagen, Daimler-Benz and BMW. Utilities (11 per cent), electricals (mainly Siemens with 9 per cent) and engineering (9 per cent) were the next largest sectors. Shares in advertising, financial services and consumer goods did not feature significantly.

Apart from a handful of blue chips, most of the shares are traded so infrequently that share prices are fixed for the day, though trading time was extended from two to three hours in 1990. Not surprisingly, therefore, the equity market is small relative to the bond market.

Prior to the start of 1987, the level of equity investment by individuals was low, with only some 5 per cent of households owning shares, and insurance companies holding only about 6 per cent of their funds in equities. In addition, relatively few pension funds exist in western Germany, a remnant of the post-war period when companies had little spare cash for such luxuries. Although individual citizens have traditionally been good savers, squirreling away on average some 14 per cent of disposable income, they have also been conservative and risk-averse. The convention has been for them to put their money into local and regional savings banks or hold government bonds. Since the beginning of 1987, however, the number of shareholders in western Germany has jumped by more than two million to almost six million, or about 10 per cent of the population. Many of the new-comers are in their twenties and early thirties, more cosmopolitan than their parents and less cynical about shares. Moreover, they belong to a generation which, for the first time this century, will inherit wealth not diminished by war or hyperinflation.

The equity market in western Germany is the world's fourth largest and concern about **Finanzplatz Deutschland** (Germany as a financial centre) has at last brought about a number of changes. 1983 was declared the Year of the Share, and eleven new companies were launched onto the market. This number rose to twenty-seven, worth some DM 4.9 billion, in 1986. Before the stockmarket crash in October 1987, nineteen maiden share issues and thirty-seven capital stock increases were made. 1988 saw a mere eight new issues, but this number rose to twenty-four in 1989. There were twenty-three such issues in 1990, and a further twenty-two each in 1991 and 1992. A total of one hundred and sixty-six new issues in ten years may not sound impressive, but this has been accompanied by other significant developments.

One helpful factor was the introduction in May 1987 of a new tier to the market. This might appear strange in a market which already distributes a low turnover over three tiers, but there were good technical reasons. The top tier, **amtlicher Handel** (full listing), involves heavy costs. The next, **geregelter Freiverkehr** (regulated free market), has modest reporting requirements but is hardly policed. The bottom tier, **ungeregelter Freiverkehr** (unregulated free market) has no rules governing disclosure or admission and consists entirely of off-the-floor trading between banks. The new **geregelter Markt** (regulated market) comes immediately below the topmost tier. It involves about half the costs of a full listing, imposes fewer admission and reporting requirements, and is open to firms with a lower minimum nominal capital. The new market immediately attracted more than fifty existing shares and many of 1987's stockmarket newcomers.

The best news of all came for the stock markets in January 1989, when the cabinet approved a bill to revamp the Stock Market Act, which goes back to 1896, and to set up a **Deutsche Termin-Börse** (options and futures exchange). The bill passed through the Federal Parliament in autumn 1989, and the new-look stock exchange and the new futures market started operating in 1990. Although other financial centres have futures exchanges, in western Germany such trading was long regarded as tantamount to gambling. So why the change? The western German experience has been that the absence of an effective hedging instrument was magnifying the swings in their stockmarket, and foreign competition was taking business away from Frankfurt-am-Main. The new Act also implements EC guidelines under which a company accepted for a stockmarket listing in one member state can be listed in western Germany without further bureaucracy.

However, the attraction of Finanzplatz Deutschland has not exactly been enhanced by two particular Federal government policies. In January 1989, it introduced a 10 per cent **Quellensteuer** (witholding tax) for foreign investors, many of whom responded by preferring London as a base from which to deal in western German securities. After intense lobbying, the tax was removed in July 1989. The Federal government also displayed marked reluctance to abolish the notorious **Börsenumsatzsteuer** (stockmarket turnover tax), which was levied at a rate of 0.1–0.25 per cent on all local market secondary trading in western German stocks and bonds. This it promised to do years ago, after it had been called by Karl Otto Pöhl: 'A tax with which to subsidize foreign stock exchanges.' The tax was finally scrapped in early 1991.

The prospects for Finanzplatz Deutschland were given a hefty boost by unification. Western Germany, and through it Frankfurt, so the argument runs, was set to use the strength of the DM and the economy to carve out an ever-increasing share of EC markets. As a bonus, Frankfurt would be able to play a central role in financing and exploiting the economic revolution in eastern Europe. However, the stock exchange enquiry of 1991 into alleged insider dealing and other irregularities at the Deutsche Bank cast a shadow over such ambitions. The lack of criminal sanctions for insider trading abuses, loose rules about what dealers can and cannot trade for their own account, and inadequate safeguards against trading ahead of orders from clients have shaken confidence in the system. Indeed, one former senior employee at the Deutsche Bank was quoted in 1991 as stating: 'As far as trading ethics go, this is still virtually a third-world country.'

Undeterred by such considerations, however, Theo Waigel, the Finance Minister, increased pressure in 1992 on the EC for Frankfurt-am-Main, and not London, to be selected as the seat of the future European Central Bank. The threat was implied that Germany could back out of plans for a single European currency if such were not done. The German government clearly sees the choice of Frankfurt as the price for surrendering the DM. The Bundesbank backed the policy, pointing out that Germany, with 80 million inhabitants, is the largest EC country and yet still not home to any major EC institution.

Business and the labour market

Business activities in western Germany in the 1980s and early 1990s have been conducted against the background of a declining and ageing indigenous population. In contrast, the working population has been increasing, thus contributing to higher unemployment than might be expected from such a strong economy. Special groups within the working population have been disproportionately affected by the scourge of unemployment, and they have been joined on the labour market by large numbers of **Aussiedler** (returnees of ethnic German origin from eastern Europe), **Übersiedler** (refugees from former East Germany) and **Asylanten** (asylum-seekers).

Demographic trends

According to the national census held in western Germany on 27 May 1987, the country had a population of 61,083,000, nearly a million fewer than expected, composed of 31,758,000 women and 29,325,000 men. 4,100,000 inhabitants were foreigners. The actual number of western Germans is declining. In 1970, there were 58,200,000; in 1987, the total was 56,900,000. Over the same period, the number of foreigners in the country rose by 70 per cent from 2,400,000 to 4,100,000, or from 4 per cent to 6.85 per cent of overall inhabitants.

The population is also ageing. In 1970, 23 per cent of the people were under 15 years old; in 1987, the proportion sank to 14.6 per cent, western

Germany having the second-lowest birth rate in Europe (1.4 children per woman). From 1970 to 1987, those aged over 65 increased by a fifth from 13.2 per cent to 15.3 per cent. In 1990, the so-called 'pensioner quotient' or dependency ratio (the number of old-age pensioners in relation to the number of people paying in pension contributions) was 50 per cent. In other words, two persons in employment were making contributions for every retired person receiving a pension. However, in the year 2000 this ratio will be 62 per cent; in 2010, 74 per cent; and in 2030, 117 per cent, i.e. by then every 100 employees paying in contributions will be supporting 117 pensioners!

Unemployment

The declining population figures have not been reflected in low unemployment rates, partly because the working population actually increased from 26.3 million in 1970 to 28.2 million in 1987 (Table 1.4).

Table 1.4 *Western German unemployment rates (1979–92)*

Year	(%)	Year	(%)
1979	3.8	1986	9.0
1980	3.8	1987	8.9
1981	5.5	1988	8.7
1982	7.5	1989	7.9
1983	9.1	1990	7.2
1984	9.1	1991	6.3
1985	9.3	1992	5.9

Source: OECD

There is no single factor that can be blamed for the high percentages of the dependent labour force out of work in western Germany. At the beginning of the 1980s, the effects of the second oil crisis of 1979 and the worldwide recession are clearly reflected in the steep rises in the unemployment statistics. In the mid-1980s, factors common to most OECD countries, such as rapid technological change and fierce Japanese competition, combined with particular western German circumstances to produce in 1985 the worst annual set of unemployment figures since the proclamation of the Federal Republic.

Low growth rates in the western German economy throughout most of the 1980s have already been noted, and these have no doubt been partly responsible for the high unemployment figures. So why was no attempt made to reflate the economy and thus reduce the number of jobless? The test of reflation is whether greater domestic demand would improve output rather than increase prices. In addition, between 1965 and 1985, the country witnessed a rise in the rate of unemployment relative to capacity utilization. This indicates, as *The Economist* observed on 26 October 1985: '. . . that even if capacity were fully used, unemployment might remain high. The reason is familiar: too much capital deepening (men replaced by machines) and too little capital widening (expansion of capacity) because of what the OECD calls western Germany's "real wage rigidity".' In effect, western German wages are less flexible than those in most European countries, and inter-industry wage differentials are virtually negligible.

Towards the end of the decade, higher growth rates did contribute to a decline in the unemployment rates, and between 1983 and 1988 one million new jobs were created. The increase in employment originated in the gradual expansion of the services sector, which has been slower to grow than in most comparable countries on account of the over-regulation already noted. The higher growth rates in western Germany were sustained into the 1990s by unification, with unemployment under 6 per cent in July 1991, the lowest monthly figure for more than a decade. Indeed, in the year from July 1990 to the first anniversary of Gemu, 600,000 jobs were created in the west. This figure contrasts starkly with the enormous number of jobs destroyed in eastern Germany over the same period, and provoked references to Schumpeter's dictum of 'creative destruction' (see page 67).

Guest workers

One segment of the labour market in western Germany which has been disproportionately affected by unemployment during the 1980s and early 1990s is that formed by the **Gastarbeiter** (guest workers) (Table 1.5).

The percentage of unemployed guest workers was lower than the national average until 1974, the year following the first oil crisis. Thereafter, it has always been significantly higher. This is because most of the guest workers are unskilled and thus regarded as more dispensable in a harsher economic climate.

The first agreement on the recruitment and placement of foreign workers was signed with Italy in 1955. Further agreements followed with Spain (1960), Greece (1961), Turkey (1964), Portugal (1967) and Yugoslavia (1968). Although the signing of an agreement with a particular country inevitably confirmed the status quo, it did not mark the date of the arrival of the first immigrant worker from that country.

Table 1.5 *Gastarbeiter (June 1991)*

	Employed	Unemployed
Turks	632,324	66,686
Yugoslavs	325,258	20,754
Italians	171,809	21,581
Greeks	105,201	11,171
Spaniards	60,649	4,330
Portuguese	46,193	2,370
Others	557,106	71,569
Total	1,898,540	198,461
Total Gastarbeiter Population		2,097,001

Source: Bundesanstalt für Arbeit
(Federal Labour Office)

The guest workers originally came to western Germany on account of the push factors in their countries of origin (high unemployment, low wages) and the pull factors prevailing in the Land of the Economic Miracle. Here they perform tasks which indigenous workers are increasingly unwilling to undertake: they work in tedious jobs (assembly lines); in dirty jobs (street-cleaning); in dangerous jobs (coal-mining); and weather-sensitive jobs (building and allied trades).

The guest workers in western Germany are very unpopular with the native population. A poll in 1981 revealed that two thirds of western Germans believed that the guest workers should return to their countries of origin. They are accused of: defiling western cities by living in ghettos; bleeding the country dry by sending home a high proportion of their wages; failing to integrate in society; and above all, taking the jobs that rightfully belong to western Germans.

One of the fundamental reasons for the unpopularity of the guest workers is the mismatch between original expectations and reality. When they first arrived, the guest workers were perceived by many western Germans as a simple solution to a simple problem. The country needed workers, and the guest workers needed jobs. In addition, the guest worker was regarded as ideal economic man. He would be a healthy individual in the prime of life, come to western Germany without family, stay for a few years, and then return home. Young and fit, he would require no medical support services; without a family, he would exert no pressure on social or educational facilities. He would naturally pay taxes and social security contributions, but he would be long gone before any benefits fell due. The reality has been quite different: although some guest workers have returned home, most have stayed. What is more, they have been joined by their wives and children, and they have had further children 'made in Germany'. In fact, they have become a permanent feature of the western German labour force, and are overrepresented in the unemployment statistics through little fault of their own.

Graduates

Another group for whom employment prospects look bleak are the graduates of western German **Fachhochschulen** (polytechnics) and universities. The total number of unemployed graduates passed the 100,000 mark in 1984, and increased fivefold from 1980 to 1985. Among the graduates registered as unemployed in 1985 were:

- 29,546 teachers.
- 22,010 engineers of all types.
- 13,168 economic and social scientists.
- 6,722 natural scientists.
- 3,728 doctors of medicine.
- 3,348 lawyers.

Unemployment rates among graduates in western Germany have continued to rise throughout the 1980s and early 1990s, and there is little hope of improvement in the situation. In fact, matters could get much worse. According to the **Institut für Arbeitsmarkt- und Berufsforschung** (Institute of Labour Market and Vocational Research), there were in this part of the country in 1980 a total of 1,501,000 graduates, 874,000 of whom will still be employed by the year 2000. There will also be a demand for an additional 627,000 graduates on account of retirements in the interim. But by the year 2000, total graduate supply will have reached 2,983,000 leaving 1,482,000 graduates unemployed!

Patterns of graduate employment are also forecast to change. Hitherto, 60–70 per cent of graduates have found employment in the public sector. But in view of government determination to cut public-sector spending at both Federal and individual state levels, it is doubtful whether such take-up rates will ever be achieved again. Economic growth rates would have to be truly phenomenal for the private sector to absorb such large increases in graduate supply.

Perhaps the best prospects for the unemployed graduates lie outside western Germany. Their chances of taking up employment in another EC state are enhanced greatly by the single market, one of the provisions of which is the free movement of labour between member states (see also page 239).

Returnees, refugees and asylum-seekers

The fall in unemployment at the end of the 1980s and in the early 1990s was accounted for by higher economic growth rates prolonged by unification and, to a disproportionate extent, by the labour force under 25 years of age, a group in which the labour supply is declining perceptibly for demographic reasons. This relief for the labour market contrasted with the increase in the labour supply resulting from a strong rise in immigration into western Germany. Thus the number of returnees of ethnic German origin from eastern Europe, numbering 397,075 in 1990, was four times higher than in 1987. The total between 1984 and 1990 was 1,173,541.

Over the same period, the returnees had been joined in western Germany by 732,223 refugees from former East Germany. Their prospects on the labour market are much brighter than those of the returnees because German is their native language, and they are mostly young, skilled, or at worst semi-skilled workers. They are likely to be snapped up very rapidly by western German companies, and their most pressing problem will probably be adjustment to the faster tempo of work in the west.

In 1987, 57,379 asylum-seekers arrived in western Germany, but one year later the figure almost doubled to 103,076. From 1984 to 1990, the total number of asylum-seekers was 853,382. The government maintains that only a fraction of them are victims of political persecution with a legitimate claim to asylum: they are fleeing from hunger and poverty and trying to establish a life in the 'golden west'. Applications for asylum are often submitted, it is claimed, because they ensure that the individual can stay at least for the duration of the recognition process. The government and political parties are looking for a solution which will not clash with subsequent EC legislation.

The total number of immigrants to western Germany in the period from 1984 to 1990 was 2,589,360. Such large numbers have given rise to outbreaks of racial tension and right-wing extremism in both parts of Germany. There were, for example, 128 assaults on immigrants in western Germany in 1990, rising to over 200 in 1991. These attacks have been condemned by all Germany's leading political figures. In addition, a nationwide campaign against racism and enmity towards foreigners was launched in Berlin's Deutschlandhalle in October 1991, with a nine-hour pop concert which was supported by leading sportsmen and entertainers.

Heinrich Franke, President of the **Bundesanstalt für Arbeit** (Federal Labour Office), is pessimistic about medium-term developments on the western German labour market. In an interview with **Westdeutscher Rundfunk** (West German Radio) on 15 February 1989, he said that unemployment would remain at high levels, between 1.5 and 2 million, until the second half of the 1990s. According to Franke, the EC's single market only serves to exaggerate movements on labour markets. Assuming western

German annual economic growth of 2.5 per cent, the number of people in employment by the year 2000 will total just over 26 million, a level similar to 1988.

Business and trade unions

The trade unions in western Germany can look back over the 1980s and early 1990s with a certain satisfaction. Despite the presence in Bonn for much of the time of a centre-right coalition ostensibly committed to free markets and deregulation, the strength of the unions remains virtually unaffected. In 1991, approximately 43 per cent of the dependent labour force were still organized in unions. Although the unions' reputation as entrepreneurs in their own right has suffered severe setbacks, they have achieved notable gains in collective bargaining, and successfully contributed to the system of **Mitbestimmung** (worker co-determination). However, their demands for a 35-hour week and commitments to certain rigid working hours are coming under pressure from employers. Moreover, the trade unions are concerned about the EC's single market. Not only its significance for manufacturing jobs in western Germany but also its implications for the rights and agreements which they have established over so many years have given rise to anxiety.

Organization

After the Second World War, the tradition of a multiplicity of small craft unions was abandoned in western Germany, and blue-collar workers were organized in sixteen large unions, one for each major 'industry'. Every one of these industrial unions affiliated to the **Deutscher Gewerkschaftsbund** (DGB) (Confederation of German Trade Unions), as subsequently did the **Gewerkschaft der Polizei** (GdP) (Police Trade Union).

The DGB was formed in Munich in 1949 and is now located in Düsseldorf. As the umbrella organization for the seventeen industrial unions, its role is to coordinate the activities of the member unions, provide advice on legal and social security matters, contribute to education and training programmes, and to act as spokesman for the unions in national affairs. It is not affiliated to any of the political parties, nor is it associated with any of the churches.

The DGB is run by its Federal Board, which consists of twenty-eight members: the President of the DGB; two Vice-Presidents; the seventeen Presidents of the member unions; and eight full-time DGB officials, who are the heads of its special committees, and two of whom have usually been card-carrying members of the CDU or CSU. The DGB meets every three years for its Federal Congress.

Entrepreneurial activities

One of the features which distinguishes the trade unions in western Germany from those in comparable countries is, or rather was, the extent of their activities as entrepreneurs. Although union subscriptions, at 2 per cent of gross wages or salary, and unions' individual contributions to the DGB, at 12 per cent of revenue, are in themselves modest enough, the DGB and its affiliated unions had succeeded, by the early 1980s, in building up considerable business interests. Through a holding company, they controlled, inter alia, the Volksfürsorge life-insurance company, the third largest of its type in western Germany; Neue Heimat, the biggest construction company in Europe; the Bank für Gemeinwirtschaft, the fifth most powerful non-state bank in the country; and the co op based in Frankfurt.

The trade unions justified these large company interests by referring to them as an attempt at an alternative form of business activity based on the cooperative principle – **Gemeinwirtschaft**. They pointed out that their experiments at capitalism with a human and acceptable face dated back to the early part of the century, with the foundation of the Volksfürsorge in 1912 to combat the high premiums being demanded by existing insurance companies. Neue Heimat, founded in 1950, was established in order to alleviate catastrophic conditions on the post-war housing market.

In the mid-1980s, however, the whole concept of Gemeinwirtschaft received a series of blows from which it has never recovered. Neue Heimat was shattered by allegedly corrupt management practices to such an extent that this massive company was sold in September 1986 to an obscure West Berlin bakery-owner, Horst Schiesser, for a token DM 1. The banks, however, to whom some DM 12 billion were owed, out of total liabilities of DM 17 billion, forced the trade unions to take it back. Because of the financial effect on them of the Neue Heimat affair, the unions were obliged to sell 51 per cent of the Bank für Gemeinwirtschaft to the Aachener und Münchener insurance group.

Mismanagement on a massive scale, including alleged presentation of falsified balance sheets, credit fraud, and tax evasion shook another union-owned company, the Frankfurt-based co op, in 1988. Total debts were estimated at some DM 600 million, and a consortium of foreign banks bought 72 per cent of the shares. The evident inability of the trade unions to manage their companies adequately has thus forced the DGB to re-think their strategy on Gemeinwirtschaft. In 1989 plans included the sale of 25 per cent of the unions' holding in the Allgemeine Hypothekenbank and even the disposal of 75 per cent of their stake in the Volksfürsorge. At the 14th DGB Federal Congress held in Hamburg in May 1990, an historic decision was taken to abandon Gemeinwirtschaft in view of the damage caused to the unions by the series of corruption scandals.

Collective bargaining

A high percentage of employees in western Germany are covered by collective agreements. Such agreements are primarily industry-based and, sometimes, also regional within an industry. There are basically two types of agreements: the **Lohn- und Gehaltstarifvertrag** (wages and salary agreement), which affects solely pay; and the **Manteltarifvertrag** or **Rahmentarifvertrag** (framework conditions agreement), which regulates in addition such matters as hours of work, holidays, benefits, dismissal and redundancy provisions. The former has traditionally been concluded for 12 months at a time; the latter for several years. Recently there has been a move towards longer-term pay agreements.

Collective bargaining for industry-level or sector-level agreements takes place between the trade union and the corresponding employers' association. Once signed, these agreements are legally binding on companies and employees alike. An agreement can, however, be extended to cover all employees in the relevant sector by being declared **allgemeinverbindlich** (generally binding). This can be done by the Federal Minister of Labour or the state Minister of Labour if companies employing at least half of all the employees in that sector have signed it. In practice, however, employers apply the terms of an agreement to all employees regardless of union membership.

After the 1991 pay negotiations had been completed, the trade unions in western Germany were accused of attempting to punish Chancellor Kohl for his pre-unification 'tax-lie' (see page 8). They were responsible, it was claimed, for launching a wage–price spiral in the west and contributing to mass unemployment in eastern Germany through insisting on wages equalization there (see pages 76–77). As for the first accusation, in 1990 real net wages per worker in western Germany rose by 4.8 per cent which, on account of tax cuts, was the largest annual increase since 1970. In 1991, due in part to the tax increase to pay for German unification, real net wages declined slightly, the seventh year of negative real pay since 1981. Between 1980 and 1990 workers' purchasing power rose by only 7 per cent. Wage claims averaging 9 per cent for 1992 were a reflection of the unions' determination to achieve improved standards of living for their members despite the recession.

Indeed, the eleven-day strike by the union of **Öffentliche Dienste**, **Transport und Verkehr** (ÖTV) (Public Service and Transport Workers) in April and May 1992, western Germany's biggest since the end of the Second World War, provided further evidence, if such were needed, that ordinary workers' patience with the high price of unification was running thin. Claims that western Germans had at last contracted the dreaded 'British disease' were, however, much exaggerated.

Industrial democracy

The business culture and the business climate in western Germany have both been favourably affected by the degree of integration of the trade unions into corporate structures. Although this integration was not always welcomed by employers, at least not initially, they have come to accept it as a fact of business life. Moreover, possibly as a result of close trade union involvement in corporate decision-making processes, employers and trade unions in western Germany refer to themselves collectively as **Sozialpartner** (social partners), thus avoiding at least the adversarial rhetoric encountered in other countries, and indicating a higher degree of consensus than is found elsewhere.

Industrial democracy in Germany looks back over a long history:

1920: Works' councils recognized as bargaining counterparts of employers in companies with more than 20 employees.

1951: Parity codetermination introduced for the mining, iron and steel industries. Capital and labour representatives have equal voting strength on supervisory boards. Voting deadlock is prevented by an addition 'neutral man', appointed by the state, if the board is split.

1952: Companies with over 500 employees forced to allocate one-third of the seats on their supervisory boards to labour representatives.

1972: Companies with five employees permitted to have a works' council. In addition, works' councils are given full codetermination rights on issues of working hours and the introduction of new technology, unless these matters are already covered by wage negotiations between unions and employers' associations.

1976: Mitbestimmungs-Gesetz (Codetermination Act) passed through Parliament. It embraces AGs and GmbHs normally employing over 2000 persons, which must have a supervisory board composed of half shareholders' and half workers' representatives. Companies with between 500 and 2000 employees have supervisory boards with one-third worker representation.

The trade unions are not entirely happy with the 1976 Act for several reasons. First, it affects only relatively few, large companies, and not the vast majority of small and medium-sized firms in the country. Second, the unions claim, the Act does not deliver true parity codetermination. It ensures that, in the event of voting deadlock, the capital owners will prevail because the Chairman of the supervisory board is always a shareholders' representative with a casting vote. Moreover, one of the worker representatives must be a 'senior manager' who, it is alleged, is likely to side with the shareholders.

The employers were not happy with the 1976 Act either. In June 1977, just as the Act was due to come into force, nine companies and twenty-nine employers' associations submitted a complaint to the **Bundesverfassungsgericht** (Federal Constitutional Court) in Karlsruhe to the effect that it contravened the Grundgesetz (Basic Law). In March 1979, the Court published its decision and rejected the employers' injunction.

Since 1979, companies in western Germany have come to terms with the provisions of the Codetermination Act, which has been the subject of minor amendments in the interim. Most will admit that worker representatives on the supervisory board make a positive contribution to the smooth operation of companies. This has been achieved both through their direct inputs in the decision-making process and through the dissemination of information on decisions taken at high levels in the company, although the works' councils in western German companies were already privy to large amounts of company information. Indeed, for ordinary workers in the average company, the focus of industrial democracy lies neither with their representatives on the company supervisory board, nor with their trade union, but with the works' council. Works' councillors need not belong to the trade union represented in a company but most of them do.

Areas of disagreement

The social consensus between trade unions and employers in post-war western Germany, as graphically illustrated by the relatively few working days lost through strikes, has continued, for the most part, throughout the 1980s and early 1990s (Table 1.6). Moreover, it is significant that the issues which have divided them most over this period are those concerned with working hours. This is undoubtedly a reflection of the sea-change taking place today, away from the erstwhile **Leistungsgesellschaft** (high-performance society) and towards the **Freizeitgesellschaft** (leisure society).

The older generations rarely tire of recalling how Germans in the west used to work: women in headscarves passing bricks from hand to hand as they toiled in the rubble to rebuild a country devastated by war; men who

Table 1.6 *Working days in western Germany lost through disputes (1980–91)*

Year	Working days lost
1980	128,386
1981	58,398
1982	15,106
1983	40,842
1984	2,921,263
1985	34,505
1986	27,964
1987	33,325
1988	41,880
1989	100,409
1990	363,547
1991	153,587

Source: Bundesministerium für Arbeit
(Federal Ministry of Labour)/
Bundesanstalt für Arbeit (Federal Labour
Office)

laboured long hours in the factories and fashioned an economic miracle; unions that used to sit down with employers, not to argue over a shorter working week, but to hatch out strategies for greater efficiency and higher output. But as western Germany has prospered and achieved the **Wohlstandsgesellschaft** (affluent society) attitudes have changed. People are taking things easier. They want more time to spend the money they are earning, and are more interested in holidays abroad than in overtime in factories at home. What has happened to the good old western German hard-work ethic?

Opinion polls provide an answer of sorts: young people are more interested in being with their families. They do not believe that they should produce ever more and work ever harder; and they are increasingly unwilling to trade off leisure for more pay. Such findings have led some commentators to deduce that the Germans in the west are becoming idle, a notion abhorrent to the older generation. But this is not even part of the real answer. The circumstances of the post-war reconstruction period were very special. Not only were enormous efforts necessary to make the country habitable again; hard work was a form of guilt expiation for the atrocities of the war, a way in which western Germans could regain their dignity in their own eyes, and the respect of the rest of the world. The nature of work in the 1980s, however, changed radically. The introduction of large numbers of numerically-controlled machine-tools and industrial robots into manufacturing plants in western Germany alienated many and left them feeling ill at ease at the workstation.

It is against this background that the altercations between employers and trade unions over shorter working hours should be viewed. In 1984, the **IG Metall** (Metal Workers' Union) went on a strike lasting eight weeks for the 35-hour week. They successfully broke the 40-hour week barrier and settled for 38.5 hours. In May 1990, they achieved their first major agreement for the introduction of the 35-hour week, to be phased in over a period of five years. The working week would be cut to 36 hours in April 1993 and finally to 35 hours by April 1995. Also in May 1990, a similar agreement was concluded between **IG Medien** (Print Workers' Union) and the **Bundesverband Druck** (Printing Employers' Federation) to introduce the 35-hour week over a similar period of time.

While the working week has been shortened in western Germany, holiday entitlement has risen. In 1989, holiday entitlement averaged 27.3 working days; in 1990, average length of holidays was 27.5 working days. Where age is used as a criterion, thirty, thirty-five or forty is the age at which employees usually attain their maximum holiday periods, while maximum service-related entitlements are between five and fifteen years' service. Overall, 99 per cent of all employees had at least four weeks' annual holiday in 1991; 94 per cent had at least five weeks; and 66 per cent had six weeks or more.

In 1991, 94 per cent of employees received additional holiday pay in one of three forms. 44 per cent of all employees averaged 47 per cent of basic pay; 31 per cent of employees were given a flat-rate cash payment to cover the entire holiday period amounting to DM 677 on average; 19 per cent of employees received a flat-rate cash payment for each day's holiday which averaged DM 25. Moreover, some 92 per cent of employees received an annual bonus, usually expressed as a percentage of a month's salary (the so-called thirteenth month's salary), and in 1991 this percentage averaged 69 per cent of gross monthly pay. Taken together, additional holiday pay and 13th month's salary averaged 92 per cent of a month's normal salary, while about two-thirds of all employees received a total bonus equivalent to at least one month's salary.

Given fringe benefits such as these, it is hardly surprising that an area of growing strife is that of weekend working. Working on Saturday or Sunday separates not only employers and unions but has also sown divisions amongst unions themselves and between unions and local works' councils. In the 1950s and 1960s, the unions succeeded in gaining acceptance of the 40-hour, five-day working week. Recently, there has been renewed pressure by employers to re-introduce weekend working, particularly Saturday working.

In 1988, both Opel in its Kaiserslautern plant and BMW in the new Regensburg works brought back Saturday working. Similarly, Siemens and IBM introduced weekend working to permit continuous production of megabit chips at their factories in Regensburg and Sindelfingen respectively. Goodyear insisted that a DM 100 million investment at Fulda was made dependent on the acceptance of Saturday working by the works' council.

In the autumn of 1990, Mercedes-Benz inserted Saturday shifts at its plants in Sindelfingen, Untertürkheim and Bremen.

Article 139 of the Basic Law states: 'Sunday and the public holidays recognized by the state shall remain under legal protection as days of rest from work and of spiritual edification.' Exceptions included in the **Gewerbeordnung** (Trading Regulations) cover mainly utilities, transport and health services, as well as the leisure sector. In contrast, there are no legal restrictions on Saturday working: wage agreements expressly stipulating a Monday-to-Friday working week apply to some 265,000 employees only.

Employers maintain that weekend working is necessary because overall working hours have become shorter, thus leaving expensive equipment idle for long periods. This, they say, places western Germany at a competitive disadvantage in relation to other countries. The inclusion of Saturday as part of the normal working week would allow employers to incorporate more effective equipment working times. Dr Werner Stumpfe, President of **Gesamtmetall** (Engineering Employers' Federation), has stated that, whereas the incorporation of Saturday as a normal working day was a necessity, Sunday working was required for technical reasons and not on economic grounds.

The engineering and print-workers' unions are opposed to either Saturday or Sunday working. They claim that weekend working isolates employees from friends, sport and culture; disrupts family life; and places further strain on the environment. The chemical workers, traditionally a more moderate union than the engineers or printers, maintain that although works' councils initially rejected the introduction of weekend working, in many cases ensuing arbitration found in favour of employers. The union consequently decided that where Saturday working seemed likely, it would attempt to trade this off against shorter working hours and reductions in overtime. In 1991, 17 per cent of blue-collar employees regularly worked on Saturdays and 8 per cent on Sundays.

In view of the large differences between the various parties, it appears unlikely that this conflict will be resolved in the short term. At present, the employers appear to be winning, partly because they can often drive a wedge between official union policy and local works' councils. They also point to increased competition from Japan, where employees put in an average of 42 hours per week, including weekends, and to some countries in the EC with similar working practices.

Medium-term concerns

The trade unions in western Germany are anxious about developments in the EC over the medium term. As the *Financial Times* observed on 31 October 1988: '. . . with the highest pay and best fringe benefits in Europe, they have most to lose from the greater mobility of capital.' The unions are confident that they can retain most of the skilled-labour and high-value-added jobs on account of the outstanding system of education and vocational training – a theme to which further reference will be made (see below). But they have worried that some lower-skilled manufacturing jobs could be exported to relatively low-cost countries such those in the Iberian peninsula.

Many of their fears could be groundless. Since the very large companies, particularly in the car industry, have already moved to Spain and Portugal, the completion of the single market has not had much of an effect. Moreover, the swift modernization of these two countries in the south of Europe has also entailed an equally swift increase in labour costs. But the single market has inspired a few smaller companies, particularly car-component makers, to emigrate south after the multinationals.

Finally, the trade unions in western Germany were worried about what they call the 'social dismantling of Europe'. They claimed that 1993 merely marked the advent of a 'Europe of capital' and focused on the opposition of such countries as the United Kingdom to the Community Charter of Fundamental Social Rights as tabled by Jacques Delors (see page 243). They pointed to the rejection of the Vredeling initiative in the early 1980s, which incorporated much of the western German system of worker participation, and feared that, yet again, what would be adopted in Europe is the lowest common denominator. These fears have now dissipated to a certain extent since every member country in the EC, with the notable exception of the United Kingdom, accepted the provisions of the Social Chapter at the Maastricht summit.

Business, education, training and development

The business culture in western Germany has been constantly enriched by the existence of a highly-trained and well-educated workforce. Education at school, vocational training in the **Duales System** (Dual System), job-related courses at polytechnics and universities, and management development in companies all make their own unique contributions to the formation of this 'human capital'. Currently an attempt is being made to have the widespread training ethos underpinned yet further by the concept of life-long learning through extra paid holidays for self-improvement. The concept itself is welcomed by the employers but they are putting up stiff resistance to the notion of even more holidays!

Vocational training

The vocational training system in western Germany is the envy of many of its competitors and a cornerstone of business success. It has also helped to keep youth unemployment down to approximately 5 per cent during the 1980s and early 1990s. In 1991, almost 550,000 young people embarked on apprenticeship courses which mostly last three years and link in-company training with specialized and general education in **Berufsschulen** (vocational schools) – the so-called Dual System. In 1991, there were approximately 1,650,000 apprentices undergoing initial vocational training.

Of the young people taking up vocational training after leaving school in 1991, 39 per cent came from **Grundschulen** (general schools) – in 1977 the figure was 54 per cent – 46 per cent had attended **Realschulen** (intermediate schools) (40 per cent), and 15 per cent of applicants for such traineeships had gone to a **Gymnasium** (grammar school) (6 per cent). The apprentices entering such schemes had behind them eight, ten and thirteen years of education at the respective schools.

In the Dual System, the individual states run the vocational schools, but the **Industrie- und Handelskammern** (Chambers of Industry and Commerce) or the **Handwerkerkammern** (Craft Chambers) are responsible for inspecting the approximately 500,000 approved training firms on a regular basis as well as for monitoring the training content of the 439 recognized training occupations. Apprentices are also registered, supervised and examined by the Chambers.

As the *Financial Times* of 25 August 1988, revealed, a comprehensive system of vocational training such as this is not cheap. AEG, for instance, spent almost DM 70 million on apprenticeship training in 1987. Training just one apprentice costs AEG approximately DM 24,000 per annum. 'Multiply this throughout the economy and the annual sum spent by industry on **Ausbildung** (initial vocational training) for its 1.6 million trainees is around DM 35 billion, though the net figure is around DM 25 billion allowing for trainees' contribution to production'.

In 1991, young people in western Germany were attracted mainly to office work. Four white-collar occupations stood at the head of the list of the most popular apprenticeships. Of every 1000 youngsters signing such contracts, 193, or almost 20 per cent, opted for apprenticeships in retailing, commerce, administration and banking. The next most popular careers were in motor mechanics, electronic engineering and hairdressing.

At the end of the apprenticeship courses, in which 90 per cent of candidates pass the final examination at the first attempt and the drop-out rate over the average three-year course is less than 5 per cent, the erstwhile trainees become **Facharbeiter** (qualified skilled workers). Now they have gained social status and possess a qualification which they can show to their present, or any future, employer. Qualified skilled workers also earn more than the unskilled, even when working in trades or crafts not their own. But equally important, the possession of this qualification gives access to a range of higher vocational awards.

In theory, any qualified skilled worker with two years' experience of his or her trade could go on to **Fortbildung** (higher vocational training) and take one of the higher qualifications; in practice, the average age for those taking the **Industriemeister**, **Fachwirte** or **Fachkaufleute** examinations is approximately thirty years. In 1990, 7,124 qualified skilled workers passed the Industriemeister, 5,432 the Fachwirte and 4,016 the Fachkaufleute examinations. The possession of a higher vocational award affords opportunities for career progression into supervisory and even management positions. In fact, the presence in lower and middle management ranks of practice-oriented employees who have emerged from the apprenticeship system, alongside more theory-oriented graduates from the country's polytechnics and universities, represents one of the major strengths of management in western Germany.

Management education

Most managers come, however, from the polytechnics and universities, where they will have studied a subject which is directly related to their future careers in business. The emphasis is, therefore, firmly placed, from the outset, on the acquisition of relevant knowledge and functional skills. The average age of a graduate leaving polytechnic at diploma level is twenty-six years, and twenty-eight years for university graduates. The 14,000 continuing their studies at university to the doctorate level are aged thirty on completing their dissertation.

In the 1960s, some 100 polytechnics were established in the country offering shorter (three to four-year), more vocationally-oriented courses than universities. In 1991, there were over a quarter of a million students at polytechnics, with 1 per cent per annum more students with the tertiary level entrance qualification opting for a polytechnic in preference to a university. The main subjects in order of popularity are: mechanical and production engineering; economics and **Betriebswirtschaft** (business economics); and social studies. In most programmes, there is a period of placement in industry or commerce. To distinguish polytechnic from university awards, some of the states insist that their polytechnic graduates designate themselves **Diplom-Ingenieur** *(FH)* or **Diplom-Kaufmann** *(FH)*, the abbreviation in brackets denoting **Fachhochschule**.

There are in western Germany some sixty-eight universities which were attended by some 1,250,000 students in 1991, giving a grand total of 22 per cent of age group in tertiary education. University courses are more academically demanding and thus longer than their polytechnic equivalents, with economics students taking 6 years and engineering students 6.5 years to complete to diploma standard.

Business regards university graduates with the diploma as good abstract thinkers but believes that they require two years of 'apprenticeship' before they become really useful to the company. In contrast, the more practically-educated polytechnic graduates are considered to hit the ground running from the very start of their careers. This is possibly why such a high percentage of polytechnic graduates find employment in medium-sized companies where induction training is rare, while university graduates tend to be recruited by large companies.

If a university graduate aspires to the topmost ranks of management in western Germany, he would be well advised to take a doctorate in a relevant subject. In 1985, 36.7 per cent of management board members in all the country's AGs possessed the doctor title; 41.5 per cent of management board members in the AGs quoted on the stock exchange also sported the title; and 53.8 per cent of the management board members of the 100 largest AGs had the right to be addressed as 'Herr Doktor'.

Management development

Large companies in western Germany conduct most of their **Weiterbildung** (management development) programmes in-house. They are fully committed to the training and development ethos and firmly believe that nobody can develop their managers more effectively than they can. Moreover, they possess their own lavishly-equipped short-course centres and are resolved to make maximum use of them. In addition, they perceive their own programmes as a means of stressing their particular corporate culture and thus persuading the individual manager to identify more closely with this culture. In other words, one of the spin-offs of in-house development programmes is their usefulness as a management retention tool.

The pattern in large companies is for lower management to receive more development than middle or senior managers. Among the lower managers would also figure the **Industriemeister**, **Fachwirte** and **Fachkaufleute** who have come up from the shop floor. Programmes at this level would be product-specific or function-specific. Typical examples for Industriemeister would be courses on safety at work, or quality assurance. Programmes for middle managers would be company-specific and have a high management information content. Senior managers concentrate on objective management techniques, subjective management behaviour and, increasingly, the company and its environment – another theme to which further reference will be made (see pages 50–56).

Medium-sized companies lacking the appropriate human, physical and financial resources look outside the firm for their management development courses. Indeed, the cost of management training starts to become significant for this size of company, and here the programmes run by the Chambers of Industry and Commerce are particularly attractive. Since all companies paying **Gewerbesteuer** (trade tax) must be members of their local Chambers and must pay membership fees, these value-for-money programmes are particularly popular.

The Chambers offer a range of development programmes for all levels of management from entrepreneurs to lower managers. Teaching staff are bought in from large companies, polytechnics or universities. Programmes are taught either in the Chambers' own short-course centres or in hotels.

The management development programmes organized by the Chambers should not be regarded as second best to those run by the large companies. In fact, the Chambers have very sensitive radar for company development needs because of their close contacts with firms of all sizes. They are ideally placed to identify the latest development trends in the large companies and subsequently to provide similar, or even better, programmes for other large, medium-sized and small companies.

Indeed, the Chambers of Industry and Commerce and the Craft Chambers in western Germany represent the key element in training and development for so much of business activity. As was noted earlier, they are closely involved in initial vocational training and higher vocational training, and the natural progression of their activities into the field of management development during the 1980s has with almost universal acclaim.

If management education and management development in western Germany can be faulted at all, criticism would have to focus on the heavy emphasis on functionality found in both areas. There is little room in western German management for the generalist: the whole system is geared to producing functional specialists. MBA (Master of Business Administration) courses turning out generalist managers do not exist. Nor perhaps were such courses necessary in the past when companies were operating mainly within their own business culture, but in the light of increased outward investment by western German companies (see pages 14–15) a more generalist approach to management education and development has now become desirable.

Lifelong learning

Higher vocational qualifications and management development programmes should be viewed against the background of a concerted attempt in the country to promote the concept of lifelong learning. It is claimed that 25 per cent of the population between the ages of nineteen and sixty-five take part every year in some form of continuing education. Participation rates are, however, disproportionate. Only 9 per cent of unskilled workers were in any way involved in 1990, and in the same year there were six times fewer participants with the general school-leaving certificate than with tertiary level entrance qualification.

To rectify these imbalances, the notion of **Bildungsurlaub** (extra paid holidays for self-improvement) has been mooted. Six of the individual states have legislated in favour, and Bildungsurlaub has formed part of a few tariff agreements between trade unions and employers' associations. While welcoming the concept of lifelong learning and actively supporting the process of adjustment to new technologies, the vast majority of companies oppose the notion of extra paid holidays. They argue that their employees already work the shortest number of hours in Europe, enjoy the longest holidays, retire as pensioners at the lowest age, and receive the best education, training and development. It is difficult to disagree with them.

Business and the environment

In the past twenty-five years, the business culture in western Germany has become increasingly affected by issues connected with the environment. Although this concern is perhaps most visibly evidenced in the country at large by the presence of Europe's most prominent ecological party, The Greens, all western Germans are worried about air, water and ground pollution. Business now shares this concern. While companies in western Germany were never exactly ecstatic about the massive investments they were forced to make to clean up their act, they realize that this capital expenditure has placed them at a competitive advantage vis-à-vis most of their neighbours in Europe. The issue of the environment will not go away in any of the European countries, and foreign companies will subsequently be obliged to purchase pollution-control equipment, much of which has been researched, designed and made in western Germany.

The origins of the problem

Western Germany is one of the most densely-populated areas in the world. More than 60 million people inhabit the 250,000 square kilometres between the North Sea and the Alps, giving some 247 persons per square kilometre compared with 24 in the United States of America. Approximately 10 per cent of the land is built up, and there are only 120 areas measuring 10 kilometres by 10 kilometres which are not crossed by main roads or rail networks.

After the Second World War, industrial reconstruction progressed at a rapid pace. Economic growth rates in the 1950s and early 1960s were phenomenal; ever more manufacturing industries were set up; increasing numbers of citizens moved from the land into the new conurbations. The economic miracle duly occurred. But the miracle was built on the steel, steel-processing, chemical, pharmaceutical, and machine-tool industries, all of which took their toll of the physical environment.

In addition, the affluent society created in western Germany permitted the citizenry to indulge in a love affair with the motor car, and the high-performance car in particular, matching the high-performance society in which they were living. One of the results is that even today there is no general speed limit on the motorways. Another is that there are some 30 million private cars on the road.

The political response

The first voices were raised in protest at the damage being done to the environment in the mid-1950s, but they were ignored. The initial hesitant response came from the legislators in the mid-1960s.

1965 First Clean Air Act passed by the Federal Parliament. Fears were still widespread about the effect which more radical legislation might have on the competitiveness of western German industry.

1969 Protection of the environment accepted for the first time in a Federal government declaration in Bonn.

1971 First comprehensive environmental programme published by a Federal government. In the course of the 1970s, a whole series of Acts were passed for the protection of the environment. The lead content of petrol was reduced; refuse disposal was placed under legal controls; the use of certain additives in detergents was restricted.

1975 Environmental consciousness began to spread rapidly through large sections of the population. The number of citizens' initiatives grew considerably.

1980 The Greens established themselves as a political party.

1983 The Greens entered the Federal Parliament for the first time.

1986 The **Bundesministerium für Umwelt** *(BMU)* (Federal Ministry of the Environment) was founded. It is supported in its work by two Federal agencies, the **Umweltbundesamt** (Federal Environment Office) and the **Bundesforschungsanstalt für Naturschutz und Landschaftsökologie** (Federal Research Institute for the Protection of Nature and Countryside Ecology).

Environmental damage

The passing of laws, the establishment of an ecology-oriented political party, the founding of a dedicated Federal Ministry, even enhanced public consciousness of the importance of a clean environment represent only the first steps in the struggle to re-introduce equilibrium in the balance of nature in western Germany. So much was destroyed or damaged in pursuit of the ideal of the affluent society, via the high-performance society, that the damage is truly immense.

In the opinion of many experts, 50 per cent of the bird species in western Germany's Central Uplands are threatened with extinction. The damage done to the woods and forests by air pollution is responsible for their plight. In 1982, approximately 8 per cent, in 1983 approximately 34 per cent, and in 1990 approximately 50 per cent of all the country's woodlands were either damaged or suffered from reduced vitality as a result of the effects of acid rain. This is caused after the combustion of coal, petrol and heating oil, when sulphur dioxide and nitrogen oxides combine in the air to descend as an acidic precipitation on the leaves, needles and roots of trees.

Air pollution has contributed in its turn to water contamination. Precipitations have deposited phosphates, heavy metal and halogen compounds in rivers and lakes. The nitrates used in intensive farming and present in factory effluents have only served to exacerbate the problem. The worst-affected areas in western Germany are found in the Bavarian forest, the Fichtel Mountains and the Northern Black Forest. In some of these areas, the water has become so acidic that the ph-value has fallen by one or two degrees since the 1950s, which corresponds to a ten to twenty-fold rise in acidity.

Every inhabitant of western Germany produces annually 375 kilograms of refuse which have to be disposed of, domestic waste accounting for approximately 32 per cent of the country's total refuse of 250 million tonnes per year. The 365 domestic refuse disposal areas can no longer cope with such quantities, and many towns and cities have begun to incinerate on a large scale, using the excess energy for district-heating schemes. The disposal of industrial waste products is, however, more problematical, and the construction of incineration plant for special industrial waste has led to protests from the citizens most immediately affected. Even western Germany is not immune to the NIMBY (Not in My Backyard) syndrome which has prevented the construction of dozens of much-needed waste-burning facilities.

The first successes

According to the Federal Environmental Office, crimes against the environment are responsible for some DM 20 billion of damage every year. Here not only large companies which introduce poisonous effluent into a river or stream are to blame: equally culpable are those drivers sneaking off into the woods to change the oil in their cars and tipping the waste onto the ground. Western German police statistics in 1987 registered approximately 18,000 cases of air pollution, water contamination or environmentally-harmful waste disposal. The clear-up rate for the approximately 16,000 cases in 1986 was 75 per cent.

The most spectacular successes have been achieved in the area of air pollution (Table 1.7).

Table 1.7 *Emissions in western Germany (in millions of tonnes)*

	1966	1974	1982	1986	1992
Sulphur dioxide	3.4	3.6	2.9	2.2	0.9
Carbon monoxide	12.3	13.7	10.1	8.9	7.9
Nitric oxide	1.9	2.6	2.8	2.8	2.5
Dust	1.8	0.9	0.6	0.5	0.4

Source: Globus

Mainly responsible for the improved air quality in western Germany are the 165 so-called desulphurizer plants which had been installed at the seventy-two sites for coal-burning power stations by 1988. The operators of such plants will have spent DM 22 billion by 1995 on the installation of sulphur dioxide and nitric oxide filters. In 1992, these measures had led to reductions of sulphur dioxide emissions of 33 per cent and nitric oxide emissions of 37 per cent. What is more, the technology was invented, designed and refined in western Germany, with Deutsche Babcock being particularly successful in this field. In 1991, the country's environmental technology sector registered the largest worldwide share (29 per cent) of new patents.

The reaction of business

Even at the beginning of the 1980s, protection of the environment was considered by both employers' associations and trade unions to be hostile to employment. It was assumed that the additional costs of measures for the protection of the environment would lead to reductions in the incomes of employees if not actually to job losses. In the meantime, there has been a change of heart on both sides. Protection of the environment is no longer regarded as a job-killer but as job-neutral, and latterly even as job-creating.

In 1985, it was calculated that approximately 300,000 employees were engaged directly or indirectly in work connected with protection of the environment. The sector of the economy associated with environmental protection was growing at 14 per cent per annum above the average for other sectors. Even back in 1980, gross sales of DM 16 billion had been achieved, 25 per cent of which were exported. This resulted in the preservation of 170,000 to 180,000 jobs.

In March 1985, the Confederation of German Trade Unions presented its programme on protection of the environment. It demanded for the following five years environmentally-effective investments of DM 50 billion. The aim of the demands was to avoid further stress on the environment and to bring about a drastic reduction in existing stresses. Protection of the environment was, according to the Confederation of German Trade Unions, to be achieved by 'quality growth', and not by a virtual renunciation of industrial society as proposed by The Greens.

The myth that protection of the environment, because of the expense involved, destroys jobs was finally laid to rest in western Germany by 1989 at the latest. It was revealed then that the immediate production of goods for environment protection accounted for 190,000 jobs in the country. The production value of goods and services connected with the environment was estimated at DM 23 billion annually. Again in 1989, 7.2 per cent of total investments by manufacturing industry were earmarked for investments in environmental measures. A total of 440,000 jobs were associated either directly or indirectly with protection of the environment. Growth estimates for further employment in this sector of the economy were approximately 16 per cent per annum.

In April 1990, Klaus Töpfer, the Environment Minister, introduced his

Packaging Ordinance to combat the throw-away society. From December 1991, companies had to take back and recycle 'primary' packaging used during transport or arrange for someone else to do it for them. From April 1992, the law was extended to 'secondary' packaging, such as gift wrapping. From January 1993, it covered all packaging from baked bean tins to margarine tubs. By July 1995, 80 per cent of packaging waste must be collected, with 90 per cent of glass and metals, and 80 per cent of plastics, laminates, board and paper having to be recycled.

To comply with this apparently draconian law, companies have established the **Duales System Deutschland** (DSD), a non-profit-making organization, which operates its own waste-collection system. About 400 companies have taken a nominal share in DSD. Producers of consumer goods have to pay at least two pfennigs per packaged item, which allows their goods to sport a DSD green dot. Firms which do not join DSD have to make their own arrangements.

Companies in western Germany have been finding the system frustrating, partly because the costs and benefits of the green dot are distributed rather arbitrarily from sector to sector. Plastic, for example, is more difficult to recycle than aluminium. Companies exporting to western Germany have found the Packaging Ordinance even more exasperating, and foreign goods have been turned back at the borders for non-compliance with the Ordinance.

Western Germany has been accused of breaking ranks with the EC on the question of recycling, but domestic companies are gradually coming to terms with the tough rules and regulations. In 1990, Mercedes-Benz launched a huge campaign to make its cars recyclable. In so doing, the company is developing new technology which could spread to millions of family cars. BMW and Volkswagen-Audi are also investigating procedures to encourage car-owners to return their vehicles at the end of their useful lives so that they can be stripped down and re-used. Engineers in the car companies maintain that even if the 600 different materials in a car cannot be taken back into the vehicle-manufacturing process, they can go into other industries.

In 1993, almost 50 per cent of company capital expenditure in western Germany was devoted to the environment and to safety. Moreover, the country currently has the highest standards of pollution control and ecological awareness in the EC. As legislation throughout the EC becomes harmonized, this is one area where standards will not be reduced to the lowest common denominator. On the contrary, standards will be forced to rise as the degree of environmental consciousness common to the citizenry in western Germany spreads throughout EC countries and beyond. What western Germany is investing today, others will eventually have to match – and almost certainly at higher costs. Moreover, the western Germans were the first in the field and are better placed than anyone else to export not only their products but their services as well.

The response of business to the EC's single market

The response of business in western Germany to the EC's **Binnenmarkt** (single market) appears to have been a muted one. Up to March 1988, there had been no large-scale publicity campaign, and a French business journal even went so far as to accuse the western Germans of a 'conspiracy of silence' on the subject. But such accusations ignore the discretion favoured by the business culture in the country. Despite the late start to the nation-wide publicity campaign, preparations went ahead quietly at the individual state level, with conferences organized by employers' associations and trade unions. Moreover, coordinating efforts at the national level were placed in the all-pervasive hand of the Chambers of Industry and Commerce.

Many western German business people perceived little need for large publicity onslaughts. They were confident of their strengths; aware of their weaknesses; looked forward to the opportunities; and were only mildly concerned about the threats. What is more, certain strategies had already been put in place and appeared to be auspicious.

Strengths

The Germans have fostered a strong domestic manufacturing base ever since the country first became industrialized. They never ruled over a large colonial empire, and very few industrial goods were actually produced in the colonies which they did possess. Production was retained back home in Germany. The consequence today is that manufacturing in, and exporting from, western Germany represent two of the country's undeniable strengths.

The concept of Technik, the art and science of manufacturing useful arte-facts, is so widespread that western Germany can be regarded as a manu-facturing-friendly society. Indeed, this is borne out by the contribution of manufacturing to the economy which, together with construction, accounts for some 40 per cent of GDP. Moreover, the lion's share of the 2.9 per cent of GDP spent on R & D is targeted at applied research in manufacturing, thus underpinning the production orientation of the economy.

Manufacturing and exporting are synonymous for firms of all sizes, so the completion of the EC's single market held few terrors for large produc-tion companies. Western Germany is already responsible for over half of all intra-EC exports, and companies are confident that the figure of 54 per cent can be maintained or even improved. Given that western Germans export more per capita than any nation in the world, including the Japanese, this confidence appears to be justified.

A third area of strength is to be found in the country's financial institutions. The record of the Bundesbank in protecting the currency and in combating inflation is probably superior to that of any other central bank in the twenty-four OECD countries. Moreover, the Big Three private commercial banks are held to be among the fourteen most powerful banks in the world in terms of their financial strength and security. Nor were they dilatory in adopting certain strategies for the completion of the single market, as has already been seen.

Human capital represents a fourth area of strength. Western Germany's workforce is probably the best equipped in Europe to withstand the challenges of the future. Starting with an excellent public education system, and continuing with either vocational training or entry into higher education, only some 5 per cent of young people fail to progress to one or the other. In addition, the whole of the education and training effort is supported by business through a deep commitment to the development ethos of its employees.

Perhaps this same commitment is partly responsible for a western German strength in a fifth area – that of industrial relations. Here the consensus between employers and trade unions, though brittle at times, has produced a business climate which is envied by many other countries. The western German record on industrial disputes is matched in Europe only by Switzerland and Austria. Moreover, the long-established tradition of industrial democracy through powerful works' councils has been reinforced by a system of worker codetermination on supervisory boards which, despite initial serious misgivings on the part of employers and trade unions alike, has accomplished much over the period in which it has been in existence.

A final area of strength is represented by western Germany's geographical location at the very heart of the EC. This part of the country has common borders with five of the EC member states – Denmark, the Netherlands, Belgium, Luxembourg and France. The physical proximity to markets, with all its implications for transport and distribution costs, could assume even more significance if Austria and Switzerland, another two of western Germany's immediate neighbours, eventually join the EC. Indeed, Germany could become without question the dominant economic power in Europe if Hungary and Poland succeed in forming closer economic links with the EC.

Weaknesses

Western Germany's weaknesses in the manufacturing sector are primarily associated with a decline in profitability over recent years. Here high corporate taxation at 70 per cent of retained earnings contributes little to the attraction of western Germany as a location for industry. Company profitability, especially in the manufacturing sector, is not enhanced either by high real unit labour costs or by inflexible labour markets. Small wonder, then, that domestic companies failed to match erstwhile high rates of investment, and foreign companies have not invested proportionately during the 1980s and early 1990s.

Taxation is also detracting from western Germany as a financial centre. The on-off 0.1–0.25 per cent stock exchange turnover tax and the 10 per cent withholding tax on dividend and fixed interest payments have both prevented Frankfurt-am-Main from competing effectively with London as Europe's premier financial marketplace.

The services sector is bedevilled by over-regulation. The **Güterfernverkehrsamt** (Road Haulage Office) has a staff of 900 to monitor the activities of domestic and foreign trucking companies. Similarly, the Bundespost still enjoys a virtual monopoly in the telecommunications field despite recent changes in its status. These are just two of the areas of the service sector which must be opened up to international competition by the EC's single market.

While the manufacturing and finance sectors were granted some fiscal relief from the much-vaunted 'tax reform of the century', which occurred in 1990, the companies in the services sector were looking forward to the report of the deregulation commission, which was delayed until 1991. It was expected that Federal government action would then follow after due consideration and consultation. It is probable, however, that the services sector will be affected more by legislation arising from Brussels than from Bonn or Berlin.

One area of weakness in the western German business culture which is reputed to be as serious as any concerned with the individual sectors of the economy relates to the alleged lack of a spirit of entrepreneurship. Critics point to the country's entrepreneurs at the bottom of the management buyout league in Europe, with only forty-six recorded by the end of 1991, and speculate that western Germany is failing to take full advantage of the single market because the business community is risk-averse.

The critics are wrong. Western Germany's business culture was enriched after the Second World War by many entrepreneurs. Without them there would have been no economic miracle. But in western Germany today the older entrepreneur is sometimes regarded as a capitalist, exploiting workers and bribing politicians. Nevertheless, many older entrepreneurs still exist, and they want to leave their businesses to someone! These are the entrepreneurs who developed their businesses after the Second World War and who now wish to retire. Very often they have no members of their family willing to continue their businesses because their younger relations have taken up different careers. But they do want their businesses to survive, and here opportunities present themselves for domestic or foreign companies to acquire these firms.

The attitude of the manager towards entrepreneurship is different. The manager's over-riding attribute is loyalty to the company-owner. He – and it is predominantly he – would never dare ask the owner if he wanted to sell the company to him because this would be construed as disloyal and could constitute grounds for dismissal. Moreover, the manager is looking for security for both himself and his family. Being a manager means belonging to the workforce and enjoying the same privileges of security. Finally, contemporary western German society values the social standing of a senior manager more highly than that of an entrepreneur. A position as a member of the management board of a large company is more prestigious than being the owner of a medium-sized company.

Nonetheless, the number of new businesses established in western Germany has been rising steadily over the past decade, though many quickly fail. In 1980, there were approximately 160,000 start-ups; in 1985, 290,000; and in 1990, 320,000, of which one in three companies was founded by a woman (cf. 1975 when only one in ten had a female founder). Western Germans, it would appear, still possess an entrepreneurial spirit, but prefer to set up their own businesses rather than indulge in complex buyouts.

Opportunities

Large companies, it is commonly believed, are the ones that will profit most from the EC's single market. Here western German business is well placed, with 3,600 officially-designated major companies. Apart from the sheer number and critical mass of these companies, it must not be forgotten that the equity holdings of the Big Three banks in many major firms render them virtually immune to hostile takeover bids. Conversely, many large companies are cash-rich as a result of western Germany's accountancy and taxation provisions, so they can take over companies at home or in other EC countries without recourse to either bond or equity markets, provided they do not fall foul of mergers and acquisitions legislation. If the big spend on R & D by the major companies does not produce the desired results, then ideas or even brands can be bought with cold cash.

Although success will differ from one sector to another, most large western German manufacturing companies are supremely confident of their
chances in the market. To name but one sector, the large chemicals companies, Hoechst, Bayer and BASF are absolutely sure that they are unbeatable
in the EC's single market.

Threats

In contrast, the **Mittelstand** (small and medium-sized businesses) are
slightly more anxious about prospects in the single market. Here, 1,900,000
companies, each with fewer than 500 workers, are responsible for roughly
half the GDP, employ two-thirds of the workforce, train four-fifths of all
the apprentices, and register most of the patents. Although they may have
been innovative, resilient, and export-oriented in the past, they are now
mildly nervous about the new competition which they face in their home
markets. They worry about foreign penetration of these markets and are
only just beginning to realize how protected they have been hitherto by
standards and norms so painstakingly concocted.

Prior to the completion of the single market, western Germany rigor-
ously enforced a plethora of competition-frustrating industrial standards,
the most notorious of which were the **Deutsche Industrie-Normen** (DIN)
(German Industrial Standards). Any country wishing to export manufactured items to western Germany was obliged in the past to have the product tested for compliance with the appropriate standard. In the single
market, industrial standards are harmonized, so that exporters from one
country do not feel disadvantaged by spurious regulations imposed by
others.

Some small and medium-sized western German companies feel threatened because the protection of their standards has been taken away from
them. They fear that, in the harmonization of industrial standards, agreement has been reached, yet again, at the level of the lowest common
denominator. But here the western Germans took pre-emptive action: they
saw to it that over half of the 120 separate EC standards committees were
chaired by their fellow-countrymen! The outcome is that many of their
cherished standards have been adopted and retained.

Nonetheless, 25 per cent of small and medium-sized businesses are forecast to close or be swallowed up by larger companies between 1991 and
1996.

Strategies

The strategies of western German companies in anticipation of the single market were two-fold: secure the home base by diversification, and expand abroad, especially in EC countries.

To secure the domestic position, acquisitions and mergers rose steeply in the late 1980s and early 1990s. There were few takeovers anywhere in the world in recent years as phenomenal as Daimler-Benz's of AEG, Dornier, MTU and MBB, but the number of smaller deals also increased. In 1990, there were 1296 completions, and in 1991 1223 mergers and acquisitions were registered with the Federal Cartel Office, with concentration becoming particularly intense in the food sector. They were occasioned by the conviction that size is what is needed to face the challenges of the single market.

Expansion abroad saw 78 acquisitions by western German companies in 1986, 137 in 1987, 180 in 1988, 183 in 1989, 186 in 1990, and 246 in 1991. Though most of western Germany's outward investment in Europe goes to the United Kingdom, as already noted (see page 219), the focus of much of the merger and acquisition activity has been France. Feldmühle, Europe's largest paper manufacturer, bought out two competitors there; Klein, Schanzlin & Becker, market-leading pump-makers, acquired Pompes Guinard; Bosch took a holding in Jeumont-Schneider; Degussa purchased Sarget; Daimler-Benz acquired a holding in Matra.

Western German companies were not the most active in Europe in terms of acquisitions in other countries in anticipation of the single market, but they were very selective. Circumspect as ever, they were at pains to play to their strengths. In general, however, they appear very confident of their prospects in the single market. The Bonn correspondent of *The Economist* stated in the 12 November 1988, issue of the journal: 'Western German businessmen seem pretty smug about 1992. Many companies reckon they are so good at selling to foreigners . . . that the creation of a single EC-wide market will mainly mean scope to sell more.' Little has changed in the meantime to shake this basic confidence, even the biggest 'acquisition' of them all – eastern Germany.

Part II Eastern Germany

Introduction

While constant attempts are being made to imbue eastern Germany with the business attitudes, values and norms as cherished in western Germany – those of conservatism and strength noted in the first part of the chapter – it is still too soon, in the early 1990s, to claim that this process has been completed. After all, the Berlin Wall only crumbled on 9 November 1989; Gemu (German economic and monetary union) occurred on 1 July 1990; and political union was achieved on 3 October 1990 – a bewilderingly swift series of events allowing little time for changes in the business culture to take root.

When reflecting on the business culture in eastern Germany, it is therefore necessary to take into consideration the old values as well as the dazzling array of new initiatives emanating from western Germany.

Business and government

The central state

The former **Deutsche Demokratische Republik** (DDR) (German Democratic Republic), or East Germany, was recognized as economically the most successful of the COMECON states. Indeed, it was held by many to be the showcase economy of the eastern European countries. Its inhabitants enjoyed a standard of living higher than anywhere else in the Communist bloc, and its business institutions appeared to radiate success and stability.

Relations between business and government were extremely close. The economy was overwhelmingly state-owned: in 1988, only 3.6 per cent of GDP originated from private enterprises. It functioned in accordance with five-year plans which were disaggregated into detailed one-year plans. These were put together by the State Planning Commission on the basis of priorities handed down to it by **Sozialistische Einheitspartei Deutschlands** (SED) (Communist party) reports and, to a lesser extent, by proposals made from below by the almost 300 locally-administered **Kombinate** (state-owned conglomerates) in industry, construction and transport. The conglomerates themselves were made up of some 8000 **volkseigene Betriebe** (VEBs) (nationally-owned enterprises) which were integrated, either vertically or horizontally, into the conglomerates.

Thus the economy of former East Germany was, like many others in the eastern bloc, a fairly self-sufficient one where business was commanded to produce a range of goods and services for domestic consumption. External trade was limited and skewed towards the countries of eastern Europe, where East German manufactured goods were exchanged for fuel or raw materials. Exports to western countries, with West Germany the main trading partner, were primarily intended to earn hard currency.

The unravelling of the eastern bloc in 1989 started not only to threaten East German exports but also to frustrate citizens eager for the economic and political reforms sweeping the rest of eastern Europe. In the summer of 1989, East Germans began to flee their country through states whose borders were newly open to the west. In East Germany itself, the firework display celebrating the fortieth anniversary of the foundation of the DDR turned out to be merely a harbinger of the end. Mass demonstrations emerged favouring reform.

As defections, and protests in Leipzig, Dresden and East Berlin partially paralyzed the country, Erich Honecker, the East German leader, resigned in favour of Egon Krenz, his protégé in the SED. Yet Honecker's resignation could neither prevent the government's subsequent demise nor delay the event that would symbolize the end of the Cold War, the fall of the Berlin Wall.

Soon after, Hans Modrow became head of a caretaker government which began to negotiate with West Germany on the basis of the issues raised by West German Chancellor Helmut Kohl's ten-point plan for German unification. The first free democratic elections were scheduled in East Germany for May 1990, as the five East German states prepared to join West Germany. Yet so intense was the pressure for change that the local elections were rescheduled for March 1990, thus encouraging East German political parties to lean heavily on the support of their West German counterparts. East Germany's Christian Democrats won the elections, with promises to establish a favourable exchange rate and protect savings during negotiations for economic and monetary union.

Gemu duly took place on 1 July 1990, and further reference to the process will be made later in the chapter (see pages 73–74). Political unification followed on 3 October 1990. As of this date, the German Democratic Republic acceded to the Federal Republic. The five new states of Brandenburg, Mecklenburg-Western Pomerania, Saxony, Saxony-Anhalt and Thuringia as well as East Berlin, which was reunited with West Berlin, became constituent parts of the enlarged Federal Republic of Germany with equal rights. On their entry the five new states automatically joined the EC, with the same rights and duties as all other parts of the Community, though transitional measures applied until the end of 1992.

The pan-German elections of 2 December 1990, made official unification complete. Helmut Kohl's Christian Democrats emerged as the winners, partly as a result of his promise to turn eastern Germany into a '**blühende Landschaft**' ('blossoming landscape'), under western German management, within four years – before the next general election.

The conversion of a former command economy into a social market system – as much 'market' as possible: as much 'state' as necessary – could not be completed in one stage. In addition to the passing of laws, to which subsequent reference will be made (see pages 71–73), far-reaching steps towards restructuring and modernizing the economy were launched throughout eastern Germany. Intensive efforts were begun to convert and streamline rigid and often outdated production facilities.

The initial effects of this conversion process have been reflected in an acute fall in the growth rates in eastern Germany. Since reliable statistics are not available on what has gone before, the figures in Table 1.8 should be treated with caution.

Table 1.8 *Eastern German growth rates (1990–92)*

Year	%
1990	–13
1991	–15
1992	–10

Source: Statistisches Bundesamt
(Federal Statistical Office)

Incentive programmes offered by the Federal, state, and local governments are, however, promoting investment, which is aimed at renewing production potential, increasing productivity, and creating much-needed new jobs in competitive industries. In 1991, Federal investment in eastern Germany totalled approximately DM 65 billion. Some 80 per cent of the total investment was spent on developing the road, rail and telecommunications infrastructure. In 1992, the Federal investment rose to a staggering DM 180 billion.

The special role of the **Treuhandanstalt** (government trust agency) in privatizing former East German industry will be discussed in a later section of the chapter (see pages 69–71).

The five new states

In addition to Federal assistance, the five new states have each launched their own incentive programmes, which embrace both direct financial support as well as tax breaks. The new states are:

Brandenburg

This is the largest of the new states, lying in Germany's northeast corner and surrounding the city of Berlin. It is home to the automotive, steel and microelectronics industries as well as metal-working. Tourism plays an important part in its economy, and the capital is Potsdam. Cottbus, Brandenburg and Frankfurt-an-der-Oder are other major cities.

Mecklenburg-Western Pomerania

Here is the second largest of the new states in terms of land area. It is the northernmost of the eastern states and contains large tracts of farm and timberland. Its industrial areas specialize in capital-goods manufacturing, ship-building, motor-vehicle production, and food processing. Tourist centres can be found along the Baltic coast. The principal cities are Rostock, Schwerin, Neubrandenburg, Stralsund, Greifswald and Wismar.

Saxony-Anhalt

Saxony-Anhalt is the third largest of the new states in terms of area but the second in population. It is located in the south-central part of Germany and has a well-diversified industrial base. The dominant industries are chemicals and building-supplies. The Harz Mountains are a traditional year-round tourist area. Magdeburg is the state capital, with Halle and Dresden representing major cities.

Saxony

This is the second smallest of the new states but, with a population density of 264 persons per square kilometre, Saxony is by far the most densely-populated one. It is located in the south-eastern corner of Germany. A traditional industrial and business centre, it remains the most heavily industrialized of the new states. Its key industries include textiles, capital goods and motor vehicles. Other important sectors are energy, non-ferrous metals, mining, food processing, electrical engineering, electronics, glass and porcelain manufacturing (including the famous Meissen works). Dresden is the capital, and Leipzig, Chemnitz, Zwickau, Görlitz and Plauen are other important centres of population.

Thuringia

Thuringia is the smallest of the new states. Situated in the southwest of former East Germany, its economy features key modern sectors such as microelectronics, engineering, construction and optical supplies as well as more traditional industries like mining, textiles and glass manufacture. Thuringia boasts a large number of spa resorts in the Thuringian Forest. Erfurt is the capital, and other significant cities are Gera, Jena and Weimar.

One of the ways in which the Federal government has attempted to change the former state-dependent business culture and to introduce a more entrepreneurial approach to economic issues is by exporting former western politicians eastwards to key government positions. Thus it was announced in January 1992 that Bernhard Vogel, ex-Minister President of Rhineland Palatinate, was to take up the post of premier of Thuringia. He becomes the third top western politician to assume such a task. Though one westerner, Kurt Biedenkopf, has met with considerable success in shaking up his state government and attracting external investment to Saxony, Werner Münch in Saxony-Anhalt has registered only modest achievements.

Such policies represent calculated risks at galvanizing the new states. The danger is that they will further aggravate opinion in eastern Germany, which is often bitter about the way westerners have imposed the social market economy on their failed Communist system. The benefit is that such experienced politicians could provide new leadership to Christian Democrats in the east who have so far not produced outstanding personalities capable of engendering cooperation between tainted former Communists and zealous young reformers with little experience of political office.

Reactions to such appointments have varied between accusations of typical **Wessi** (western German) arrogance towards the east in foisting candidates on the local party and frank admissions from **Ossis** (eastern Germans) that they do not trust anyone from their own land.

Indeed, Volker Rühe, general secretary of the Christian Democratic Union at the time and subsequently defence minister, has spoken of: '. . . two societies in one country', though he did express the hope that by the end of 1994, the date of the next general election, the two would be better mixed. Others are not so optimistic. Robert Leicht, deputy editor of *Die Zeit*, has stated: 'If you put an east German and a west German together, you will find that they are more different than a German is from a British person . . . The traditions and habits of these people are impregnated more than they realize.' Hans-Wolfgang Pfeifer, chief executive of the *Frankfurter Allgemeine Zeitung*, goes further: 'You have to recognize that these people have been living in a completely different world . . . A not inconsiderable part of our newspaper is incomprehensible to them.'

Perhaps a more auspicious and discreet form of west–east assistance is to be found in the 'state-twinning' system. Here North-Rhine Westphalia has sent over 2000 officials and advisers to Brandenburg, its adopted 'twin' state in the east. Lower Saxony is lending personnel to its eastern neighbour, Saxony-Anhalt; while Baden-Württemberg is helping Saxony, and so on.

Business and the economy

The area of the five new states is an old industrial region where business enjoys a long tradition. But during the period of transition from forty years of a state-planned economy to a social market system, much of industry is having to start more or less from scratch. The absorption of a closed, Communist economy into former West Germany's social market economy has thus resulted in what Joseph Alois Schumpeter, the celebrated Austrian economist, called, in a different context, 'creative destruction'. To date, western Germany has experienced the creation and eastern Germany the destruction!

The main reasons for this in the east are the outdated machines which hamper the necessary improvements in productivity and which cannot provide the desired product quality. According to a study by the **Institut der Weltwirtschaft** (IWW) (Institute of International Economics) in Kiel, at least 21 per cent of industrial machinery and equipment in the area of former East Germany are more than twenty years old – compared with only 5 per cent in former West Germany. Only 27 per cent of new plant were commissioned there in the last five years (40 per cent in the old Federal Republic).

Manufacturing

The structure of the industrial sectors in the five new states shows a predominance of mechanical engineering and the manufacture of vehicles, in addition to food and chemicals.

Mechanical engineering

It is estimated – because of a lack of reliable statistics – that mechanical engineering production of East Germany in 1989 amounted to DM 20 to 25 billion. But calculations by the **Verein Deutscher Maschinenbau-Anstalten** (VDMA) (Association of German Machinery and Plant Manufacturers) in Frankfurt-am-Main point to a doubling of the production value of the industry by the end of 1994. This is to be achieved mainly from joint ventures with companies in western Germany: by the end of 1990, 25 per cent of the VDMA's members were negotiating with a partner in the new states.

Vehicle building

According to information from the **Verband der Automobilindustrie** (VdA) (Association of German Automobile Manufacturers) in Frankfurt-am-Main, there were approximately 4.8 million units of passenger cars on eastern German roads at the beginning of 1991, 23.5 per cent more than a year before. During the same period, the number of trucks rose by almost 6 per cent to 775,000 units. The overall increase was due mainly to 70,000 new cars from western German and foreign production.

Future demand will increasingly be met as a result of investment in new plant in the east. In 1990, Volkswagen began to establish a new car-production facility in Mosel, near Zwickau, with manufacturing due to start in 1994. Also in 1990, Adam Opel joined with Automobilwerk Eisenach, which was formerly part of the IFA-combine, to found a new plant west of Eisenach. Finally, Mercedes-Benz is building a new facility for the production of light and medium-sized trucks at Ludwigsfelde, south of Berlin.

Chemicals

Most of the chemical plants in eastern Germany are not state of the art. According to information from the **Verband der Chemischen Industrie** (VCI) (Association of the Chemical Industry) in Frankfurt-am-Main, the situation in 1990 was characterized by production of a high percentage of basic and standard chemicals in old facilities with low productivity. In the meantime, however, the two largest chemicals companies, Leuna AG and Buna AG, have begun to implement modernization programmes. This has not been accomplished without considerable assistance from western Germany. Hoechst, Bayer and BASF have all been involved in varying degrees.

Food, beverages and tobacco

According to a study by the **Deutsches Institut für Wirtschaftsforschung** (DIW) (German Institute of Economic Research) in Berlin, this industry is the one faced with the harshest structural changes. Compared with western Germany, an insufficient range of goods is on offer, and inferior product quality is also problematic.

Many companies in this sector will have to rely on cooperation from western Germany or abroad if they are to survive. The degree of interest to date in takeovers, mergers or joint ventures has been somewhat disappointing.

Agriculture

Agriculture in former East Germany was dominated by state-owned and co-operative farms. In 1989, more than 80 per cent of all agricultural workers were employed in such establishments, cultivating 95 per cent of all agriculturally productive land, growing 75 per cent of the crops, and tending 75 per cent of the livestock. Only approximately 5 per cent of agriculturally-productive land was cultivated by 3500 farmers and their families.

In 1989, the total number of people working in agriculture was 820,000, or some 9 per cent of the labour force. This represents a high degree of overmanning, and labour will have to be shed if the sector is to become competitive in international markets.

It is assumed that a varied agricultural sector will now develop, with different types and sizes of farms. The number of co-operatives will probably decrease sharply as the number of private family farms rises. In 1990, more than 2000 farmers in eastern Germany applied for assistance to establish a family-run farm.

To facilitate the transition from a command to a social market economy, the German government set up the Treuhandanstalt. Overnight, title to the 8000 former state-owned enterprises was transferred to this body, thus making it the largest holding company in the world.

The statutory duties of this body are defined in the **Treuhandgesetz** (Trust Authority Law) of 17 June 1990, and can be summarized as follows:

- Privatization
  - rapid and comprehensive reduction of the state's role as entrepreneur
- Structural adjustment
  - restoration of competitiveness
  - reconstruction of companies
  - promotion and development of effective company structures
  - asset management
  - application of state assets according to the principles of the social market economy
- Securing and creation of employment opportunities
- Relief and support of public finances

More detail on the Treuhandgesetz can be found later in the chapter (see page 72).

When first established, the Treuhandanstalt was staffed mainly by former East German functionaries, who were less than enthusiastic about privatization. In an attempt to add weight to its commitment to privatization, and to maximize efficiency, the German government soon placed experienced executives from the west in the top posts. However, the first of these, Rainer Gohlke, resigned in August 1990, after just over one month in the job, using the word 'chaos' to describe the state of the economy in eastern Germany. He was replaced as head of the Treuhandanstalt by Detlev Rohwedder, who was brutally murdered on 1 April 1991. The current president is Birgit Breuel.

At first it was calculated that one-third of the original 8000 state-owned companies would survive without undue problems; one-third would make the transition to the social market economy, but only with substantial outside investment; a further third were held to be beyond redemption. By the beginning of 1992, the first two of these ratios had been revised downwards as more realistic estimates of the potential of the companies were made.

By far the largest number of acquisitions in eastern Germany to date have been made by companies with headquarters in western Germany. Among the first acquirers, who did not escape accusations of both 'gun-jumping' and 'cherry-picking', were the Deutsche Bank, which was quick to grasp the major share of the existing commercial banking network in a joint venture with Deutsche Kreditbank, the former East German banking monopoly. Deutsche Bank took 122 branches. Similarly, the Dresdner Bank secured 72 Kreditbank branches which, together with its own new outlets, put its representation in eastern Germany at 107 branches. Likewise, Allianz, the largest insurer in Europe, secured 51 per cent of the former East German state instance monopoly, much to the consternation of the Federal Cartel Office.

By 1 February 1992, 5584 of the former state-owned companies had been sold by the Treuhandanstalt, but fewer than 200 had been acquired by foreign companies. Among the foreign buyers were British Gas, Agip, Lafarge Coppée and Coca-Cola. Problems facing potential foreign acquirers range from company valuation difficulties, uncertainty over the ownership of land (1,100,000 property claims outstanding in March 1992), to the heavily-polluted state of factory sites. Many of them are also obliged to hesitate by the consideration: 'If it's any good, why haven't the western Germans bought it first?'

The sale of former East German companies represents only one aspect of the trust body's work: it is also obliged to close down companies which it deems to be beyond rescue. By the beginning of 1992, some 850 companies had been liquidated, among them Pentacon, the Dresden manufacturer of Praktica cameras and arguably former East Germany's most famous company. Interflug, the ex-state airline, suffered a similar fate.

Most western German companies acquiring in eastern Germany have only been prepared to make major investments at the cost of large-scale redundancies. Robotron, an electronics firm now owned by Siemens, was obliged to reduce its staff from 68,000 to 15,000. Carl Zeiss Oberkochen buying its namesake in Jena insisted on redundancies on a similar scale.

Wholesale company closures and the downsizing of workforces have inevitably led to huge rises in unemployment in eastern Germany, a phenomenon which will be treated later in the chapter (see pages 75–76).

Business and the law

In principle, the law of the old Federal Republic of Germany also applies now to the five new states. A comprehensive **Einigungsvertrag** (Unification Treaty) concluded between the two German republics on 31 August 1990, laid down all the details for the changeover to a social market economy, as well as the limited application of special parts of former East German law, and the newly-drafted regulations for transition.

Even during the period after the first free elections and the creation of the first-freely elected East German government in March 1990, comprehensive new regulations for the preparation of the conversion to a social market economy were adopted. A vast number of laws had to be passed for which there were no precedents, not only for the restitution of land and companies to their former owners but also for the modernization and privatization of state-owned companies.

The adaptation of the social system to that of western Germany required its complete reorganization. This could only take place with the establishment of proper institutions, and in several stages, so that no excessive burdens were placed on the population in either part of Germany. The new citizens of Germany enjoy, thus, the right to equal treatment, e.g. in the field of labour law and in finding employment. A rapid expansion of Labour Offices alone would not have sufficed: the number of courts in all sectors had also to be increased. Administrative courts, for example, where the decisions of the administration are subject to judicial review, were totally alien to the concept of a state economy. Nor could the judges working in civil and criminal jurisdiction be expected to administer justice at short notice under a new legal system. For the adaptation of the Grundgesetz (Basic Law) of western Germany, administrative authorities had to be reorganized as well as the entire legal and administrative structure.

Reorganization comprised not only all aspects of economic life but also cultural and public life as well. The aim of the conversion process is an economic system based on private ownership, which also applies to the means of production, freedom of trade, with no regulation of prices (by all persons involved in business), but within a legal framework for the protection of free competition and social security. Therefore, the organizational structure of companies had to be changed completely, and real estate reviewed.

The following measures were significant for business:

- The Treuhandgesetz, to which reference has already been made (see page 69), was adopted by the transitional government of former East Germany. It formed the basis of the complete transfer of all state-owned enterprises into the trust property of the Treuhandanstalt. By act of law, therefore, as of 1 July 1990, all state-owned enterprises were converted into AGs (corporations) and GmbHs (limited liability companies) according to the German Commercial Code, the shares of which were lodged with the Treuhandanstalt.
- Enterprises converted into private companies had to present information required for the **Handelsregister** (company registry) at the appropriate **Registergericht** (registration court) by 16 July 1990.
- The newly-founded AGs and GmbHs were also required to present to the Treuhandanstalt by 31 October 1990, draft articles of association in compliance with the German Commercial Code as well as an **Eröffnungsbilanz** (opening balance sheet) retrospective to 1 July 1990. The basic principles for the establishment of the opening balance sheet were laid down in the **DM-Bilanzgesetz** (DM Balance Sheet Law) as stipulated in the Unification Treaty.
- General principles for the re-transfer of land and enterprises to their former owners were established in the **Gesetz zur Regelung offener Vermögensfragen** (Law on the Settlement of Open Questions as relating to Assets). These principles allow for **Wertausgleich** (value equalization) and damages in cases where assets no longer exist to their former value.

Despite the passing of laws and the wholesale transfer of judges from western Germany to administer them, anyone expecting to encounter the same law-abiding, indeed law-revering, business culture as in the western part of the country will be bitterly disappointed by what they experience in the east. The Business Crimes Office of the Treuhandanstalt registered some 500 cases of bribery, accepting bribes, offences under the German Official Secrets Act, and fraudulent bankruptcy in the course of 1991. Hans Richter, the head of the Office, is quoted as saying: 'The control mechanisms are for the most part just not in force in the east'. According to Jutta Limbach, Berlin's justice senator, the German capital city was cheated out of DM 4.5 billion from 1 July 1990, to the end of 1991. Indeed, the prevalence of commercial fraud in eastern Germany provoked *Der Spiegel* of 9 September 1991, into commenting: 'The risk of business criminals being caught in the east is scarcely greater than in a Latin American banana republic.'

Business and finance

The most significant single event affecting the business culture in eastern Germany in terms of finance has been Gemu.

The whole process was surrounded by controversy from the outset. Early in February 1990, Karl Otto Pöhl, President of the West German Bundesbank at the time, described the idea of monetary union between West and East Germany as 'fantastic'. It was, he said: 'an illusion to believe that even one of East Germany's problems could be solved', either by monetary union or by some alternative kind of parallel currency arrangement. Yet in the very same week, he was obliged to retract this statement and declare that he supported Helmut Kohl's policy of monetary unification. The retraction was a demonstration of the limits of the Bundesbank's much-vaunted independence: constitutionally, it is bound to support the government's general economic policies (see page 22).

In April 1990, the Bundesbank recommended an exchange rate of one West German DM for two Ostmarks, except for the first 2000 Ostmarks of a person's savings. President Pöhl argued at the time that there was no further room for generosity because higher instant spending power in East Germany would prove to be inflationary, and the Bundesbank is obliged to protect the value of the currency (see page 23). Again, the Bundesbank was rebuffed, its proposals being subsequently amended by Chancellor Kohl, who insisted on an exchange rate of one DM for one Ostmark for salaries and pensions, as well as for the first 4000 marks of savings for all those between 14 and 60. Children were only permitted to exchange 2000 marks at this rate, while for pensioners the ceiling was 6000 marks. All other savings were converted at one-to-two, and company debts were also halved at a rate of one DM to two Ostmarks.

Gemu occurred on these terms on 1 July 1990, to the accompaniment of much celebration throughout eastern Germany. The currency switch was handled with brilliant technical precision, but the repercussions for eastern German industry were grave. From Gemu onwards, goods made in eastern Germany were priced in DM, and many of the country's trading partners in eastern Europe were no longer able to pay at the high, hard-currency exchange rate. The result was a virtual collapse of the export economy. Internally, productivity levels in eastern Germany were approximately 30 per cent of those in western Germany and product quality was usually inferior. The outcome here was that western German goods were sucked into the east of the country in ever greater volumes. Many parts of the domestic economy in eastern Germany were adversely affected. Inflation rates soared.

Even the cost of dying skyrocketed. The demise of state-run funerals left thousands unable to afford a decent burial. By 1991, coffins were almost 25 times dearer than under the old Communist system, and the total cost of a funeral was often the equivalent of two months' wages. No wonder Karl Otto Pöhl subsequently described the terms of Gemu as 'a disaster'! (Table 1.9).

Table 1.9 *Eastern German inflation rates (1990–92)*

Year	%
1990	4
1991	10
1992	9.2

Source: Deutsche Bundesbank (German Federal Bank)

In May 1991, Herr Pöhl. announced his resignation as President of the Bundesbank, emphasizing his desire to devote more time to his family. It was, however, an open secret in Germany that he still harboured deep misgivings about the wisdom of grafting a Trabant economy onto a Mercedes business culture. Moreover, there was widespread speculation that he was not in agreement with the EC plan to found a European Central Bank under political control.

Helmut Schlesinger, Pöhl's deputy, took over as President of the Bundesbank on 1 August 1991, after almost forty years' service there. He has the reputation of a monetary hardliner and can be counted on to pursue the same vigorous, anti-inflation policies as his predecessor while protecting the Bundesbank from undesirable political interference.

Business and the labour market

Demography

Recent years have revealed a decrease in the population of former East Germany. By the end of 1989, it amounted to 16.3 million. While the total population in the eleven former states of the Federal Republic declined on account of a negative birth rate since 1972, the main reason for the population decrease in former East Germany lay in migration to West Germany. In 1988, 39,832 easterners moved to the west; in 1989, the figure jumped to 343,854; in 1990, it dropped back to 238,384. The reasons for such migrations were enhanced job prospects and standards of living in the west.

At the end of 1989, 47.9 per cent of the resident population were male and 52.1 per cent female. Population density at the same time amounted to approximately 140,000 citizens per square kilometre. It is lower in the rural areas of Mecklenburg-Western Pomerania and Brandenburg and increases towards the more highly-industrialized south.

Unemployment

It is, of course, unemployment in eastern Germany that has borne the full brunt of Gemu as factories were closed and labour forces drastically cut. Even the 600-person, 100-animal East German state circus had to fold its tents. The army ballet, orchestra, cabaret and ensemble suffered a similar fate, but the army choir was allowed to remain.

On 1 July 1990, the number of registered unemployed in the east rose from 270,000 (approximately 2.8 per cent of the unsustainably large labour force) to 1,060,000 (12 per cent) in October 1991. The number on short-time work rose from 660,000 (6.7 per cent of the labour force) to 1,450,000 (13.5 per cent) over the same period. In addition, approximately 450,000 easterners were commuting daily to the west of the country (Table 1.10).

Table 1.10 *Eastern German unemployment rates (1990–92)*

Year	%
1990	5
1991	12
1992	14.5

Source: Statistisches Bundesamt (Federal Statistical Office)

The reaction of the German government to such alarming rises in unemployment in the east has been to increase investment in a number of schemes. 2000 Labour Office employees were dispatched to the east to assess needs and set up appropriate programmes. By October 1991, the number of easterners on training schemes was 320,000; work-creation schemes accounted for a further 280,000; and early retirement schemes for 566,000. 4,324,000 citizens in the east were in full-time employment.

Perhaps the most controversial of the government's policies are the job-creation schemes. Here some 400,000 workers were employed in 1992. Under these programmes, the state pays people between 90 and 100 per cent of their previous wages. This makes work-creation schemes more attractive than the training schemes, where wages of only 70 per cent of previous levels are offered. The fear is that job-creation schemes might crowd out private investments and therefore prolong the agony of the unemployed.

The first signs of an upswing, and with it slight relief for the labour market, were visible in early 1992 at the latest. By then, small and medium-sized western German firms had begun to invest. Vofa, a specialist company employing approximately 1000 people making cables for the automobile industry, was building a new plant at Gehren in Thuringia. Henkel, the chemicals, cosmetics and detergent manufacturer, another family concern but at the big end of the medium-sized scale, had also started investing in the east.

If real jobs are to be created in sufficient numbers, many more Mittelstand companies, the backbone of western Germany's economy, will have to follow Vofa's and Henkel's examples. Investment cannot be left to the state and to the large companies alone. Unfortunately, some Mittelstand companies in the west are experiencing their own special problems, as was noted earlier (see page 60). Equalization of unemployment rates between the west and east of the country will take a considerable time to achieve, and will certainly not be accomplished by December 1994, the date of the next general election.

Business and trade unions

It is perhaps a matter of some regret that the DGB (Confederation of German Trade Unions) has not given a stronger lead in helping to refashion the business culture in eastern Germany. Instead, it has been embroiled, since unification, in an unseemly wrangle over the ownership of assets which belonged to the former **Allgemeiner Deutscher Gewerk-schaftsbund** (ADGB) – the main trade union confederation prior to 1933. A commission ruled at the end of 1991 that the DGB is not the legal successor of the **Freier Deutscher Gewerkschaftsbund** (FDBG) – the union confederation of former East Germany – and therefore is not entitled to take over its assets. The DGB's view is that property which belonged to the ADGB prior to 1933 should be transferred automatically to the DGB, and that property acquired by the FDGB after 1945 should be sold to the DGB at a 'fair price'.

The main contribution to the business culture in eastern Germany which the individual trade unions have made to date appears to be in the area of high wage claims. These have met with varying degrees of resistance from employers' associations, but wage awards have risen considerably since Gemu, partly though not entirely, as a result of high inflation in the east (see page 74). **Tarifunion** (the harmonization of pay and conditions with workers in the west of the country) has also been one of the major driving forces.

In fact, it could be argued that it is in the area of wages that the economies of the two parts of the country have grown closest together. The ratio of wages per employee in the east to that in the west rose from 32 per cent in the second half of 1989 to about 50 per cent in the first half of 1991. On account of declining output, labour costs per-hour-worked in eastern Germany increased by 73 per cent between the second and fourth quarters of 1990.

The first signs of industrial unrest appeared in November 1990, when 250,000 Reichsbahn workers walked out for two days, bringing all rail traffic in the five new states, including 550 goods trains, to a grinding halt. The railway workers, whose numbers were expected to be halved, secured a forty-hour week as from April 1991, and a phased harmonization of pay with workers in western Germany.

In December 1990, insurance employees marched through Leipzig and Berlin, protesting at the low level of their salaries. The **Deutsche Angestellten-Gewerkschaft** (German White-Collar Workers' Union), based in western Germany, promised to back their cause. Eastern German insurance employees were earning approximately 40 per cent of their western counterparts.

It was, however, the settlement achieved by IG Metall (Metal Workers' Union) that set the pace for wage deals in the new states. In their 1991 negotiations for the east, the union secured wage rates, from April 1991, of 62.5 per cent of their western equivalent, an outcome much nearer the 65 per cent claim than the 50 per cent offer by the employers. Moreover, the negotiations provided for an increase to 71 per cent of western German pay as from April 1991; a further increase to 82 per cent of rates in the west from April 1993; and finally an increase to 100 per cent of western German pay by April 1994.

The race to catch up with wages in the west is proving a boon for some unions eager to increase their membership. By January 1991, IG Metall had 35 offices in eastern Germany, through a merger with its counterpart in the east, and was targeting one million new members, or 12.5 per cent of the total workforce in the five new states, by March 1991. Other trade unions based in the west have not been so successful in persuading the citizens of eastern Germany that subscriptions of 2 per cent of their hard-earned salaries represent a good investment. The pressure is on these unions to produce results in the form of handsome wage settlements. Increased membership will then be their reward.

Business, education, training and development

It is perhaps in the area of education, training and development that the business culture of former East Germany was most deeply inculcated into its citizenry. As a consequence, the attitudes and values acquired over so many years are proving to be the ones most difficult to change. These are, therefore, worth looking at in some detail.

The whole of the education system in former East Germany was founded on the state's claim to the right of the education of children within the Communist world order. A child's education was not a parental right. Consequently, the essence of the education to which all children were exposed was heavily influenced by the tenets of Communism. This resulted in the ideological homogenization of all schools, colleges and universities.

Even the **Kindergärten**, which were attended by 93 per cent of age cohort, were run either by the state or by state-owned companies and thus subject to Communist party ideology. Political indoctrination continued in the so-called Polytechnic Upper School, attended by all children from the age of six to sixteen. This school was regarded as the pre-selection stage for the profession to be chosen. Indeed, every school was closely tied to its own godfather company, with 80 per cent of pupils doing voluntary work in the factory during school holidays. Entry to the Extended Polytechnic School to take the **Abitur** (the German counterpart of 'A' levels) was restricted by the state to some 8 per cent of age cohort.

Very few young people in former East Germany failed to take an apprenticeship. Thus, after completing the tenth class in the Polytechnic Upper School, 87 per cent of age cohort were exposed to a two-year vocational training course, with 85 per cent of these youngsters signing an apprenticeship contract on first application, usually with the school's godfather factory. The practical work was done in this factory and the theory learned in the factory's own vocational school.

Tertiary studies at university or college were held to be a high social distinction and the personal duty of the student to the working class and the state. Access to university or college education was on the one hand determined structurally by the economic and social needs of the state. On the other, access was personally determined by political loyalty, e.g. membership of the Free German Youth movement or by 'volunteering' for three years' military service as opposed to the normal 18 months'.

By the end of the 1980s, a system had been established whereby the six universities and nine technological universities provided the people for the top management functions in all aspects of the state. The nine engineering colleges and two economics colleges provided the technical or back-up staff. Most engineers and technicians, then, formed a middle stratum between the intelligentsia and the working class.

It was the members of the intelligentsia who took over not only the running of the state, the party, its planning institutions but also its combines and the companies integrated into them. The top managers, or directors general, of the combines received their management development at the élite Central Institute for the Socialist Economic Experience. Middle managers, or higher industrial functionaries as they should be called, were developed at the Institutes for the Socialist Economic Experience attached to the fourteen ministries running the various sectors of the economy.

The directors general of the largest state-owned combines had arguably more power than the presidents of companies in the United States of America. Eight of them actually sat on the SED's central committee. They were thus even more powerful than the industry ministers to whom they reported. Their elevated position gave them the freedom to break many of the rules and regulations, and afforded them priority in the allocation of precious resources and access to hard currency.

'Middle managers' is not the correct term for the next layer of management: higher industrial functionaries is more apposite. Their power was restricted not only by the one-man management practices of their directors general, but also by the trade unions and local SED party. Indeed, they were even impaired by the realities of commercial life in the system. Profits were only regarded as genuine if earned within the plan; raw materials had to be bought in at costs laid down by the state; and prices for finished goods were similarly dictated by the state. In other words, these people did not manage: they functioned by taking orders from above and executing them.

As a result of their limited education, highly-specialized training and development, and above all the erstwhile management practices, former East Germany's managers are not held in high regard by western Germany companies acquiring in the east. Many of them have been dismissed, especially former Communist party officials and members of the **Stasi** (state security police). Others have been demoted for incompetence. Yet some, especially sales managers, have been retained because of their deep acquaintance of, and contacts with, markets in eastern European countries.

In 1990, an attempt was made by Mülder & Partner, a Munich firm of management consultants, to ascertain whether, despite all the evidence to date, there was an untapped pool of top management talent in the east. 250 eastern German managers were surveyed for their suitability as management board members in companies in western Germany. Of the 250, only seven would qualify. The other 243 would fail on account of their lack of market knowledge, lack of creativity and lack of flexibility.

Even the seven successful candidates, however, would face an uphill task, not least on account of their acceptability in the west. There is a widespread conviction in western Germany that: 'The Ossis (eastern Germans) are all turncoats: yesterday Karl Marx; tomorrow Ludwig Erhard.'

It is for all the above reasons that education, training and development are being reformed in the east of the country. The five new states now

enjoy the same autonomy in matters of education and culture as their western counterparts. Because the state governments in the east are predominantly CDU-controlled, the western German selective school system has
been taken over lock, stock and barrel, with the **Gesamtschule** (comprehensive school) being very much a minority experiment.

Likewise in higher education, restructuring goes on apace. From the
mid-1970s, higher education in East Germany was fairly static, with student numbers remaining around 130,000 in total throughout the 1980s. In
West Germany, by comparison, total student numbers in tertiary education
rose from one million to one and half million over the same decade.
Following unification, much freer access to higher education has been
allowed, and this has resulted in a marked increase in student admissions.

Greater participation rates at the tertiary level have led to a deterioration
in student:staff ratios, which at the time of unification were approximately
4:1 (compared with 14:1 in the west). Staff in universities and colleges have
had to re-apply for their jobs, in competition with candidates from both
parts of Germany. Some staff who were officially employed by the Stasi
have been purged, and there are many cases outstanding which involve
allegations of unofficial collaboration with the former security forces.

In vocational education, eastern Germany's biggest problem is that only
50,000 apprenticeships were on offer in 1991 to the 120,000 young people
wanting them. The Federal government is cajoling companies to offer more
places, as it did successfully in West Germany in the early 1980s, and giving DM 5000 per year subsidy per training place in the east. Even so, the
state is having to train on a large scale, contrary to the ethos of the Dual
System in the west (see pages 46–47).

Business and the environment

Any consideration for the protection of the environment was totally lacking in the business culture of former East Germany. Indeed, the main environmental theme for the united country in the foreseeable future will be
the raising of standards in polluted eastern Germany. The costs are estimated by the DIW in Berlin to total some DM 30 billion. The task will take
until the end of the millennium to complete: so great was the physical
destruction wrought in forty years of neglect.

Origins of the problem

Although environmental protection laws had been in existence since 1986
in former East Germany, measures governing permissible emissions,

concentrations, and penalties for infringements and failures to comply were introduced only towards the end of the 1980s. Even then, they were honoured more in the breach than in the observance. Moreover, key sectors, such as the energy industry, were exempted from existing standards by special provisions.

The major causes of the present catastrophic environmental situation are:

- Many years of maintaining an energy and structural policy characterized by large-scale use of brown coal; heavy industry involving intensive application of energy and raw materials; high energy consumption and outmoded production processes.
- Long-term neglect of environmental precautions and excessively low funding for environmental protection measures.
- An underdeveloped industry for the production of environmental technology which was unable to meet demand.

Particular areas of concern are air, water, waste, and nature protection.

Air

With emissions of sulphur dioxide and dust affecting 36.1 per cent and 30 per cent of citizens respectively, air pollution levels are classified as very high or extremely high. In certain areas with the latter levels of pollution, the number of respiratory diseases among children rose between 1974 and 1989 by 111 per cent. Indeed, doctors in Halle issued a statement in 1990, declaring: 'Of the three possible types of illness caused by environmental pollution – eye infections, respiratory diseases, skin disorders – almost every local inhabitant has one.'

Air pollution is created mainly by the energy, chemicals and transport sectors. Exhaust emissions cause the death of forests, and it was estimated in 1989 that 54.3 per cent of former East Germany's forests were already severely damaged.

Water

After air pollution, water pollution is the most significant environmental problem facing eastern Germany. Of the approximately 17.7 billion cubic metres of water available each year, 19 per cent cannot be used for drinking or for irrigation on account of pollution.

In 1988, approximately 450,000 inhabitants of former East Germany were drinking water, over sustained periods, with a nitrate content above the World Health Organization limit value. The figure rose to 1,200,000 by the end of 1989.

The water pollution capital of former East Germany was the town of

Bitterfeld. When added together, all the liquid waste produced by Bitterfeld's factories amounted in 1989 to an annual total of 70 million cubic metres of poisonous by-products, containing dangerous salts and acids, phenol, chlorohydrocarbons and mercury.

Waste

In former East Germany, there were very few plants to reduce the volume of waste or even to provide preliminary treatment to eliminate pollutants, and those which did exist failed to meet international standards. The pollution of the environment by uncontrolled and inappropriate dumping of waste occurred mainly through contamination of the groundwater.

In view of the uncontrolled dumping of household and special refuse in over 7000 unregistered sites, and the additional imports of waste from western countries (including 5,000,000 tonnes of waste per annum from western Germany), a comprehensive waste disposal system is an initial priority.

Nature protection

The ecological dangers to the natural environment indicated above have led to the extinction of many plant and animal species. The number of animal species threatened with extinction increased between 1970 and 1989 from 203 to 302.

Initial projects

Since 1990, it has been agreed to launch six major environmental initiatives in former East Germany. These are:

- The installation of a smog early warning system.
- The establishment of a heating plant for untreated brown coal in Magdeburg.
- The construction of a small heating plant in Staaken.
- The building of several plants to recover chlorohydrocarbons and mercury in Buna.
- The incineration of pharmaceutical residues at high temperatures in Dresden.
- The establishment of a plant for the production of chlorine in Buna.

By late 1991, the first of these projects was well under way. Three new air pollution monitoring units and thirteen container stations fitted with automatic monitoring equipment were set up between the Baltic Sea and the

Thuringian Forest. The aim is to permit long-term forecasts of atmospheric pollution and the travel-range of pollutant particles caught by high-altitude airstreams. These data are of vital importance for the smog alarm system in the winter months. A similar system, providing early warning of elevated ozone levels in summer – 'summer smog' – is currently undergoing trials. To keep the public informed, arrangements are in hand to publish the latest environmental data on BTX, the German PTT's interactive videotex system.

Business prospects

Carl Hahn, the head of the Volkswagen management board, summed up the problem most accurately: the conversion of the centrally-planned economies of the former Communist countries to market economies on the western model is an extremely difficult and expensive task. Professor Horst Siebert, director of the IWW in Kiel, believes that the process of transformation in eastern Europe, as opposed to former East Germany, will take not years but decades.

The problem for western Germans is that their fellow citizens in the east will not be willing to give them many years, let alone decades, in which to convert their part of the country into the promised 'blossoming landscape'. Unless progress is visible and swift, they will continue to migrate westwards in ever-increasing numbers, with the intelligent, the young and the fit in the vanguard.

The conversion process for the economy began promptly after Gemu, but with a two-year period, of 'creative destruction', the like of which not even Schumpeter could have imagined. The economy in the east went into virtual free fall. In the problem sectors such as ship-building, chemicals and electronics, factories were closed, workers made redundant, placed on short-time working, or encouraged to retire early. At the same time, institutions for the future were put in place and vast amounts of money invested by the German public purse and private companies alike. However, little inward investment was made by foreign companies.

Nonetheless, by the beginning of 1992 at the latest, signs of the long-awaited upswing became visible in the east. Queues of vehicles with western German registration plates on the autobahns and scaffold-shrouded towns attested to a palpable feeling that help and reconstruction were under way. This was also reflected in the 20 per cent increase over the year in the output of the construction industry.

By the same time, the Treuhandanstalt had privatized approximately 5500 of the original 8000 state-owned companies, some of which had been broken up into more manageable units, giving an overall total of approximately 11,600 for sale. Acquisitions in the east were led by the major companies based in western Germany, with medium-sized and smaller companies there showing more reluctance to take the plunge.

Yet if the economy in eastern Germany is to experience a full recovery, the citizens there cannot rely solely on their fellow countrymen in the west: they will have to learn to help themselves. Signs of an enterprise culture in eastern Germany are beginning to emerge. In 1988, there were only 182,000 self-employed people in the workforce in the east, including family members helping in the businesses (2.1 per cent of the workforce compared with 12.6 per cent in former West Germany). In 1990 alone, 350,000 applications to establish businesses were received by the appropriate authorities.

The business prospects must be more auspicious for eastern Germany than for any of the other ex-Communist states in central and eastern Europe. The citizens of this part of Germany can rely on continued, massive financial and technical aid from their fellow countrymen in the west, not least because it is in their own self-interest. But the eastern Germans possess a further significant advantage over their former Communist comrades in the shape of the successful business culture in western Germany to which they can aspire. If they can come to terms with, then gradually absorb its attitudes, values and norms, business should, in the fullness of time, flourish as it does in the west. Speculation about a second, pan-German economic miracle, even by the end of the millennium, would appear, however, premature.

References and suggestions for further reading

Ambrosius, G. (1984), *Der Staat als Unternehmer*, Göttingen: Vandenhoeck and Ruprecht.

Ardagh, J. (1987), *Germany and the Germans*, London: Hamilton.

Böhler, W. (1984), *Betriebliche Weiterbildung und Bildungsurlaub*, Düsseldorf: Centaurus.

Burtenshaw, D. (1984), *The Economic Geography of Germany*, London: Macmillan.

Capital, various issues between 1982 and 1992.

Childs, D. (1992), *Germany in the Twentieth Century*, London: Batsford.

Childs, D. and Johnson, J. (1981), *West Germany – Politics and Society*, London: Croom Helm.

Conradt, D.P. (1978), *The German Polity*, New York: Longman.

Cullingford, E.C.M. (1976), *Trade Unions in Germany*, London: West View Press.

Economist, The, various issues between 1982 and 1992.

Economist Intelligence Unit (1992), *Germany Country Profile, 1991–92*, London: The Economist Intelligence Unit.

Economist Intelligence Unit (1992), *Germany Country Report*, London: The Economist Intelligence Unit.

Financial Times, various editions between 1982 and 1992.

Handy, C. et al. (1988) *Making Managers*, London: Pitman.

Hübner, E., and Rudolfs, H.-H. (1992), *Jahrbuch der Bundesrepublik Deutschland 1991/92*, Munich: Beck/DTV.

Investor's Chronicle, various issues between 1982 and 1992.

Jäkel, E. and Junge, W. (1978), *Die Deutschen Industrie- und Handelskammern und der Deutsche Industrie- und Handelstag*, Munich: Droste.

Kloss, G. (1989), *West Germany: An Introduction*, Basingstoke: Macmillan.

Koch, K. (1989), *West Germany Today*, London: Routledge.

Lawrence, P. (1980), *Managers and Management in West Germany*, London: Croom Helm.

Manager Magazin, various issues between 1982 and 1992.

OECD Economic Surveys, West Germany and Germany, various years between 1982 and 1992.

Oldham, K.M. (1981), *Accounting Systems and Practices in Europe*, London: Gower.

Owen-Smith, E. (1983), *The West German Economy*, London: Croom Helm.

Price Waterhouse (1992), *Doing Business in Germany*, London: Price Waterhouse.

Randlesome, C. (1992) 'East German Managers – From Karl Marx to Adam Smith?' in *European Management Journal*, Volume 10, Number 1, March 1991.

Römer, K., Dreikandt, U.K. and Wullenkord, C. (1987), *Facts about Germany*, Gütersloh: Bertelsman.

Schuster, D. (1977), *Der Deutsche Gewerkschaftsbund*, Düsseldorf: Droste.

Smith, G. (1982), *Democracy in Western Germany*, Aldershot: Gower.

Spiegel, Der, various issues between 1982 and 1992.

Times, The, various editions between 1982 and 1992.

Wall Street Journal, The, various editions between 1982 and 1992.

Watson, A. (1992), *The Germans: Who are they now?*, London: Thames Methuen.

Wirtschaftswoche, Die, various issues between 1982 and 1992.

Witte, E., Kallmann, A. and Sachs, G. (1989), *Führungskräfte der Wirtschaft*, Cologne: Poeschel.

Zeit, Die, various issues between 1982 and 1992.

Lille •
ARTOIS

Rouen • Amiens • PICARDY

NORMANDY
ILE DE • Reims
Paris ■ FRANCE CHAMPAGNE
LORRAINE
Nancy • Strasbourg •
ALSACE

BRITTANY
MAINE
Le Mans • Orléans •
ANJOU ORLEANAIS
Nantes • Tours • FRANCHE
Bourges Dijon • Besancon • COMTE
TOURAINE NIVERNAIS
BERRY
POITOU BURGUNDY
Poitiers • BOURBONNAIS

AUNIS
SAINTONGE MARCHE LYONNAIS
ANGOUMOIS Limoges • Lyon • SAVOY
Clermont •
Ferrand Grenoble •
LIMOUSIN AUVERGNE
DAUPHINE
Bordeaux •
GUYENNE
Monaco •

GASCONY Toulouse • PROVENCE
LANGUEDOC
BEARN Marseille •

Perpignan •
ROUSSILLON

2 The business culture in France
Colin Gordon

Introduction

As in the United Kingdom, in the 1980s business in France was faced with a drastic upheaval in both the political and economic environment. In the United Kingdom, emphasis on the supply-side of the economy throughout the Thatcher years led to the enterprise culture with companies experiencing fewer and fewer constraints, particularly in terms of finance and labour relations. In France, however, the sea-change was of a different order which is typified by the French obsession with the idea that since the first oil shock of 1974, France was in a state of **crise** (crisis) from which it has only now just emerged.

During that time business had to come to terms with the realization that the **Trente Glorieuses**, thirty years of constant growth since 1945 which in the 1960s even exceeded that of former West Germany, were over. Profits and investment rapidly declined in a country which obstinately refused to wake up to reality and to cut back on paying its citizens enough to maintain their sacrosanct standard of living. Businesses, and not individuals, were made to pay for this 'crisis' through indexed wages and spiralling debt and social charges.

An ill-timed reflation of the economy by a Socialist government in 1981 brought yet more grief and it was only in the mid-1980s that French business began to recover slowly from the changed circumstances of the previous ten to fifteen years and to adapt to the competitive challenge of a wider European market. Now in the 1990s there is a general awareness that some considerable catching-up has been achieved and France has rapidly closed the gap on its major industrial competitors.

So, change was not gradual in France, but marked by a long period of deeply disturbing events shaped both by external developments and domestic policies.

Yet despite the setbacks to an economy which, according to a Hudson Institute report of the early 1970s, was set to become the Japan of Europe, France has bounced back energetically and has underlying strengths on which to draw:

- The fourth-largest economy of the OECD countries behind the USA, Japan and Germany, but ahead of Italy and the United Kingdom.
- A highly-successful policy of deflation through maintaining the strength of the franc within the EMS which, in spite of the recession, has led France to have one of the strongest economies in the EC, with a rate of inflation of 3.5 per cent and growth of 2 per cent in 1992.
- A strong growth in industrial competitiveness which at last seems to be overcoming a nagging trade deficit, as exports grow strongly.
- A nationwide consensus on the importance of education and training.
- A degree of cooperation between industry and government.
- A concerted effort by many companies to become more internationally oriented. Overseas investment increased by a factor of five over the late 1980s, as companies increased market share by external acquisition.
- A greater willingness to take risks – management buyouts are now more common currency – in a general climate of public opinion which has grown to accept the business world and the idea of profit-making after a long tradition of aversion.
- A new type of self-made business leader is emerging to challenge the highly élitist structure of French management.
- Increasing use by large companies of share capital in preference to debt, thus creating an upsurge in the importance of Paris as a strong financial centre.

Considerable concern and question marks remain, however, in a number of areas:

- In politics, although the situation is relatively stable, the popularity of both the President and the government are at an all-time low, the right-wing parties are split over many issues, and the National Front has dramatically grown in strength.
- There has been a worrying increase in social tension as a result of problems with ethnic minorities, principally North African, in France's major cities.
- Although numerically weak, trade unions have begun to flex their considerable muscle in the public sector, particularly over increased pay after some years of wage restraint.
- Although stabilized in 1992 at 10 per cent of the working population, unemployment will still prove difficult to contain without sustained growth over the coming years.
- The tax structure is badly in need of reform, since high social security contributions, a minimum wage (**le SMIC**) and local business rates all act effectively as taxes on jobs.
- The élitist management education system may not be turning out the right calibre of flexible, international manager, capable of responding quickly enough to shorter product life cycles.

- The same system, with its rigid equation of qualifications with hierarchical grades, is suppressing the aspirations of the supervisory and lower grades to management status.
- Many French companies, albeit dynamic, are undercapitalized and lack the critical size necessary to compete in the European and global markets post-1992. They are therefore easy prey to foreign corporate raiders.
- In spite of the increased overseas investment, managers lack the international vision and experience of their counterparts in Germany, the United Kingdom, USA, etc.
- The level of R & D investment in private companies is insufficient.
- In its attempt to reduce its budgetary deficit, the state is increasingly short of cash to inject into the sizable nationalized sector to enable it to make necessary overseas acquisitions. In addition, any attempts to aid the public sector are increasingly coming in for close scrutiny by the EC Commission.
- Is the state therefore going to be forced into a further bout of privatizations in the almost certain event of a right-wing government in the forthcoming general election?
- Is France really prepared to accept a Europe in which its pivotal role has been both challenged and weakened by the unification of Germany, the possible accession of new members and a thorough reform of the Common Agricultural Policy?

The scene has been set in France, however, for an almost complete restoration to full health of the economy and for a transformation of traditions, values and strategies which will enable France to benefit more substantially, not only from the European single market but also from the globalization of markets.

Business and government

It has often been said that in France market forces have never been allowed to function freely due to a long succession of interventionist policies in all aspects of economic and industrial activity. Perhaps more than in any other OECD country, central government, therefore, has played a crucial and all-pervasive role in determining the major directions in which business activities have moved. Decentralization in the 1980s shifted some of the centres of decision-making but nevertheless central government continues to be the major determinant of policy.

Central government

Three features in particular stand out when examining the role of central government since the Second World War. Firstly, the importance attached to a system of five-year economic plans, especially during the Trente Glorieuses. Secondly, largely in response to the former West German economic miracle and the American challenge of the 1960s, the French authorities devised a system of industrial policies specifically designed to convert inefficient industries and develop those of the future. This took the form of mergers and takeovers engineered by a policy of tax incentives, medium and long-term credits allocated through a state-directed financial sector, and direct government intervention. This was the policy of 'national champions' and such present-day companies as CGE, Péchiney, Saint-Gobain, Rhône-Poulenc, SNIAS (Aérospatiale) were all moulded during this period. Thirdly, the fact that from 1945 until 1981, with one or two minor exceptions, France enjoyed an uninterrupted period of one-party rule, the rise of the Socialist party as an alternative government being of quite recent date – the early 1970s.

The initial plans were limited to building up industry after the devastation of war but in the boom years of the 1960s they became so sophisticated and all-embracing – they covered not only all macro-economic variables but also industrial inputs and outputs – that they generated much interest abroad and France was considered to have discovered the secret of managing effectively the complexities of a national economy. Internal crises – the return of one million **pieds noirs**, the white settlers of Algeria, in 1962, for example – and international constraints such as that imposed by the first oil shock, eventually blew some of the later plans off course. Planning lost much of its importance, and the 1970s were typified by erratic stop-go policies implemented in reaction to the new conditions of reduced growth. Under ex-President Giscard d'Estaing and his Prime Minister growth slumped to -2 per cent in 1975 (the first minus figure since the war), investment fell sharply and both bankruptcies and unemployment increased dramatically. Under Raymond Barre, Chirac's successor, there was an attempt both to combat the immediate crisis with an austerity programme of higher taxation and a temporary freeze on wages and prices and to initiate a longer-term restructuring of the economy to bring it more into line with the country which increasingly became France's obsession, former West Germany. (Even today, all leading indicators are compared avidly with those of Germany.)

The result was a dramatically-high level of unemployment (1½ million in 1981) and the austerity programme did not reduce inflation (13 per cent in 1980). The franc held steady, however, due partially to a growth rate slightly above the Western average (GNP grew by 1½ per cent in 1980). A healthy surplus in the trade balance was wiped out by the second oil crisis of 1979.

This, then, was the situation inherited by the in-coming Socialist government, with François Mitterand as President. There is some argument about the opportuneness of the economic policy of reflation which he then decided to pursue. Most observers consider reflation against the stream of a severe world recession was akin to harakiri. Others, particularly the French themselves, deem it to have been purely unlucky in its timing. Certainly, its objectives were clear and laudable: increased growth, reduced unemployment, reduced wage differentials, and maintenance of purchasing power. To achieve these objectives, there was an increase in the SMIC, an increase in social benefits, a reduction in the working week, retirement for all at sixty, and a fifth paid holiday week – a heady cocktail which rapidly led to increased production costs, yet more inflation, and the resulting loss of competitiveness combined with the increase in demand led to a chronic trade balance deficit and three devaluations of the franc. For the business world, the effects were catastrophic. Profits and investment levels had been steadily declining throughout the 1970s and the recourse to crippling bank borrowing to cover ever-increasing costs led to a lack of profitability from which companies emerged only in the mid- to late 1980s.

One other aspect of Socialist policy must be mentioned, the extension of the already considerable nationalized industrial and financial sectors. Classical Socialist ideology no doubt played its part but there was also some sincerity in the conviction that private industry had failed to invest in the 1970s and that the state would have to take control, if France was to maintain a powerful industrial presence in the world, with the necessary financial support to sustain it.

Nationalization was no stranger to France. Whereas the issue aroused passionate opposition in the British parliament in the immediate post-war years, a similar programme in France during the same period aroused little debate, a **dirigiste** industrial policy (whether through planning or nationalization) becoming an acceptable, even desirable, norm to back up private industry. Even under the continuing domination of parties of the right in government, and particularly during the 'national champion' years of the 1970s, nationalization via takeovers by existing state companies continued unabated. Despite their shortcomings the existence of state companies was never challenged, particularly since investment was considerably greater in the state than in the private sector (particularly in energy and telecommunications) and many firms depended on it as subcontractors. But in 1982–83, the process reached its zenith with eventually, in 1984, the public sector representing:

- 16 per cent of the working population (excluding agriculture).
- 28 per cent of turnover.
- 36 per cent of investment.
- 23 per cent of exports.
- 91 per cent of bank deposits.

The whole vast experiment of the early Socialist years failed catastrophically, however, and in 1983, the Socialists were forced to execute a spectacular U-turn by freezing prices and incomes, tightening exchange controls and increasing taxation, including a compulsory loan. Many jobs created in the state sector were precisely those to go first and perhaps the greatest sign of the true significance of the U-turn was the new-found belief by the Socialists that only companies, not the state, could create wealth and therefore jobs. Indeed, it can be said that the recent love affair of the French with the world of business can be traced to this period. They would not have believed parties of the right but if Socialists said business was acceptable then they would accept it.

By the time of the general election in 1986, then, the economy was being nursed back to health, with the slower rate of increase in costs of the factors of production and the fall in imported raw material prices gradually contributing to lower inflation. Reduced demand plus an effective policy to reduce energy imports through the substitution of nuclear energy (80 per cent of electricity in France is now generated by nuclear means) transformed the trade deficit in both goods and services into a surplus by 1986.

The new right-wing government under Jacques Chirac (with a Socialist president still in power, however) was an ardent advocate of less state spending and deregulation and liberalization. Privatization of not only the newly-nationalized companies but also of those which had been in the state sector since immediately before or after the war, became a burning issue, with CGE, Saint-Gobain in the industrial sector, Société Générale and Paribas in banking, Agence Havas (advertising) and the television channel TF1 reverting into private hands before the October crash of 1987. Since then Indosuez and Matra have also been privatized.

Liberalization in particular meant a dismantling of supply-side rigidities, particularly the necessity for companies to seek the authorization of the local Inspector of Labour before shedding labour, reduction in taxation and total freedom in prices except for pharmaceuticals and oil products. The reduction of the government deficit, business efficiency and market forces became the driving forces and many in France, with its long tradition of dirigisme, became concerned whether these were right policies for France.

The highest marginal rate of personal income tax fell from 72.4 per cent in 1986 to 56.8 per cent in 1988, the rate of corporation tax was reduced from 50 per cent to 42 per cent (now 42 per cent if dividends are paid, 37 per cent if not) and the **taxe professionnelle** (payroll tax) has been progressively cut. Offset against this, however, social insurance contributions were increased in 1987 and these, combined with other forms of taxation, both direct and indirect, contribute to France having the heaviest burden of taxes among the major OECD countries. This is of growing concern as growth falters and the social security system creaks under the weight of an ever-more-costly pay-as-you-go scheme which has the effect of a severe brake on employment.

The resolve to continue a public sector pay policy which has a knock-on effect in the private sector increasingly led to business making greater profits and beginning to reach investment levels of the early 1970s. Unemployment still stubbornly refused to fall, however, as growth in 1986–87 remained sluggish when France failed to take as much advantage of the upturn in the world economy as other OECD countries. Fear of another dramatic turn of events as witnessed in 1983, together with the chastening discipline of membership of the EMS and being hence locked into former West Germany's own meagre growth performance, forestalled any idea of expansion through reflation.

In 1988, President Mitterand was elected for a second term and a general election was called. A landslide victory was predicted for the Socialists but they surprisingly failed to win an overall majority and are forced to seek the support of members of the centrist parties. The party's popularity slumped severely, however, particularly under the Prime Ministership of Edith Cresson, who managed to antagonize most sections of public opinion with both strident and ill-advised remarks and a penchant for a heavy-handed dose of interventionist industrial policy. President Mitterand fared little better, being wrong-footed by the coup attempt in Moscow (which he supported), the unification of Germany (which he opposed), and the Gulf War (when he wavered). He is seen as being increasingly out of touch and losing his grip on both domestic and world events, and there have been demands for him to reduce his Presidency immediately from a seven- to a five-year term (the next Presidential election is timed for 1995). With the steadying hand of the new stolid Prime Minister, Pierre Bérégovy, the architect of the strong currency and competitive disinflation policy, Mitterand has bounced back to some degree, however, but almost certainly not enough to save the Socialist party, rocked by accusations of corruption, from defeat in the national elections in 1993. The parties of the right, despite their differences, seem poised for victory. Despite the country's solid economic performance, the French are not happy, however, and are undergoing a period of some considerable malaise, fuelled by stagnating buying power, cynicism over the whole political arena and a feeling that their role in influencing European and, indeed, world events is no longer as decisive and clear as it was. Immigration policy is a running sore, too, particularly with the threat of a massive invasion of new immigrants from Yugoslavia, and, to a lesser extent, other Central European countries. The racist policies of the National Front, the extreme right party, and its leader Jean-Marie Le Pen are hence gaining credence and even forcing leading members of the traditional right to make compromising remarks in an effort to jump on the electoral band-wagon and woo voters. The overall mood is a mixture of boredom, frustrated disenchantment and apprehension. Preoccupation with individual well-being and a relatively high level of general prosperity make it implausible, however, that events will lead to a social conflagration as has occurred so often in French history.

In industrial policy terms, Mitterand declared there would be no more nationalizations nor more privatizations and that a mixed economy would prevail, giving the best of both worlds. There is much evidence to support the view that, although day-to-day management of the state sector is at arm's length, the government still takes vital decisions in the so-called strategic sectors such as electronics, particularly on acquisitions or mergers, where further capital is needed, although such decisions are coming in for much closer scrutiny by the EC Commission in Brussels.

Overall, however, direct government ownership appears to be on the wane: companies in the state sector can now seek up to 49 per cent private capital (mostly non-voting stock, however, apart from in the case of the intended sale of 98 per cent of total, when normal shares are to be offered). Siren voices are nevertheless still heard, warning of Japanese rocks on which European industry will be wrecked. Alain Gomez of Thomson and Jacques Calvet consider the United Kingdom utterly wrong in its encouragement of massive Japanese investment: salvation can only come in their eyes, through Europe promoting European (usually French) champions and providing them with enough breathing space and resources to compete on equal terms with the Japanese.

In economic terms, in spite of being hit by the recession, France considers itself to have recovered much of its former strength. In fact, with Denmark and Luxembourg, it is one of the few countries to meet the convergence criteria of the Maastricht Treaty. Domestic demand is still comparatively weak but exports boomed since the beginning of 1992, thus drastically reducing the persistent trade deficit and underlining the restored competitiveness of certain sectors of the economy. Growth in 1991 was a creditable 1.2 per cent and forecast to exceed 2 per cent in 1992, thus outpacing that of most other G7 countries. Inflation has risen slightly to 3.1 per cent from a low of 2.9 per cent but in spite of such hopeful signs, industrialists are still sceptical. Profits fell by 12 per cent in 1991 (27 per cent in 1990); many companies are heavily in debt and hence investment refuses to pick up. Unemployment has risen to 10 per cent. Everything now depends on an upturn in the world economy and without its export record, growth would be zero in France.

Business and the economy

The tertiary sector, as in the United Kingdom but less so, has grown rapidly in France to represent some 60 per cent of GDP. Manufacturing

Table 2.1 *French growth rates (1979–92)*

Year	%
1979	3.2
1980	1.6
1981	1.2
1982	2.5
1983	0.7
1984	1.3
1985	1.7
1986	2.1
1987	2.3
1988	3.7
1989	3.5
1990	3.5
1991	1.2
1992	1.9

Source: OECD

industry has inexorably declined to around 30 per cent of GDP but France has not allowed whole swathes of industry to go to the wall, considering it strategically vital to retain interests, not only in aircraft-manufacturing, electronics and defence equipment but also in space, consumer electronics and a sizable indigenous car industry.

Manufacturing

It is only quite recently (1992) that French products finally ceased losing market share, due to increased price and quality competitiveness. Failure to invest in the 1970s and early 1980s on account of excessive wage costs, as has been seen, had previously been the direct cause of lack of competitiveness. Another was the hitherto poverty of capital, resulting from lack of profitability and limited external sources. Whereas former West Germany's manufacturing investment increased between 1975 and 1987 by 44 per cent, France could only manage 14.3 per cent. R & D has fared better in recent years rising from 1.46 per cent of GDP in 1975 to 2.28 per cent in 1987, figures which again are a poor comparison with West Germany's 2.1 per cent and 2.71 per cent between the same two years. This is only part of the picture, however, since a large proportion of that R & D expenditure was by the state in a highly-targeted narrow band of industries (e.g. electronics) and was not across the board by both state and private companies, as in West Germany. Small and medium-size companies (**Petites et Moyennes Entreprises** – PMEs) in particular have lost out, with very little benefit accruing to them from vast national projects. In 1983, however, the government introduced a research tax credit scheme which increased the number of PMEs investing in R & D. In 1989, there was yet more discussion of how to bring PMEs' efforts up to German standards, with priority areas being JESSI, high-definition TV, the 'lean-burn' engine, agribusiness and new materials. Other forms of investment, in marketing, for example, have been inadequate, too, with French goods not enjoying good press in either Germany or Switzerland in terms of sales promotion and advertising.

Compared with other major OECD economies, France has few real strengths in the manufacturing sector, except in transport equipment and metal-working. Indeed, France's gradual loss of comparative advantage revealed another weakness of its manufacturing sector – failure generally to spot in which sectors world demand was growing and prices falling. According to the OECD it has thus had a tendency to remain specialized in exporting highly-priced, high-technology goods for which world demand is relatively declining. In addition, it shunned head-on competition in the more dynamic markets of the USA, Europe and Japan in favour of the often-captive markets of its former colonies in Africa where a greater relative percentage of its high-technology goods are exported. To redress the balance and to gain market share by rapid external growth, however, in 1989–90 French companies such as BSN, Rhône-Poulenc, and St. Gobain, went on a veritable acquisition binge, primarily in Europe and North Africa.

Iron and steel

Although hard hit by Barre's attempt to restructure industry in the late 1970s and in spite of record losses in 1983, France's and Europe's leading steelmaker in terms of production, state-owned USINOR SACILOR matched the profits of British Steel (4.5 billion French francs in 1988). 1987–9 were boom years throughout Europe but the beginning of the 1990s saw a fall in worldwide consumption, bringing a sharp drop in Usinor Sacilor's profits. Like British Steel, it has continued to concentrate on basic steel and, in the process, has drastically cut costs and increased R & D expenditure. Both companies have expanded overseas with Usinor Sacilor making the largest investments, a situation which has led British Steel to call 'foul' since it believes that the French company is being unfairly subsidized by the state, particularly through state-owned Crédit Lyonnais' purchase of one-tenth of the company in 1991.

Vehicle building

Despite domestic shares of 24.2 per cent for Renault and 35.3 per cent for PSA (Peugeot-Citroën), leading positions among the European car manufacturers (number six with 10.5 per cent and number 3 with 12.4 per cent respectively) and a return to healthy profits, the French car industry still faces a number of problems.

Protected by a 3 per cent annual limit on new Japanese registrations, Peugeot and Renault have fought a losing battle to keep out British-made Nissan cars. They have accepted the inevitability of a sharp increase in Japanese penetration to maybe 8–9 per cent with the dismantling of trade barriers, but have succeeded in concluding a deal for a transitional quota after 1992 (4 per cent in 1993, including transplants) to enable them to adopt new manufacturing methods, speed up product development and launch more joint ventures as R & D costs soar, leading to further industry concentration. Both firms support higher debt levels than their other European counterparts and, despite drastic labour reductions and other cost-cutting measures, may well be vulnerable over the next three to four years particularly if unrest in Peugeot over wages and conditions spills over into Renault, too. Finally, underlying all this, there is an already perceptible increase in import penetration (40 per cent) by foreign makes, giving the lie to the often-heard statement that 'the French only buy French'. An interesting comment on the situation is that any merger between the two is considered completely out of the question in Paris, with each side preferring joint ventures with foreign manufacturers to attempting a marriage between the state-run, highly-centralized Renault and the private, more-dispersed Peugeot. The most likely solution to Renault's problems is a complete merger with Volvo of Sweden, which would inevitably lead to its reversion to the private sector, a position long demanded by Peugeot. Renault-Volvo would then be Europe's fourth-largest group with 12.1 per cent of the market.

In commercial vehicles, France shows a weakness characteristic of many other sectors, its overconcentration on the domestic market, with RVI, Renault's truck division, having 42 per cent of the French market, but only 12.3 per cent of the European market. Despite a creditable comeback from the abyss of the early 1980s, and being Europe's number two manufacturer in production terms, both technically and in terms of reliability, RVI trucks are not up to Mercedes and Volvo standards. In addition, if **cabotage** (permission to pick up and set down loads within another country) is allowed in the EC, this will particularly favour Dutch road haulage firms with their lower labour and fuel costs and therefore their vehicle suppliers DAF, Mercedes, Volvo and Scania, to the detriment of RVI. Here again, the linkup with Volvo will bring much needed know-how and a much bigger share of the European and world market (RVI-Volvo would be the world's number two behind Mercedes).

Electronics

With an annual turnover of FF 50 billion, Alcatel (part of CGE) is the world's largest manufacturer of telecommunications equipment and represents one of the flagships of the French economy.

Thomson, now world number two behind Hughes-General Motors, in defence electronics and number one in Europe for radar and sonar equipment, again is considered to be too French, with 95 per cent of its employees in France and 60 per cent of production exported in a sector where customers are requiring more and more local production and where not only overall size counts, but also size per market.

A major disadvantage to France's policy of the 1960s to withdraw from NATO and to plough its own furrow for reasons of national independence has been that French arms manufacturers have not had access to NATO specifications. While Third World markets were buoyant, this situation was of less significance but as they become more and more saturated, French companies must turn to acquisition in Europe (e.g. Thomson's takeover of Philips' defence interests) to plug the gap. France has traditionally seen the whole defence industry as one of its strengths to be pursued, but as other leading manufacturers are divesting themselves of their defence interests in a climate of greater détente and arms limitation talks, questions are being raised about the wisdom of Alain Gomez' strategy of continued expansion. This strategy looks even more risky as Thomson, in parallel with its defence interests, relentlessly pursues ever-increasing size in the consumer electronics sector which it dominates in Europe, together with Philips.

Aerospace

The merger of Thomson's and Aérospatiale's avionics divisions puts the new company Sextant Avionique in fourth position in the world and points to the state's role (both companies are nationalized) in galvanizing key industries into assuming internationally-competitive positions.

The sector as a whole represents one of the stars of the French economy (number three in the world, number one in Europe in terms of turnover and exports) and remains firmly in state hands (Aérospatiale, SNECMA, Dassault). France's resolute intention to remain in the space sector with the Ariane launcher points to its deeply-held conviction that Europe cannot neglect its spin-offs (e.g. manufacture in space of new products) unless it wants to become a mere subcontractor of the USA (the old bogey of the

1960s and the American challenge). As Michael Heseltine commented in 1987 in his book *Where There's a Will*: 'We would not have a major civil airframe manufacturer in Europe today if it were not for France . . . the role of the government is a manifestation of French will'. Sweeping redundancies are planned, however, as France cuts back sharply on military expenditure and Airbus orders plummet. But the first six months of 1992 saw France's trade deficit dwindle dramatically, largely due to Airbus exports and so it remains to be seen just how well the aerospace sector will ride out present uncertainties (in terms of size and employment).

Chemicals

The chemical industry in particular was one of the industries completely restructured by the Socialist government in 1982 but in spite of now showing a profit after many years of losses, there is still a considerable gap between the French chemical industry and its main competitors. Rhône-Poulenc, the largest of the French companies, is for example only half the size of BASF, Bayer and Hoechst. Size is less important, however, than position in each speciality market, but even here France is not so strong. Paradoxically, therefore, France is the second-largest producer of plastics in Europe but no one French group is number one or number two in its field. In pharmaceuticals, Rhône-Poulenc is only number twenty in the world.

The industry is in for yet another bout of restructuring, therefore, with Rhône-Poulenc aiming to be number five in the world and, as has been seen to be a recurrent theme in French industry, a general intention to break out from being too concentrated on the French market. With Europe restructuring, France sees it imperative to be part of the trend but, fearful of losing its independence, is not seeking alliances with other European companies, particularly the Germans. The most notable acquisition was of the American company Rorer by Rhône-Poulenc, for which many considered it paid too high a price, leading yet again to suspicions of state feather-bedding.

In the sector overall, the state has the whip hand, owning six French chemical companies (Rhône-Poulenc, Atorkem, Orkem, Entreprise Minière et Chimique, Total Chimie, Société Nationale des Poudres et Explosifs): a neat illustration of the ambiguity and dilemma of state control in France. The government is determined to allow heads of state companies to use their initiative in restructuring the industry but as long as competitiveness is reinforced. Heads will roll if it is thought that companies are sitting back on old, protected positions – **chasses gardées**, as they are known in French, the term for protected hunting grounds. Thus the autonomy of the chairmen of these state companies has its limits, with the government determined to have the final say, and particularly since it has to stump up extra capital.

Luxury goods

Perfumes, bags, scarves from companies such as L'Oréal, Yves St-Laurent, Hermès, Vuitton – for many, these are the traditional image of France at its best and certainly recent results and trends underline French strength. With the explosion of sales worldwide, turnover in the sector in France increased by 18 per cent in 1988, with value added standing at 40 per cent of turnover and gross trading profits at 13 per cent. In 1988, luxury goods as a whole (including château-bottled wine) showed a positive trade balance of FF 36 billion, considerably more than the FF 25 billion for military equipment. When Yves St-Laurent sought a listing on the Paris stock exchange, it had to be delayed because the issue was oversubscribed some 260 times! Indeed, the wheel went full circle: French ministers once considered that modern France had much more serious things to offer than perfume and wine but became so alarmed at seeing the jewels of the French luxury industry falling into foreign hands that they blocked Japanese attempts to buy into the distribution of the exclusive Romanée Conti wine. But the nature of the industry has changed, moving to a blend of high-tech processes and traditional craft skills with companies generally preferring to re-invest profits than distribute dividends. It is also breeding a new generation of managers, typified by Bernard Arnault, the mercurial head of LVMH (Louis-Vuitton-Moët-Henessy), which is ousting the old family owners and replacing maintenance of traditions with more emphasis on modern management techniques and profitability.

But coinciding with the Gulf War, storm clouds began to appear on the clear horizon of the French luxury goods industry. Recession in the USA and the fall in the value of yen were just two of the more obvious causes. More fundamental was increasing competition, from the USA and particularly from their own backyard, Italy. Already, France's share of the world luxury goods market had fallen from 75 per cent in 1975 to 50 per cent in 1989. France's leadership is still impressive but Italian brands in sectors such as food, jewellery, haute couture and luxury off-the-peg clothing are achieving superior growth rates. Even French fine wines are not spared: chemical contamination scares, drink-and-driving campaigns, competition from Californian and Australian wines, and from branded spirits have all seriously dented France's supremacy.

The clothing industry's answers to the problems are direct control of distribution by abandoning franchising, better training and design. An underlying problem in the luxury goods sector is one of much-needed finance, however, as more and more companies fall into foreign, especially Japanese, hands. This points to a constant French dilemma: does foreign ownership of French companies matter or is it the value added in France that counts? Nationalism and market truths make uneasy bed-fellows in present-day France.

Whereas, as a percentage of exports, the figure for manufactured goods remains absolutely stable over the 10 years to 1989 (77 per cent), OECD reports show that the corresponding figure for manufactured goods as a proportion of imports rose dramatically (from 54 per cent to 73 per cent). There has been, therefore, an inexorable decline in the export/import ratio, with drops in exports recorded, not only to both EC and OECD countries, but also to non-OECD countries. Possible reasons for this have already been discussed but there was firm conviction in government circles that capacity investment in the right areas was enough to narrow the deficit, although this may have seemed optimistic in view of the fact that for capital goods alone, the real export/import ratio fell from 143 per cent in 1984 to 106 per cent in 1987. After a trade deficit of FF 30 billion in 1991, the first five months of 1992 showed a surplus of FF 13 billion, including a surplus in manufactures of FF 6 billion in April 1992. With above-average growth, some French commentators consider France has turned the corner of competitiveness, whereas others point to low investment and rising unemployment as proof that much more evidence is needed. Problems of high real interest rates dictated by the German Bundesbank and a sluggish world economy need to be resolved before French manufacturing industry can really show its paces.

In the first quarter of 1992, investment shrank for the sixth consecutive quarter and as far as inward investment is concerned, government officials are beginning to speak of missed opportunities. There is much talk of Japanese investment in France, but in reality there is very little (1.5 per cent of total foreign investment in France in 1989), according to the national planning agency DATAR (Direction à l'Aménagement du Territoire et à l'Action Régionale). Point-blank refusals and the imposition of draconian conditions meant, for example, that the Japanese invested a meagre FF 1.7 billion in France in 1988, whereas the three car-manufacturing groups, Toyota, Nissan and Honda, alone spent FF 18 billion in the United Kingdom, with Honda preparing to invest another FF 3.3 billion (see page 218). In contrast, Subaru negotiated for three years to build a site near Angers but finally threw in the towel, in spite of the last minute and ironic concession by the Ministry of Industry to reduce the amount of local content demanded from 80 per cent to 60 per cent. An interesting development has been the increase in Korean investment in France, even in the automotive sector. This paradoxical situation, given France's anti-Japanese investment stance, is explained by the official government line that the real bone of contention with Japan is lack of reciprocity. In return for allowing Korean investment, France is well placed to win a TGV contract in Korea and it is through such trade back-scratching that the French government seeks to normalize relations with Japan. France is heavily supporting the Korean alternative for its investment in Asia and is even rumoured to be contemplating a Franco-Korean axis in the electronics industry to combat the Japanese.

In 1988 France succeeded in attracting FF 32 billion of inward investment and in terms of acquisitions is the second-largest target for foreign investors in Europe, but still way behind the United Kingdom ($2.3 billion compared with $6 billion). According to the French Ministry of Industry one company in nine is now under foreign control (20 per cent of capital).

According to the same report, in 1988 American (22 per cent of total), German (20 per cent) and Swiss (15 per cent) investments 'created or pre-served' 13,000 jobs in France as opposed to 44,000 in the United Kingdom.

Opinion is divided over the potential benefits of such investment. Some see it as nibbling away at French industry whereas others point to the bet-ter performances recorded by foreign-controlled companies, where produc-tivity is some 20–25 per cent higher than in their totally French counterparts. In 1986, FF 35,000 per employee were invested in foreign-controlled companies, as against FF 27,000 in French companies. Their export record is far superior, too: 32 per cent of production compared with 26 per cent.

The biggest constraint on inward investment has no doubt been the Ministries of Finance and Industry. They may well vaunt their policy of selectivity as having served French interests well but the severity of the policy has been enough to dissuade many overseas companies from bring-ing yet more investment to France. In order to improve this situation the Ministry of Finance has abolished the procedure requiring potential investors to submit a prior declaration and the right exercised by the Treasury to defer any decision. Such procedures caused Northern Telecom to wait thirteen years before building a plant in Eastern France.

One barrier has been removed, but another has appeared in its place, a monthly meeting of a Treasury committee to discuss investment by foreign companies in France, particularly those involving acquisition of more than 20 per cent of French companies. The avowed objective is to find a Franco-French solution. An example of what may occur is that investment oppor-tunities in France were hawked by the Minister of Finance, Mr Bérégovoy (now Prime Minister), in New York only for a proposed takeover of Spontex by 3M to be rejected in favour of the nationalized group, Total.

One further possible factor in deterring potential investors and one which seriously constrains the competitiveness of French companies are social charges. France is one of the most heavily taxed of the OECD coun-tries (45 per cent of GDP compared with 38 per cent for Germany and the United Kingdom, 35.8 per cent for Italy and 29 per cent for the USA). In terms of hourly wage costs, France seems to be reasonably well placed compared with some of its European neighbours. The overall cost of labour in June 1991 was 21 per cent higher in Germany and 20 per cent higher in Belgium (but for a lower level of productivity). The United Kingdom was 24 per cent lower, however, the USA 13 per cent and Japan 10 per cent. But it is the social charges and minimum salary which cause the big difference however. As a proportion of the total cost of labour (33 per cent, as compared with 24 per cent in Germany, 15 per cent in the United Kingdom and only 4 per cent in Denmark), they are much higher and are currently seen as a major brake on unemployment.

In its determination not to allow the Americans, Japanese, British and even Swedes foothold in Europe without doing the same, France is the largest investor in Europe in terms of mergers and acquisitions, the major purchases being:

- BSN's acquisitions of pasta-making concerns in Italy, of HP and General Biscuit in the United Kingdom.
- Compagnie Générale d'Electricité's acquisition of Kabelmetall and ITT Europe.
- Carnaud's purchase of Metalbox.
- Various purchases by Pernod, Elf, Rhône-Poulenc, SGS-Thomson.

In addition, in 1988, France was the fourth-biggest international investor behind Japan, USA and the United Kingdom and ahead of former West Germany. In five years overseas investment multiplied by a factor of five, from FF 14 billion in 1983 to FF 71 billion in 1988. This growth of investment is undoubtedly explained by the better profits being turned in by private companies but against this background must be seen the ability of state companies to make similar purchases. Most have become profit-making but profits have been used more to repay debt than to build a war-chest. The undercapitalization of these large groups makes them financially dependent on the state.

If domestic investment is beginning to pick up, its geographical spread remains highly uneven. Efforts by DATAR since the war have ensured that there is no North–South Divide and that, apart from parts of the Lille-Tourcoing conurbation and Marseille, there are no real areas of great urban decay or deprivation. Some regions have inevitably progressed faster than others and there are some signs that a French version of the Sun Belt is being created along the French coast from the Pyrenees to the Italian Border. Montpellier has, for example, the highest rate of start-ups, and the most successful of the **technopoles** (science parks) is at Sophia Antipolis near Nice. Technopoles are a good example of the way in which decentralization has loosened the grip of Paris as the centre of all decisions, particularly regarding regional development aid. Regions and municipalities now enjoy greater financial freedom, through a redistribution of state tax income and greater freedom with levying local taxes, and now compete fiercely to set up the latest technopole, with its attendant research centres, university or business school and small company 'nurseries'. Many may well find success difficult for two reasons.

First, the communication infrastructure in France is still such that many regions, if not inaccessible, at least require lengthy journey times to reach them. This explains why France has embarked on such a massive programme of improvement in all areas of transport, but particularly in road and rail. More East–West motorway links are planned, and a comprehensive network is to link the French end of the Channel tunnel both to the rest of France and to its immediate neighbours. 20 September 1989 in France witnessed the inauguration of a new 300 kph TGV service between Paris and Le Mans, costing FF 18 billion. This TGV-Atlantique will eventually link the capital with the West and South-West and, it is hoped, bring the same advantages as the present TGV has created for passenger traffic to Lyon. Deregulation of air transport constitutes a major threat to the French national railway company, SNCF, which it is countering with a vigorous policy of extending the TGV network, including links to the major capitals of Northern Europe and a by-pass system around Paris and Lyon to ensure more rapid transit to the South. Eventually, not even some of the most far-flung cities of France (Toulouse, Perpignan, Nice, Biarritz) will be more than five hours by train from Paris. The whole project represents a considerable challenge to France's biggest employer (200,000 employees), not only in terms of better communication but also in terms of the technological spin-off for transport equipment of France's most important industrial sectors.

Second, for the same population as the United Kingdom (approximately 56 million), France is three times the area, with only six towns having more than half a million inhabitants. There are large, wide open spaces between its small and medium-size towns and therefore the ready markets of concentrated hinterlands, as in the Ruhr, Northern Italy and in the South (and parts, too, of the North) of the United Kingdom do not exist. However, many companies, particularly those from the Scandinavian countries are beginning to see France as a European crossroads and giving particularly good access to the booming Mediterranean markets. But commercial reasoning will decide where to invest. Saint-Gobain's decision to build a new float-glass factory in the Grenoble area had more to do with the desire to be near its markets in South-East France and Italy than to benefit a particular region, either at the behest of the state or a technopole. The same applies to the car manufacturers compelling their subcontractors to set up close to their assembly plants; to Pechiney installing new plant at Dunkirk to benefit from ease of delivery by sea of raw materials and access to cheap nuclear power; to Coca-Cola setting up, again in Dunkirk, to serve the whole of the European market; and to Arthur Andersen software, going for the proximity of analogous industries in Sophia Antipolis.

One striking feature of the upsurge in investment in the late 1980s, particularly in the production of basic materials, was the new lease of life given to the old smokestack areas of the North, a welcome move for the area ahead of completion of the Channel tunnel. Coca-Cola and Pechiney at Dunkirk have already been mentioned. Usinor-Sacilor is renovating its steelworks, Saint-Gobain its glassworks in the Aisne département.

But despite DATAR's past achievements, the present blossoming of the South-East and South-West, the incipient renewal of the North and the energetic attempts of technopoles to attract customers, the Paris region still acts as a magnet, especially in the area of services. There still has not been in France a spreading of high-level functions between several towns as in Germany, the United Kingdom, Switzerland and Italy. In 1964, Paris had 14,766 group headquarters with only 1325 in Lyon, the second-largest town in France. Twenty years later, the geographical concentration of power still remained very strong. Paris still had 77 per cent of top management posts in the tertiary sector, 83.5 per cent of the headquarters of the top 200 French companies. In terms of investment credit, the greater Paris region (Ile-de-France) accounted for 59 per cent across all sectors, 66 per cent of all loans to the service sector, 84 per cent for transport and telecommunications and 91 per cent for energy. 89 per cent of export credit alone also went to the region, up from 79 per cent in 1975.

In industry, the Ile-de-France region lost a third of its workers between 1962 and 1985, but unemployment remains at 8.4 per cent (as against the national average of 10.1 per cent) and the region's contribution to national added value has remained at a steady 22 per cent, thus underlining the fact that although other areas have benefited from industrial growth, there has been no real deindustrialization of the Paris region.

In education, too, Paris remains preponderant, having 34 per cent of the university population, and in R & D, although the region's share of public sector research fell from 61 per cent in 1973 to 52 per cent in 1983. In the private sector there has been virtually no change (62.4 per cent to 61.7 per cent).

All this points to the continuing monopoly of the Paris region in many areas and to the relative failure to develop sufficient regional poles of activities to attract particular services away from Paris. Only the signing of the Single European Act compelled France to realize that not only countries but also regions will be competing with one other, hence the decision to implement the overall policy to improve the basic infrastructure and thus open up more space to allow more regions on the margin of industrial and economic activities to benefit more fully from a *Europe sans frontières.*

Services

As in most other industrialized countries, the contribution of the services sector to added value has grown rapidly in France, standing at 63 per cent in 1986, compared with 55.2 per cent in 1973. 60.4 per cent of the working population are in service industries, compared with 49.3 per cent in 1973. The most spectacular growth has been in the retail sector, where concentration has been the most prominent feature, with the rise of Europe's largest retailer, Carrefour and other groups such as Casino, Auchan and Mammouth. Yet, in spite of the presence of 747 hypermarkets, the retail sector still remains more fragmented than in the United Kingdom (see page 221). No one group has more than 5 per cent market share and the top forty groups account for only 37 per cent of the retail trade's total turnover. Independent retailers as a whole still account for 46 per cent of retail distribution as opposed to 25 per cent in the United Kingdom, thus underlining the fact that whereas in the United Kingdom the chief buyers of the top twelve major chains need to be persuaded to buy a product before it appears on shelves from Lands End to John O'Groats, in France even contacting all of the top purchasing organizations will not ensure that a product will reach the twenty-five largest centres of population.

It is a sector, too, where there is very little sense of mutually-beneficial cooperation between manufacturers and retailers. Relations are on more of an open-war footing as price margins are pared to the bone in a highly-competitive sector. In its drive to contain inflationary pressures, the government is not displeased to see advantages gained from manufacturers passed on to the consumers by the large hypermarket groups. Profits are consequently low: for the same turnover as Carrefour, Marks and Spencer makes seven times more profit (although profits may be understated in France, accounts being prepared only for the tax authorities). The average profit margin can be as low as 1 to 1.5 per cent, with as much as 80 per cent of this profit margin deriving from managing the cash flow. On average, hypermarket stock rotates once every twenty-four days, while sixty days are normally taken to pay suppliers, thus providing thirty-six days of cash to invest.

The **Loi Royer** of 1973 established regional commissions to regulate the building of new hypermarkets and, as a result, the commission being heavily weighted in favour of local small retailers, a firm brake was put on any extension to the market. This led most major groups to set up abroad with no fewer than 100 French hypermarkets to be found as far apart as Brazil (15) and Spain (53). French hypermarket chains have indeed excelled precisely in countries with a highly-fragmented distribution system, but on the whole failed in the more concentrated systems of North Europe (e.g. the United Kingdom).

The question of Sunday trading brings into sharp relief how the public authorities shape economic policy. Shops already open for some 100 hours in France, as opposed to sixty hours in Germany, but there has been a strong lobby to increase this even further by allowing Sunday trading. A report published in August 1989 suggested that hypermarkets should not be allowed to open, but furniture hypermarkets should be restricted, however, to those in the Ile-de-France region! The Swedish group Ikea is particularly pleased since 25.8 per cent of its turnover is taken on Sundays, in a market which is generally stagnant (+1.5 per cent in 1988) but where the hypermarkets groups have a market share of 33.6 per cent and annual growth rates of 4.6 per cent. The trade balance in furniture was negative in 1988 by FF 11 billion so what easier than to allow Ikea to continue trading on Sundays, particularly since the group is purchasing ten times more from French sources than in 1984? A decision made all the more desirable since French manufacturers are beginning to adapt to selling to the large discount stores.

In the tourism sector, record revenues of FF 90 billion were expected in 1989 with a healthy foreign trade surplus which has remained stagnant since 1984, however. This has greatly benefited French hotels and particularly the largest hotel group Accor (Sofitel, Novotel, Ibis, Mercure) which currently ranks as number four in the world. Despite its presence, however, the hotel market remains highly fragmented with 55 per cent of hotels having less than 25 rooms, and 65 per cent of the French never or rarely staying in a hotel. Only 18 per cent of hotels are in the hands of the megachains, compared with 60 per cent of the market in the USA. The pattern of holidays in France is anarchical, too, not so much in terms of the periods in which they are taken – no other nation seems to compress its holidays into so short a time between mid-July and August, plus a week's skiing during the winter – but in terms of the type of holiday the French take. France has one of the highest numbers of people going on holiday, but 80 per cent take their cars and go and stay with friends or relatives. By contrast, 43 per cent of Germans go to hotels. Only 16 per cent of the French go abroad, as against 33 per cent for the rest of Europe.

Of those going abroad, only three million take package tours as against ten million in Germany and the United Kingdom. The top four national tour-operators – of which there are over 200, again in a highly-fragmented market – only account for 29 per cent of total demand as against 80 per cent in Germany. Thus, lacking the commercial clout of the big German and British tour operators, Touropa of France, for example, charges 73 per cent more than Thomson in the United Kingdom for the same holiday, half-board in the same hotel in Benidorm in Spain.

Vertical integration is the key, the most important aspect being air transport. Most tour operators have their own fleets (Britannia, owned by

Thomson is the largest of its kind in the world) and if deregulation becomes a reality in air transport, these same operators could well take a long hard look at the French market where both tour operators and charter airlines are much smaller. As with road haulage, cabotage could be the key. It is not too fanciful, for example, to imagine a Britannia airliner taking off half-full from Luton and landing at, say, Beauvais to pick up the other half of its passengers, en route for Spain. A new trend on the part of the largest United Kingdom tour-operators to move up market could be another spur.

As for travel agents, there are some 3000 points of sale in France (Havas Tourisme, Wagon-Lits and Selectour being the largest) but 1000 of these were forecast to go by 1992, either through restructuring from within the industry itself or through acquisitions by foreign predators. They live off 10 per cent commissions, have low levels of productivity and are generally of a poor quality of service, with a low penetration rate. As has been seen in connection with other sectors, size is the all-important factor again (with the exception of Club Med), together with less navel-contemplation on the domestic market. In-fighting is another problem, too – it has been recently said that, generally speaking, there is a lack of solidarity among French industrialists, compared with their German counterparts. Whereas in Germany links between distributors and producers are important, the French are almost proud to sell out to a foreign purchaser and thereby thwart a domestic rival, particularly if it is felt that the foreign purchaser is a leader in its field, that it has the right level of technical and professional know-how and is not just a financial holding company.

Business and the law

In Germany, the concept of the Rule of Law is emphasized: the same is true of France, except that having devised a whole series of complex and arcane laws and decrees, the French are most anxious to find ways round them! Written detailed contracts are paramount in business but whereas the British are content with accepting more general and simple rules, the French businessman will constantly be seeking reinterpretation and loop-holes. This legalistic environment holds good for the system of public administration (ultra-bureaucratic in nature), commercial law and labour law to which further reference will be made later.

The advent of 1992 brought the legal profession into sharper focus, particularly in matters concerning cross-border mergers and acquisitions. Until recently, the profession was fairly compartmentalized with every sector having different areas of responsibility and expertise. There was a general feeling that the system, particularly in terms of ease and accessibility, was very backward in comparison with its Anglo-Saxon and German counterparts. The legal environment of French companies was indeed once described by the journal *L'Entreprise* as 'under-developed, incoherent, ill-adapted and archaic'. Whereas a German competitor might go to one organization to carry out a simple legal act, a French director had to go through the hands of many different professionals who were often all necessary and all jealous of their prerogatives. Overall, France had fewer legal experts than any other Western countries (1 per 2000 inhabitants, as against 1 per 1200 in former West Germany and 1 per 500 in the USA) who in the main, still looked after individuals whereas corporate law is more lucrative. The **avocats** provided advice in all areas of the law and had a monopoly of pleading before the courts. The **notaires** had a monopoly in drawing up an **acte authentique** (authentic document) necessary for all transfers of property, wills and marriages. They enjoyed no monopoly in matters of consultancy or advice. Anyone could become a **conseil juridique** (legal adviser), however, who enjoyed no monopoly and did not necessarily have to belong to one of the liberal professions (**avocat** or **notaire**) hence banks, insurance companies, chambers of commerce and employer organizations would offer such a service. This was also true of the big eight accountancy firms which in France were allowed to do both legal and accounting work, whereas they are kept rigidly apart in the United Kingdom and USA. Fidal is the largest legal advisory firm in France and is a subsidiary of KPMG which claims that no confusion arises between the two professions. Whereas its legal activities only represent 15 per cent of turnover, it is considered that, whereas the auditing side is coming up to maturity, legal advice shows the biggest potential in the present climate of acquisitions, takeovers, etc.

Urgent reform of the profession was seen to be sorely needed with the result that there has now been a merger of the conseils juridiques and the avocats, thus establishing a monopoly in legal advice and a new profession similar to that in the USA.

The most common forms of business enterprise are:

1 Société Anonyme – SA (corporation)

This is the most common form adopted by large companies and may be quoted or unquoted. A minimum of seven founder shareholders is required with a minimum legal share capital of FF 250,000 of which 25 per cent must be paid up at incorporation. Most corporations issue one class of common shares, but two other classes exist: preferred and non-voting, the latter being limited to 25 per cent of share capital. It is possible to limit the number of votes per shareholders' holding of the same class of share, and double votes are also possible but limited to fully paid-up registered shares for at least two years by the same shareholder.

The issuing of double voting rights is quite frequently used as a defence mechanism against a takeover bid (**Offre Publique d'Achat** – OPA) together with the right to buy back shares (**autocontrôle**) as long as they are for cancellation (reduction of capital) or for employees' share acquisition plans. Cross-shareholdings also exist up to ceilings of 10 per cent.

As recently as 1987, very few financial directors or heads of companies were concerned about their shareholder structure but since that time acquisitions, both by French and foreign companies, have snowballed to such an extent that even the French President issued a dire warning of possible consequences for French industry early in 1989. The facts are, however, that French companies have not been slow in going over to the offensive, making 143 acquisitions in France, as opposed to 129 by foreign companies. Most have been straight, friendly acquisitions since takeover bids are still comparatively rare in France, in spite of the media attention surrounding such companies as LVMH, Bolloré and the insurance company Victoire, recently the subject of a bid by Suez, the largest ever seen in France. In 1988 there were only 29 stock exchange battles in France, compared with 186 for British companies in London. Until 1992, the law allowed takeover bids to be for either 66 per cent or 100 per cent control. All bids must henceforth be for 100 per cent control, a change calculated to dissuade corporate raiders and to protect minority shareholders' interests by giving longer response times.

French companies do not enjoy the same solid backing of banks as they do in Germany and defence measures are therefore more limited. Some have already been mentioned, others include:

- The Act of 7 June 1987 allows companies to write into their statutes the obligation for all shareholders above 0.5 per cent of share capital to be declared. Only some 5 per cent of listed companies have not availed themselves of this provision.
- It is perfectly legal to limit the number of votes. In CGE individual shareholders are not entitled to more than 8 per cent of votes, whereas in Lafarge-Coppée, now the world's second-largest cement producer, the limit is as low as 1 per cent. The technique is common in Germany, the Netherlands and Switzerland but hitherto has only been used in France by the two companies quoted.
- BSN, Schneider, Lafarge-Coppée and Saint-Gobain have used another far more expensive ploy, that of buying a financial institution (**Etablissement de Crédit**). Under French law, any raider making a bid for a company owning more than 10 per cent of such an establishment must have the prior backing of the authority which oversees all banking operations, the **Comité des Etablissements de Crédit**. Companies using this method thus kill two birds with one stone. They gain time to marshal their defence and they provide themselves with an efficient tool for managing their treasury or juggling with exchange controls.

- The last resort for many companies are the institutional investors (**les zinzins**). The main problem here, however, is that the French institutional investors are not as rich as their German counterparts, for example, to be able to afford significant shareholdings in French companies, mainly due to undercapitalization. The insurance companies, however, precisely through their insurance activities, do have capital to invest. These are the state-owned companies, UAP, AGF and GAN, which between them held a share portfolio of some FF 60 billion at the end of 1988, in 140 different companies. These sums are small, however, in relation to the capitalization of French companies and hence their room for manoeuvre is accordingly limited. Their objectives are twofold: either purely to make a trade investment like unit trusts or involvement in the management of a company, in which case they ask to take a seat on the board of management. Even here, however, holdings are of the order of 4–6 per cent. French insurance companies do not have the financial clout to own 50–60 per cent of a company's capital, like British insurers.

Banks find themselves in a similar position for the same reason of lack of capital, with BNP, Crédit Lyonnais and Société Générale having holdings of a total value of FF 32 billion. Such activity is increasing rapidly, however (Société Générale has increased its shareholdings by 179 per cent in three years), both to defend their clients and to help them make their own acquisitions. With a further bout of privatizations predicted for 1993, it will be interesting to see whether the French government will promote a policy of banks taking large stakes in the newly-privatized companies, based on the German model. The fact that the three insurance groups and two of the banks are state-owned must be of considerable importance here and it is difficult to believe that certain governmental preferences are not stated in those boardrooms where state representatives are present. This is particularly true, given the close-knit nature of the relationships between senior managers in large groups, both state and private, senior civil servants and government ministers. This relationship is a key ingredient in France's business culture and will be discussed at greater length later in the chapter (see page 129).

Of the top 200 companies, 62 are still actively family-controlled including such names as Michelin, Peugeot, Carrefour, Casino, Matra, LVMH, Pernod, l'Oréal. Foreign companies are slowly but surely making their presence felt, with 44 French companies in 1987 and 61 in 1989 controlled by overseas concerned (mainly American and German).

As far as management structure is concerned, French commercial law allows for SAs to have either the two-tier management structure of a Supervisory Council (**Conseil de Surveillance**) and Directorate

(**Directoire**),based on the German model or a single Board of Directors (**Conseil d'Administration**) whose chairman (**Président**) is often general manager as well (hence **Président Directeur Général**).

In reality the two-tier structure is virtually confined to the state sector in which the trade union movement is more powerful and is allocated seats on the supervisory councils.

2 **Société à Responsabilité Limitée – SARL (limited liability company)**
The SARL, the most popular form of company, is suitable for small French business. Registration requirements are identical to those for SAs but, in contrast, a SARL need only have a minimum of two and a maximum of fifty shareholders, with a minimum share capital of FF 50,000. When an SARL has only one shareholder it may be transformed into an EURL (**Entreprise Unipersonnelle à Responsabilité Limitée**) in which the single shareholder exercises all the rights and powers of shareholders in general meetings. Shares (**parts sociales**) are freely transferable among existing shareholders but cannot be transferred to third parties without the assent of three-quarters of the shareholders. There is no board of directors in this form of company which is managed by one or more managers (**gérant**). Statutory auditing requirements depend on size in terms either of turnover or of numbers employed.

3 **Société en Nom Collectif – SNC (general partnership)**
All partners in an SNC are called **commerçants** and have unlimited liability for all debts and obligations of the partnership. They may appoint a manager (gérant) who is not necessarily a partner.

Since reporting or regulatory standards of SAs and SARLs are almost identical, interest in SNCs and other structures has been rekindled, principally because of the great degree of control which can be exercised.

4 **Société en Commandite (limited partnership)**
This may take one of two forms: by guarantee (**société en commandite simple**) or with shares (**société en commandite par actions**). It is a form rarely used in recent times and considered to be antiquated, but the prestigious manufacturer of luxury goods, Hermès, has recently decided to adopt the form to guarantee family control over the company. The principle is simple: the law provides for a **commandité**, the representative of the shareholder, to have the sole right to oversee the managing body and cannot be relieved of its powers unless 75 per cent of the shareholders so decide, a provision which guarantees almost total security. In the case of Hermès, the commandité an SARL controlled by members of the Hermès family. Along with Yves St-Laurent, which decided on the same route to avoid the fate of LVMH, the subject of

tough takeover bids, Hermès is determined to remain private to provide more long-term management of a quality product and not to fall prey to institutional investors in search of short-term profits, which have become more of an accepted word in France with the gathering strength of the **Bourse** (stock exchange).

5 **Groupement d'Intérêt Economique – GIE (economic interest grouping)**
This is a form of joint venture with a legal personality. Generally they are cost and not profit centres and are used for exports, R & D, joint sales or distribution agents for their members who set their rules by agreement.

6 **Entreprise Individuelle (sole trader)**
The sole proprietor of such an entity is personally liable for all debts and obligations and must be registered with the Clerk of the Commercial Court (**Tribunal de Commerce**).

Business and finance

Two notable changes occurred in the French financial scene in the 1980s: a gradual but fundamental reform of the banking sector and a general shift away from reliance on debt towards equity as a source of external finance. These two changes have been underscored by a whole paraphernalia of new financial instruments and engineering methods which are leading to radically-changing views on ownership, management and structures of companies.

The period of greatest expansion in the banking sector occurred between 1967 and 1975, following the reform of 1966 which allowed banks more flexibility to set interest rates and to open new branches, with the aim of shifting the burden of providing investment funds from the state to the banking sector. Until the 1960s some 80 per cent of investment financing emanated from state sources. During the late 1960s and 1970s the financing of investment by banks increased from 38 per cent (1965) to 60 per cent (1974), while the capital markets played a very minor role. The banks were essentially the main financial intermediaries.

The concentration of industry was mirrored by a similar process in the banking sector, as many local banks disappeared (245 in 1945 and 63 in 1975), together with a number of merchant banks (43 in 1946, 17 in 1975). The period was dominated by the deposit banks Banque Nationale de Paris, Crédit Lyonnais, Société Générale (all nationalized) and the two merchant banks Paribas and Indosuez, but the mutualist and cooperative banks also expanded rapidly to compete both on interest rates and number of branches.

By the 1980s, there was a growing crisis in the financial system:

- The increasing number of clients using cheques (for which there is still no charge in France) was rapidly increasing overheads.
- There was growing unemployment in banks as those hired in the 1960s and 1970s were laid off to make way for new technology.
- There were some 65 privileged loan schemes, 68 different types of subsidy being offered by different privileged compartments of the system (e.g. Crédit Agricole which had a monopoly of preferential loans to Agriculture), which led to 48 per cent of credit to the economy being allocated through specialized and diverse lending establishments. All had so many different statutes, rights and privileges that competition became hopelessly distorted with a resulting high cost of credit. Because of such distortions the task of the Banque de France regulating the economy by interest rates was infinitely more difficult than that of its much more independent German counterpart, the Bundesbank. Until joining the ERM, France's attempts in controlling inflation had hence been much less successful (Table 2.2).

Table 2.2 *French inflation rates (1982–92)*

Year	(%)
1982	9.7
1983	9.3
1984	6.7
1985	4.7
1986	2.1
1987	3.4
1988	3.5
1989	3.5
1990	3.4
1991	3.2
1992	2.5

Source: OECD

- The growing importance of the capital market, particularly after the tax incentives of 1979, started a gradual tendency for savings to move from shorter to longer types of investments (unit trusts – SICAV – became particularly attractive and still represent one of the most vigorous markets in Europe).
- The low equity base of French banks was of continuing concern.

This crisis was characterized by a gradual process of disintermediation, i.e. less indirect and more direct financing via the capital markets which large companies were finding more profitable. French firms increasingly switched to building up equity and reducing debt, with the result that the proportion of new equity issues rose from 8.4 per cent of new external resources in 1982 to 25.5 per cent in 1987, although in 1988 and 1989 there was a sharp upturn in short-term credit after the October crash in 1987.

All this meant less custom for the banks at a time of growing costs (labour in the early 1980s representing two-thirds of overheads) and led to an overall drop in profitability.

Most of the banking sector was nationalized in 1982, a process which involved thirty-six banks (thirty-four deposit and two merchant banks) and provided the state with control of over 80 per cent of both loans and credits. Reasons for such nationalization were partly classical Socialist ideology, but there was a genuine concern to introduce a more efficient system of monetary control, by decompartmentalizing the system and allowing all of the various types of establishment to offer the same services in terms of loans and deposits. This process had already started under the previous government in 1979 with the introduction of the savings accounts and the Livret d'Epargne Populaire (LEP) and the Compte de Développement Industriel (CODEVI) which all banks were entitled to offer. Two acts, one in 1982 and a second in 1984, made all establishments covered by the same law, excluding the Treasury, the Banque de France and the powerful **Caisse des Dépôts et Consignations** (a state financial institution responsible for the collection and distribution of all funds through the **Caisses d'Epargne** – national savings banks – and a major institutional investor). In reality, the many different networks have not disappeared, but they can all offer the same products. There are still four big categories:

- The high street and merchant banks.
- The mutualist and cooperative sector.
- The Sociétés Financières, specializing in leasing, hire purchase, etc.
- The specialist state-controlled financial institutions, e.g. Crédit Foncier, Crédit National which are still the main distributors of state credit for industrial investments and whose loans are often subject to the National Plan.

The final main chapter in the recent history of French banking was the bout of privatization under the right-wing Chirac government of 1986 which planned to sell off Société Générale, Crédit Lyonnais, BNP, Paribas, Indosuez and Crédit Agricole. Only three reverted to the private sector, Société Générale, Paribas and Indosuez. As has been seen, it is essentially these six banks, together with the insurance companies, which make up the major institutional investors. The partial success of the privatization programme, however, posed the fundamental question of how effective the programme could possibly be when some of the major shareholders of these same privatized companies were still in state hands and thus subject to a degree of inevitable manipulation. To this issue was added another, that of the **noyau dur**, the hard-core of faithful investors approached by the Chirac government to acquire stakes in the newly-privatized companies. The in-coming Socialist government of 1988 accused the Chirac government of approaching those companies which gave financial support to the right-wing parties, and there was some debate over ways of dismantling the noyau dur before the expiry of the legal time limit imposed on these shareholders to retain the shares. Certainly the ensuing saga points to the very thin line which exists between the influence of political and financial clans and the workings of the marketplace in France.

Life for the two **vieilles dames** (old ladies) – Crédit Lyonnais and BNP – still left in state hands has not been made easy by the difficulty of finding new capital from a government intent on reducing its central borrowing requirement in a climate of tax harmonization (and hence loss of tax revenue as France will inevitably be forced to lower its VAT rates). Crédit Lyonnais' failed attempt at an equity swop with Commerzbank in Germany was a clear example of the difficulty. But state-owned companies can now issue up to 49 per cent of their capital in non-voting **certificats d'investissements** and are now experimenting (e.g. Rhône-Poulenc) with perpetual notes which are considered as close to equity.

In spite of recent attempts to bring some order into banking and finance, France still has a bewildering array of specialist financial institutions ranging from leasing companies to the newly-formed **banques de trésorie** whose prime function is to improve the workings of the reorganized financial markets by market making and arbitraging.

But, although the 1970s saw an opening of so many bank branches that many began to talk of France as being overbanked, foreign banks are particularly anxious to buy into the number of small but rich regional deposit banks. The savings rate of French households at present stands at 12.2 per cent of disposable income and indicates a market of some potential, particularly for medium-size banks capable of offering more sophisticated services to their customers. In addition, it is considered to be the only way to have a presence in France for the single market.

Although there is not the same degree of closeness between banks and industry in France as in Germany, as holders of equities in companies (see page 25), it has been seen that some measure of influence over corporate strategy is possible. During takeovers, special arrangements often exist whereby banks have an option to issue special subordinated loans which count as equity.

As has already been pointed out, privatization in 1993 may well bring a closer relationship between banks and industry, as recommended by Michel Albert, the head of the state-owned insurance company AGF in his recent book *Capitalisme contre Capitalisme.*

In addition, bilateral consultation and exchange is extensive together with multilateral consultation through the national planning bodies. Banks also share a common feature with large industrial groups in that their PDGs are often ex-top treasury officials, thus pointing to an even closer triangular relationship between banks, industry and government, such a big feature of the business culture in France.

Stock markets

The growing importance of the bourse has already been alluded to as the direct result of tax changes favouring equity investments by individuals (particularly through unit trusts) and of disinflation and the consequent switch by companies from debt to equity. The privatization issues of 1986 greatly swelled the ranks of private investors from 1.5 million in 1986 to 7.5 million in 1988. Major structural reforms have accompanied this evolution with the addition of new financial instruments and markets, one of the overall major aims also being to make Paris the major financial centre for Europe, after London, and to attract back securities business which has leaked to London.

France has seven stock exchanges: one in Paris (the seventh largest in the world) and six in various towns and provinces, the second most important being Lyon. Since January 1991, all quotations on the regional bourses have been integrated into a national system centred on the Paris bourse. In Paris, the old outcry method on the forward market (**à terme**), which accounts for the greatest value of trading, has been replaced by a computerized system giving continuous quotations. Prices are still fixed daily on the spot or cash market (**comptant**), which comprises a greater number of stocks, although capitalization is less than the forward market. For those companies wishing fewer strict formalities, there is the over-the-counter market (**marché hors côte**).

The big success story, however, has undoubtedly been the equivalent of the unlisted securities market – the **second marché** which was set up in 1983. Its popularity has largely been due to the less onerous conditions imposed on companies than on the official market. Only a minimum of 10 per cent of shares have to be offered and a complete prospectus is not required. New issues have been frequently oversubscribed many times, making it the largest market of its kind in Europe.

There have been changes, too, in the system. The previous stockbrokers (**agents de change**) were all appointed by the Ministry of Finance, which also fixed commissions. They alone could deal in shares on the stock exchange – there were no market-makers – and they also monopolized the market for French government bonds. The break-up of their monopoly started under the Socialists but to speed the process of reform a new market was set up in 1987 to deal with government bonds. This business transacted by twelve market-makers is now proving more lucrative than the equivalent London market shared by double the number of dealers. Since 1988, any French or overseas concern has been able to buy one of the stock-broking firms (now called **Sociétés de Bourse**) whose monopoly was set to end in 1992 (fixed commission went in 1990). Many are in dire need of such an injection of funds having lost vast sums of money on the new futures market, the MATIF, whose regulations have now been accordingly tightened up. Principal buyers of the stockbrokers have been the banks, which have long fretted at the commission they paid the brokers although the majority of orders come through the banks.

Other financial instruments now commonly used by banks and industrial companies are commercial paper (**billets de trésorerie**) and certificates of deposit (**certificats de dépôts**).

The Paris financial scene is much changed then, since the early 1980s, with many expecting it to be the most important financial centre in Europe after London. But old traditions and cultures die hard, and foreign banks have great difficulty in making money in Paris, unless their staff are completely French and fully conversant with the close network of treasury officials, bankers and industrialists who will all have been educated and trained in the same élite establishments.

To complete this picture of dramatic metamorphosis, according to *Science, Vie, Economie*, junk bonds began to make a halting entrance onto the financial scene in France until the financial scandals hit the American junk-bond market. Unlike the USA, only companies which are sufficiently well known and powerful issue bonds. These are mainly the state-owned or newly privatized concerns. Most of the others, particularly the small and medium size companies, borrow from banks. The idea of French rating agencies is also in its infancy, only one being in existence thus far, the Agence française d'évaluation financière, which was established in 1986, and hitherto has rated just 47 issuers of bonds.

In addition, whereas such bonds were commonly used in the USA for hostile takeover bids, such bids, as has been seen, are rare in France, where it is forbidden to endanger the existence of a company which one does not yet own, and therefore to guarantee a raid with the assets of the target company.

Junk bonds were commonly used for leveraged management buyouts (RES – **rachat d'entreprise par ses salariés**) however, and it is in this activity that the French equivalent of junk bonds appeared. Such LMBOs have rapidly increased since 1986, both in numbers and value. In 1986, no LMBO was greater than 400 million francs. In 1988, three operations (Darty, Saunier-Duval and Fruehauf-Trailor) exceeded this sum, using financing similar to that used for LMBOs in the USA, although only one true junk bond has been recorded so far in France, that issued for the SICLI group (industrial cleaning, maintenance) when buying the American company, HP Cleaning. Any 'mezzanine' transactions are mainly in the form of bank loans rather than bonds.

But the potential market was thought to be small in France (several hundreds of millions of francs) compared with the United Kingdom (FF 2 billion), these two being the only two European countries where there were experiments with the formula. Such issues require a liquid market and hitherto, most institutional investors in France seemed unwilling to invest their clients' money in such risky ventures. With an increasing number of mergers and acquisitions, a market for subordinated debt might well have emerged and Paribas seriously contemplated a special investment fund for this purpose. Of significance is the fact that Moody's, the American credit-rating agency, set up in France, thus considering it a country which is increasingly prepared to envisage financial innovation.

Indeed, there is a new younger generation of managers in France who refuse to adopt the negative attitude of those who blame la crise for France's ills and carp continuously about the Socialist experiment of the early 1980s and its effect on the competitiveness of industry, but who have a growing and passionate faith in industry and in growth. The number of heads of companies aged over fifty-five has dropped by 13 per cent since 1980, proof that this generation is taking over the reins. In so doing they are not hesitating to use the most up-to-date methods of financing: management buyouts, stock-options, second market, venture capital, etc.

Business and the labour market

Demographic trends

According to the national statistical office, INSEE, at 1 January 1988 the population was estimated at over 55.7 million persons, compared with 55.5 million in 1987, thus growing at a rate of 0.4 per cent, compared with -0.2 per cent in former West Germany and 0.1 per cent in the United Kingdom. The fecundity rate at 1.8 children per woman has dropped since the 1960s, but if this rate continues the population will grow to 58 million in 2000. As in Germany and elsewhere, the population is ageing, however: in 2000, there will be 15 million people less than 20 years old, 1.1 million less than today, 12–13 million aged more than 60, representing 2 million more and one million aged over 80, compared with 680,000 in 1983.

The geographical spread will look different too, with 35–6 per cent of households living in rural communities, compared with 27 per cent at present. Taking the population as a whole, nearly 40 per cent will live in rural communities, contrasting sharply with today's 29 per cent.

The number of immigrants is growing too. In 1985, France had 3.8 million foreign inhabitants, 21 per cent more than in 1972 and representing 8 per cent of the total population.

Unemployment

The working population has been increasing at a rate of 1 per cent annually, reaching 24.5 million in 1987. 190,000 more seeking work are predicted annually until 1991 and more than 100,000 annually until 2005. The working population will then stabilize at around 26.5 million and decline slowly thereafter. One of the key current questions about the French economy is, therefore, how to create enough employment for these new arrivals on the job market, when growth rates, although much improved, need to maintain a strong upward trend. This is particularly disturbing to a nation which has seen its unemployment figures obstinately refuse to fall during the 1980s, as they have in many other European countries (Table 2.3).

The working population is growing, as has been seen, but not at the same pace as in other countries and this cannot therefore explain higher

Table 2.3 *French unemployment rates (1979–92)*

Year	(%)
1979	5.8
1980	6.3
1981	7.3
1982	8.3
1983	8.3
1984	9.9
1985	10.2
1986	10.4
1987	10.5
1988	10.0
1989	9.5
1990	8.9
1991	9.4
1992	10.3

Source: OECD

unemployment. According to OECD reports, the underlying cause is a failure to create enough corporate employment in the 1980s due to rigid labour costs (high social charges, indexed wages, the SMIC), in marked contrast to France's main trading partners. Such employment picked up in 1988, but mainly in the tertiary sector, whereas only in 1989 did industry start to create jobs with the upsurge in investment in production capacity (particularly in metal-working, rubber, plastics and building materials).

Youth unemployment causes the most concern, 23.0 per cent of the 16–25 age group currently being out of work (7.8 per cent in West Germany, 17.4 per cent in the United Kingdom). Various youth employment schemes have been funded by government schemes such as the TUC (**Travaux d'Utilité Collective** – community work contracts), work-familiarization placements and social security relief for employers hiring young people, but such schemes are unlikely in the long run to halt rising unemployment. Apprenticeship schemes are far fewer in France than in Germany and hence a larger proportion of young people either leave the education system with no qualification at all, or with unwanted qualifications. Generally speaking, for example, there is a shortage of engineers, technicians and skilled workers as production techniques progress, but a waning demand for unskilled workers, hence explaining the apparent contradiction between industry beginning to create jobs and unemployment remaining at 10 per cent.

Particularly disadvantaged at present are the PMEs (small and medium-size companies) which are most in need of more labour and increasingly having to employ managers (**cadres**) and technicians, often for the first time. They are losing out, however, to the large companies towards which cadres and technicians naturally gravitate.

In regional terms, in 1992 the areas most affected by unemployment (between 11 per cent and 13 per cent) are the whole of the North-Eastern area, the South-Western départements of Charente-Maritime and Gironde in the Bordeaux area, Loire-Atlantique and, worst of all (13 per cent) the départements of Pyrenées Orientales, Hérault, Gard and Bouches-du-Rhône in the South (also the areas which have seen a veritable population explosion).

One rigidity in the labour market which was removed in 1986 was the obligation for companies to seek the authorization of the local inspector of labour before making employees redundant 'for economic reasons'. A new Act, the so-called **Loi Soisson**, modified the measures enacted in 1986 and allows the labour courts (**Conseil des prudhommes**) not to have an *a priori* check on redundancies but to seek *a posteriori* justification of their necessity. French employers could now face the real prospect of checks on all redundancies after the event, following the principle of the benefit of the doubt is with the employee.

Paris has a significant role to play in the labour market, too. In spite of its continuing economic significance, French managers are beginning to show considerable signs of disenchantment with life in the capital and to express growing preferences for a pleasant lifestyle in the South and South-East where sun, sea and the ski-slopes offer obvious attractions. In a survey in 1989, Aix-en-Provence, Toulouse, Montpellier, Annecy and Grenoble were put at the top of a list, ahead of Paris, of towns where managers would accept to live. Towns of the North and North-East (Lille, Reims, Le Havre, Nancy, Amiens, Calais) were, not surprisingly, the least popular.

One of the main reasons for this trend is the cost of a career in Paris, both in terms of energy and money. Two-thirds of housing is in the East of Paris, two-thirds of offices in the West. Constant traffic-jams and annual strikes in the public transport system make life hard for workers in Paris, with the rush-hour increasing by a quarter-hour annually since 1985. Rents are three times those to be found in the provinces and, not surprisingly therefore, there has been a move away to villages and towns of fewer than 20,000 inhabitants. 36 per cent of managers still live and work in the Paris region, however, with the Rhône-Alpes and Mediterranean areas still way behind with 18 per cent.

These are various reasons for the pull of Paris:

- By accepting a job elsewhere, a manager might greatly reduce his potential on the labour market.
- Selling a house in some areas of Paris could bring some into the bracket of wealth-taxpayers. In addition, Paris prices until recently increased dramatically, making it difficult to return and buy housing.
- Children's education in a city in which there is a disproportionate number of both universities and particularly of the highly prestigious and élitist engineering and business schools.
- The tradition that, unless a manager has done a stint in Paris, his career could suffer thereby, particularly in the large companies in the banking and insurance sector. Amongst the young, if any preference is given for working elsewhere, it is not in the provinces but abroad, with the USA far ahead of the EC countries as the main preference.

Once again, improvements in the transport infrastructure are bringing about change. With the Paris-Lyon TGV full at the beginning and end of the day, commuters in both directions are now quite commonplace, with managers living in Lyon and working in Paris and vice versa. Passenger traffic between Paris–Lyon–Grenoble has increased by 7 per cent yearly, with over a quarter being managers.

Immigrant workers

By far the largest group are those from the Moslem countries of North Africa – Algeria (780,000), Morocco (520,000) and Tunisia (212,000), although there are considerable numbers of Portuguese (860,000), Italians (425,000) and Spaniards (380,000). Although many will have entered the country quite legally, most after 1945, a considerable number were illegal, a situation which particularly suited employers who could thus pay lower wages, hire and fire at will, and pay less attention to working conditions.

Many of the original immigrants also arrived without their families, hoping to find a job and save up enough money to go home and set up in business. The majority stayed in France and were later joined by their families (as was also to be later the case with many illegal immigrants who regularized their position). Thus family groupings are on the increase, with women representing 38 per cent of the Algerian and Tunisian population. More than 80 per cent of immigrants in France today have residence permits and work permits valid for ten years, but automatically renewable.

The bulk of the immigrants arrived in France without qualifications and took jobs on building sites, as unskilled workers on assembly lines, particularly in the car industry or the less salubrious jobs, such as emptying dustbins, which the French disdained to take.

With the onslaught of **la crise**, many immigrants were the first to suffer, representing two-thirds of redundancies in the construction industry and the greater part of the massive lay-offs in the car industry, particularly of Talbot, in 1983. Today, more than a third of them are to be found in local grocery stores or as waiters in cafés and restaurants.

The immigrant is often the first to be laid off and the young often leave school with few qualifications and hence find it difficult to find jobs. For the older ones, reconversion is difficult, at times impossible, as many are still unable to read or write French. This led directly to the failure of plans to reconvert Talbot workers and miners recruited directly in the Atlas mountains.

In the Ile-de-France region, 30 per cent of the long-term unemployed are immigrants and hence in 1977, the government introduced its first plan to encourage immigrants to return home. Some 60,000 – mostly Portuguese and Spanish – took advantage of the scheme between 1977 and 1982, and in 1980 50,000 Algerians benefited from a special Franco-Algerian agreement to provide travelling expenses and training centres in Algeria. The scheme was revived in the car industry in 1984 but, after some initial success, rapidly can out of steam, most immigrants viewing acceptance of aid to return home as acceptance of failure and preferred to stay in a country in which they are not always welcome. Racial friction often erupts as the French accuse them of taking their jobs, committing the majority of crimes and of forming filthy ghettos. Islam is now France's second religion and this alone is a source of much tension, particularly over the claim, much-publicized at the time, to the right for girls to wear the traditional Islamic head-scarf, the tchador, in schools – anathema to the highly anti-clerical teachers' union which jealously protects a lay state system and brooks no recognition of religious affinities. Islamic fundamentalism is taking a firm grip in the Algerian education system and many see the tchador affair as being a fundamental exercise in surreptitiously spreading Islamic propaganda. The numbers of immigrants are still being swollen, too, by illegal entrants who prefer indignities at the hands of unscrupulous employers to poverty in their native lands.

The situation of ethnic minorities came even more sharply into focus in the early 1990s with the resurgence of the National Front, under its leader Jean-Marie Le Pen. Once thought to be a spent force after an initial ignominious attempt to become President, he is now recognized as representing the forces of disaffection, and many apparently respectable French would not disagree that his beliefs have some appeal. His growing success is such that, on immigration issues, the other political parties are beginning to echo his sentiments, in a shabby attempt to win more of the popular vote. Of overriding significance to the French is the EC's stance on immigration. Tougher all-round policies which can be implemented in neighbouring countries, through which illegal immigrants easily pass, are seen as a key element.

Le Pen failed in his turbulent attempt to become President of the Provence-Alpes Maritimes region but as unemployment refuses to abate and the situation in certain Central European countries leads to the wholesale exodus of ethnic minorities to the countries of the EC, he is set to continue to be a figure to contend with in the coming years.

Business and trade unions

The trade unions in France experienced a dramatic dwindling of their numbers in the 1980s, down from a fairly low figure of 20 per cent in the early 1980s to around 10 per cent in 1989. Too close an identification with the hard-line Communist party which refused to condemn the Russian invasion of Afghanistan was one reason for the decline. Other causes put forward have been:

• Growing unemployment in large sunset industries more likely to employ unionized labour.
• The unions are out of step with the aspirations of an increasingly wealthy working population.

- They are too fragmented to be effective.
- They are generally too politicized.

Although the law provides for various forms of worker representation, overall the picture of labour relations in France is far from being one of basic agreement between management and employees for the good of the company, as in Germany. But there are growing signs that neither the unions nor employees are happy with this state of affairs as industrial conflict begins to increase in France, particularly in the public sector, especially as wages continue to stagnate, under the effect of the government's tough anti-inflationary monetary policy.

Organization

The bodies representing workers are confederally organized and have no umbrella organization to which they jointly belong, such as the TUC in the United Kingdom or the DGB in Germany (see pages 242 and 37). Each confederation comprises separate unions and federations which horizontally represent different industrial sectors and vertically the administrative units, from the **département** through the region to national level. The three largest, in order of size, are:

- The CGT (**Confédération Générale du Travail**) founded in 1895, which is particularly strong in most of the state-owned sectors such as steel, electricity and gas (EDF and GDF) and the railways. Its leaders are members of the Communist party.
- The CFDT (**Confédération Française Démocratique du Travail**) which has strong Socialist allegiances and is still committed to workers' control (**autogestion**), a principle rejected by both the other unions, unless ownership of the company is shared too, as in state companies (in which employees' representatives sit on the board), cooperatives, local government, etc. This latter point underlines a basic tenet which FO shares with the other unions and that is of complete opposition to capitalism.
- The FO (**Force Ouvrière**) is the most moderate of the three, believing in direct negotiation rather than conflict with government authorities.

Before 1982, it was possible to create a union branch only in companies employing more than fifty persons but since then, even in the smallest companies, there exists the right to establish a branch. The only condition laid down is that one or several employees notify the head of the company, who must agree to meet the unions at least twice yearly. Japanese and other investors cannot demand single unions and must therefore resort to creating a small company or one in a low-unionized region.

At shop floor level, the unions nominate a shop steward (**délégué syndical**) and all workers in companies employing more than ten people elect a **délégué du personnel** whose task it is to solve individual problems, but not negotiate with employers as does the délégué syndical.

At plant and company level, a works' committee (**comité d'entreprise**) is necessary in companies of over fifty people and must be informed on planning, results and changes in organization and consulted on redundancies, working hours, wages and health and safety.

All of these different representatives are protected by law, are allocated specific hours to conduct their business, and cannot be fired. Over and above these representatives, new laws (**les lois Auroux**) in 1982 allowed for 'expression groups' which the government (even though Socialist!) considered necessary to counteract what they saw as too much potential influence of the unions in the existing structures and to give the shop floor more effective consultation at company level. They were intended as a means whereby workers can talk directly to management without necessarily going through the unions. In this they resemble quality circles, and both bodies aroused the hostility of the unions, particularly the CGT. Quality circles have become extremely widespread, particularly since 1985 when France had more than the rest of Europe together. In 1987, there were 30,000 such circles which varied considerably in their degree of effectiveness. One special problem is that they threaten traditional hierarchies in the firm – particularly middle managers, hence cadres are often blamed for being indifferent to them.

Collective bargaining (conventions collectives)

Many salaries, rights and conditions are laid down in collective agreements drawn up either on an industrial sector or local/regional basis. Employers bound by these agreements, either through their employers' federation or through being a direct signatory to them, must respect their minimum provisions.

Such agreements lie at the very heart of a form of traditional corporatism in France which perpetuates a highly-fragmented patchwork of rights and privileges pertaining to all forms of profession, trade and even employee status. The very composition of the workforce is made up of a scale of coefficients which correspond to levels of specified duties and tasks and specific qualifications enabling those duties and tasks to be fulfilled. A night watchman in the oil industry who does no rounds is coefficient 100, for example; one who does have rounds is coefficient 120; a fork-lift driver is 130; whereas a light vehicles driver is 150. The minimum salaries, periods of leave, seniority, bonuses, promotions sanctioned by these agreements are fiercely defended by unions and non-union workers alike and not infrequently cause stoppages, particularly if a company wishes to rescind an agreement covering one industry to sign an agreement covering a different industry, affording more flexibility and lower costs.

Such a system leads to rigid hierarchies which can prevent advancement of workers on merit and no more clearly is this seen than in the case of technicians aspiring to managerial grades, a case which will be discussed later in the chapter (see page 132).

Until the mid-1980s, nearly all salaries rose by the same fixed amounts according to the industry, but this system, much to the chagrin of the unions, and again particularly the CGT, is progressively being replaced by two-part awards, one part being fixed and the other based on merit and performance. In addition, an Act of 1986 has enabled companies to pay generalized bonuses based on a whole new set of flexible criteria: productivity, quality improvement, cost reductions, sales, etc. Such money (**intéressement**) is immediately available, unlike profit-sharing schemes (**participation**) which are frozen for five years before any payment is made. In general, the unions favour such payments, except for those linked to productivity, which is still taboo to the CGT.

Industrial relations in the public sector

Many jobs in the public sector – SNCF, PTT – are guaranteed for life since they confer the status of civil servant on their holder. Other privileges include advantageous pension and health schemes, automatic advancement, but in strict line with the hierarchy laid down in the **convention collective** and various bonuses. Wages are often low, however, and since the rigorous deflationary policy pursued by the government since 1983 has particularly held down salaries in the public sector, many state sectors – banks, air-traffic controllers, taxmen, nurses, teachers, postmen, railwaymen – are undergoing a period of extreme social tension. Add to this the fact that the unions are numerically strongest in these sectors, and there is reason for some concern. Whatever the strength of the unions, however, the unrest is characterized by outbreaks of spontaneous stoppages called by groups of individuals determined to voice their grievances. Such outbreaks the unions are finding hard to control and, indeed, there is a growing conviction amongst some employers that a strong and ordered union is easier to deal with than 10,000 individual grievances.

Unrest also led to difficulty in making necessary structural changes in certain sectors. This was particularly true of the combined postal and telecommunications organization, PTT-France Telecom, which was, until comparatively recently, still officially a government department (but the world's fourth-largest telecommunications operator). Its head and five principal senior managers were appointed by the Council of Ministers, negotiations on salaries, staffing levels were at state level and even the state representatives in the regions – the **préfets** – had a say in its affairs. Prices were set by the state, not only for basic telephone call units, but also for telephone equipment (while FNAC and DARTY, two large consumer electronic retailers, were offering special deals on the same equipment). It needed new investment but could only obtain such from the Ministry of Finance which continuously milked its profits, since 1982 for national budgetary purposes and for investment in the electronics sector, an industrial policy priority area. Now France Telecom has become a company in its own right, albeit still state-owned and influenced by state policy (it was *invited* to take shares in Bull, for example).

Reform was needed, therefore, if it was to compete with companies which had already adapted to global competition, particularly through deregulation and privatization as in the United Kingdom, Spain, Italy and The Netherlands. France was one of the exceptions in Europe and one of the major reasons holding it back was its highly-unionized labour-force (430,000 employees) who adamantly refused to accept any split between the post and telecommunications sectors or, worse still, any attempt to turn the organization into a company, albeit state-run (a **régie** like Renault) which would possibly herald loss of their sacrosanct status, rights, privileges and rigid hierarchies.

Attention has now switched to ports in France, where the government is attempting to change the status of dockers. A tense conflict is looming, reminiscent of the British government's own confrontation with the dockers over the same issue.

Business, education, training and development

In line with its 'dirigiste' tradition, France has a unique higher education system which was originally designed to produce the engineers and administrators needed to implement state policy. The universities were seen as too mediaeval and uninterested in the realities of state requirements and hence in the middle of the eighteenth century, the 'Ecole des Ponts et Chaussées', the engineering school, was created, the first in a whole succession of so-called **grandes écoles** (there are now over 170) which provide education specifically geared to technical, administrative and business needs in the civil service, and state and private industry.

Unlike the universities to which any student with a baccalauréat (the equivalent of British 'A' levels but more broadly based) can gain access, competition to enter these grandes écoles, particularly the top engineering and business schools, is fierce and eliminates all but the very best – that is, in terms of mathematical prowess (a French obsession and the main admissions criterion) and abstract, logical thinking. Only 6 per cent of those going on to higher education make the grade, some 15,000 graduating annually from the engineering schools and 8,000 from business schools. There is now considerable pressure to increase the output of engineers and to this end, more grandes écoles and, significantly, university departments accredited to award **diplômes d'ingénieurs** are contemplated, together with some measure of flexibility in entrance requirements (e.g. more direct entry from university). Growth is to be limited to 4 per cent annually, however, since it is argued that demand should exceed supply otherwise there will be unemployment among engineers, as there is among doctors.

Large companies focus their graduate recruitment on the grandes écoles, on a student population which is highly gifted and trained, although much criticism is often heard of their arrogant view of their own infallibility and their lack of some of the 'softer' personal skills. This is the price to be paid in a system which breeds a narrow élite which has been and still is to some extent the lynchpin of French economic and industrial activity and a vital constituent part of business culture.

The élite is not purely intellectual, however. It has been argued by John Ardagh in *France Today* that the French failed to do away with its aristocracy in 1789 because the meritocracy which replaced it has not eliminated power and privilege. To this extent the management class has become far more of a hereditary class than in comparable countries, with one-quarter of managers in the top 200 German firms coming from rich families, just one-tenth in the USA but over three-quarters in France. The grandes écoles system perpetuates this situation with a student population which is overwhelmingly middle-class and Parisian. With over 80 per cent of senior managers in large companies having a grande école qualification, it is not hard to see the true extent of the power and privilege which the system bestows.

Although no longer seen as the nadir of career aspirations, state service was long a laudable and acceptable goal in France, and top civil servants are as much a product of the grandes écoles as their counterparts in industry. Indeed, it is still a current tradition for civil servants, particularly Treasury officials, to move over into banking and industry, whether state or private, and to retain the right to revert to government service as members of one of the **grands corps** which resemble collegiate bodies acting as old boys' clubs and dominating selection of the upper echelons of the civil service. So contact between business and government is close, with the main actors being cast in the same mould of the grandes écoles and preserving a lasting web of interlocking formal and informal relationships, which have served France well over the last three to four decades.

And these relationships are used. Before the world of business was rehabilitated, to reach the top of the civil service was a primary career ambition
for the young because top civil servants who were noticed by their
Ministers ran departments, formulated policy and influenced decisions to
nominate heads of both public and private companies. Both sectors existed
in a mixed economy in which the grands corps pulled the strings through
personal relationships and positions of influence and power. Such a system
underlines the strength of **colbertisme** in France, the idea of a strong interventionist state which, particularly back in the 1960s and 1970s, had to be
researcher, investor and financier. It alone had the necessary global vision.
The heads of major companies connived with this view – it allowed them
to share out markets between them, fix rules to avoid competition and constitute monopolies to serve the state. Hence even nationalization was seen
in a different light. An interventionist industrial policy which it implies
was to their advantage in sustaining the incestuous relationship with the
state.

With the accession of the Socialists to power in 1981, nationalization
assumed a new ideological hue, however, although there were solid
grounds for believing that, with a virtually non-existent bourse and no
banks as in Germany to provide major sources of funding, the state had to
make up for the growing deficiencies of the private sector. The enthusiasm
of the ideology of a party dominated by a majority of ex-teachers led to a
fundamental disturbance of the hitherto-cosy relationship between the
state and private industry and, although some nationalized companies
recovered dramatically from a state of near bankruptcy in 1981, over-zeal-
ous interference replaced mutual self-interest, and imperious commands
were substituted for arm's-length surveillance.

The success of the privatizations of 1986 forced the Socialists to realize to
what extent they had cut themselves off from reality with their brand of
nationalization – many of the valid arguments of 1981 had gone, with a
reinvigorated bourse capable of bringing capital to companies requiring it.
The recent Société Générale affair (one of the top deposit banks privatized
in 1986) revealed, however, that even privatizations in France were potentially unhealthy, with the formation of a hard core of friendly investors
which supported the Gaullist RPR party, and would prefer a return to the
comfort of the 1960s and 1970s, when the 'establishment' which they constituted went hand in glove with the state, and takeovers, markets and
strategies were decided by a few civil servants and heads of companies
behind closed doors. A failed attempt to split up this hard core of investors
and replace it with a group more amenable to the Socialist position pointed
to the opposing view of state intervention in France. During the affair, Jean
Peyrelevade, head of UAP, one of the three nationalized insurance companies, refused to submit to a request by the Minister of Finance to buy shares

in Société Générale and for some commentators, this constitutes a highly significant turning point in the history of state intervention in France. The head of a state company refuses to be the lackey of ministers and civil servants and this could well be a marked shift to a more Anglo-Saxon view of business, with its concepts of raising capital independently on the bourse and enjoying freedom to determine strategy on purely business grounds. The stage is set for a battle between this new view of running a business and the all-pervading wisdom of a narrow clique of civil servants and the 'establishment' determining major directions of industrial policy – a battle which could well see the demise of the remaining nationalized companies and their eventual privatization.

The élitist nature of the management of large companies is also prevalent in the number of places held on different boards of directors by heads of both state and private companies. Jean Peyrelevade, for example, also sits on the board of the private Banque Stern, of which he was once chairman, of the Lazard group, Roussel-Uclaf, BNP and CGE. Jean-Marc Vernes, head of the Compagnie Industrielle, sits on the board of no less than twenty-six companies and Ambroise Roux, head of Générale Occidentale, has seats on the boards of CGE and nine other companies. Between them, they symbolize the concentration of power which is characteristic of large French companies and acts as another powerful tool in the event of unwanted takeover bids. This power is reinforced by the role of the boards and their chairmen. General meetings of shareholders have virtually no teeth and the board is only formally answerable to its shareholders. In their turn, members of the board are only there to back up the chairman (le président). The system is almost a carbon copy of the French parliamentary system, with extensive powers vested in the State President. Some have called it management by divine right, with chairmen not answerable to anyone – votes are rare and, indeed, if a proposal is put to the vote, it is seen virtually as a sign of no confidence in the chairman and time for him to resign.

By law, no more than eight seats on different boards may be held by any one person, but in reality many get round this by representing people who do officially have a seat. The inevitable result in many cases is only scant knowledge of the detailed workings of a company's business and hence greater reliance on the authority of the chairman. Absenteeism is rife, as in French law there is no obligation to mention attendance at board meetings in annual reports. The notion of working committees is also virtually unknown, and board members are very rarely taken to court for negligence. Add to this the fact that in both private and state companies, the main decisions are not taken during board meetings, but as a result of discussion between a few key board members, and the picture of the extensive cross-linking powers of board chairman is complete.

Elitist status is nowhere better exemplified than in the distinction between technician and engineer. Whereas the word 'manager' in English is informal and loose, the corresponding word in French, 'cadre' is stricter in definition. To become a cadre, employers may come up through the ranks (but usually with no transferability of the status to another company), graduates may join a company directly but with a qualification gained after four (increasingly five) years of study after **baccalauréat** (bac +4/5 in French parlance) or after some years on technician grade (with the qualification of BTS – **Brevet de Technicien Supérieur** – or DUT – **Diplôme Universitaire de Technologie**: both bac +2) The latter are increasingly sought after with the increasing emphasis on automation of production and designing and running of automated systems. They have virtually cornered production management jobs which engineers shun for Design Offices and R & D. They are highly praised by employers and there is little unemployment at this grade. Precisely because of their increasing importance, however, they have aspirations to cadre status and that is precisely where the shoe pinches, because having reached the top of the technician grade, the majority find it impossible to become engineers, i.e. cadres. Companies prefer their engineers to have the generalist's more theoretical training of a grande école – 'you can't have a plethora of generalist in a company, you've got to have some rank and file'. However good a technician they are, a technician is what companies want them to stay. Many drift towards the small and medium-size companies where they immediately become cadre. Some large companies have grasped the nettle, however, and particularly prompted by the findings of the Decamps Commission report, instigated training programmes allowing technicians to gain an engineer's qualification (IBM, in particular) or implementing a policy of bringing their status close to that of engineer and cadre, even if they do not have the same responsibilities. Rigid differentiation is still the order of the day for most companies, however, and is yet one more symbol of the attachment the French feel for rights and privileges accorded to status and positions. Even the French language allows for such distinctions, the form *tu* being used instead of *vous* in some design offices by engineers when talking to non-cadre technicians, to denote their inferiority (*tu* was always used to address servants and is still used to insult). The situation has even caused considerable industrial unrest in some companies and as individuals demand more and more responsibility and freedom in the workplace in France, such attitudes could well provoke some discontent in the future.

Perhaps the last comment on this aspect of élitism lies with the company spokesman who said '*un technicien supérieur ne pourra jamais faire valoir les compétences d'un Supélec*' (a senior technician will never be able to display the same abilities as a Supélec engineer [the grande école for electrical engineers]).

The response of business to the EC's single market

France was almost certainly the first of the EC countries to start public awareness campaigns on the subject of 1992. Every business and every individual in the land has hence been long aware through national, regional and local conferences, debates and seminars of the issues involved. The chambers of commerce and the employers' federation (CNPF – **Confédération Nationale du Patronat Français**) have been particularly active. The coping stone has been the Xth National Plan, which is entitled 'France and Europe' and which devotes separate commissions to seven different areas: technology in Europe, finance, social policy and employment, social protection, education and training, quality of life, and state efficiency. Various luminaries from the other EC countries were appointed to an advisory European board (Robert Maxwell(!) and Theodore Zeldin from the United Kingdom, de Benedetti from Italy, Hahn from VW in Germany among others).

Initially, 1992 was spoken of in France in tones of fear and foreboding, particularly given certain structural and economic weaknesses. As economic strength appears to be growing, so optimism is now more characteristic of France's approach. Optimism, that is, tinged with the knowledge that weaknesses there still certainly are, together with certain real threats but that the opportunities outweigh them both, as industry begins to invest again, to reorganize and expand. The confidence lacking in 1986 has been refound.

With the referendum over the Maastricht Treaty, however, for the first time, seemingly, there was much debate about the issue of possible loss of sovereignty implied in a common monetary policy and closer political union. The outcome was a narrow majority in favour of the Treaty. This is widely interpreted, however, not only as a cry for more public discussion but also as an anti-Mitterand vote of discontent.

Strengths

Many sectors still show the traces of a long history of fragmentation, late development and protectionism. But of late, through increased levels of investment engendered by greater profits, there has been a strong industrial recovery, particularly in some of the basic industries such as steel, chemicals and aluminium. In the strategic high-technology areas, too, such as aerospace, nuclear and telecommunications investment, restructuring is proceeding at a fast pace. Agribusiness, luxury goods, civil engineering, transport equipment and computer software continue to maintain their traditional strength. And this investment brings new capacity to increase exports and stem haemorrhaging imports. Indeed, as has been seen, in 1992 the trade deficit began to fall sharply. Overall, France is the world's fourth-largest industrial power.

Second, French society has been reconciled with its industry. The image of companies has been rehabilitated and the new entrepreneurs enjoy the same limelight as actors and footballers, as they juggle with the new instruments of financial engineering offered by a rapidly-developing capital market. Control of inflation, principally through containment of wage increases, has added to the attraction of increased profits.

Third, France will not suffer the same traumatic effects as Germany and other countries as their ageing populations dwindle. While not completely renewing its generations, its fecundity rate is higher than any other European country, except Ireland. The presence of sizeable populations of North Africans, however, is not without significance in this respect.

Fourth, the level of agreement between top civil servants, government and the heads of large state and private companies, which is such a prominent feature in the economic and industrial management of the country, is ensuring that areas of weakness are recognized and acted upon in a cohesive manner.

Fifth, France's geographical location is seen as an area of strength and explains in part, the government's determination to provide the country with a much-improved and expanded road and rail network. Its central position between North and South Europe, particularly the hitherto dynamic markets of Spain and Italy is seen as an advantage to be nurtured. The Channel tunnel and the importance this will bestow upon the north eastern area of the Nord-Pas-de-Calais for combined manufacturing and distribution purposes are also often stressed and explain the whole-hearted enthusiasm expressed by France for the tunnel.

Weaknesses

In stark contrast to its high-technology industries, which some commentators would conclude France has emphasized too much, many others are inward-looking, fragmented and small by world standards. The state oil companies, Elf and Total, are still too firmly entrenched in their domestic markets and are dwarfed by such giants as BP and Shell; Rhône-Poulenc is half the size of the German chemical giants BASF, Bayer and Hoechst; the car industry is still protected by an unofficial import limit of Japanese transplants; the Renault truck division's sales are predominantly concentrated in France; even, in aerospace, there is some doubt whether France can afford two major airframe manufacturers, Aérospatiale and Dassault, particularly as the latter goes it alone with the construction of the 'Rafale', France's alternative to the European Fighter Aircraft, and for which there is no other market as yet, except the French Air Force. In the tourist sector, too, the tour operators are small and lack the vertical integration of their United Kingdom and German counterparts: the top four companies account for only 29 per cent of a market of three million taking package tours, compared with the top four in the United Kingdom and Germany accounting for 80 per cent of a market over three times the size. Overall, there is no French company which figures in the world's ten largest companies and only fifty in the top 500. A survey conducted by Bain Consultants in Paris, for the Ministry of Industry, among 300 companies in the turnover range FF 1–35 billion (i.e. between the top twenty groups and the PME) showed that the average turnover of the top 250 French companies is 35 per cent and 40 per cent less than that of British and German companies respectively. 52 per cent of this turnover was generated in France and 60 per cent of their manpower worked in France. Hence the realization that they must quickly become more international, particularly since the companies concerned realized that only one-third of their growth would come from France over the following three years.

Second, as a result of this preoccupation with the domestic market, relatively few French managers enjoy the international experience and vision of their British and German colleagues.

Third, the managerial class is well trained but the general workforce overall lacks the right training and qualifications, a fact underlined by the high unemployment amongst the young. In addition, among the managerial class, technology is confused with a few high-tech areas. Production and the German notion of 'Technik' are the cinderellas in French technical culture, and research, unless focused on such prestigious areas as Ariane and the TGV, enjoys little status.

Fourth, the structure of companies is still too hierarchical, and autocratic decision-taking is the norm, thus stifling initiative and consensus.

Fifth, France has pursued certain elements of its industrial policy up a blind alley. Some regret is now being expressed, for example, that Japanese investment, especially in the car sector, has been kept out. The 3 per cent limit on Japanese car imports was loosened in 1993, which inevitably led to job losses.

Sixth, a high level of social security charges and the existence of the minimum wage weigh heavily on companies and are effectively holding back employment. Change is urgently required but only if some of the strain is taken up by tackling the taboo subject of income tax, currently paid by only 50 per cent of French families and with a top marginal rate of 56.8 per cent, considerably in excess of those in competitors' countries. Private pension schemes, too, are urgently needed to bail out the alarming social security deficits. Equally, the local business tax, is in urgent need of reform for two fundamental reasons. It is calculated partially on the basis of numbers employed and therefore affects employment; it has a negative impact on investment, since the amount of plant employed is another basis for taxation.

Last, low levels of trade union membership are leading to anarchical claims on the one hand, and on the other, the strong concentration of membership in some state sectors, e.g. the ports, is stifling long-overdue reform and flexibility in the labour market.

Opportunities

The large companies, in many sectors, have primarily appreciated the opportunities of an enlarged EC market as a springboard for global markets. Indeed, perhaps in realization of their former weakness, French companies were until recently the biggest investors in Europe in terms of mergers and acquisitions, the United Kingdom being their number one target. France is investing more overseas than is being invested by overseas buyers in France but it still only ranks as number six in terms of overall international investment. Thomson in defence equipment, GCE in both telecommunications and transport equipment, Rhône-Poulenc in chemicals, Lafarge in cement, BSN in food manufacturing and Financière de Suez in banking and insurance, are some of the big names which have moved fast to reach critical size and market share via acquisition of brands, joint-venture agreements and mergers.

Even more capital injected into the state companies, if privatized in 1993–4, will provide much-needed scope for further investment.

Threats

The main threat is to the myriad of small and medium-size companies which are top of the range through their high value added and often incomparable know-how. France is viewed as a veritable gold-mine for brands and labels built up over many generations in a wide spectrum of sectors from baby soaps (Monnot) to ladies stockings (DIM). British companies have been most avid, quadrupling their acquisitions to a value of FF 12.5 billion in 1988, followed by the Italians and Americans. Because, in the main, French companies are not as cash-rich as many of their German and British counterparts, they cannot afford some of the prices being offered. Many, indeed, may disappear themselves through lack of size: in plastics, for example, out of 3800 companies, only thirty have more than 500 employees and only 1500 exceed ten employees. In public lighting, three of the major companies are in British hands in an area rapidly expanding, with the construction of new motorways and where, being subject to national and local procurement traditions, trading under a French name is crucial.

Strategies

The larger French companies are having to pursue a parallel course of action embracing consolidation at home and acquisition abroad to enable them to reach the critical size they so often lack. Thomson, for example, has merged its avionics interests with those of Aérospatiale while at the same time acquiring the defence interests of Philips in Europe. Reydel, Plastic Omnium and Sommer-Allibert in the automotive equipment area have all installed major sites near car manufacturers in the United Kingdom, thus shadowing a move already made nearer car manufacturers in France. The chemical groups, Rhône-Poulenc, Alsthom, Orkem, etc., are reorganizing in France but also seeking overseas partners. The plastics side of the chemical industry is indicative of a common French problem – France is the second largest producer in Europe but no one group is number-one or number-two producer.

In the Bain report quoted above, all companies intended to go over to an offensive strategy in search of expansion, better performance and innovation. Concern was expressed over the need to catch up, and over their vulnerability, in terms of both their size and convalescent profits. A sense of urgency was common to them all, as they face stiffer competition both at home and abroad. As France moves to the top of the EC league in terms of growth, it remains to be seen whether French companies can continue their encouraging export performance of the first quarter of 1992. Profitability is the key, however, and being still shaky, hampers any really vigorous upturn in investment.

References and suggestions for further reading

Albert, Michel (1991), *Capitalisme contre Capitalisme*, Seuil.
Albertine, Jean-Marie (1988), *Bilan de l'économie française*, Seuil.
Ardagh, John (1987), *France Today*, Penguin.
Baliste, Marcel (1989), *L'économie française*, Masson.
Drevet, Jean-François (1988), *1922–2000 Les Régions françaises entre l'Europe et le déclin*, Souffles.

Eck, Jean-François (1988), *Histoire de l'Economie Française depuis 1945*, Armand Colin.

France 300 (1989), Bain et Compagnie, Paris.

Heseltine, Michael (1987) *Where There's a Will*, London: Hutchinson.

L'Entreprise, various issues between 1988 and 1992.

L'Expansion, various issues between 1988 and 1992.

L'Express, various issues between 1988 and 1992.

Le Nouvel Economiste, various issues between 1988 and 1992.

OECD Economic Surveys, France, (1988/1989).

L'Usine Nouvelle, various issues between 1988 and 1992.

Price Waterhouse (1989), *Doing Business in France*, London: Price Waterhouse.

Science, Vie, Economie, various issues between 1988 and 1992.

VALLE
D'AOSTA

Aosta

TRENTINO-
ALTO ADIGE

Trento

FRIULI-
VENEZIA
GIULIA

LOMBARDY

Milan

VENETO

Venice

Trieste

Turin

PIEDMONT

EMILIA-ROMAGNA

LIGURIA

Genoa

Bologna

SAN MARINO

Florence

TUSCANY

Ancona

THE
MARCHES

Perugia

UMBRIA

Pescara

LATIUM

ABRUZZO

Rome

MOLISE

Campobasso

CAMPANIA

PUGLIA

Bari

Naples

Potenza

BASILICATA

SARDINIA

Cagliari

CALABRIA

Palermo

Reggio Calabria

SICILY

3 The business culture in Italy
William Brierley

Introduction

Business culture in Italy is informed by three principal factors: the size and importance of the state sector (and the concomitant importance of politics and client–patron relationships); the large number of family concerns (and hence a preoccupation with social values including but also beyond those of the profitability of the enterprise); and the scale of the small-firms sector (which requires for its survival a finely balanced mix of both highly cooperative and highly competitive attitudes). These factors have led to an extraordinarily-rich mix of corporate cultures, with interesting spillover effects for both the big and small industrial sectors: for example, in the recent large-scale reorganization of the public-sector industries, profit rather than social engineering has emerged as the driving force, but in striving to retain the synergies identified as the benefit of being big, the newly-reorganized companies are also seeking to achieve the flexibility of smaller companies and thus the ability to respond more quickly to shifts in market demand. Business culture must, therefore, be explored in relation to these basic factors. But first an overview of the Italian political and economic system is called for.

At the end of the 1970s, after a decade of terrorism, political and social strife, and obvious industrial weakness, the words most commonly used to describe the state of Italy were 'chaos', 'shambles' and the most common of all, 'crisis'. Yet, by the end of the 1980s, the scourge of both left- and right-wing terrorism had been eliminated, industrial restructuring involving the loss of 700,000 jobs in manufacturing had been accomplished with relatively little pain, and a new relationship had been established with the trade union movement. All of this despite a political and administrative system which remained the least adapted to the needs of modern and efficient government in the late twentieth century, where clientelism and political patronage were rampant in every sector from nationalized industry to the arts and media. These contradictions and paradoxes became particularly apparent when, in November 1987, by including the 'black economy' in the official statistics, the Italian economy overtook the British economy as the third largest in Europe and the fifth largest in the Western world, yet the then Italian President, Francesco Cossiga, had to cancel a state visit to Britain because he had to stay at home to sort out the collapse of the 47th post-war government. How, the question was asked, could a country have such an apparently strong and resilient economy and at the same time such a weak and unstable political system and a corrupt and inefficient bureaucracy?

In the late 1980s the Italian economy had some clear successes:

- Exports were at an all-time high.
- State industry had embarked on a relatively successful process of restructuring and reorganization.
- Italy's large private firms continued to be European leaders (Fiat, Olivetti, Montedison, Ferruzzi).
- Its small and medium-sized enterprises bedazzled observers (Benetton is the best-known, but far from only, example).

At the end of the 1980s an air of prosperity pervaded the country, but a series of problems remained, and seemed set to threaten the durability of that prosperity:

- High unemployment (the national average is 11 per cent, but ranges from 8 per cent in the North to 19 per cent in South).
- Relatively high interest rates (prime lending rates stood at 22 per cent in 1982, and fell to 13.5 per cent in 1991, but are consistently among the highest in Europe).
- Italy's labour costs have risen faster than those of its neighbours and although it still enjoys a 5.5 per cent advantage over Germany and 17 per cent over the United Kingdom, Italian labour costs are 7.3 per cent ahead of France's and 2 per cent ahead of Spain's.
- Relatively high inflation (16 per cent in 1982, falling to a fairly constant 5 per cent from 1986 to 1989, and now set firmly at about 6.5 per cent).
- Vast public expenditure (in 1991 the budget deficit was 12 per cent of GDP).
- A staggering public debt (in 1991, 102 per cent of GDP, or 25 million lire (£11250) for every Italian).

In the early 1990s, it has become clear that the inability of successive governments to deal with these and other problems has brought Italy to the edge. 1992 is clearly a critical year in the history of the republic.

Business and government

One often-expressed view suggests that such successes as the Italian economy has enjoyed (and there have been many) have all been due to the geniality, imagination and flair of the individual Italian entrepreneur. Another, slightly more sinister, view sees the Italians as lovable rogues, living on their wits, exploiting chance circumstances and the ineffectuality of the state in a black economy devoid of responsibility and beyond the control of the authorities. In fact, the picture is a good deal more complicated, as we shall see below.

In any analysis of the Italian business culture, a clear understanding must be gained of the link between the political and economic systems, and hence the link between the public and private industrial sectors. Before we analyze the relationship between the public and private sectors, it is necessary to describe recent political developments, which are dramatic, even by Italian standards.

Italy operates a system of proportional representation: following a referendum on electoral reform in 1991, electors vote for a party list and may express a further preference for one candidate on that list. For electoral purposes, the country is divided into large electoral colleges. Given the multiplicity of parties (small parties are encouraged by the lack of a threshold below which they are denied representation in parliament, such as operates in Germany), the Italian elector is presented with a bewildering abundance of candidates – in the Rome electoral college for the April 1992 elections over 25 parties were represented, with more than 20 candidates on most lists.

The **Democrazia Cristiana**, DC (Christian Democrats) have been in power uninterruptedly since 1946, and since the 1960s have shared that power in coalition with the **Partito Socialista Italiano**, PSI (Socialist Party) and an array of smaller parties, including the **Partito Socialdemocratico Italiano**, PSDI (Social Democrats), the **Partito Liberale Italiano**, PLI (Liberals) and the **Partito Repubblicano Italiano**, PRI (Republicans). The popular perception outside Italy is of a country of great political instability: the country has had 50 governments since the war. But, in fact, this instability has hidden a deeper-seated problem: before the elections in 1992, the same political parties, and the same political leaders, had been in power for over thirty years. The dominant characteristic of the Italian political system, therefore, is stagnation, rather than instability. A change of government, though often described as a crisis, has simply meant a minor adjustment in the distribution of seats in cabinet to reflect a shift in the balance of power among the coalition party secretaries (a system dubbed **partitocrazia** or party-ocracy). Typical of this process was the government crisis of 1989: the prime minister, Ciriaco De Mita, on the left of the DC, and who had ruffled too many party feathers with his efforts to reform and modernize the party, was replaced as prime minister by the foreign minister, Giulio Andreotti, from the DC old guard and five times prime minister in the 1970s. After two months of haggling, a 'new' government emerged based on exactly the same party configuration as before, with a handful of new faces but with no new policies or ideas, and whose only purpose seemed to be to survive until the scheduled general election in 1992.

There has been no credible alternative to this system, no possibility of an alternative left-wing coalition, since the failed attempts to involve the **Partito Comunista Italiano**, PCI (Communist Party) in a grand coalition (the so-called **compromesso storico**, or historic compromise) in the late 1970s, when the PCI agreed to abstain in parliament, rather than vote against the government, in exchange for consultation on the legislative pro-gramme. The PCI and the left generally have been further weakened by the knock-on effects of the collapse of the Berlin Wall: the PCI had gradually disassociated itself from Moscow in the 1960s and 1970s, but the collapse of Communism in the East forced a complete review and re-focusing of the PCI, which led to a split of the party into a new **Partito Democratico della Sinistra**, PDS (Democratic Party of the Left), and a rump of Stalinists, the **Rifondazione Comunista** (Reformed Communist Party).

This lack of an alternative government coalition has allowed the DC the luxury of a high degree of factionalism. Indeed, the only thing that kept the DC together was Catholicism and fear of the extremes of Communism and Fascism. During the last twenty years both of these aspects of Italian life have seen change: the referenda on divorce (1974) and abortion (1981) have demonstrated a divergence between Italian public and private morals, and a considerable loosening of the grip of the Catholic Church over political life; the spectre of Communism has now disappeared in the aftermath of the collapse of the Berlin Wall, and Fascism (in the form of the neo-fascist **Movimento Sociale Italiano**, MSI (Italian Social Movement) has never emerged as a serious alternative, despite right-wing inspired terrorism in the 1970s.

Thus, coalition government, previously a system to eliminate the possi-bilities of extremism, has become a device to serve the interests of the par-ties. The factions of the DC have long been funded by corruption and **lottizzazione** – the practice of dividing the spoils of public sector jobs along party political lines. A rake-off from the award of public contracts is shared systematically according to formula among the parties, principally the gov-ernment parties (DC, PSI, PSDI, PLI) but even the parties with 'clean' images (PRI and PCI/PDS) have recently become tainted. From lottiz-zazione stems the system of **clientelismo** or patronage whereby jobs, posi-tions of influence, even the provision of telephones, hospital beds and school places are manipulated and distributed on the **raccomandazione** (recommendation) of a party official.

In the face of such large-scale political corruption, and of the evident inability of the political class to deliver the long-overdue economic and political reforms, Italian voters might have been expected to demonstrate their disaffection and scepticism through abstentionism and non-participation in the 1992 elections, but turn-out, at 87.2 per cent, remained high. Rather, the electors delivered a body-blow to the system by breaking years of habit and voting for new and untried political alternatives (Table 3.1).

Table 3.1 *General election results*

Party	1987		1992
DC	34.3		29.7
PSI	14.3		13.6
PSDI	2.9		2.7
PLI	2.1		2.8
Government coalition	53.6		48.8
PCI	26.6	PDS	16.1
		Rifondazione	5.6
MSI/DN	5.9		5.4
PRI	3.7		4.4
Northern Leagues	1.3		8.7
Radicals/Pannella	2.6		1.3
Greens	2.5		2.8
La Rete	–		1.9
Others	3.8		5.0

Source: *Corriere della Sera*
La Rete = anti-mafia rebel Christian Democrats led by the former mayor of Palermo, Leoluca Orlando.

If 'crisis' was a much-overused word in describing Italian politics before 1992, in the aftermath of the elections it is barely adequate to describe the confusion and devastation wrought on the political scene. There are now more parties in parliament than ever before (16); with the collapse in vote of the DC and the PSI, the government coalition lost its overall majority. The winners of the election, undoubtedly, were the Northern Leagues, principally the **Lega Lombarda** (Lombard League), led by the rabble-rousing Umberto Bossi, who criticizes the corruption of the system and demands a federal constitution for Italy. The League became the largest party in Milan, toppling the PSI in their stronghold. However, the victory of the League, in signalling the defeat of the old order, gave little indication of a possible alternative. Given the fragmentation of the left, and the declining share of the vote for the former PCI, no alternative majority seemed possible. Italy was immediately judged by many commentators to be ungovernable.

The effects on the party old guard were immediate: Prime Minister Andreotti, DC Party Secretary Forlani, and State President Cossiga all resigned. The Socialists were in even deeper disarray than the Christian Democrats. In May 1992, senior Socialist Party officials and politicians, including Carlo Tognoli (minister for tourism and former mayor of Milan), Bobbo Craxi (Bettino Craxi's son) and Paolo Pillitteri (former mayor of Milan, and Bettino Craxi's brother-in-law) were placed under cautionary arrest and charged with taking bribes from businessmen in return for awarding public contracts for work in the health service, airports, football stadiums and transport systems. Pillitteri was also under investigation by an inquiry into mafia investment in Milan. Further arrests of PDS and DC politicians followed, as did the arrest of the managing directors of Italy's two largest construction companies: Lodigiani and Cogefar-Impresit (Lodigiani built the hugely expensive San Siro football stadium in Milan, Cogefar, now part of Fiat, built the Milan metro and the Louvre Pyramid). Following these arrests, more than 150 businessmen volunteered further information, partly hoping thereby to avoid arrest, but also seeking the opportunity to unburden themselves of the weight of political corruption which had spread even to the efficient and European north of the country. As investigations progressed, the scale and extent of corruption began to be revealed. Italian has a wide vocabulary for describing bribery: **bustarelle**, **mazzette**, **pizzi**, or the word of the moment **tangenti**. These bribes had been paid to politicians for the award of public contracts, from as little as £50 for the contract to bury the dead from a local authority hospice, to £10 million allegedly paid to the head of the Milan Metro authority. Milan has been renamed **Tangentopoli**, but it is by no means the only city to be infected. By July 1992, the scandal had spread to Venice, Florence, Rome and Naples, implicating politicians from most of the political parties, including out-going PSI foreign secretary Gianni De Michelis.

Despite the clear demand for reform expressed by voters in the election, the political parties settled into their normal pattern of haggling over jobs in the political structure. The election of the new State President had already gone through 16 inconclusive rounds when the mafia intervened. The murder of Giovanni Falcone was a cold, cynical act, designed to show the mafia's total freedom of operation outside the control of the state. Falcone was the director general of criminal affairs in the justice department. As a judge in Sicily he was responsible for many of the most effective blows against the mafia, including the discovery of the **super-pentito** (supergrass) Tommaso Buscetta in 1984, and the 1987 **maxi-processo** (super trial) which saw over 350 **mafiosi** sentenced to long terms in prison. Already the target of a previous assassination attempt in 1988, Falcone, his wife and body guards, were blown up by a two thousand pound bomb on the Palermo–Trapani motorway. Falcone was returning from Rome to his family home in Sicily. On such journeys, Falcone used special air transport wholly controlled by the Italian security services. High-level involvement in leaking information concerning his movements is not in doubt. Falcone, at the time of his murder, was investigating the link between the mafia and the Milan corruption scandal, and had recently begun investigations into a series of Swiss bank accounts.

At his funeral, the caretaker President (the entirely respectable Republican, Giovanni Spadolini) and other party leaders were jeered and booed by the crowds. The party leaders were shamed into immediately electing a compromise candidate as State President. Oscar Luigi Scalfaro, a 73-year-old Christian Democrat, is a devout Catholic. More to the point, he is also a committed parliamentarian. His election puts to an end former President Cossiga's (and Craxi's) designs for constitutional reform based on a presidential model. Scalfaro also left vacant the position of speaker of the Chamber of Deputies. This was awarded to the right-wing PDS deputy, Giorgio Napolitano. With Spadolini as President of the Senate, the way was thus open for a Socialist Prime Minister. Without the Milan scandal this would have undoubtedly gone to Craxi, but his close connections with persons already arrested on corruption charges precluded him, so his close friend Giuliano Amato (former treasury minister) was chosen to form a new government. Although Amato is close to Craxi, he is more open than his friend to the possibility of collaboration with other parties to the left, especially the PDS. Amato's declared priorities on which he hopes to build a new government are: public finance, the fight against crime, morality in public life, and electoral reform. In early July 1992, Amato managed to form a government consisting of the old four-party coalition (DC, PSI, PSDI and PLI), with a slender majority of 24. Serious doubts must exist as to whether it will be able to address the problems, and further elections in 1993 remain a strong possibility. Of the urgent problems facing the new government, the most important, and intractable, is the problem of public finance.

The deficit problem

The government deficit for 1991 was over 150 thousand billion lire, and the accumulated national debt stood then at 1,439,000 billion lire or 102 per cent of Italy's annual GDP and in comparison with the national income, three times the national debt of the United States. Interest payments on the debt account for 11 per cent of GDP. This is a significant problem on its own, but it is compounded by the fact that the government deficit is funded almost entirely by domestic private-sector saving which is traditionally higher in Italy than in other countries. Italians are sitting on a mountain of **buoni del tesoro** (state savings bonds) to the tune of 1.5 million billion lire – the same amount as the public debt. On average, at 1987 prices, every Italian family has 35 million lire in savings and investments, of which 13 million are in savings bonds and 17 million in bank accounts. They are held by Italians irrespective of class, age, educational background or geographical location. So any attempt to reduce the public debt by reducing returns on savings bonds will affect large numbers of voters. Furthermore, now that all restrictions on capital movements have been removed, Italian capital is free to leave the country if investors feel a lack of confidence in the government's economic policy, or simply because they see the possibility of better returns elsewhere. In either case, the exchange rate would come under pressure and the government would be required to act to sustain the value of the lira within the Exchange-Rate Mechanism (ERM) of the European Monetary System (EMS). Managing the exchange rate has become a more precise operation since the lira joined the narrower 2.5 per cent band in the ERM in January 1990. Given these sorts of pressures, a traditional approach would be to raise interest rates. By so doing, however, the government would be shooting itself in the foot: since the Italian debt is largely held by Italians, paying higher interest on the debt would strengthen domestic consumption whilst at the same time reducing industrial competitiveness, thus worsening the balance of payments problem. There continues to be a real fear, therefore, that the scale of the problem could force the lira out of the ERM and bring about the reimposition of capital controls.* In such a case, the problem would be as severe a test of the effectiveness of the EMS as it is of Italian government policy.

Guido Carli, former governor of the Bank of Italy and DC Treasury Minister until he lost his seat in the 1992 election, made several proposals for dealing with the problem, aiming to limit the deficit to about 10 per cent of GDP by raising revenues and cutting expenditure. His proposals included: the reduction of the number of state employees and reduction of wages for those remaining; reform of the health service and pensions system; increased privatization; reduction of state subsidies to industry; improvement of financial procedures; and increased taxes. These objectives are easier stated than achieved. Tax evasion in Italy is still rampant – in 1989 it was calculated at 260,000 billion lire, equivalent to about 28 per cent of national income – and there are still no credible restraints being placed on health and pensions expenditure. Deficits in the national health service and in social security, as a percentage of allocations, rose form 5.4 per cent in 1985 to 22.1 per cent in 1990. Expenditure on health, social security and pensions is universally recognized to be completely out of control. The proceeds from the government's tentative privatization programme are likely to remain extremely modest. Even if the government were to achieve the apparently impossible

---

* In fact, this is precisely what happened in September 1992.

and restrict the deficit to 10 per cent of GDP, this is still way behind the target of 3 per cent set by the European Community at Maastricht. The government must cut 100 thousand billion lire from the 1992 budget and increase revenue if it is not to be excluded from the next stage of monetary union and thereby relegated to the European second division.

The new treasury minister, Piero Barucci, a financial technocrat, announced the Amato government's plans for tackling the problem in July 1992: the discount rate was to be raised from 12 to 13 per cent, and the commercial lending rate from 13 to 14.5 per cent; charges for telephone, electricity and gas services were frozen, as were motorway tolls and train fares (in an attempt to curb inflation); increases in income tax to net an additional $4 billion, and controls on the state pensions schemes were announced. Whether such reforms can be passed through parliament and taken into effect must still be open to question, given the general lack of political will to force through such painful measures.

Table 3.2 *Italian growth rates (1981–92)*

1981	1.1
1982	0.3
1983	1.1
1984	3.0
1985	2.6
1986	2.5
1987	3.0
1988	4.1
1989	3.0
1990	2.0
1991	1.0
1992	1.2

Source: OECD

The nub of the political and economic problem facing the country lies in the close links between the political parties and the public sector, both industrial and administrative. In any analysis of contemporary Italy, much relies on an understanding of the relationships between the public sector and the political parties, and between the public and private sectors and how the public sector has been used to provide a basis for the growth of the private sector. It is necessary, therefore, to understand how this system works.

The **Istituto per la Ricostruzione Industriale** (IRI) was set up by the Fascists in 1933 as a temporary measure to handle a number of bank insolvencies and industrial bankruptcies. The agency was to take temporary control of these concerns and sell them back to the private sector when conditions had improved. By 1937, when it had become clear that reselling the firms would be impossible, IRI was given a new role in the autarchy objective – that of reinforcing the state's direct control over the economy. After 1945 its role became one of sustaining the national economy, maintaining the basic sectors considered crucial for the development of the country's *private* manufacturing capability. IRI now accounts for three-quarters of employment in the state holding system, and is the largest service and investment company in Europe. Its activities are so vast that they are split up into sectorally-defined sub-holding companies, the most important of which are Finmeccanica (mechanical industries, including aerospace and railway rolling stock), Fincantieri (shipbuilding), Finmare (shipping lines), STET (telecommunications, divided between Italtel and SIP), Italstat (infrastructure construction), and ILVA (formerly Finsider, steel production). IRI also controls RAI (the national television and radio broadcasting corporation), Alitalia (the national airline), SME (the food conglomerate with the Motta, Alemagna, Pavesi and Autogrill brand names), together with a variety of banks including three of Italy's top ten banks (Banca Commerciale Italiana, Credito Italiano and Banco di Roma).

Ente Nazionale Idrocarburi (ENI) was set up in 1953 with the initial objective of disposing of the assets of AGIP (Agenzia Generale Italiana Petroliferi), which had also been founded by the Fascists. Under the dynamic leadership of Enrico Mattei, by 1962 AGIP had expanded into an organization dealing with oil exploration, drilling, importing and marketing, natural gas exploitation and petrochemicals. In 1978, ENI accounted for 13.5 per cent of state sector employment and 29 per cent of its fixed capital investment. ENI now controls AGIP Petroli (oil refining and petrol distribution), AGIP (petrol and minerals research), SNAM (natural gas distribution), Enichem (chemicals), and a variety of companies involved in engineering and services.

Ente Partecipazione Finanza Industria Manufatturiera (EFIM) deals with manufacturing industries in difficulty and is the least purposeful and least profitable of the state holding companies. It has interests in transport, aeronautics, glass, weapons production and computers. It seems to owe its existence to the fact that, in the carve-up of the public sector, it was traditionally the preserve of the Social Democrats, although with the presidency in 1992 of Gaetano Mancini control has now passed to the PSI.

There is little logic to the activities of the three companies; their activities are as much a result of historical accident as political (but never industrial) design. All three are involved in informatics and tourism; and duplications occur in railways, air transport, construction and insurance.

The state holding sector, of which IRI, ENI and EFIM are the principal components, has a pyramidal structure. At the top is the **Ministero per le**

Partecipazioni Statali (Ministry of State Holdings), which issues directives and is responsible to parliament. Below the Ministry come the principal **enti** (boards), which are wholly government controlled in the sense that all their equity capital is put up by the state. At the base of the pyramid come the various firms and enterprises in which the enti have a controlling interest but whose capital can also be partly privately subscribed. Given the fragmented nature of private shareholding in many firms, the state can maintain a controlling interest with as little as 15 per cent of the equity capital. Thus the state holding sector differs from the Italian nationalized industries which are wholly state financed.

This network of public and semi-public bodies dominates every aspect of Italian life: state corporations control 80 per cent of Italy's banking, 25 per cent of industrial employment, 50 per cent of fixed investment. The state sector is a vast array of hypothetically independent entities (some with private shareholders), but in receipt of public funds and, since the late 1950s, increasingly under the control of political appointees. Other western states have large public sectors, but none has such a breadth of economic power with such a depth of national influence.

The achievement of IRI and ENI was that they succeeded in the 1950s and 1960s in establishing those industrial infrastructures essential for rapid economic growth (cheap steel, cheap petro-chemicals, cheap energy and a motorway system). Thus the public sector, instead of competing against private monopolies and/or adopting a strategy in favour of collective needs, ensured instead the expansion of the private sector.

By the 1970s, however, the state sector had become a political instrument in the hands of the DC, its economic functions entirely subordinated to the objective of enabling the survival of the party and the kind of economic structures which had grown with it. Between 1965 and 1977, the DC factions were estimated to have received $100 million from public corporations. Between 1974 and 1984, IRI ran a $200 million slush fund largely for the benefit of the DC. In recent years, the PSI has imitated and often outdone its coalition partner in the manipulation of the public sector, and the recent scandals have demonstrated that no political party can any longer claim to have '**le mani pulite**' (clean hands) – the PCI boast in the 1970s.

Thus, from being the foundation stone of the economic miracle in the late 1950s and early 1960s, the public sector had by the mid-1970s become a major drain on the country's resources and an authentic power centre in its own right. Most of the public corporations are now in permanent debt. There have been major scandals in the banking sector (the collapse of Italcasse in 1980 and the Banco Ambrosiano in 1982 are the best-known examples) and the DC has seen its grip on the public sector loosened. Nevertheless, the DC has to keep supplying the public sector with state funding, which it hopes will continue to be used to ensure political support for the DC. It is estimated that in 1989, IRI received 31,000 billion lire in state subsidies; ENI 9,000 billion.

The captains of Italian industry (not unnaturally) object because private enterprise is being squeezed:

- High wages in the public sector create high demands in the private sector.
- Wage indexation has constrained bargaining power.
- Excessive union power has constrained the ability of management to manage.
- High social costs have been imposed on employers.
- The bribes required by political party bosses in exchange for public contracts have become an intolerable burden for Italian businessmen.

Hence the increasingly strident demand for the break up of the public sector, which eventually got under way with the sale of Alfa Romeo to Fiat in 1986.

Privatization

Romano Prodi, professor of economics at Bologna University and former DC economics minister, was appointed to head IRI in 1982. His strategy for dealing with the holding company was in the medium term to re-establish control over the management and solvency of IRI firms while in the longer term seeking to take IRI out of sectors in which private industry could do better than the state, in order to concentrate on service networks and high technology in which, because of the huge investment involved, he believed the state still had a part to play. In pursuing this latter objective, Prodi had to move towards an internationalization of the public sector in order to improve efficiency, especially in advanced sectors. The new IRI strategy required at the outset the privatization of firms acquired during the period of crisis which were not crucial for (or were counter-productive to) the achievement of IRI's objectives.

Two early attempts at privatization were made, both of which failed. In 1982 the proposed sale of Maccarese (agricultural holdings) was blocked by the trade unions, and in 1983 the proposed sale of the SME food conglomerate to Buitoni-Perugina (part of the De Benedetti group) was blocked after disagreement within the government. The SME sale would have made SME-Buitoni the largest food group in Europe and by far the largest in Italy but it fell through after sustained pressure from Barilla and Ferrero provoked the opposition of the PSI. This sort of party political interference in the management decisions of both public and private sector industry is commonplace. For example, Marisa Bellisario, Italy's top woman executive and managing director and chief executive of Italtel (the Milan-based telecommunications switchgear manufacturer) was blocked by Fiat's managing director as chief executive of a joint venture with Fiat's Telettra because of her Socialist party affiliation.

The first successful privatization was that of Alfa Romeo in 1986. Alfa had been in trouble since the early 1970s. Originally the company had produced higher-class cars and aimed at a lower-volume market, unlike Fiat which had always targeted a mass market. In the late 1960s, however, Alfa was required, as part of the government's policy of direct investment in the South, to build a new production plant. Construction of the new plant at Pomigliano d'Arco near Naples began in 1968, and production of the new Alfa Sud model came on line just in time to coincide with the slump in demand which followed the first oil crisis. In 1986, Alfa Romeo was employing 36,000 people, of whom 28,832 in the automobile sector. Despite gradually increasing sales, the company was running huge losses.

Alfa was sold to Fiat in November 1986 for 1,050 billion lire, although payment for the company in five annual instalments is not due to start until 1993, by which time the cost in real terms will have halved and Alfa should in any case be paying for itself. As a result of this successful, and the previous-failed, privatizations a number of ground rules for future privatizations in Italy seem to have been established:

- It is up to the agency that effectively controls the stock of the company to be privatized to work out an agreement with the purchaser.
- This agreement must meet objective criteria.
- IRI has to ratify the sale based on an overall evaluation of the objectives of the public sector.
- The government must agree to the deal based on a consideration of the overall economic well-being of the country.

Although the procedures are slightly clearer as a result of the Alfa privatization, other attempts at privatization have not achieved even these modest successes. Probably the best-known recent example of a failed privatization is that of Enichem, the wholly-owned chemical subsidiary of ENI. The company's privatization through a sale to Raul Gardini's Montedison was vetoed by the Prime Minister, Giulio Andreotti, in 1990. A joint venture between the two firms (called Enimont) subsequently collapsed, and Enichem has been struggling ever since. In 1991 the firm lost 722 billion lire, and this loss cannot be entirely explained by the recession which has hit chemicals companies hard across the world. The company has also been affected by political interference and union objections to trimming its sprawling operations, which are scattered throughout Italy. Enichem is not immune to scandal: both the company itself and its parent, ENI, are fiefdoms of the PSI. An 80-kilometre pipeline, built to link two

Enichem plants at Ravenna and Ferrara in northern Italy was planned to cost 80 billion lire, but finally cost 200 billion. Enichem's own investigation blamed the subcontractor (who was loyal to Andreotti's faction in the DC) for the project's mismanagement. Andreotti appointed a further enquiry, seeking to place the responsibility on the Enichem board. Whatever the outcome of the enquiry, Enichem's problems remain. In 1992, ENI announced a 1,300 billion lire investment programme aimed at turning the company round and returning a profit by 1994, and further talk of mergers or alliances (Union Carbide and Montedison are possibilities) has been put off until then.

Privatization, however, is not the answer to all the public sector's problems. In the 1980s, IRI and ENI were controlled by technocrats (Romano Prodi (DC) at IRI and Franco Reviglio (PSI) at ENI), and some restructuring did take place. Prodi and Reviglio turned the sector round: in 1983 IRI and ENI between them lost 4000 billion lire, but in 1987 they made a profit of 900 billion. IRI shed 125,000 jobs in six years (1983–8), privatized 29 'non-strategic' companies and as a result of mergers and internal streamlining, the number of IRI-controlled industrial concerns was reduced from 467 to 361 and the number of banks from 82 to 54. The share of IRI equity held by private shareholders increased to 37.7 per cent. Prodi and Reviglio did nevertheless have their difficulties. Prodi's major failure was his inability to sell SME, the food conglomerate, to De Benedetti. Reviglio's moment of torture was in the summer of 1986 when a dangerous manoeuvre in the exchange market failed, causing a sudden collapse of the dollar–lire exchange rate.

These difficulties apart, the periods in office of Prodi and Reviglio were generally judged a success. But as their mandates came to an end in late 1989, the old party struggles for the succession began anew. Now that the companies were profitable again, they represented rich pickings for the parties and the DC and the PSI soon demonstrated that they had become tired of the independence of their previous nominees and they wished to give the jobs to more amenable candidates. In 1990, Franco Nobili was appointed to head IRI and Gabriele Cagliari at ENI.

Issues remaining to be resolved in the public sector include the choice of foreign partner for Italtel, the telecommunications equipment manufacturer; the rationalization of telecommunications services under STET (currently divided among SIP, the telephone company, Italcable, the international carrier, and ASST, a telephone company which is part of the postal service); a swap of IRI's Alfa Avio aero-engine components company for Fiat's Savigliano subsidiary which produces railway bodies and rolling stock; an agreement between IRI and ENI over the production of gas turbines; the rationalization of aerospace and defence equipment manufacturers (Aeritalia (IRI) and Agusta, Oto Melara and Galileo (EFIM)); and a re-grouping of Termomeccanica (EFIM), Italimpianti (IRI) and Snamprogetti (ENI) in the heavy plant and equipment sector. Discussion of the industrial logic of these proposals has been swamped by political objections to their main effect – the strengthening of DC-controlled IRI.

In 1992, the government planned to raise 15 thousand billion lire from privatization, but the election and subsequent uncertainty placed even these modest plans under threat. Even if they were to succeed, the effect on the budget deficit or the public debt would be minimal, but they are nevertheless fiercely opposed by the trade unions who fear massive lay-offs as the enterprises are rationalized post-privatization. The management do not support the plans either. State industry is one of the largest sources of patronage available to politicians and the careers of many state sector managers are dictated by considerations other than the profit-and-loss account of the companies they manage. There is also the question of who would get the money from the disposals: since most state industries are owned by the holding companies (IRI, ENI or EFIM), the treasury has had to concede that proceeds should go to the holding companies. In turn, the treasury could sell off the holdings. Both IRI and ENI own potentially attractive companies, and prefer stock market listings to direct sales to private buyers. This has led to accusations that they are attempting to nationalize savings rather than privatizing state industries.

In July 1992, the government announced plans to liquidate EFIM after a parliamentary commission had refused to sanction emergency funding to bail out the holding company after record losses of 867 billion lire in 1991. The company has total debts of over £4 billion, of which almost half is held by foreign banks and financial institutions. Although some of EFIM's holdings are sound and marketable, many are not. The row over the responsibility for EFIM's debts will be long and bitter, and is unlikely to enhance Italy's international image.

Business and the economy

Manufacturing

The private sector economy is proportionately the smallest in Europe, accounting for only 35–40 per cent of production. It is also remarkable for its large number of small producers (90 per cent of firms employ fewer than 100 employees, the average number of employees in an Italian firm is 7.6). Italy has the largest number of shopkeepers in Europe. Nevertheless, in the 1980s the private sector blossomed, to a considerable extent replacing the state sector as the dynamic segment of the Italian economy. But the private sector, despite the vast number of small firms, is dominated by a handful of dynamic industrialists: Gianni Agnelli (nicknamed l'**Avvocato**, the lawyer, at Fiat), Raul Gardini (**il Contadino**, the farmer, formerly at Ferruzzi-Montedison), Carlo De Benedetti (**l'Ingegnere**, the engineer, at Olivetti) and Silvio Berlusconi (**Sua Emittenza**, his '**emittence**' – a pun on a Cardinal's honorific – owner of the TV network Canale 5 and the super-market chain Standa, amongst other things). A review of the activities of these extremely influential men and their organizations is therefore appro-priate.

Agnelli and Fiat

Fiat had to face the same crisis in the 1970s as all the other European car producers, but the company emerged in the late 1980s as the largest and most successful European car manufacturer. Fiat's problems were of two types: one to do with the management of the workforce, the other to do with production of the right product.

Along with other big employers after 1969, Fiat found itself beset by the problem of handling a well-organized and disruptive workforce. Fiat's response to this problem was to develop and perfect its sub-contracting strategy: unable to reconstruct the social peace of the 1950s inside the fac-tory after 1969, the firm opted for the fragmentation of labour power into a multitude of small supplying firms. Fiat decentralized many of its sub-processes and components to subcontracting firms. In the early 1970s, for example, Fiat had been criticized for not investing in the South. When it finally did begin to invest, three years after Alfa, it was able to learn from Alfa's mistakes (principally, setting up a large factory in an urban–indus-trial area). Fiat took better advantage of regional incentives and rather than set up large plants in urban industrial areas it opted for smaller factories in conservative rural areas with high unemployment, creating a scatter of medium-sized plants in a range of locations. This multi-plant strategy, which also included plants outside Italy, prevented a strike from suddenly paralyzing the whole of production, since major components such as engines or gearboxes could be obtained from several sources.

At the height of Fiat's decentralization, it was estimated that there were some 8,000 supporting satellite firms which were in some way subordinate to the main industry; Fiat determined the supply of these firms' products, the level of prices and, by implication, the investment and staffing levels. Together with the introduction of robots in labour-intensive tasks such as welding, this meant a large reduction in the Fiat workforce. Fiat laid off 23,000 workers in 1980. The lay-offs were bitterly opposed by the unions, but in October of that year, 40,000 workers marched through Turin, in defiance of their union leaders, demanding the right to work. This moment was a significant one in worker–management relations at the national level as well as at the level of the company. It signalled the end of the militant postures adopted by the unions since their victories of 1969 and marked the beginning of the end of trade union unity. The significance of the events was noted all over Italy. Industrial tribunals began upholding dismissals for absenteeism and **Confindustria** (the employers' federation) challenged the **scala mobile** (wage indexation system) which had been in operation since 1945.

Fiat, then, has an important role in the national political scene as well as in the industrial scene – this is hardly surprising, given that the company accounts for 4 per cent of Italy's GNP. In the 1950s Fiat worked closely with the political authorities and was able to influence the economic strategy of the DC and hence of the government. The Italian state helped Fiat by providing the infrastructure for the development of a large car market: building motorways, keeping down the price of petrol, running down public transport. Externally, Fiat presented a progressive image, but internally it was repressive towards the unions, especially the Communist-inspired CGIL. Throughout the 1960s and 1970s, however, Fiat dissociated itself from the DC, attacking the clientele system and demanding (when Agnelli became President of Confindustria in 1974) a central role for industry in the management of the economy, planning, and a clear separation between the state and the private sector. Agnelli's line did not prevail, mainly because the sheer size of the public sector makes it difficult for private industry to emerge as a political protagonist. Nevertheless, Agnelli is not averse to making his political views known (he is a member of the Italian Senate), and he has expressed enthusiasm for Craxi's 'modernizing' approach.

Much of Fiat's commercial success is due to the ability of the car section to capture larger market shares, mainly through its most successful models, the Uno and the Tipo. 60 per cent of Fiat's 38,000 billion lire turnover in 1988 came from cars, and cars generated 2000 billion lire profit – two-thirds of all Fiat's profits from 48 per cent of its 270,000 employees. In 1988, Fiat became Europe's largest car manufacturer with over 2 million sales.

Agnelli's announcement in November 1988 that Vittorio Ghidella, the **amministratore delegato** (managing director) of Fiat Auto and previously tipped to succeed Cesare Romiti as the chairman of the Fiat Group, was to leave the company and his functions to be assumed by Romiti himself, may seem puzzling in the light of Fiat Auto's success. In fact, 1988, as well as being a year of outstanding success for the company, was also a year of deep and bitter internal struggle over the basic strategy of the group. Ghidella believed that to survive and prosper into the 1990s, a successful car producer would have to be able to compete in 'two out of three' of the world's major markets (Europe, the USA and Japan). Fiat's domination in Europe would not be enough to safeguard its future. The group would therefore have to concentrate more of its resources on car production and/or enter into large-scale production and commercial agreements with US manufacturers. Fiat's agreements with Lee Iacocca's Chrysler was a start in this direction, but for Romiti, this was already too much. For Romiti, car production is a 'mature sector' and investment should be limited to that strictly necessary to maintaining market share. Romiti is much more interested in the financial sector and banking, media and telecommunications, and diversification into other industrial sectors (operations such as Snia-Bnp who produce missiles and munitions). Ghidella had been supported by Umberto Agnelli in demanding restrictions on Japanese imports, but such demands were out of step with political developments and unlikely to find favour in government circles.

Under Romiti, Fiat would not buy out other car manufacturers (BMW was mooted at one time), but rather diversify into electronics and aerospace, even though its experience and success in these sectors were limited (a modest agreement with IBM produced less than expected; Fiat withdrew from Westland after less than two years). Even more, Fiat would attempt to expand into banking and finance. Fiat has the money to buy banks, mainly because its recent acquisitions have cost it very little (see the Alfa purchase above), but the group must first overcome the strong resistance of the Bank of Italy, which is firmly opposed to the mixing of industrial and financial interests.

Many questioned the wisdom of dispensing with such a successful manager as Ghidella, and of concentrating the whole of Fiat management in one person's hands, and of radically changing a strategy which had paid such dividends, particularly at a time when the highly-protected Italian car market (car imports from Japan have been limited to a meagre 14,000 units per year) was about to be opened up as a result of Project 1992. But Romiti responded vigorously to the challenge, signing an historic deal with the Soviet Union in November 1989 to build a £1 billion car plant in the USSR, setting up a merger between Lancia (Fiat's luxury car subsidiary) and the car division of Sweden's Saab to create the largest luxury car manufacturer in the world, as well as making the running in two other deals, the first to take over the Spanish state-owned truck manufacturer, ENASA, and the second to build a replacement for the existing Fiat-backed FSM factory in Poland.

In the early 1990s, Fiat's performance has been mixed: profits fell from 1,417 billion lire in 1990 to 871 billion in 1991, total sales remaining fairly static at 58,000 billion lire. Fiat Auto made profits of 386 billion lire on sales of 27,506 billion, despite the stagnant market. During the same period, Fiat's total number of employees was reduced from 303,238 to 287,957. Financial services, Toro Assicurazioni and Rinascente (department store) made good profits, whilst Iveco (industrial vehicles) and Magneti Morelli (components) made losses. Nevertheless, in 1992, Fiat completed a $2 billion takeover of FSM, giving it a significant stake in the Polish market with its popular 126 and Cinquecento models.

Gardini and Ferruzzi-Montedison

The Ferruzzi agri-business group, headed until 1991 by Raul Gardini, is the major shareholder of the Montedison chemicals company. In 1988, Gardini, with the not-inconsiderable assistance of Enrico Cuccia at Mediobanca, put together a consortium to re-finance Montedison and consolidate the chemicals activities of the state-owned Enichem and of Montedison into a new company, Enimont. Before the reorganization, Ferruzzi and Montedison had combined debts of 12,000 billion lire; rationalization and the selling off of many of Montedison's assets gave the group considerable liquidity and greatly-reduced debts. Enimont (by adding Enichem and Montedison's market shares together) had 34 per cent of the domestic Italian chemicals market and employs 52,000 people (7–9000 jobs are set to go in rationalization). Sales were estimated at about $10 billion per year. The collapse of the joint venture in 1990, for political rather than economic or business reasons, disgusted Gardini, who left Italy in 1991, highly critical of both the Ferruzzi family and the Italian system, and vowing never to return. After spending several months engaged in the Americas Cup yacht race, however, he seemed reinvigorated and prepared to use his 505 billion lire golden handshake from Ferruzzi to entrepreneurial advantage. Together with Giulio Malgara, president of Quaker Europe, he established a joint venture company called Garma, aimed at carving out a slice of the oils market – traditional Ferruzzi territory. After striking a products and distribution deal with Quaker, Garma entered the market with Cuore and Topazio oils, and sales of 200 billion lire and distribution rights worth a further 300 billion. Gardini also had his sights set on Café Hag and Levissima mineral water, which would raise his turnover to 800 billion lire. The challenge to Ferruzzi is clear.

De Benedetti and Olivetti

Carlo De Benedetti resigned as Chief Executive of Fiat Auto in 1976 (at the age of 41) when his plan for revitalizing the auto group was rejected by Agnelli. He immediately bought CIR (Compagnie Industriali Riunite) and used it to start buying small manufacturing companies. He took over the loss-making ($8 million a month) typewriter manufacturer in 1978 and transformed Olivetti into Europe's second-biggest information technology company, after IBM, with sales in 1988 of $4.8 billion. Just under half of Olivetti's sales are in Italy, followed by France, Germany, Britain, Spain and Switzerland. Olivetti has 40 per cent of the domestic personal computer market (25 per cent to IBM) and 23 per cent of the mini-computer market (33 per cent to IBM). Olivetti's relationship with AT&T proved problematical especially on the issue of technical standards. De Benedetti has dreams of a Europe-wide industrial and financial empire to which diversification is the key, and in the pursuit of which he has been repeatedly frustrated, first in his failed attempt to take over Société Générale de Belgique, then in the SME fiasco, and more regularly in competing with Siemens of Germany, who produce almost everything that Olivetti produce. Olivetti went through a shake-up in 1988 both in production and in organization, with a new corporate structure and a new product range. The prospects for Olivetti in the 1990s seemed brighter. In 1989, Olivetti won the contract to supply computers and terminals to the French post office, a contract worth 40 million francs. However, the recession and the glut of computers on the world market has had a serious effect on Olivetti. With all the major companies making losses, many of the European companies were forced into mergers with, or even taken over by, American or Japanese competitors (ICL was taken over by Fujitsu, Bull has sold stakes to NEC and IBM). De Benedetti (who owns 42 per cent of Olivetti) resisted this trend for as long as possible, seeking ways of going it alone in Europe. 1991 was Olivetti's worst year on record, however; the group recording a loss of 460 billion lire, and laying off 18 per cent of its staff between 1990 and 1991. In his attempt to shore up losses and build a stronger base outside Italy, De Benedetti went in search of partners, but the European players were simply not strong enough. In 1992, Olivetti announced that Digital Equipment Corporation (DEC) would take an immediate 4.03 per cent stake in the company, building up to 10 per cent by the end of 1994. The alliance with DEC augurs better than the AT&T fiasco, since it provides DEC technology for a new generation of Olivetti computers, thus relieving Olivetti of research and development costs and assuring DEC of a wider market for its chips. The announcement was one of the few things to have gone right for De Benedetti in 1992: during the same year, he was found guilty of fraud and sentenced to six years imprisonment for his role in the Banco Ambrosiano scandal (he has appealed).

De Benedetti has long believed that entrepreneurs cannot limit themselves simply to the search for profit, but that they must also accept wider social and political responsibilities, such as the development of new relationships with the trade unions and the political parties in an attempt to renew the political forces of the country. His position has not enjoyed widespread support.

Berlusconi

The Berlusconi empire is built on suburban housing and B-grade television. Silvio Berlusconi began his career in the early 1970s building Milano 2, a development just outside Milan which claims to have 'everything to cater to the social, commercial and leisure interests of man'. In 1976, he bought a small commercial TV station for Milano 2, more or less at the same time as the Italian high court was ruling that private local TV stations could compete with the national RAI network. Berlusconi succeeded where many others failed by buying local stations up and down the country and shipping out to them pre-recorded programmes on cassettes which were then transmitted simultaneously, thereby creating a pseudonational network to compete directly with RAI. Having established this national network, Berlusconi hammered home the advantage by offering advertisers twice as much time for their money. By buying out two competitors who tried to beat him at his own game, Berlusconi created the three networks he now owns.

Berlusconi has subsequently diversified his activities. The purchase of the Standa supermarket–department store chain in 1988 (for details see below) put Berlusconi in a unique position with a mutually supportive advertising, distribution and sales network. By giving TV advertisers guaranteed shelf space he has effectively obtained a stranglehold on large areas of consumer retailing. Berlusconi also now controls the Mondadori publishing house and, together with his TV operations, this means that his companies now control about 60 per cent of the national advertising market.

More recently, however, Berlusconi, and his holding company Fininvest, have suffered a series of setbacks. After a successful expansion of his broadcasting empire outside Italy (to establish Telecinco in Spain and Telefünf in Germany), his proposed rescue of La Cinq in France and his bid for Channel 5 in the UK both failed. Furthermore, there is suspicion in Italy that Fininvest is dumping advertisements and that the group is abusing its dominant position in television advertising: Italy has roughly three times the European average of television advertising, yet TV advertising revenue is only 40 per cent above the European average. Fininvest is now Italy's third-largest private-sector concern, but it is not a quoted company and does not publish accounts. It is estimated that the group has debts in excess of 3000 billion lire, and it seems likely that the group will find it difficult to continue servicing such a large debt. The post-election uncertainty is particularly serious for Berlusconi, who has relied heavily on the influence his powerful friend Bettino Craxi has exerted on his behalf. A recent news media law has not yet been implemented, but according to its provisions three of the proposed twelve national channels would be reserved for RAI, and other existing positions would be preserved. However, if in different political circumstances RAI were required to divest itself of one of its channels, Berlusconi could hardly justify keeping three for himself.

Machine tools

Italy is the world's fourth-largest manufacturer of machine tools, after
Japan, Germany and the former USSR, but ahead of the USA, Switzerland,
the United Kingdom and France. The largest companies in the sector are
COMAU-Fiat, Berardi, Mandelli and Dea. These and other companies in
the sector have won markets on the basis of their flexibility and creativity,
producing machines to match the quality and price of their competitors,
but offering the additional benefits of a 'made-to-measure' approach,
designing or adapting machines in collaboration with the purchaser.
However, the engineering sector as a whole had a bad year in 1991: production fell by 5.6 per cent, plant use fell to 75.4 per cent, and employment
fell by 2.7 per cent.

Textiles and clothing

Textile manufacturing is Italy's third-biggest business after engineering
and construction. Textile sales account for almost 14 per cent of the value of
Italian manufacturing and one-third of the entire textile turnover of the EC.
Exports account for 20,000 billion lire, more than double the value of textile
imports. Italy has about 840,000 textile workers. Italy is also Europe's leading exporter of clothing, with exports in 1987 totalling 5360 billion lire. Italy
accounts for 38 per cent of the clothing imports of the members of the EC.

   The jewel in an already glittering crown of clothing manufacturers and
exporters is Benetton. The Benetton company was formed in Treviso, near
Venice, in 1965 as a family concern involving the three Benetton brothers
(Luciano, the director, Gilberto, the financial director, and Carlo the technical director) and their sister Giuliana (the designer). The market identified
by Luciano Benetton was the clothes market in a consumer society where
clothes are an expression of personality and mood, and change as often.
The Benetton production system therefore had to respond to the demands
of this market: creativity in design and immediate response to changes in
taste were the essential parameters of his production and distribution system. Since it is not possible to predict what colours will become or remain
fashionable during the season, Benetton began to produce clothes in neutral colours, to be dyed at the last minute when the demand for particular
colours was confirmed by information gathered from computerized tills in
his shops.

   Addressing the casual market, rather than the fashion market, Benetton's
annual sales are now over $1bn, of which about 35 per cent are in Italy, 15
per cent in North America, 13 per cent in Germany, 11 per cent in France
and 6 per cent in the United Kingdom. Benetton's current group strategy in
the clothing market is to achieve a geographical spread of sales that will see

one-third of its revenues coming from North and South America, one-third from Europe and one-third from the Far East. Benetton is also diversifying into other markets, such as perfumes with its 'Colors' range. Benetton continues to challenge and occasionally outrage, as with their advertising campaign in early 1992, which featured images of national and personal tragedies, such as the Vietnamese boat people, and, most controversially, an AIDS victim. Luciano Benetton (like Gianni Agnelli) has also begun a political career as a Senator in the small but influential Republican Party (PRI).

The fashion market is smaller but no less sparkling. The top five fashion houses – Valentino, Armani, Versace, Krizia and Ferré – have combined sales of about $1 billion, of which just over half comes from the sale of clothes. The business strategies of the top fashion houses do not differ greatly: they have all realized that there is money to be earned both in Italy and abroad by lending their names to the manufacture of an array of goods, from sunglasses, watches and perfumes to less exotic umbrellas and even kitchen tiles. And almost all have also launched cheaper secondary lines in ready-to-wear clothes as well as the ubiquitous designer jeans.

The food industry

The food industry in Italy is small scale and fragmented and wide open to foreign takeovers. The inability of the industry and the government to handle the privatization of SME is an indication of the fragmentation of the sector and the dangers of government interference. The original proposed sale of SME (which includes companies like Cirio, Motta, Allemagna and Pavesi) to Carlo De Benedetti's Buitoni-Perugina company was blocked in government by the Socialists. Having been frustrated in his efforts, De Benedetti sold off Buitoni to Nestlé. SME's profits between 1984 and 1987 rose from 65 billion lire to 115 billion. The IAR group (an alliance of Barilla, Ferrero and the broadcasting magnate Silvio Berlusconi) began to show interest in acquiring SME. Berlusconi, having acquired the Standa national department store chain from Raul Gardini in 1988, was seeking to build up a supermarket and store network to rival Rinascente (part of the Fiat group). He was interested in the highly profitable Autogrill (which has a monopoly of motorway cafés) and Generale Supermercati supermarket chain. Berlusconi was not interested in the food-producing side (presumably to be left to Ferrero-Barilla), but sought to take his profits from advertising (food producers now spend more on TV advertising than car manufacturers, and Berlusconi has Canale 5 ready to provide them with air time), and distribution via the GS supermarket chain. Berlusconi was too keen, however, and his close relationship with the Socialists antagonized the Christian Democrats, who ensured that the deal did not go through.

The food industry in Italy is an easy target for foreign investment and takeover.

Domestic appliances

Zanussi (23 per cent of the domestic market, 20 per cent of the European market), Merloni (Indesit and Ariston brands, 20 per cent of the Italian market, and 10 per cent of the European), and Candy (14 per cent in Italy, 5 per cent in Europe) are the main firms in this sector. Zanussi now belongs to the Swedish Electrolux group, and its factories in the Veneto region are among the most highly robotized and productive in the world. Merloni, too, uses high technology in every phase of design, development and production. Vittorio Merloni, who controls the group, aims to export two-thirds of his production, concentrating on new markets in the former USSR and China, where he hopes to build factories. Both Merloni and Candy are now developing new design ideas, such as refrigerators with different temperature compartments.

Design

Italian designers and Italian design are among the most celebrated in the world. The names of car designers like Pininfarina and Giugiaro are well established throughout Europe and the USA. Pininfarina designs cars for Fiat and for General Motors too. Giugiaro has designed some of Europe's best-selling motors: the VW Golf, the Fiat Uno, the Audi 80 and the Saab 9000.

Although industrial design may be big business in image terms, in revenue terms individual designers tend to be small and compact operations. Giugario, for example, had a turnover in 1987 of 65 billion lire. Small-scale home and office furniture designers are proliferating as all the major companies now farm out their design problems to an army of creative individuals.

Cooperatives

Cooperative ventures are a particular feature of central and northern Italian economic organization. The movement has its origins in the nineteenth century utopian socialist view that the roles of owner (shareholder), provider of work and worker could be harmoniously combined. Cooperatives group together into associations which reflect their political and social aspirations, thus there are Catholic associations (especially in the north-east, the so-called 'white' cooperatives), lay associations, left-wing associations (the 'red' cooperatives of the central regions, Tuscany, Emilia-Romagna and Umbria) and, more recently, green associations. The cooperative movement is extremely important to the economy: the turnover of the red cooperatives, for example, is estimated at 25,000 billion lire, roughly equivalent to the turnover of Fiat-Auto. The economic activity undertaken by cooperatives is broadly based: about 25 per cent is concerned with distribution, 23 per cent with agriculture and fishing, 20 per cent with building, but cooperatives are also active in tourism, culture, services, informatics and insurance.

The origins of the cooperative system are ideological, and the operation of cooperatives has in the past had a clear ideological purpose. The system is currently threatened by both economic and ideological shifts: the small-firm system as a whole faces a series of challenges (see page 192), and the apparent collapse of socialism as a political ideology creates tensions for a system of work organization now seemingly based on false ideological premises.

Tourism

Tourism remains something of a Cinderella of the Italian economy. During the late 1980s there was a gradual decline in net receipts from tourism, although this decline was arrested in 1990, reflecting the effects of the soccer World Cup and a gain in the competitive position of the Italian tourist industry in comparison with other Mediterranean countries (Greece, Spain and Yugoslavia). Even so, the surplus on tourism amounted to only 0.5 per cent of GDP, 1 percentage point lower than in 1985. This decline is partly attributable to the behaviour of Italian residents, who now travel abroad in greater numbers assisted by the progressive liberalization and final abandonment of exchange controls. Even so, Italian families spent only 1.7 per cent of their income on tourism in 1990, compared with 0.5 per cent in the early 1980s, and 3.5 per cent for the average OECD country in the late 1980s. The Italian tourist industry has been unable to respond to the increasing differentiation of international tourist demand, and there have also been problems in preserving the country's vast artistic heritage. Some problems have also been caused for tourism by environmental conditions, such as algal blooms in the Adriatic during recent summers. Tourism is also highly concentrated in the centre-north, with the south being, as usual, largely undeveloped. Of the 38,000 hotels in Italy, only 4800 are in the south. Emilia-Romagna alone receives more visitors than all the eight regions of southern Italy and the islands put together. These same regions have only twenty five-star hotels between them – the same number as the two northern regions of Lombardy and Liguria.

North–South divide

The recession of the early 1970s restricted the expansion of industry in the North, but the effect on the South was even more dramatic. As the recession hit both the north Italian and the European economies, leading to higher unemployment in these areas of traditional labour shortage, the usual safety valve for southerners – emigration – was blocked. At the same time both the population and the labour force in the South continued to grow faster than in the rest of the country. The slowdown in economic growth was accompanied by high inflation which limited the effectiveness of public expenditure programmes on which the southern economy had come to depend. As the scale and value of investment stagnated, so did growth in the South. Between 1974 and 1988, the South's overall contribution to Italy's GDP remained between 23 and 24 per cent (whereas the southern regions account for 36 per cent of Italy's population). More significantly, per capita GDP declined from 69 per cent of the Italian average to 64 per cent, whereas in the centre-north per capita GDP rose from 116 per cent of the Italian average to 120 per cent. The South's contribution to Italy's exports also declined, from 13.7 per cent to 9.6 per cent, while imports from both the centre-north and from abroad continued to grow. The effect on employment was dramatic: employment in agriculture, industry and construction continued to decline, but was not balanced by the expansion of employment in the service sectors, as happened in the centre-north. Italy's average unemployment rate is around 12 per cent, average unemployment in the South is almost twice that rate, and in the 15–30 age group it reaches 36 per cent.

Government policy to address the problems of the South has seen some changes but the main arm of policy throughout has been the development of infrastructures. In the 1950s and 1960s (with the creation of the **Cassa per il Mezzogiorno** (Fund for the South, semi-autonomous regional development fund), as Italy transformed from a rural to an industrial economy, there seemed to be sense in a policy of infrastructure development to facilitate private industrial investment. Of the 94,000 billion lire (at 1987 prices) spent between 1974 and 1988, almost 70 per cent was spent on infrastructure and only 23 per cent on direct investment in production. Even so, much of this money was wasted in ineffectual bureaucratic monitoring procedures: by 1988, of the 39,000 public works programmes initiated under government intervention schemes, only 13,000 had reached completion. Moreover, the regions had been unable to spend all the money allocated to them, some 25,000 billion lire remaining in regional treasuries.

The mafia

Of the major problems facing the South, perhaps the most dramatic is organized crime in its various manifestations (**mafia** in Sicily, **'ndrangheta** in Calabria and **camorra** in Naples), which poses a grave threat to civil life and a major disincentive to legitimate entrepreneurial activity in some areas of the South. These criminal forces not only threaten public order, but they also destabilize the economy. They have now become dominant forces in these three regions; they control bidding on public-works projects and launder money obtained illegally (especially from drug trafficking). Estimates of the scale of organized crime and of its significance in economic terms vary widely, from $750 million per year (equivalent to a company the size of ITT) to $10 billion (equivalent to the activities of Exxon). These would seem to be conservative estimates, given that the value of heroin traded in Italy in 1988 is put at $35 billion, and the trade seems set to continue to grow to satisfy the demand from Italy's 300,000 addicts (three times as many as the USA, on a per capita basis).

The traditional pattern is for the organization to make money from prostitution, protection and more recently and more lucratively from drug trafficking and to 'invest' their gains in property speculation and construction work. A cosy relationship has existed in the past between the mafia families and the political parties, particularly the Christian Democrats, but this has recently been torn apart as the government and regional authorities have been forced to confront the organization, with bloody consequences. Political leaders and senior policemen, once considered immune from the attacks of the assassins of the **onorata società** (honoured society), now fall victim with sickening regularity. Just three tragic examples will suffice to demonstrate that no part of the establishment is now safe: 1980, Pier-Santi Mattarella, Christian Democrat leader of the Sicilian region, murdered for attempting to clean up his party by exposing mafia links; 1982 Pio La Torre, leader of the Communist group in the Sicilian parliament, prominent opponent of cruise missiles and mafia involvement in the building contracts at the nuclear base at Comiso in Sicily, murdered for passing legislation sequestrating mafia profits; 1982, Carlo Alberto Dalla Chiesa, Prefect of Palermo, sent to Sicily to take on the mafia after defeating the **Brigate Roses** (Red Brigades terrorist group), murdered at the point where he had begun to piece together a full picture of mafia financing from information in bank accounts. The list of murdered magistrates would fill pages. The arrest of **superpentito** (super-grass) Tommaso Buscetta in 1984 led to a series of **maxi processi** (super-trials) as cracks in the wall of **omertà** (the rule of silence) began to appear (hence the vengeance exacted on the promoter of these successes, Giovanni Falcone). But the mafia is deeply rooted in the social fabric and its extirpation is a matter of social and cultural renewal, not only of criminal investigation and prosecution.

Organized crime used to be a plague only on the South, creating a negative business atmosphere and blocking useful investment. Concerns about the criminal ramifications of the completion of the European internal market entered national consciousness recently when the Governor of the Bank of Italy told a parliamentary committee that the mafia had billions of dollars ready for laundering and investment throughout the European Community. Antonio Gava, at the time Minister of the Interior, revealed how the mafia was underwriting Italy's national debt by buying up treasury bonds through foreign banks. The **Guardia di Finanza** (Finance Police) believes that the mafia has enough of a representation on the Italian stock market to manipulate companies and even destabilize the lira. Giovanni Falcone, two years before his murder, ridiculed the notion that the mafia was symptomatic of a 'southern problem' and that the mafia was dividing Italy into north and south. In Falcone's view, the mafia unites Italy, with its export investment in the northern economy and stock exchange, drug dealing, construction and financial operations throughout Italy and abroad.

For the rest, the South suffers all the problems of modern Italy but in a more concentrated form – urban degeneration is more pronounced, the transport network is less efficient, the banking system is more costly and less efficient, research and development are almost non-existent (of Italy's already low R&D investment – barely 1.5 per cent of GDP – only 7 per cent is spent in the South), vocational training is declining in all regions except Sicily and Sardinia.

Some rays of hope do exist: the high quality of the potential labour force, for example. Of the 758,000 young unemployed in the South, 45 per cent have diplomas or degrees. Also, the population in the South continues to grow, whilst that in the centre-north is declining (it is projected that the South will account for 45 per cent of Italy's population by 2005). The South is therefore set to repeat its role as source of labour for the North as the North fails to produce sufficient labour for its growing economy. Southerners also display great flexibility and very high productivity – often diverted into the black economy and therefore not revealed in official statistics.

The Cassa per il Mezzogiorno has been wound up and replaced by a new **Azienda per il Mezzogiorno** and a series of special provisions including law 64 of 1986, which allocated 120,000 billion lire to the South over a nine-year period. Few improvements are to be expected as a result, however, since the problems of bureaucracy and lack of control which prevented the old system from being effective have not been addressed. Some large-scale investments have taken place, for example Fiat and Olivetti have been given 2500 billion lire for projects in the South (a state contribution of 60–70 per cent of the total investment), but the impact on employment will be limited: Fiat proposes to provide only 1200 new jobs (each job therefore costs 1.5 billion lire) and Olivetti will use its money simply for restructuring just to preserve the current jobs. The prospects for Southern Italy are not encouraging.

Business and the law

The means of incorporating a business enterprise as a legal entity in Italy are laid down by the **Codice Civile** (Civil Code).

The most usual types of company are as follows:

- **Società per Azioni** (SpA), which is the same sort of organization as a United Kingdom public limited company. The minimum share capital is 200 million lire with special permission being required from the Italian Treasury if the capital is to exceed 2 billion lire.
- **Società a Responsabilità Limitata** (Srl), which is similar to a United Kingdom limited company. The minimum capital requirement is 20 million lire, but otherwise the formation procedures are the same as for a public limited company.

For both the SpA and the Srl, 30 per cent of the initial capital must be paid up on incorporation. There is no restriction on foreigners being shareholders or directors.

- **Partnerships.** There are three main types of partnership: a general partnership in which the liability of the partners is not limited (Snc, **Società in Nome Collettivo**); a partnership in which the liability of individual partners is limited by agreement to the amount of their capital contribution (Sas, **Società in Accomandita Semplice**); and an incorporated partnership in which the liability of certain partners is unlimited (SapA, **Società in Accomandita per Azioni**). In a partnership, there must be at least two partners, but there is no legal maximum. There is no legal minimum of capital to be subscribed except in the case of the incorporated partnership which follows the same rules as the corporations and must have the same minimum capital of 200 million lire. This latter form of partnership is very rare.

All business concerns in Italy must be registered with the local **Camera del Commercio** (chamber of commerce). Taxes on companies are levied both by central government and by local authorities. The rate for corporate income tax (IRPEG, which is levied on all income, whether produced in Italy or abroad) is 35 per cent and for local income tax (ILOR) 15 per cent. There are withholding taxes on dividends, interest and royalties. A double taxation agreement exists between Italy and the United Kingdom.

Imposta sul Valore Aggiunto (Iva) (VAT) was introduced in Italy in 1973 and is levied at a basic rate of 19 per cent (raised from 18 per cent in July 1988) with special low rates for food and other essential products and higher rates of 20 and 38 per cent for luxury goods.

Labour law and social security legislation are complex and extensive.

Italian law recognizes four basic categories of employee: **dirigenti** (senior managers); **quadri** (middle managers); **impiegati** (staff employees, white-collar workers); and **operai** (manual workers, blue collar workers). A range of laws regulates employment conditions and individual and collective rights, the most important of which is Law 300 of 1970, the **Statuto dei Diritti dei Lavoratori** (Law on Workers' Rights). Other legislation regulates the engagement and dismissal of employees; maximum normal working hours (40 hours for a five-day week) and overtime; employee's rights to reasonable remuneration, annual bonus, one day's rest per week, annual paid holidays and severance pay. In general, firms employing more than three persons must recruit their employees with the approval of the local Employment Office of the Ministry of Labour, and half of all recruits are nominated by these offices. Grounds for dismissal are limited by statute, especially for firms with more than fifteen employees. Discrimination in employment on ground of race, sex or religion is illegal, as is discrimination based on trade union membership or activity.

Business and finance

Another of the anomalies of the Italian business culture is that whilst the nation's industry is moving forward, its financial markets are 'backward, incestuous and dangerously underregulated' and the financial system is 'anachronistic, even feudal' (Alan Friedman, in the *Financial Times*).

Banking system

Italy has some 1200 separate banks with around 12,000 branches. The system is the least concentrated in the world and the least competitive, not least because a large proportion of the banks are in the public sector and most top jobs are handed out as part of a lottizzazione (division of political spoils).

The need to rationalize the system, demanded by the Governor of the Bank of Italy, Carlo Azeglio Ciampi, and by the then Treasury Minister, Giuliano Amato (PSI), awoke in the minds of the two main government coalition parties not the need to find the best people for the jobs, but simply the need to carve up the jobs between themselves at the expense of the smaller political parties and to ensure that their relative political strengths would be preserved in any future rationalizations (Table 3.3).

Despite the political shenanigans, some rationalizations were planned in early 1989. The model on which restructuring was to take place was the so-called 'universal' banks of Germany (see page 25). The Italians use the term

Table 3.3 *Italy's top banks and their political controllers (1988)*

Rank	Bank	Assets ($million)	Political control
1	Banca Nazionale del Lavoro	96,072	PSI
2	Instituto Bancario S Paolo	73,477	DC
3	Monte dei Paschi di Siena	67,183	DC
4	Banca Commerciale Italiana	62,539	Technocrats
5	Banco di Napoli	59,343	DC
6	Banco di Roma	56,361	DC
7	Cariplo	53,891	DC
8	Credito Italiano	50,448	Technocrats
9	Banco di Sicilia	31,140	PRI
10	Istituto Mobiliare	23,386	Technocrats

With the exception of the Cassa di Risparmio di Venezia (PSI) all the other major savings banks were also controlled by Christian Democrats.
Sources: *The Banker* and *L'Espresso*, 23/10/88

plurifunzionale (polyfunctional) to describe the new system: holding companies control commercial banking, medium-term corporate finance, securities underwriting, investment banking and financial services including insurance. Italian bankers and financial groups have made progress in the area of bancassurance: the notion that banks can profitably sell insurance products and vice versa. The state-owned insurance company Istituto Nazionale delle Assicurazioni (INA), with 20 per cent of the national market in May 1992, announced plans to form an alliance with the Banca di Roma (a new banking group formed by the merger of the Cassa di Risparmio di Roma, the Banco di Santo Spirito, and the Banco di Roma). Other insurers and bankers have also formed alliances – Fondiaria with Istituto Bancario San Paolo di Torino; Assibanca (Toro, Generali and RAS) with Banca Commerciale Italiana; SAI with Banca Popolare di Novara.

So, the banking houses seem to be getting in order, but they have a long way to go in providing an acceptable retail banking service. As any tourist knows, the service offered to bank customers in Italy is appalling. Lengthy queues and indolent bank clerks are the order of the day. In-built inefficiencies abound, such as the civil service status of bank employees; the difficulty of achieving restructuring by means of redundancies; and the way banks have got used to the cushy money earned on cheques which take up to a month to clear. A nationwide cash dispenser system

(Bancomat) has recently been introduced, and this has begun to ease the problem. Indeed this aspect of the banking system is the one that has seen most progress in the past few years: cash dispensers accepting a wide range of cards are now to be found on almost every street corner of larger towns and cities and many machines accept paper currency from 17 countries (Sweden to Japan) for instant conversion into lire. Some problems remain: the lack of a nationwide banking network, and the poor standard of service in bank branches. Before things can improve, top bank executives must undergo a cultural change in the way they perceive individual retail customers. Italian bankers have not yet recognized that value-added retail services can generate substantial revenues, as well as improving efficiency and reducing cost structures.

In restructuring bank services, the Italians are uncertain which model to choose: the German model (Eurocentric, close to business) or the British model (offering strongly international financial services). However, further major banking reforms seem unlikely in the near future, given that most interest in the financial sector seems to focus on the more glamorous aspects of corporate finance. Most major Italian industrial companies are flush with cash and everyone recognizes the need for Italian banks to be made more efficient in order to remain competitive in the single internal market. Why, then, not allow the industrialists to take over the banks and run them as efficiently as they have been running their companies? This is the question posed by Cesare Romiti of Fiat (though he always wears his hat as chairman of Gemina when talking about banking), Carlo De Benedetti of Olivetti and Silvio Berlusconi. The principal obstacle to their ambitions is the Governor of the Bank of Italy. Ciampi does not oppose the idea of industrialists buying minority shares (up to 15 per cent) of banks, but he sees the possibility of serious conflicts of interest if their shares go higher and they start to control the banks. The debate has been very heated and critics have said that Italian industrialists could better use their time and company cash balances to concentrate on achieving Europe-wide economies of scale, while the central bank could make better use of its resources to press for priorities such as faster cheque-cashing, a stronger inter-bank market, and more cuts in government spending. One cannot help feeling that the critics might have a point. See Table 3.4.

In all this, the Bank of Italy has managed to maintain a reputation as the most authoritative, least political, most independent and internationally-experienced institution in Rome. The Bank is an organ of government and cannot, therefore, always behave as though it were immune to the caprices of politicians and powerful corporate interests. Unlike politicians and managers of state industry, however, the Governor of the Bank of Italy is appointed for life, and he therefore enjoys a greater deal of security than many of his opponents. This security lends him authority and also allows

Table 3.4 *Italian inflation rates (1981–92)*

Year	%
1981	17.8
1982	16.5
1983	14.7
1984	10.8
1985	9.2
1986	5.8
1987	4.7
1988	5.1
1989	6.3
1990	6.5
1991	6.4
1992	5.2

Source: OECD

him to take a longer view of the time scale for change. The Bank in recent years has encouraged greater competition among banks and relaxed its rules on the freedom of banks to alter their branch networks. It has promoted improvements in the efficiency of the payments system and tightened restrictions on general-purpose loans to industry (loans which were then re-lent on the financial markets). The Bank has also been active at the international level on issues such as Third World sovereign debtors and the European System of Central Banks. The fact that Governor Ciampi enjoys the fierce opposition of both politicians and industrialists is the surest sign that he is doing a good job. In January 1992, a new law was approved by parliament giving the Bank of Italy greater independence in monetary policy-making. The central bank was given full responsibility for setting the discount rate. Its full independence also limits the government's ability to run an overdraft: Italy is now in line with the Maastricht treaty provisions which are aimed to prevent the granting of credit or account overdrafts by central banks to governments as well as their acquisition of government debt.

At the other end of the banking spectrum lies the relationship between small firms and their local banks. In this area, as in so many others, Italy shows a marked difference from the United Kingdom. A large part of the banking system is made up of **Casse di Risparmio** (local savings banks). These banks derive their funds from local investors and savers and lend to local firms. They have a strong local identity. Their directors and managers have a close working relationship with the firms in their area and a personal knowledge of anyone setting up in business and needing to borrow money to do so. In some cases the bank may be involved in the decision-making of the business and may even lend staff. Some banks subsidize centres to provide specialist services to small firms, but equally important is the fact that the decisions of the bank will be based on an understanding of the local economy rather than on rules laid down by a distant head office. There are clearly implications for this system, which is obviously of benefit to Italy's small firms, in the moves to rationalize the banking system to meet the challenges of the EC's single market.

Stock market

In 1985, fewer companies were quoted on the Milan bourse than in 1975 (145 compared with the earlier 155), but in the next two years the number jumped by over 40 per cent to 210. However, to say that the Italian stock market is now the fifth largest in Europe, after the United Kingdom, Germany, France and Switzerland, is to give the wrong impression. Milan's total market capitalization in 1988 stood at around 160,000 billion lire. This represented between 16 and 17 per cent of Italy's GNP, whereas the capitalization of the London stock exchange was equivalent to 98 per cent of UK GNP and Wall Street amounted to 55 per cent of US GNP. The Italian stock market's value was equivalent to only 12 per cent of the country's total financial assets. But even this may mislead. Among the 200 or so quoted companies, the average proportion of company stock that is actually traded on the Milan bourse – the float – was 25 per cent of issued share capital. So the actual capitalization of Milan could be considered to be one-quarter of its total 160,000 billion lire. Moreover, the market sees active trading in only 40 or 50 shares – again one-quarter of the total. Some 40 quoted companies do not even have as much as 25 per cent of their shares available on the market, even though this is the legal minimum. The stock market regulatory body believes it would be 'unrealistic' to suspend trading in so many shares just to conform with a legal nicety. Final confirmation of the limited nature of the bourse, if such were needed, is given by the fact that one-third of the stock market's value is accounted for by just two companies: Fiat and Generali. In macroeconomic terms, then, the Milan bourse is tiny. It is also riddled with insider dealing.

The retiring Chairman of the Milan Stock Exchange, Ettore Fumagalli, in December 1988 said: 'The bourse in Milan is a club of insiders, made up of the big groups, a few shareholders and the brokers . . . The big groups have manipulated the market, prices have been rigged and the share deals have generally hurt the small investor.'

Consob, the stock market and securities industry regulatory body, was founded in 1974, but it still remains without the legislative backing which might allow it to play a more positive role in protecting the interests of the 4 million small investors on the Milan bourse. Italy still has no anti-trust legislation, no monopolies and mergers commission, no rules on company takeovers, no laws to restrict insider trading and no law that would even require companies to put out full results, including net profit figures on a half-yearly basis. One example should suffice: when Berlusconi bought 70 per cent of the stock of the publicly-quoted Standa retail chain from Ferruzzi he paid nearly double the quoted market share price. United Kingdom law would have required a public offer to be made. Italian law does not, so thousands of small investors were left holding just under 30 per cent of the shares at a price well below that paid in the takeover.

The Milan bourse, is not, therefore an attractive place for Italian investors. As a result, a real fear exists that, with the establishment of the EC's single internal market and the relaxation of restrictions on investing abroad, Italian investors will look to bigger and better markets elsewhere. The 'corner shop' image of the Milan bourse has been reinforced as the major Italian companies have been quoted on other exchanges as they seek to gain access to international finance.

A solution to this problem may lie in persuading some of the estimated 800 Italian companies which are legally qualified but not quoted to float themselves on the stock market. If only half of them decided on this course of action, the market would become immediately more varied, more attractive and more competitive. It is unlikely that they will be persuaded, however, for mainly cultural reasons: most of the companies are family businesses, in the black, and quite happy with the way things are; quotation on the stock market brings with it lots of obligations such as providing information for shareholders and for regulatory authorities, without any immediate and obvious return. These smaller family firms have never seen or appreciated the value of, or need for, a stock market quotation. Perhaps elsewhere the banks might have played a greater role in this development, but as we have already seen, the relationship between small firms and the banks is quite cosy too.

Business and the labour market

Demographic trends

In 1988, Italy had the lowest birth rate in the world. Zero growth rate implies a birth rate of 2.05 children per woman: Italy's national average was 1.29 children per woman. At this rate, Italy's population would fall from its current 57.4 million to 41.6 million by 2033. Such a decline would imply dramatic burdens on the social and economic structure of the country: by 2033 more than half the population would be over 70 years old; there would be one pensioner for every person of working age. These predictions may be too dramatic, however, since attitudes in the present childbearing generation have changed rapidly. In 1983, most Italians thought a falling birth rate was 'a good thing'; now more than half see it as a problem, and 90 per cent of Italians think that the 'ideal family' should have two or more children (2.2 on average).

Employment and unemployment

Unemployment in 1992 fell to its lowest level since the mid-1980s – to around 10.9 per cent (Table 3.5). Overall, 200,000 new jobs were created in 1991, all of them in the small and medium-sized enterprise sector. In contrast, the situation in large companies (over 500 employees) continues to deteriorate: 25,000 jobs were lost in 1991, largely in the industrialized North and Centre of the country. In the South, unemployment has stabilized at about 20 per cent.

Table 3.5 *Italian unemployment rates (1981–92)*

Year	%
1981	8.5
1982	9.2
1983	10.0
1984	10.1
1985	10.2
1986	11.2
1987	12.1
1988	12.2
1989	12.1
1990	11.0
1991	10.5
1992	11.0

Source: OECD, ISTAT

These figures, however, disguise sizable differences according to region and age group. Whilst unemployment declined in the North and Centre, where virtually full employment has been reached among prime-age males

(25 to 59-year olds), unemployment in the same age group in the South was 9.2 per cent in 1989, and the rates among unemployment-prone groups (women and young people) were much higher (for example, 55.4 per cent of the youth labour force, compared to 15 per cent which is the OECD average; unemployment among women in the south was 31.8 per cent in 1990). Since sectoral wage agreements are negotiated nationally and labour mobility is low, wage pressure in the North spreads throughout the economy, thus making employment prospects in the South even worse.

Migration

Outward labour migration is no longer the easy answer to Italy's problems that it was in the 1950s, at least in part because welfare assistance is now so much more adequate and available in the South. More investment is required directly in the South if the country is to make full use of its labour force. Some believe that this will happen automatically as labour markets tighten in the North, but it could equally be that with the opening of the EC's single market, investors will look to place their capital in more productive and accessible regions in the centre and north of the Community. In any case, the model of migration facing Italy is now quite different from the previous one: for Italians, internal migration is still a possibility, although tensions of a pseudo-racial character have built up, and often exploded, in the past few years. Attacks on southerners (offensively dubbed **terroni**), and even second- and third-generation migrants, have become increasingly common in the North, as have attacks on non-EC immigrants in a country where racial tensions have been previously virtually unknown. Italians have always perceived theirs as a poor country, with a large number of outgoing migrants, and they are struggling with their new image as a wealthy country which is the target or pole of attraction for incoming migrants, with all the implications this would have for an Italy with a multiracial character.

The black economy

In 1987, by re-evaluating the value of the black economy, Italy overtook the United Kingdom as the fifth-largest economy in the world. The black economy is notoriously difficult to identify and value. Nor is it geographically constrained, although Naples is often cited as the home of the submerged economy. In the late 1980s, the value of income declared by Neapolitans was 6000 billion lire, whereas their estimated expenditure was in the region of 18,000 billion, and in addition they had an estimated 23,000 billion lire deposited in banks and savings accounts. In some parts of Italy, the black economy is probably not too dissimilar from the pattern in the rest of Europe, where it is estimated to account for about 12 per cent of the gross domestic product. But for the country as a whole, ISTAT (the official government statistical agency) estimates that it accounts for 20 to 25 per cent of the GDP, with 6.5 million people having second jobs, and 2.5 million 'unemployed' people at least partly engaged in economic activity.

Theorists will argue about whether the black economy is a pre-modern or a post-modern phenomenon. The phenomenon is so diversified that there are activities which will fit either, both or neither category. The least one can say is that it represents the attempts of individual Italians to escape the controls (bureaucratic, legal, social, fiscal, trade union) of a state and society in which they have rapidly decreasing confidence.

Graduates

In 1987–8, 19.8 per cent of the Italian population was in full-time education, of whom 10 per cent (1.1 million) were at university. 13.7 per cent of the 19–24 age group was attending university. 67 per cent of high school graduates go on to university. The most popular faculty is economics and social studies (29 per cent of the first-year intake), followed by literature (19 per cent), law (17 per cent), engineering (15 per cent) and science (11 per cent). The intake to economics and social studies is growing steadily, while intakes to literature and law are slowly declining.

This rosy picture is belied, however, by an examination of the number of graduates produced. More than two-thirds of the first-year intake of over 250,000 drop out, to leave an annual graduate cohort of about 75,000. This happens because there is no selection of university entrants. To some extent, first-year exams constitute the selection procedure, but in fact studies have indicated that as many as 70 per cent of first-year drop-outs do not even take these exams.

The distribution of graduates is, as a consequence, rather different from the distribution of first-year intake. Literature accounts for the largest proportion of graduates (20 per cent) followed by medicine (16 per cent of graduates, but only 4 per cent of the intake), economics and social studies (also 16 per cent), science (13 per cent) and engineering and law (both 12 per cent). The drop-out rate in economics should concern business employers, but they may find consolation in the fact that the number of economics graduates has more than doubled over the past ten years.

A study carried out by IBM Italia in 1987, and confirmed by subsequent studies, showed a considerable imbalance between the supply and demand for graduates in industry, especially for graduates of scientific and technical disciplines. Generally speaking, the university system does not produce the types of graduates in the sorts of subjects that industry believes it needs. (See below for a discussion of business, education and training.)

Women and part-time work

Part-time work is growing in all western economies and now accounts for about 15 per cent of total employment on average, but reaches 25 per cent in some north European economies. Part-time work has been seen as one of the weapons in the battle against unemployment, especially amongst women. It is also seen as attractive to other previously-marginalized groups (older workers, the disabled); and it may also appeal to a growing number of people more concerned with the 'quality of life', in search of a new relationship between work, pay and leisure. In this sense, part-time work has actually opened up new areas of the labour market, rather than offering a solution to the problem of traditional 'official' unemployment. But the growth in part-time work cannot be explained simply by changes in the labour supply. It is also dependent on a change in the type of work demanded, the new flexibility in production, and therefore a demand from employers for new working methods and practices.

Part-time work in Italy has had formal recognition and legal control only since 1984 (Law no. 863). (The concept is still both new and foreign, such that Italians refer to **il part-time**, rather than use the Italian phrase **il lavoro a tempo parziale**). The law was clearly intended to provide an entry point into the labour market for young people, and also to provide a less traumatic (and cheaper to the state) alternative to laying workers off when industries restructured. This clouds the discussion of part-time work, since the ILO definition of part-time work includes the notion of choice, whereas the Italian legislation dealing with part-time work is aimed at resolving employment difficulties. It is therefore dealing with the problem of under-employment rather than with part-time work as such. In terms of business culture, part-time work is seen not so much as a factor contributing to flexibility and modernization, but rather as a way of reducing the size of the workforce and the attendant labour costs.

Even so, the phenomenon in Italy is less well-developed than in other European countries. In 1985, Italy had about one million part-time workers (5 per cent of the total workforce), compared with the United Kingdom's 5 million (21 per cent) and former West Germany's 3.3 million (13 per cent). In the 1980s throughout the rest of Europe, both unemployment and part-time work have increased at the same time as the proportion of women in the workforce has also increased. In Italy, however, the entry of women into the labour force has had a less dramatic effect on full-time employment. In fact, women are entering the full-time labour market in Italy, rather than the part-time market. Participation rates among the group normally most attracted to part-time work (married, middle-aged, middle-class women) are particularly low (only 80 per cent of the EC average), and part-time employment in Italy is found more commonly in the industrial and agricultural sectors, rather than in the service sector where it is encountered in the rest of Europe.

Women currently account for about 5 per cent of engineers, 13 per cent of public sector managers, and 18 per cent of journalists. About 20 per cent of small and medium-sized enterprises are managed by women.

Business and trade unions

Employers' organizations

Most employers in the private sector belong to the appropriate employers' association:

- Confindustria (industrial employers).
- Confcommercio (merchants).
- Confapi (small firms).
- Confagricoltura (agricultural producers).
- Confartigianato (craft industries).
- FTA (Federazione del terziario avanzato) (service sector).

Intersind is the employers' organization for public sector employers.

Confindustria, led by Gianni Agnelli (1972–6), promoted political consensus and accommodation with the PCI and the trade unions. Since 1980, first under Guido Carli and then under steel-producer Luigi Lucchini (1984–8), a conservative counter-revolution has taken place, with a demand for the re-establishment of free-market principles. Sergio Pininfarina was president of Confindustria from 1988–92. President from May 1992 is Luigi Abete.

Organized labour

There are three main trade union confederations in Italy, the **Confederazione Generale Italiana del Lavoro** (CGIL, basically Communist (PCI/PDS) but with a substantial Socialist (PSI) minority), the **Confederazione Italiana Sindacati Lavoratori** (CISL, basically Catholic (DC)), and the much smaller **Unione Italiana del Lavoro** (UIL, an amalgam of the Socialists (PSI) and the smaller lay parties). In 1983, 45.5 per cent of Italy's 14.8 million wage earners were members of trade unions. The working members of the trade unions totalled 6.75 million divided as follows: CGIL 46.8 per cent, CISL 34.9 per cent, UIL 18.3 per cent. There is also a philo-fascist trade union, CISNAL, which has 2–300,000 members. By 1989, total membership had fallen to 6.1 million: 44.79 per cent CGIL, 35.46 per cent CISL, and 19.66 per cent UIL. Between 1980 and 1989, membership of unions by active workers was in general decline (22 per cent down in the CGIL, 17 per cent in the CISL and 6 per cent in the UIL), but overall membership grew by 10 per cent, due to the increasing membership of unions by 3.8 million pensioners and other non-workers.

The issue at the heart of Italian trade unionism is: how to reconcile political power and responsibility with the partisan defence of workers' wages and conditions. The influence of the unions in the political and economic spheres has shifted periodically.

1945–48: The unions were strong politically by weak economically.
1948–62: Weak in both respects.
1963–69: Weak politically, strong economically.
1969–80: Strong in both respects.
1980– : Declining influence in both spheres.

These shifts need some explanation.

Land workers from the South flooded into the northern factories in the late 1950s and 1960s. Permanent employment in the prosperous factories did not come to them easily, however, and when it did, they discovered that the work bore little relationship to that to which they were accustomed. They felt they were treated as unskilled and resented strangers who were putting pressure on the already scarce stock of housing resources. The southern immigrants wanted to be accepted and to have some sort of social standing which at that time no union or political party offered them. They needed to make a convincing gesture to show that they were willing to take on the values of northern industrial workers and to do this they adopted a militancy and a trade union loyalty not known in the North before. In their militancy they had four main objectives:

• To become accepted by northern workers as good trade unionists.
• To demand and obtain better working conditions and better housing (demands for better working conditions and higher wages were always bound up with wider demands for better living conditions, better housing, better public services).
• To remove the (to them) wounding distinction between skilled and unskilled work, at least by removing wage differentials (hence the demand throughout the 1970s for flat-rate increases which naturally reduce differentials).

- To ensure that wages were high enough for them to transfer residues to families left behind in the South.

The great achievement of trade union militancy, and especially of the **autunno caldo** (hot autumn) of 1969, was the **Statuto dei Diritti dei Lavoratori** (Statute on Workers' Rights) of 1970. The **Statuto** was the first of a series of legislative measures which provided almost cast-iron security of employment in larger firms (small firms were exempt from many of the provisions of the Statuto, see below) and also gave unions the right to organize elections in factories and set up factory councils.

Throughout the 1970s, the united CGIL-CISL-UIL Confederation achieved a series of major victories, including the extension of the **scala mobile** (wage indexation system), significant wage increases, the forty-hour week, the reduction of wage differentials (**ugualitarismo** – partly the result of the flat rate increases awarded under the wage indexation system), the establishment of a common job classification system (**inquadramento unico**), and the setting up in 1975 of the **Cassa Integrazione Guadagni** (CIG – a national government fund to make up the wages of workers who were temporarily laid off). The CIG was of at least as much benefit to industrialists as it was to workers. Much industrial reorganization in the late 1970s and early 1980s was made possible by the CIG, which paid laid off workers up to 95 per cent of their wages. By September 1985, 436,000 workers were in receipt of CIG benefit. Such funding will not be available to Italian industry after 1992, as state subsidies of this kind will be outlawed under the EC's competition rules. Nevertheless, even during 1991, there were 77,000 workers in the Cassa every month.

Trade unions also won the right from 1975 onwards to have access to information about the firm's condition and investment programmes. As a basis for worker participation, however, these rights were never built upon, since, though the unions could agree that some form of worker participation was a good thing, they could not agree on what form such participation should take. The CGIL took a global view, saying that the union should have an input into factory plans, but that these factory plans should form part of a wider strategy of economic planning. The CISL and the UIL took a narrower view, believing that all trade union action should be directly related to shopfloor demands.

By 1978, the trade unions were increasingly identified as one of the major contributing factors to the chaotic state of the Italian economy. Their position (to demand a role in the management of the economy as a whole) was seen as untenable in the light of their refusal to moderate their claims for higher wages which the nation could not afford. In an impressive display of unity and restraint, they modified their position (the so-called **svolta dell'EUR** of 1978), indicating a willingness to exercise restraint in bargaining over wages and conditions in return for an increased say in national economic policy-making, but for many it was too late. Government and industry were already beginning to regain the upper hand.

The most significant moment in this struggle came in 1980 when Fiat announced the dismissal of 14,000 workers, in an attempt to re-establish the profitability of its automobile division. The FLM (the metalworkers sections of the unified CGIL-CISL-UIL Federation) called an all-out strike which lasted thirty-five days but which was ended when 40,000 workers marched in protest against the strike, demanding the right to return to work. The terms negotiated for the return to work – 23,000 workers to be laid off with 93 per cent of their wages to be paid by the CIG – were drastic and the reaction of the workforce was violent, since the call for a return to work had been far from unanimous. But the tide had clearly turned. After protracted and bitter disputes between the unions and the employers, the dismantling of the scala mobile began in 1984, and the acrimonious break-up of the trade union federation followed. A referendum on the scala mobile, forced by the PCI in 1986, led to the ignominious defeat of the party and by association of its trade union ally, the CGIL. Demoralization set in: between 1981 and 1987 membership of the CGIL fell by 23 per cent. New autonomous trade unions and Cobas (**comitati di base** – grass roots committees) also sprang up, fragmenting the union movement.

It is too early, however, to write off the Italian trade union movement as a force in Italian industry and the economy as a whole. 1988 saw an overall up-turn in membership and new ideas are emerging, at least in the union leadership. The general secretary of the CGIL, Bruno Trentin, identified a failure to understand the implications of new technologies as the major failing of both unions and management in the 1970s. New technologies were misunderstood by management (who often sought to take advantage of the situation by increasing pressure on workers) and by unions, who failed to grasp the fact that the implicit drawbacks (mobility of labour, discontinuity of employment) could also be opportunities for workers to construct more varied professional careers.

Managers and workers are clearly in search of a new culture for industrial relations to replace the aggressively conflictual culture (on both sides) of the 1970s, a culture which made **c'è sciopero** (there's a strike) the commonest excuse for the inefficiency of production or the inadequacy of public services. One view, inspired by Romiti at Fiat, would see the unions having a recognized role in the firm, but as representatives of the lowest paid and defenders of minimum conditions, leaving other issues to direct negotiation between managers and individual workers. (At least part of the reason for Ghidella's marginalization at Fiat was his desire to see a more participative form of management in response to the introduction of new technologies. This view conflicted with Romiti's predominantly financial view of things.) In recent years, several companies have put forward ideas for linking a part of wage increases to the performance of the company. The idea was first floated by Fiat but has since been taken up by other employers: Zanussi, Olivetti, Aeritalia, Enichem, Snia, etc. All want to go further than old-fashioned production bonuses but stop short of a direct link between salary and company profits. Olivetti, for example, wants to link profits to its **margine operativo lordo** (MOL) (net operating margin) which is the value obtained by subtracting from the value of company sales the cost of materials, labour, fixed costs and stocks. Part of the annual wage increase would be made dependent on Olivetti's MOL being above the average of its international competitors. The MOL is not the same as the company's profits, and De Benedetti says that company profits should not be used as a measure for awarding even a part of wage increases because the unions are not yet ready to deal with the problems of company balance sheets that this implies (amortization policy, management of financial resources, company tax strategy, etc). The unions, in particular the CGIL, reject the notion of linking wage increases to company profits and even less to company competitiveness, because these things are influenced by management decisions, investment strategies, by the market and by the behaviour of the firm's competitors far more than by anything the individual worker can do.

However this debate turns out, it will not lead to the complete marginalization of unions in Italy. The Italian world of production offers a wealth of possible solutions. The worst culture (both for the management and for unions) would be one which simply defends past practice. An alternative might be what Bruno Trentin calls 'una codeterminazione in una fase sperimentale' (experimental worker participation) where unions and management share responsibility for new work practices, training programmes, job enrichment and greater efficiency. Whether the workforce is ready for these new responsibilities when all the pressures of the system are for sectoral retrenchment is an open question. In this, the unions are not helped by their changing structures and membership: the high numbers of non-working members are forcing unions to address wider issues, as a result of which they may lose their representational appeal to manufacturing and industrial workers.

In 1992, the differences between the trade unions and between unions and industrialists on broad issues of industrial relations were no closer to resolution. The 1986 law reforming the scala mobile (index-linked wage rises of about 25,000 lire, paid six-monthly) expired at the end of 1991. The CGIL, led by Bruno Trentin, wanted to see a replacement system introduced; the CISL, led by Sergio D'Antoni, sought index-linking of a minimum wage of 900,000 lire, plus a two-tier system of national and local bargaining for wages above the minimum. Confindustria is uncertain whether to exploit the differences between the unions, or to wait until they agree a common position before attempting a negotiated solution. The caretaker government is unlikely to attempt to rock the boat.

Collective bargaining

Pay and most other terms and conditions of employment are negotiated nationally between the national trade union confederations and the relevant employers' federation. Contracts are negotiated nationally, industry by industry, though supplementary plant-level agreements may also be negotiated, especially where minimum rates do not attract skilled personnel. National sectoral agreements last for three years and also stipulate annual holidays (normally at least four weeks plus 10 statutory public holidays), working hours and permissible levels of overtime. Most national agreements also stipulate thirteen months' wages (fourteen in the case of commerce). Although the national agreements are binding only on those employers and unions who sign them, they tend to be applied to other analogous occupations, either because of custom and practice, or because of court judgments, or because Employment Offices are required to ensure that terms and conditions on offer are no worse than in the appropriate national agreement before authorizing recruitment. The system of centralized bargaining has been placed under strain in recent years, and the tendency towards the fragmentation of Italian industrial relations and the growing strength of the Cobas' rank and file committees could generate increasing disorder in the labour market. The consequence of this would be a further decline in centralized sectoral bargaining and an increase in wage drift.

Indirect labour costs

Non-wage labour costs are among the highest in Europe (over 40 per cent of total labour costs according to the OECD), although Italian workers are among the worst paid in Europe. This apparently paradoxical statement is explained by the high social and fiscal costs, the main elements of which are contributions to the social security agency (INPS) for pensions and to the Cassa Integrazione Guadagni for compulsory lay-off insurance, and whose reform many industrialists have long demanded. However, these same industrialists have been very reluctant to sacrifice the Cassa Integrazione since this has allowed them to lay workers off without actually dismissing them. The CIG and the high cost of labour are the opposite sides of the same coin.

The main burden of contributions falls on employers. Normal retirement age is 60 for men and 55 for women, but pensions may be drawn when 35 years' contributions have been paid. Employers are also required to pay in full during sickness or maternity leave, though partial offset may be available from INPS. The burden of severance payments is also heavy: since 1982, 2/27 of annual pay for each year of service, subject to inflation-proofing. The entitlement to severance pay is virtually guaranteed, no matter what the grounds for termination of employment.

Business, training, education and development

Generally speaking, the situation of vocational training in Italy is very precarious. There is no binding legislative framework. No obligation is placed on the employer to provide for the training of employees, although training on a comprehensive scale is provided especially in large and medium-sized undertakings. Reliable statistics on provision are not available, and there is virtually no social research in this field. Responsibility for the training system is broken down between the school education system, for which the state is responsible, and the vocational training system, for which the regions are responsible. The long-overdue reform of the system cannot take place without an equally long-overdue reform of the secondary education system.

Education

Compulsory schooling in Italy lasts for eight years: five years of elementary education (**scuola elementare**, 6–11), followed by three years' lower secondary education (**scuola media inferiore**, 11–14). The minimum school-leaving age is 14, which is the among the lowest in Europe. Upper secondary education (**scuola media superiore**) is extremely diversified, but the basic categories are:

- Academic (*liceo scientifico, classico*).
- Technical (*istituto tecnico-commerciale, tecnico-industriale, tecnico-agrario, tecnico femminile*).
- Teacher training (*magistero*).
- State vocational training schools (*istituto professionale statale alberghiero, IPS industriale* and *artigianale*).

The **istituti professionali** used to have three-year cycles of study but now most adopt a five-year cycle like the other schools, except the **magistero**, which runs for four years. Any student obtaining the school-leaving certificate (the **maturità**) is automatically qualified to attend the university of their choice.

The secondary education system is complex. There are clearly overlaps between what the education system is trying to do and what a vocational training system might want to do, but the secondary education system is generally acknowledged to be failing to provide adequate preparation for the world of work.

Vocational training

Most of the problems which beset vocational training in Italy have existed for years. Essentially, conflicts and overlapping responsibilities between the central government and the regions (both of whom run employment services and provide vocational training), and between the Ministry of Labour and the Ministry of Education, and between the unions and the employers over the purpose and form of vocational training, coupled with the need to reform the secondary education system, have made it impossible to establish an effective and coherent system for vocational training. While some areas of vocational training within industrial firms are covered more or less adequately, major deficiencies exist in sectors such as vocational training for agricultural workers, apprentice training, vocational training for adults (as opposed to young people) and continuing education. Both the vocational training set-up and the adult education system are underdeveloped in Italy – the courses lack variety, there is no established system of leaving certificates, there are no clearly-defined aims, and the opportunities for using what has been learned are limited.

High unemployment in the immediate post-war years made the promotion of vocational training necessary and led to legislation which placed the system of vocational training under the Ministry of Labour. Many firms and public companies offered specialist courses at their own vocational training centres, some of which attracted large government subsidies. Law no. 264 of 1948 enabled the Ministry of Labour to finance training courses organized by firms or other institutions for the purpose of retraining their workers, or those looking for their first job. Although the law is quite exceptional for its time because of the prospects it opened up, its power to produce a workable system of vocational training was limited by the lack of planning for the courses, which were financed indiscriminately on the basis of applications received rather than in response to identified training needs. Development was also hindered because Italian industry, in the moderately industrialized areas, was able to achieve high profits with low wages and relatively modest technology. Furthermore, the trade unions, after the suppression endured under the Fascists and still involved in the struggle for recognition, concentrated on security of employment and wage increases, giving less priority to other objectives such as the implementation of a vocational training scheme. As a result the system which emerged was more concerned with patronage and using vocational training as a semi-educational form of welfare than with responding to the training needs of industry.

At the same time, a parallel training system was created under the Ministry of Education, but the state institutes for vocational training, developed in the 1960s within the education system, had not been devised as a means of implementing labour market policies. In fact, they were usually attended by people looking for more highly-skilled jobs.

Another reason for the lack of development in the 1960s was the failure to implement regional reform. The 1948 Constitution (articles 117 and 118) gave the responsibility for vocational and craft training to the regions. The regions were not established until 1970, and it was not until 1972 that the regions were finally given responsibility for training outside the education system. Even then, the Ministry of Labour retained responsibility for distributing resources, for relations with the EC, for social security contributions, for apprentices, for the training of teaching and training personnel and for training for special measures associated with the reorganization of production or the establishment of new industries. These functions were to be carried out by the **Istituto per lo Sviluppo della Formazione Professionale dei Lavoratori** – ISFOL, Institute for Workers' Vocational Training. Other public bodies concerned with training were disbanded and their functions transferred to the regions.

At the same time, some potentially innovatory steps were being taken in the area of educational leave. Educational leave for workers was included in nearly all wage agreements after 1973/74. This is the so-called **150 ore** (150 hours) entitlement to workers in many industrial sectors to attend school in work time to pursue studies leading to the **licenza** of the scuola media inferiore (middle school-leaving certificate). Provision is based on use of the school system. The exact nature of access to this system depends on the collective agreement between the trade union for the industry concerned and the employers. The job of selecting which workers are to enjoy educational leave is left to the **consiglio di fabbrica** (works' council), and the trade unions have developed selection criteria to ensure fairness in the selection procedure.

The '150 hours' system was set up to respond to certain needs as identified by the trade unions: in 1971, 76.6 per cent of Italians had not obtained the **licenza media**, and the figure was much higher among women, senior citizens and in the South. The '150 hours' courses were therefore aimed at correcting the deficiencies of the schooling system by making up for the general lack of educational qualifications among many employees, and also by increasing pressure for the reform of the school system as a whole. The system specifically excludes the possibility of the 150 hours being used for vocational training. The effects of educational leave provisions on the labour market in Italy are consequently virtually nil.

A 1977 law on youth unemployment acknowledged the regions' responsibilities for vocational training agreements and in general for all measures to encourage the development of training. The results have not, however, come up to expectations because of the inadequacies of the training system. An outline law was adopted in 1978, for example, which linked training to employment, made clear the distinction between vocational training and academic education and gave the regions an opportunity to plan vocational training. By 1985, thirteen of the twenty regions had adopted legislation in the area, but six had failed to take steps to bring existing legislation into line, and one region had no legislation in the area at all.

Thus, the picture that emerges is not an encouraging one: there is no established system of vocational training for adults comparable with systems in other EC member states. This is the result of:

- The general pattern of development of firms, and small firms in particular, which have tended to resist the introduction of new technologies and have therefore side-stepped the issue of re-training.
- The priority given by trade unions to equality of educational opportunity, and therefore the linking of demands for paid leave for education to the completion of compulsory general education. Unions have traditionally not demanded vocational training as part of their general demands on wages and conditions.
- Firms have been discouraged since it has not been possible to offset the costs of vocational training against grants or tax concessions.

Training activities

Only a few large private firms (Fiat, Olivetti, Montedison) and the large public enterprises have their own training services for their employees. Run mainly by personnel departments, these services take three forms:

- Training for new workers, for workers in line production or transferring to a different section within the firm.
- Re-training required as the result of company or section reorganization.
- Management training, either in-house or provided by external agencies.

There has been a basic change in the relationship between small firms and their larger sisters in the matter of training: up to the 1960s it was the small firms which provided executives for the larger firms, but nowadays, the reverse is the case. Large undertakings function as centres where skilled workers acquire initial training and social skills. They then usually find better prospects on the external market. Some of the major companies have reacted to this state of affairs and have reorganized their training departments, converting them into training agencies which cater both for the group and for the external market. Most of these activities are self-financing and are therefore not subject to external control and are difficult to quantify and assess, but it is generally thought that the qualitative level is good and well matched to the needs of the labour market.

Apprenticeships have virtually disappeared from industrial firms in Italy, though they still exist in the craft industries. Trade unions objected to the apprentice system as a form of exploitation of young labour through underpayment. Law no. 25 of 1955 established the framework for apprenticeships, combining training at work with instruction outside for eight hours per week, but the law was never properly implemented because of disagreements between the employers and the unions. In 1984, the regions stopped financing the additional eight hours' tuition and such apprenticeships as survive are now conducted entirely within the firm.

Incentives to employ young people have been made available via **contratti di formazione-lavoro** (training-work contracts) provided for by Law no. 863 of 1984. This law gives firms special concessions to employ young people (aged 15–29) for a limited period before either taking them on permanently or returning them to the labour market. 108,000 people were on the scheme in 1985. About 60 per cent of young people on the scheme are in industrial employment, the remainder in the service sector. Over 70 per cent are in small firms (with fewer than fifty employees).

Continuing training, in the sense of publicly-financed vocational training not specifically linked to work place activities or reorganization, does not exist. There is no legislative framework, nor any separate agency, nor, in some respects, sufficient expertise.

The ineffectiveness of vocational training in Italy has been at least in part the result of intransigence on the part of both trade unions and employers. The collective bargaining system is both conflictual and politicized and this has led to a disjuncture between the individual who requires training and the 'social partners' who see training either in terms of basic education, an instrument for general human and cultural betterment and for the promotion of the general political awareness of the workers, or in terms of the promotion of a narrow industrial culture, on-the-job training exclusively for the improvement of immediate profitability. Inevitably, the system as it stands satisfies none of even these narrow objectives.

Given that the unions and the employers have been unable to agree on the objective of vocational training, but given also that training must be happening because the nature of work has changed so radically, it follows that a two-tier system of training has developed: a rather ineffective explicit institutional system (that described above), and a more successful, but still inefficient, implicit submerged system based on the decentralization of production, precarious employment in small sub-contracting firms, the learning implicit in the creation (or more precisely, the creative destruction) of firms. The challenge of the 1990s is to institutionalize the submerged system, both to give a greater role to the employers and the unions in negotiating training programmes and to make the training system more effective.

There are signs that developments are occurring in this direction: trade unions are becoming more involved in in-firm training to handle restructuring (Fiat, Italtel, Alfa Romeo); large firms are re-assessing their own training centres (Elea-Olivetti, Isvor-Fiat); vocational training is becoming associated with industrial democracy (the Protocol agreements between the unions and the public-sector employers, Intersind, in 1984, 1986 and 1987). Such developments need now to be consolidated.

Management training

The **Scuola della Cancelleria del Palazzo Ducale** (Chancellery School of the Doge's Palace), founded in Venice in the seventeenth century, was arguably the world's first business school. But despite a few prestigious exceptions, like the private Luigi Bocconi University in Milan with its **Scuola di Direzione Aziendale** (Business School), Italy is a country without a supporting network of major business schools. In the 1980s, American business schools were popular with Italian students hoping to specialize in management, but they gradually realized that the American firm, around which such courses are constructed, bore little resemblance to managerial reality in Italy – at the same time as management courses in the United States were being criticized as being too mechanistic and quantitative in their approach. The MBA is not particularly well regarded in Italy because it has become associated with values (quantity rather than quality, short-termism, ambition and personal promotion rather than hard work and company development) which are inimical to the Italian management style.

Support services for updating and training managers are provided by private consultancy firms, but there is still a feeling that managers are born (and therefore skills are acquired in the process of managing a company, and cannot be acquired through abstract or theoretical study). In recent surveys, 47 per cent of managers of SMEs had never attended any training course. The managers showed an awareness of a need to update their professional knowledge, but the fact that there were so few managerial staff in small firms made taking time off to attend courses very difficult. 30 per cent of managers saw nothing to be gained from management courses. The remaining 70 per cent viewed training as a luxury to which they could treat themselves only in times of prosperity. These findings disguise the fact that many firms draw solely upon their own resources to provide training, since they doubt the ability of outside public- or private-sector training providers to make a useful contribution towards solving their problems. Given the reluctance of small firms to release employees for training, one might have expected to see the development of a distance-learning system. A CEDEFOP report of 1986 cites Italy as the only industrialized country which as yet has no distance-training system.

The rise and fall of the small business

The phenomenon of the small business in Italy is spectacular: the total number of firms in Italy grew from less than 200,000 in 1982 to more than 3.8 million in 1989. 80 per cent of business in Italy is under family management, and 40 per cent of businesses are headed by their founder. Between 1986 and 1991, new businesses were launched at the rate of almost 300,000 per month, although companies were also failing at an average rate of 120,000 per month. New business creation is stronger in the Centre-North than in the South, but this is not to say that the south is excluded from the phenomenon. How has this situation come about, and what are the prospects for the future?

One of the problems facing Italian entrepreneurs in the 1970s was how to circumvent the gains achieved by the working class in 1969–70 by reorganizing the system of production in such a way as to maintain the production of traditional goods while resisting Third World competition. It should be remembered here that Italy has never been strong at producing high-technology goods, but rather medium-technology, like television sets and washing machines, or low-technology, like clothes and shoes; electrical and non-electrical machinery and appliances accounted for 24 per cent of Italian exports in 1987, clothing and shoes accounting for a further 11.6 per cent. But how do small firms producing low-technology goods survive in a market which is elsewhere dominated by large corporations in fierce competition with one another and with low cost Third World exporters? The answer to this question is complex, but it begins with the decentralization of production.

The basic theory of the firm suggests that a firm is a system whose purpose is the organization of the factors of production. These factors are human resources (the labour market), technology, capital, raw materials and energy. In the classical theory of the firm, there exists 'one best way' to combine these factors, but this management approach has never been accepted in Italy. The Fordist production ethos and Taylorist principles of scientific management are largely alien to Italian entrepreneurs. To the extent that the firm consists of basic operations such as planning and design, production, sales, all supported by services, any one of these operations can be subcontracted out. The first thing to go is production, in favour of sub-contracting a semi-finished product (the entrepreneur no longer has the problem of controlling the workforce). Planning and design can also be decentralized. And so the cycle continues.

This phenomenon exploded in the 1970s. Why?

- Labour costs: increased rapidly after 1970.
- Raw materials and energy: Italy is a transformation economy, and so is deeply affected by the rate of exchange and the price of oil.
- The cost of money went up: 1973–4 the interest rate rose from 4 per cent to 14 per cent.
- Technology also became more expensive.

Given the explosion in costs, the entrepreneur seeks to maintain his market share by first of all adding value to his product through design. But this is not enough on its own. Production shifts from large industrial concerns to an array of small firms and cottage industries, using domestic labour, juvenile labour, part-time and casual labour. Pressures towards this type of reorganization also come from the desire to escape from:

- Trade union constraints.
- Health and safety regulations.
- Strikes.
- Taxes and social security contributions.

Many of these constraints on industry were the direct result of the Statuto dei Lavoratori, and in fact small firms now enjoy major concessions from the Statuto. Small firms (originally defined as employing 15 or fewer workers, later raised to 20) were exempted from the main provisions of the Statuto, especially those relating to trade union representation. They were exempted from VAT up to a generous limit, and from social security payments and they were to be assessed for local taxes at a lower rate than larger firms. Local authorities were also empowered to set up small trading estates and to designate certain areas as 'depressed zones' and to provide subsidies for small firms to set up in them.

In Italy there are firms which start small and remain small. The existence of small firms is permanent and structural (not always the same small firms, obviously, the turnover of small firms is very rapid). And small firms are an essential ingredient of Italy's success: almost 60 per cent of employment in Italy is in companies with fewer than 100 employees, and these firms account for 26 per cent of total manufacturing exports. Small firms dominate totally in the traditional manufacturing areas such as fabrics and clothing, shoe-making and leather goods, ceramics, carpentry and furniture.

In some areas and sectors, new low-wage economy conditions were created – but these were acceptable because wages in the black economy are often used to top up wages in the formal economy (women adding to the man's wage, moonlighting – an estimated 54 per cent of state employees have second jobs). But the survival of the small firm in the traditional low-tech industries is not solely a function of low wages and a deregulated labour market.

The flourishing of small enterprises reflects both the fragmentation of the industrial system, with specialized manufacturing and services increasingly contracted out by large companies to small operations, but also a creative entrepreneurialism in an increasingly decentralized country. At best, regional and family loyalties combine in local networks which embrace trade unions, bankers, businessmen and politicians to produce cultures that both facilitate and reward initiative. The Italian small firm is therefore more of a cultural entity than its British equivalent. It has familial, social and artistic aspects as well as economic ones, offering its workers a wide range of satisfactions besides that of simply earning a living. There are no sleeping partners or equity shareholders in the majority of small firms, so the possibility of takeover is unlikely, and small firms cannot be considered as fodder for larger, growing firms to feed on. Neither growth nor profit maximization can be considered the principal reason for existence of the small firm.

Various models have been developed to explain the phenomenon of small firms. One such is the Emilian model (King, 1987). The principal features of this model are: decentralized production in small and medium-sized rural towns; geographical specialization in the kind of product made; and a high degree of mainly female sweated labour in small factories, craft workshops and homes. In Emilia-Romagna, the region to which the model is said to apply, there are no industrial concerns employing more than a couple of hundred workers, with the exception of the petro-chemicals plants at Ferrara and Ravenna, the fruits of outside investment. But the characteristics of independent enterprise, product distinctiveness and hard work based on solid traditions of peasant farming and generations of craft skills have made the region into one of the richest in Italy. In 1983, Modena overtook Milan as the richest province in Italy.

Another model is that of 'flexible specialisation' (Goodman et al. 1989). This model suggests that within a productive system characterized by the decentralization of various stages of the production process, the small and medium-sized firm will tend towards specialization in a limited number of phases of production, but for many different types of goods. According to the model of flexible specialization radical changes in the production environment are the cause of this new structure of the industrial system. Technological innovation is no longer to be found principally in the large firms, and its effects are to be felt throughout the productive system. It helps to make machinery more efficient and more flexible, and allows the progressive substitution of machinery for human labour in the more repetitive areas of work. Above all, it enables firms to react more quickly and more efficiently to changes in product demand. The advantages which large firms have traditionally derived from economies of scale have been outweighed by the growing demands of the workforce in large firms and by the reduction in the minimum efficient size of the firm, brought about by changes in the production process as a result of the introduction of new technology.

The resulting small firms, grouping together into industrial districts, display certain characteristics:

• Flexibility of production, made even more possible by the falling costs of modern technologies.
• A dualism of competition and collaboration; in other words, the same firms may collaborate closely on the development of new tools or techniques, but will compete fiercely for contracts.

In general terms, the success of the small firm system in central and north-east Italy seems to be based on three principal factors:

• Maintaining competitiveness on international markets, where demand is determined as much by quality (and here design, 'Made in Italy', plays a significant role) as by price. Advantages that other producers may gain from long runs at high volume are offset by the ability of the Italian small industry system to produce non-standard goods and to respond quickly to short-term demand.
• Flexible production and division of labour between firms. A system of complex subcontracting allows costs and risks to be shared out among a number of firms, but it also allows production to be based on short-term contracts which can rapidly be adjusted to market requirements by switching between subcontractors when a particular type of good is required or by raising or reducing the subcontracting when the level of demand fluctuates. In turn, this system depends on the efficient circulation of goods and information between the producers. This is guaranteed by the geographical proximity of the firms as well as the frequent use of microcomputers to communicate information sometimes even to domestic out-workers.
• The unique local, social and institutional conditions provided by the

relationship between the modern market town and its once agricultural hinterland.

Within this model, the particular culture of individual firms (the way they recruit, use or remunerate labour, the technologies they apply, the marketing skills of the entrepreneurs) is of limited relevance. More important is the way the firms operate within a system of production. The firms are not free operators in a free market but part of a complex and integrated system of production. The firms derive their resilience from the stability achieved by the system as a whole. The firms described here are not independent small firms in the traditional sense, nor are they simply subcontractors for larger firms. They are inter-linked but independently owned production units, within an industrial system. The uniqueness of the system does not derive from the economic and social organization of production within the individual firms, but rather from the economics of the vertical disintegration of the production process, which has created a new set of inter-firm relationships.

Generalization about the small firms sector is difficult and dangerous since within the category a highly-diversified situation is to be found. The models described in the previous paragraphs, for example, are more or less geographically confined to the regions of north-east and central Italy. But even here, and especially in other areas, highly innovative firms operate alongside technologically backward firms. It must also be said that in their process of reorganization, large firms may take advantage of new technologies to reunite the various phases of the production process within medium and large plants. These factors may place limitations on the small firms sector and may signal the beginning of a new phase of domination by the large firm. Similar questions remain about the durability of the Emilian model. It is becoming more and more difficult to increase or even maintain the level of exports; increasing labour costs can no longer be counteracted by devaluation; markets supplied by many of these firms are becoming saturated both at home and abroad; competition from other sectors – agriculture, tourism, the construction industry – for both land and labour is intensifying; and finally, the reserves of marginal labour are also drying up.

The question must be asked, therefore, about whether the small firm can expect to continue to flourish in the face of financial pressures and inducements that are likely to arise over the next few years. In the early 1990s the social context of post-industrial and post-Communist society is becoming more clearly defined:

- Markets are becoming increasingly fragmented.
- Information flows are becoming increasingly rapid, and information rapidly loses its value.

- New technologies increasingly determine the competitiveness of firms, but new technologies are expensive.
- Automation minimizes the role of unskilled labour in production and makes the decentralization of production to the Third World less attractive.
- Firms are collaborating and cooperating both internationally and nationally in more inventive and varied ways.
- Information technologies and the creativity of individual workers become increasingly critical factors.

Further threats to the political economy of the small firm come from developments within the EC. Among the changes brought about by the single market has been the removal of restrictions in Italy which prevent foreign firms from owning more than 49 per cent of an Italian business. Possibly more alarming is the prospect of foreign banks freely entering the Italian market, and the consequent 'rationalization' of the Italian local savings bank system which, as we have seen, gives vital support to small businesses.

Areas where Italian exports have traditionally been strong, and where small firms have made significant contributions (textiles and clothing, metal-engineering, leather and footwear), which expanded strongly between 1980 and 1986, have since seen significant slowdown or even decline. As a whole, the Italian share of the manufacturing imports of the seven most industrialized nations in goods in the traditional 'Made in Italy' category fell from 12.2 per cent in 1986 to 10.5 per cent in 1989. This has resulted in a decline in the overall numbers of small firms; acquisition of small firms by medium- and large-sized enterprises; the return of external functions as internal functions; higher qualitative control over the whole production cycle; and diversified production within the single enterprise. Small may still be beautiful, but big is beginning to look good again.

The response of business to the EC's single market

All of Italy's top entrepreneurs from both the public and private sectors (Agnelli, Gardini, Prodi, Reviglio, De Benedetti) were vocal in their enthusiasm for the completion of the single market. They believed that they were strongly placed to take advantage of industrial development which will result from the complete integration of the European national economies. They also claimed, with justification, that their companies were already well established in the European marketplace and that there was no need for them to be taking additional preparatory measures to enable them to compete and prosper.

A 1988 survey of opinion among Italian and European industrialists, however, revealed that the Italians, although sharing the enthusiasm of the top entrepreneurs for the principle of a single market (72 per cent thought it represented an opportunity rather than an obstacle), were far more pessimistic about their ability to take advantage of the opportunity. 64 per cent of those interviewed thought that other European countries would benefit more from the single market than Italy, and a further 11 per cent thought that non-European countries would do better too. In other words, only one in four thought the single market was looking good for Italy. In this respect, Italian industrialists were the most pessimistic in Europe, and the gravest misgivings were expressed by those in the motor car and electronics industries. Only 12 per cent of industrialists saw exporting to the EC as a natural path of development for their company. Among their greatest fears (felt by 23 per cent of Italians, a greater proportion than in any other country), was the withdrawal of state subsidies. Seeking partnerships with other EC companies was not seen to be an answer to the problem: in the sample as a whole, 62 per cent would actively seek partnerships with other EC companies, 23 per cent with companies from their own country, and 15 per cent with companies from outside the EC, but in Italy 53 per cent thought allying with other Italian companies was the answer, only 27 per cent seeking allies in Europe and a further 19 per cent outside. Even where companies had taken action in response to the challenge of the single market, the responses had been largely confined to the marketing function; other functions such as commercial planning, production, company organization and personnel had been largely ignored.

From the preceding outline of Italian business culture it will be obvious that the threats to Italian industry posed by the completion of the internal market are not insignificant.

- Will small and medium-sized businesses cope with international competition?
- Will the country's relative shortage of high technology industries be a handicap?
- Can the fragmented and relatively underdeveloped banking and financial services sector hold its own against foreign competition?
- How will it be possible to prevent parts of the Mezzogiorno from falling even further behind industrially?
- Will industry as a whole be able to withstand the withdrawal of state aid (a 1989 European Commission report showed that in 1988 Italian state aids to industry amounted to £5.3 billion – nearly nine times the amount of United Kingdom state aid to industry)?
- Can the political system deliver the necessary reforms of the economy and the bureaucracy?

And it is this final point which, at the end of the day, may be the most telling. Italy's failures in the past to apply EC directives and even to spend its allocations from Community funds have been the despair of Brussels. Henceforth, failure on the part of government, parliament and the bureaucracy promptly to apply Community legislation will lead directly to competitive disadvantage to Italian industry.

In more general terms, there are underlying weaknesses in the Italian economy which must cause concern in the business sector. The development of the 1980s was not coordinated, so the effects were unevenly distributed, the rewards unevenly spread between the social classes and between North and South. Thus the dualisms which were identifiable in Italy immediately after the war are still there, and must remain a cloud over the undoubted successes of the Italian economy:

- Territorial dualism: which sees a prosperous industrial North expanding despite, or at the expense of, a poorer, agricultural South.
- Industrial dualism: which sees a coexistence of an advanced, modern, highly-productive sector together with a fragmented, under-technologized sector.
- Labour market dualism: wherein well-paid, secure sectors coexist with badly-paid, marginal and precarious sectors.

The problems remain, and have been heightened by such recent developments as the complete failure of the political class to renew itself; the spread of mafia violence and corruption throughout the peninsula; and the emergence of separatist movements in the North. These problems of **sistema Italia** (the Italian system) will not be solved by the flair and imagination of the individual Italian entrepreneur alone. The real opportunities for business in Italy lie in finding a new accommodation between the public and private sectors, and between the government, the employers and the workers. But first Italians must grapple with the problem which they seem to have spent most of their history avoiding: the construction of a national civil society. Unless, that is, Metternich writing in 1849 is to be proved correct, and Italy really is no more than a geographical expression!

At the end of the 1980s, it was just possible in a post-Thatcherite climate to conclude that the Italian experience showed that small really was beautiful and that a culture of democratic flexible specialization as typified by small firms in north-east Italy was the right response to the problem of post-Fordist socio-economic systems. More realistically, it would have been seen that, having been on the defensive in the 1970s, during the 1980s large firms in Italy had recovered their dynamism and determination. They undertook intensive restructuring and invested heavily in new technologies, and management regained the initiative at the expense of the workforce and the trade union movement generally. During the 1980s, big business reasserted and expanded its own control over the manufacturing system and aimed at improving its image as a promoter of both economic and socio-cultural opportunities. The ownership strategy was simply one of expansion, regardless of other strategic objectives such as consolidation or development. This strategy has changed in the early 1990s to focus more on the enhancement of quality and know-how in production, and more competitive features have emerged, forcing many firms to reappraise and return to notions of core business, rather than expansion, as the *raison d'être* of the enterprise.

By the end of the 1980s, however, most societal groups (entrepreneurs, families, state institutions, the political system) seemed suddenly to lack the insights that had allowed them to respond so creatively and dynamically to the challenges of the decade. Collective life at the time was probably fairly typified as going through a waiting stage. Collective actors (political parties, representatives of labour and business) lost their sense of whom they were representing; locally-based political movements challenged the very notion of Italy as a nation; the weakening of institutions and the inefficiency of public services further contributed to the delegitimation of the state; organized crime infected all levels of society and every sector of activity (finance, business, institutions). No strongly-felt alternative collective myths have emerged: Project 1992 has certainly not fulfilled this function, as some might have hoped. For the business world, this has led to an ethos where it is sufficient, even attractive, to 'do business' rather than to 'produce growth', but for Italian society as a whole, the consequence may be more dramatic. There are signs that Italians are deeply alienated and that 'we don't like ourselves any more' is an outspoken translation of an emerging attitude of disengagement from collective identification. It may therefore be that 1992 marked a moment of deep rupture for Italy, and not just another crisis **all'italiana**.

References and suggestions for further reading

AAVV (1992), 'Europa 1993: Sono pronte le imprese italiane?', *L'Impresa* (rivista italiana di management), 1.

AAVV (1992) (gruppo di ricerca di Nomisma), *Rapporto 1991 sull'Industria Italiana*, Bologna: Il Mulino.

Bianchi, Patrizio (1988), 'Privatisation of industry: the Alfa Romeo case', in Nanetti, Rafaella, Leonardi, Robert and Corbetta, Piergiorgio (eds), *Italian Politics: A Review*, vol. 2, London: Frances Pinter.

Bracalente, Bruno and Marbach, Giorgio (1989), *Il part-time nel mercato italiano del lavoro*, Milan: Franco Angeli.

CENSIS (Centro Studi Investimenti Sociali) (1991), *Italy Today: Social Picture and Trends, 1990*, Milan: Franco Angeli.

Ciarrocca, G. (1987), *Come Investire in Italia* (How to Invest in Italy), Milano: Pirola. (A bilingual guide to investing in Italy.)

De Michelis, Gianni, and Scognamiglio, Carlo (1989), *Come guidare l'Italia nel Duemila. Le Riforme del 1992*, Roma: Sperling e Kupfer Editori.

Department of Trade and Industry (1992), *Italy: Country Profile*, London: Exports to Europe Branch, Italian Desk, Department of Trade and Industry.

Economist Intelligence Unit (1992), *Italy: Country Report* and *Country Profile*, London: Economist Intelligence Unit.

Friedman, Alan (1988), *Agnelli and the Network of Italian Power*, London: Harrap.

Garonna, P. (ed) (12987), *The Role of the Social Partners in Vocational Training in Italy*, Berlin: CEDEFOP (European Centre for the Development of Educational Training).

Goodman, Edward, and Bamford, Julia, with Saynor, Peter (eds) (1989), *Small Firms and Industrial Districts in Italy*, London: Routledge.

King, Russell (1987), *Western Europe: Economic and Social Studies. Italy*, London: Harper & Row.

Lange, Peter, and Regini, Marino (1989), *State, Market and Social Regulation. New Perspectives on Italy*, Cambridge: CUP.

OECD, Economic Surveys, Italy, Paris: OECD.

Onida, Fabrizio, and Viesti, Gianfranco (eds) (1988), *The Italian Multinationals*, London: Croom Helm.

Sassoon, Donald (1986), *Contemporary Italy – Politics, Economics and Society since 1945*, Harlow: Longman.

Spotts, Frederic, and Weiser, Theodore (1986), *Italy: A Difficult Democracy –A Survey of Italian Politics*, Cambridge: CUP.

Vidal, Florence (1990), *Il Management all'Italiana*, Milano, Il Sole 24 Ore, 1991 (first published as *Le Management à l'Italienne*, Paris: InterEditions).

Villa, Paola, and Marchetti, Aldo (1991), *Continuing Training in Firms and Trainer Development in Italy*, Berlin: CEDEFOP.

Zanderighi, Luca (1990), *Piccole e Medie Imprese e Sviluppo Commerciale*, Milano: EGEA.

KEY – NORTHERN IRELAND

1	BELFAST
2	ANTRIM
3	CARRICKFERGUS
4	NEWTOWNABBEY
5	NORTH DOWN
6	CASTLEREAGH
7	ARDS
8	DOWN
9	NEWRY & MOURNE
10	BANBRIDGE
11	LISBURN
12	CRAIGAVON
13	BALLYMENA
14	LARNE
15	MOYLE
16	BALLYMONEY
17	COLERAINE
18	MAGHERAFELT
19	COOKSTOWN
20	DUNGANNON
21	ARMAGH
22	LONDONDERRY
23	LIMAVADY
24	STRABANE
25	OMAGH
26	FERMANAGH
27	LOUGH NEAGH

ORKNEY

SHETLAND

WESTERN ISLES

HIGHLAND

GRAMPIAN

TAYSIDE

FIFE

CENTRAL

LOTHIAN

STRATHCLYDE

BORDERS

DUMFRIES & GALLOWAY

NORTHERN IRELAND

NORTHUMBERLAND

TYNE & WEAR

CUMBRIA

DURHAM

CLEVELAND

NORTH YORKSHIRE

LANCASHIRE

WEST YORKSHIRE

HUMBERSIDE

MERSEYSIDE

GREATER MANCHESTER

SOUTH YORKSHIRE

CHESHIRE

DERBYSHIRE

NOTTINGHAMSHIRE

LINCOLNSHIRE

CLWYD

GWYNEDD

SALOP

STAFFORDSHIRE

LEICESTERSHIRE

NORFOLK

WEST MIDLANDS

WARWICKSHIRE

CAMBRIDGESHIRE

SUFFOLK

POWYS

HEREFORD & WORCESTER

NORTHAMPTONSHIRE

BEDFORDSHIRE

DYFED

GLOUCESTERSHIRE

OXFORDSHIRE

BUCKINGHAMSHIRE

HERTFORDSHIRE

ESSEX

GWENT

GREATER LONDON

WEST GLAMORGAN

MID GLAMORGAN

SOUTH GLAMORGAN

AVON

WILTSHIRE

BERKSHIRE

SURREY

KENT

SOMERSET

HAMPSHIRE

WEST SUSSEX

EAST SUSSEX

DEVON

DORSET

ISLE OF WIGHT

CORNWALL

4 The business culture in the United Kingdom
Collin Randlesome

Introduction

Business people in the United Kingdom do not have it easy. As a nation, the British are taught in school to deplore the vulgarity of wealth; in much of English literature, the villain of the piece is exposed as a ruthless businessman either deceiving aristocrats or exploiting workers. Prince Charles apart, the leading members of the Royal Family do not appear to be particularly interested in business; while the established Church of England gives the impression that it is actually anti-business. Indeed, the former Archbishop of Canterbury, Dr Robert Runcie, in an interview with *Director* magazine in 1989, castigated the country for being too materialistic and warned of the emergence of a 'Pharisee' society based on self-interest and intolerance. In March 1992, the Bishop of London, Dr David Hope, ascended the steps of the Royal Exchange to deliver a homily against greed, ruthlessness and avarice. In short, the country at large has never really learned to love business.

As a result, British business people have hesitated to proclaim their business activities as denoting something inherently good or to trumpet their many achievements. They have also been reluctant to lend an air of permanence to their business activities, too often giving the notion from their job-hopping tendencies that they are 'just visiting' rather than representing an established feature of a company. They have even tolerated for far too long the absurd caricature of the British business person as someone who indulges in protracted lunches and rounds of golf in company time.

Such values, attitudes and downright distortions have exerted a profound influence on the business culture in the country. Above all, they have contributed to the much-criticized short-termism which continues to haunt the culture. Short-termism manifests itself still in the British fascination with financial engineers in the City rather than the real thing in the country's manufacturing industries; in the preference for asset holders rather than product makers; in the exposure of the country's leading industrial companies to hostile takeovers by financial manipulators.

It is short-termism that forces British company boards to concentrate on profits now rather than investment for the future. Thus there has been a signal failure, in the past, by the country's companies to invest in human capital. Company directors have been reluctant to train their employees and develop their managers because the companies which did adopt the longer-term view and educated their workforces were in fact punished. Their shares were marked down, they were accused of damaging cash flow, and their skilled workers were poached by other companies. The result is that the United Kingdom probably has one of the poorest-trained workforces of any of the major industrial countries. Fortunately, this attitude is now changing, and training has risen towards the top of company agendas.

Equally, short-term thinking is responsible for a lack of investment by British companies in R & D. Between 1981 and 1985, British firms spent £250 per annum per employee, compared with £300 in France and $400 in western Germany. Of the top ten industrial nations, the United Kingdom ranked ninth in terms of R & D spending by industry. If rate of growth is taken into account, the country came last. Nor has business been helped in this respect by government. In fact, the government's share of civil R & D funding declined from 1.2 per cent of GDP in 1981 to 0.8 per cent in 1988, with further falls in real terms in subsequent years.

At the same time, the business culture in the United Kingdom has always been one which is receptive to new ideas, innovative and adaptable. It has inevitably been the first to try out new concepts – the good as well as the bad – originating from the acknowledged home of free enterprise, the United States of America. Nor has it been slow in inventing its own concepts and systems.

Perhaps, however, the outstanding positive feature of the business culture in the country is its sheer adaptability. Indeed, business in the United Kingdom has had to be adaptable just to survive the many changes visited upon it since the Second World War by different governments of the left and the right, and by swings in economic policy brought about by political expediency. In recent times, the adaptability of the business culture has been demonstrated nowhere more clearly than in its response to the enterprise culture since the return to power of the Conservatives in 1979. The number of companies in the United Kingdom almost doubled during the 1980s; more jobs were created in the country than in the rest of the EC countries put together; profitability improved out of all recognition. Although the enterprise culture appears slightly tarnished in the early 1990s, and both company failures and unemployment have increased dramatically, business must still be doing something right. Why else would Japanese direct investment in the United Kingdom constantly outstrip that in any other European country and total some £5 billion per year?

By the early 1990s, business in the country was doing much that was right, despite the recession. Fixed investment by non-oil companies in 1989 had reached record levels (more than double what it was in 1986), and expenditure on training and development had increased spectacularly. Moreover, the country's contribution to world manufacturing exports revealed a rising tendency, probably for the first time this century.

The highly adaptable business culture in the country changed radically during the 1980s. If business is to meet the challenges of the 1990s, including success in the EC's single market, it will have to continue the process of adaptation, but with an even greater sense of urgency.

Business and government

After the strike-ridden 'winter of discontent' of 1978–9, European newspapers and magazines appeared to be competing with one another to paint the blackest possible portrait of business in the United Kingdom. *Le Monde* forecast that the United Kingdom was on the verge of becoming 'an underdeveloped country'; *Der Spiegel* ran a whole series on 'sick England'. In May 1988, by contrast, *Fortune* magazine was declaring in its cover title that 'Britain is back' and even speculating that the comeback might qualify: '. . . as a full-blown economic miracle'. If the cold economic indicators over the period from 1979 to 1992 are compared with the country's long-term past performance, there was no miracle in the United Kingdom. However, the business climate, for which government in any country is mainly responsible, did change radically and for the better, and with it the business culture.

In May 1979, the Conservatives regained power from Labour, and their leader, Margaret Thatcher, became the United Kingdom's first female prime minister. On 6 June 1979, in a speech in Cambridge, she said: 'The mission of this government is much more than the promotion of economic progress. It is to renew the spirit and solidarity of the nation.' Economic progress, especially in terms of economic growth, was promoted for the most part, and the spirit and solidarity of much of the business community renewed, but not of the nation as a whole.

One of the ways in which business confidence has been bolstered is through continuity of government. Margaret Thatcher retained office in two general elections since 1979, thus becoming the longest-serving prime minister this century, and the longest in continuous office since Lord Liverpool in the first quarter of the nineteenth century. The stability afforded by her continuous tenure of 10 Downing Street from May 1979 to November 1990 enabled business to plan and invest, and indeed make profits, in a way which the country has seldom witnessed. While not all sectors of business flourished equally under what came to be known as **Thatcherism**, profit is no longer held to be a dirty word, and managers have been given the freedom to run companies in the way in which they, and not the trade unions, think fit. They have also received the rewards for doing so.

Since 1979, the Conservative government, led first by Margaret Thatcher, and from 1990 by her protégé, John Major, has pursued policies which are founded on a political and economic philosophy of free enterprise, competition and less state intervention. The Conservatives' top priority, from the outset, has been to furnish a framework within which private business can succeed. Margaret Thatcher's three periods of office attempted to loosen business people, the creators of wealth, from regulations and constraints, and let market forces prevail. Only in this way, she believed, could power be returned to individuals. According to Margaret Thatcher, there is no such thing as society!

While advocating similar fundamental economic policies to his predecessor, one of John Major's first speeches on becoming prime minister referred to his desire for a 'classless society'. The expectation in the country, after he led the Conservatives to victory in the 1992 general election, was that he would pursue policies with a less radical edge to those of Margaret Thatcher, despite her stout assertions in an article in *Newsweek* of 27 April 1992, that: 'I don't accept the idea that all of a sudden Major is his own man'; and 'There isn't such a thing as Majorism'.

The state of the United Kingdom's economy was indeed gruesome in 1979, the year the Conservatives resumed government:

- Economic growth for 1979 measured 2.6 per cent.
- Inflation was high at over 13 per cent, and on the increase.
- Unemployment registered 5.1 per cent according to OECD figures and 4 per cent on the Department of Employment's admission, but rising.
- The current account was in deficit.

The over-riding macroeconomic priority of the first government under Margaret Thatcher was the **defeat of inflation**. However, the policies chosen to reduce inflation by the Chancellor, Sir Geoffrey Howe, did little to enamour the Conservatives to large sections of business, especially manufacturing. A tight monetary policy was adopted, with high interest rates and a lofty exchange rate for sterling. By the end of 1980, the pound cost approximately $2.40, making imports relatively cheap but rendering the country's exports uncompetitive. These measures prompted Sir Terence Beckett, erstwhile Director General of the **Confederation of British Industry**, (CBI), in his closing speech to the 1980 conference, to call upon the leaders of industry to take up a 'bare-knuckle fight' with the government. One month later, he warned that industrial companies were 'disappearing down the plug-hole faster than we can stop them'. In 1981, as industrial output reached its nadir, 264 eminent economists signed a letter published in *The Times* demanding a change of policy.

But in many ways the first three years of Conservative government from mid-1979 to mid-1982 appeared to be a denial of much that Margaret Thatcher stood for. Despite the frequent utterances of **TINA** ('There is no alternative'), government succumbed to the threat of a coal miners' strike, conceded a 50 per cent rise in civil servants' pay over the 1979–80 period, and continued to subsidize nationalized industries such as British Steel, which was losing £1 million per day at the time. With unemployment approaching three million, 'job-creation schemes' were concocted which amounted to the complete antithesis of the Conservative philosophy. It seemed ironic in the extreme that the successful Conservative slogan in the 1979 election had been 'Labour isn't working'.

By mid-1982, there were clear signs that the worldwide economic recession was coming to an end. Inflation in the United Kingdom began to fall, as did the number of days lost through industrial disputes (see pages 228 and 244). These achievements, though modest enough in themselves, taken in conjunction with the 'Falklands Factor', helped the Conservatives to victory in the 1983 general election. They also helped mask the fact that many of the pledges on which the Conservatives had regained power in 1979 remained unfulfilled. Despite the sales of several state-owned concerns, i.e. privatizations, to which further reference will be made (see page 208), and of dwellings previously owned by local government to occupiers, the size of the public sector and public spending were increasing; and despite certain cuts, the tax burden on the majority of the working population was greater than when the Conservatives took over from Labour.

Although they do not win general elections, the leading economic indicators for 1983, with the exception of the unemployment figures, did show an improvement on 1979.

- Economic growth for the year registered 3.6 per cent.
- Inflation was below 5 per cent and falling.
- Unemployment amounted to 10.7 per cent according to OECD figures and 10.5 per cent on the Department of Employment's, with both rates still showing a rising trend.
- The current account was in surplus, thanks to North Sea oil.

The Conservative victory in 1983 was facilitated by a high level of internal dissent in the Labour Party, and the emergence of the Liberal/SDP Alliance as a real political force served to deprive Labour of some of its traditional supporters.

It was only during Margaret Thatcher's second period in office, from June 1983 to June 1987, that three of the key policies affecting business –

trade union reform, privatization and tax reform – were perceived as approaching fruition.

Victory over the coal miners in March 1985 after a strike lasting 14 months appeared, to the public at large, to vindicate the *1980* **Employment Act** which had outlawed secondary picketing. Victory over the print unions at Wapping in 1986 justified the Conservatives' struggle to introduce a measure of flexibility into the country's labour markets, which had found its expression in the *1982* **Employment Act**. The Conservatives' trade union reforms, including those passed in 1984 incorporating measures to make unions more democratic and in 1988 to tighten up the circumstances under which a 'closed shop' can operate are discussed in full, together with subsequent reforms, in a separate section of this chapter (see pages 241–242).

One of the most radical policies implemented by the Conservatives under Margaret Thatcher, and one which came to prominence in her second term of office, was the **selling of state-owned concerns to the private sector**. Just as the sales of local council homes to occupiers (1,300,000 by 1989) were used to foster a nation of property-owners, privatization was the Conservatives' main method of creating a share-owning democracy. Among the public-sector companies sold were: 50.2 per cent of British Telecom, which brought in £3.9 billion in November 1984; British Gas for £5.6 billion in December 1986; the government's 31.5 per cent stake in British Petroleum, sold for £7.2 billion in October 1987; British Steel for £2.5 billion in December 1988; and the water authorities for a further £5.2 billion in December, 1989.

By the turn of the decade, over 42 per cent of 1979's nationalized industries sector, or roughly 6 per cent of GDP, had been transferred to the private sector. In addition, the Conservatives privatized the twelve electricity distribution companies in England and Wales in December 1990 and the two generating companies in March 1991, followed by the Scottish power companies in June 1991. The second tranche of British Telecom shares was sold off in December 1991. Privatization of British Coal and partial privatization of British Rail were both announced in the Queen's Speech which opened the session of parliament beginning in May 1992.

The privatization policy has proved to be one of the government's most controversial. The Conservatives contend that companies in the private sector are more efficient than those in the public sector because they produce a better level of service, due to market forces, and have to meet profit targets. Government critics counter that, especially in the cases of British Telecom, British Gas, and water and electricity supply, private monopolies have merely replaced public monopolies, thus necessitating the establishment of watchdog bodies to protect consumer interests. Critics have also claimed that government revenue from privatizations, 'selling the family silver' as it was called by the late Lord Stockton, a former Conservative prime minister, distorts public accounts. They point to future problems once this source of revenue dries up.

The third area of policy with important repercussions for business has been that of **tax reform**. When Labour left office in 1979, the basic rate of income tax was 33 per cent and the top marginal rate 83 per cent. In his first budget in June 1979, Sir Geoffrey Howe set the tone for the Thatcher era and beyond, reducing the basic rate by 3 per cent to 30 per cent, widening the tax bands and cutting the top rate to 60 per cent. Personal allowances were also increased. In 1986, Nigel Lawson, Sir Geoffrey's successor as Chancellor, brought this basic rate down to 29 per cent and indexed personal allowances. He followed these cuts one year later to bring the basic rate down to 27 per cent, and in 1988 to 25 per cent. Five higher tax rates up to 60 per cent were replaced by a single rate of 40 per cent for taxable incomes over £19,300. In 1992, Norman Lamont, John Major's successor as Chancellor, reduced the basic income tax rate to 20 per cent for the first £2000 of taxable incomes and savings.

Reforms of company taxes were also initiated under Sir Geoffrey Howe's chancellorship and continued under that of Nigel Lawson. A reduction of 1 per cent in the hated National Insurance Surcharge was announced in the 1982 Autumn Statement, and further reductions were made in 1983 prior to final abolition in 1984. At the same time, cuts were introduced in the main corporation tax rate, which fell from 52 per cent to 50 per cent in 1983–4, then to 45 per cent in 1984–5, 40 per cent in 1985–6 and to 35 per cent in 1986–7. The rate for small companies was reduced from 38 per cent to 30 per cent in 1983–4, then 29 per cent in 1985–6, 27 per cent in 1987–8 and to 25 per cent in 1988–9.

Despite the Conservatives' attempts to create a property-owning democracy, by the time of the 1987 general election over a quarter of all householders were still public tenants; despite their attempts to create a share-owning democracy, only a fifth of the adult population aged sixteen or over possessed shares. A third of all workers were in the employment of the state, more than in western Germany or France. Worse still, government expenditure was increasing in real terms and the state was responsible for as large a share of GDP as under the last Labour administration. The popularity of the legislation introduced to curb trade union powers and the tax cuts probably constituted the most successful elements of the Conservatives' record in government, especially with business people. Managers had been afforded the freedom to manage companies and were in receipt of the rewards as well.

The leading economic indicators for 1987 were much more auspicious than in 1983, and even the unemployment rates were falling.

- Economic growth registered 4.6 per cent for the year.
- Inflation was below 3.8 per cent.

- Unemployment measured 10 per cent according to both OECD and the Department of Employment.
- The current account showed a slight deficit.

Once again, the opposition vote was split between Labour and the Liberal/SDP Alliance, which benefited the Conservatives, who remained in government with a reduced but comfortable majority. The Labour Party, however, mounted its most professional campaign in living memory.

After the 1987 election victory, the United Kingdom probably witnessed the most radical programme of change since 1945. The continuing policies of trade union reform, privatization and tax reform were joined by fresh government initiatives in reform of the **National Health Service** (NHS), education, and rates.

An area of government policy in Margaret Thatcher's third term which brought forth much opposition, from the public at large and the medical establishment in particular, was the reform of the NHS. The aim was to promote efficiency and competition within the NHS by means of a three-phase package completed by 1991. Reforms included hospitals opting out of regional health authority control, and general practitioners setting up independent practices with responsibility for their own budgets. The government was accused of attempting to privatize the NHS, and some of the measures proved to be unpalatable to those most directly affected.

The Conservatives' education reforms are discussed in full in a subsequent section of this chapter (see pages 247–248).

Possibly the most controversial of the initiatives between 1987 and 1992 was **rates reform**. The government had been committed for some considerable time to abolishing rates, the tax based on nominal property values levied to fund local authority services such as education, police and fire services, refuse disposal, and roads. Under the new legislation, domestic rates were replaced by a community charge payable by all adults. The former system of rates on commercial properties was changed to a uniform business rate. The government argued that the community charge would render high-spending local authorities more accountable to those who vote for them. Critics preferred to call the community charge a poll tax, maintaining that it was a regressive tax which disproportionately affected the poor in society. They also claimed that the poll tax was expensive to collect and difficult to administer. The community charge was introduced in Scotland in 1989, and in England and Wales in 1990. It proved to be so unpopular, however, that it was withdrawn as from April 1993, to be replaced by a council tax.

In macroeconomic terms, the most outstanding achievement of the Conservative governments between 1979 and 1989 was probably their record on economic growth (Table 4.1).

Table 4.1 *United Kingdom growth rates (1979–92)*

Year	(%)
1979	2.6
1980	−2.7
1981	−1.7
1982	2.0
1983	3.6
1984	2.2
1985	3.5
1986	3.2
1987	4.6
1988	3.7
1989	2.3
1990	0.8
1991	−1.9
1992	−1.0

Source: OECD

The *1987–1988 OECD Economic Survey* commented as follows on the post-1979 cycle: 'Measured from peak to peak, the division of nominal GDP growth between output growth and inflation was much more favourable over the 1979/1988 period than during the 1973/1979 cycle and similar to earlier experience, suggesting that there have been policy-induced improvements in supply performance. Other economic indicators confirm this picture: the deterioration in performance in the 1970s has been reversed; and, compared with other Member countries, there has been a relative improvement. Economic growth during the 1981–8 recovery, at over 3 per cent per annum, was not outstanding compared to previous upswings, but the upturn was unusually long.' In other words, peak-to-peak sustained growth outstripped the rates recorded in western Germany, France and other countries but fell short of the United Kingdom's own long-term trend rate. Growth was good and sustained, but not miraculous.

What was almost miraculous was the growth in company profits. During the 1980s, profits grew more quickly in the United Kingdom than in any other industrialized country, albeit from a low base. Average growth in gross trading profits (net of stock appreciation) of United Kingdom firms outside the North-Sea oil sector was 21.7 per cent per annum in the period from 1981 to 1987. The real rate of return on capital rose to its highest level since the 1960s and was in 1988 broadly in line with that of other major competitor countries.

Unfortunately, the good times could not last. Misjudgments made in monetary policy after the 1987 stock exchange crash, such as the lowering of interest rates, and the failure to predict the credit explosion after financial deregulation, contributed to the economy overheating in the latter years of the 1980s. Corrective action in the form of higher interest rates during John Major's chancellorship, from 1989 to 1990, led to a home-made recession, which was lengthened and deepened as other major economies throughout the world followed the United Kingdom into recession.

The depressed state of the economy, the unpopularity of the NHS reforms, and the disastrous introduction of the community charge with which she was personally identified, combined to produce serious doubts in the minds of Conservative members of parliament as to whether Margaret Thatcher was the right leader to take the party into the forthcoming general election. Her leadership was challenged in November 1990, initially by Michael Heseltine, and she resigned as party leader, and therefore as prime minister, after the first round of voting.

John Major won the leadership contest and assumed the office of prime minister with at most 19 months left before the next general election was due. He pursued the same basic economic policies yet did manage to project a more caring image. He finally decided to go to the country in April 1992, although the leading economic indicators can have given him few grounds for optimism.

- Economic growth for the previous year registered minus 1.9 per cent.
- Inflation for 1991 was 6.2 per cent but falling.
- Unemployment was at 8.7 per cent and rising.
- The current account was in deficit by $21 billion.

Although virtually every opinion poll predicted a hung parliament, the Conservatives were returned to power with a small, but workable majority. The stock market responded positively, sterling strengthened initially on the foreign exchanges, and the CBI reported greater confidence among its members than at any time during the previous three years.

Provided the Conservatives under their new prime minister can steer the economy out of the longest and deepest recession since the Second World War, business confidence will remain high. The new optimism and new business ethos engendered in the Thatcher era, in which the creation of wealth is not merely accepted but actually applauded, will then be afforded time in which to permeate the whole of the business community, including manufacturing. The sooner the new optimism and the new business ethos become permanent features of the business culture at large, the better for the citizenry of the country. Business and government in the United Kingdom can then proceed to address an issue which has yet to enter the country's business culture in any significant fashion – protection of the environment. But even here there is optimism, with the drafting of an environmental management system by the **British Standards Institution** (BSI) in 1991, and the appointment of former environment minister, Michael Heseltine, as president for the board of trade in John Major's 1992 cabinet.

Business and the economy

The United Kingdom was the 'workshop of the world', the leading manufacturing nation, in the nineteenth century. Although the value of the output of the country's manufacturing sector has been surpassed in the interim by the United States, Japan, Germany and France, it still came as a shock when, in 1983, the United Kingdom registered a deficit in manufactured goods for the first time since the Industrial Revolution. Despite great improvements in productivity and big increases in inward investment, a large trade gap remained in the early 1990s, when manufacturing accounted for only 23 per cent of GDP. Nor has an impressive increase in size of the service sector of the economy been able to offset fully the decline in manufacturing industry.

Manufacturing

'Mrs Thatcher prefers people who make money to people who make things', was a complaint by one of the delegates to the CBI conference in 1988 which was widely reported in the business press. While it is not beyond the bounds of possibility that Mrs Thatcher liked both, Sir John Harvey-Jones, former chairman of Imperial Chemical Industries (ICI), has frequently pointed out that manufacturing is still perceived, in the United Kingdom, as a less important and laudable aspect of the business culture than making deals in the City.

Almost immediately after the Conservatives regained power in 1979, manufacturing industry began to feel disadvantaged. While exchange and dividend controls were swept away by the incoming government, the detested National Insurance Surcharge remained in force. In addition, interest rates were maintained at a high level, as was the sterling exchange rate, making the country's exports uncompetitive. Whereas the index of industrial production registered a record 107.1 in 1979, it had plunged by 1981 to 96.6 as two million jobs were lost. The government's anti-inflationary policies combined with the worldwide recession to thrust manufacturing industry into deepest gloom.

In 1980, nationalized British Steel entered *The Guinness Book of World*

Records with the largest annual loss recorded up to that time – some $4 billion. It subsequently cut its workforce by two-thirds. In March 1981, Guest, Keen & Nettlefolds (GKN) reported an annual trading loss for the first time ever. In three years, GKN reduced its workforce from 69,000 to 37,000 A similar pattern was repeated throughout industry as demand plummeted and companies found themselves severely overmanned. Some of the most illustrious names in British industry went into liquidation or were taken over.

One of the effects of the 1980–1 recession in manufacturing industry was to exacerbate the **North–South Divide**. Between 1971 and 1984, the number of people employed in manufacturing industry in the Newcastle-upon-Tyne area dropped from 147,000 to 77,000. The biggest falls were in shipbuilding and engineering but practically all manufacturing sectors shed labour. A few miles away in Consett, County Durham, in six months in 1980, the unemployment rate rose from 12.3 per cent to 22.4 per cent, the highest in mainland Britain. But hardest hit of all in this recession was Northern Ireland, with its clothing industry. By November 1981, unemployment in Londonderry was 23.1 per cent and rising. Many parts of the South East of England, with their preponderance of service-based industries, were relatively unaffected (Table 4.2).

Table 4.2 *Regional growth and regional unemployment 1979 and 1985*

	Regional real gross product % change from previous year (excluding North Sea oil)		Regional unemployment rates % of working population
	1979	1985	1985
North	1.1	3.8	16.5
Yorkshire/Humberside	1.2	5.5	13.0
East Midlands	4.0	3.8	10.5
East Anglia	1.7	1.7	8.6
South East	2.5	3.6	8.6
South West	2.7	3.0	10.0
West Midlands	-0.3	4.8	13.6
North West	0.0	2.8	14.8
Wales	1.2	5.0	14.8
Scotland	1.1	3.0	14.1
Northern Ireland	1.9	1.3	17.4
UK (including North Sea oil)	3.0	3.5	11.8

Sources: BSL *Business Strategies* and *Employment Gazette*

In sharp contrast, manufacturing companies, especially in the north of the country, weathered the 1990–2 recession far better than many of the service companies. After almost uninterrupted growth in output and employment since the Second World War, and extremely rapid growth in the 1980s, the service sectors experienced falling output. This is reflected in the larger falls in regional real gross percentage changes in the South East and South West in 1991 than in the North or even in Yorkshire/ Humberside. Scotland, which had been a problem region in the early 1980s, emerged from the 1990–2 recession as one of the least-affected regions. (Table 4.3).

Table 4.3 *Regional growth and regional unemployment 1988 and 1991*

	Regional real gross product % change from previous year (excluding North Sea oil)		Regional unemployment rates % of working population	
	1988	*1991*	*1988*	*1991*
North	6.1	−1.7	12.2	10.4
Yorkshire/ Humberside	6.4	−2.4	9.8	8.7
East Midlands	6.9	−1.4	7.4	7.2
East Anglia	8.0	−1.8	4.9	5.8
South East	6.5	−3.4	5.4	6.9
South West	7.7	−3.0	6.5	7.1
West Midlands	6.3	−3.8	8.8	8.6
North West	6.2	−2.4	9.7	9.4
Wales	5.9	−2.3	9.3	8.7
Scotland	5.5	−0.6	11.7	8.7
Northern Ireland	6.0	−1.7	16.7	13.7
UK (including North Sea oil)	4.3	−1.9	8.3	8.7

Sources: BSL *Business Strategies* and *Employment Gazette*

The effect of the 1990–2 recession was to close the North–South Divide quite substantially. According to a report in 1992 by BWD Rensburg, the United Kingdom's most prosperous areas were to be found in the North. While stressing that some of the country's most distressed areas were also located in the North, the report made reference to a 'northern playground' stretching from the Lake District to the Yorkshire coast. These areas had the eight lowest unemployment figures in the country, coupled with buoyant house prices and high disposable incomes.

One of the reasons for the re-emergence of certain traditional manufacturing regions such as the North and the North West was the remarkable **rise in productivity**, and with it competitiveness, in the 1980s. Productivity in manufacturing industry increased by an average 5–6 per cent per annum in 1980–8, faster than in any other developed industrial economy, including Japan. Even in terms of what is called 'total factor productivity', or the efficiency with which business uses both capital and labour, the United Kingdom surpassed the achievements of other industrialized countries. In a study comparing the six years from 1979 to 1985 to the preceding six-year period, the OECD established that only the United Kingdom had registered a sizable increase.

In the latter years of the 1980s, the improvement continued, and United Kingdom labour productivity was less than 20 per cent below western Germany's in 1990. Measured in terms of output-per-worker instead of per-worker-hour, the productivity gap with western Germany had closed to less than 10 per cent by 1990. Companies such as ICI, Courtaulds, and even Rover, proved able to compete effectively with their western German counterparts. In the chemical industry, United Kingdom productivity levels were actually 10 per cent higher than in western Germany by the early 1990s.

Industry's critics, however, have pointed out that manufacturing output exceeded the 1979 level only in 1987, and fixed investment in manufacturing reached its pre-1979 level, in real terms, only in 1989. They have stressed that despite the rise in labour productivity in manufacturing, by 1988 the country's share of world trade in manufactured goods had dropped to 6.5 per cent in volume terms and roughly 6 per cent in value terms, compared with 8 per cent on both counts in 1979. There has also been greater import penetration in manufactured items. While finding it impossible to deny the vast improvements in labour productivity, critics have turned to the 'batting average' argument which shows that a cricket team's overall average automatically improves if several of the worst players are excluded from the calculations. It follows that if the least efficient companies go bankrupt, the performance of the survivors must appear to be better.

On balance, however, it is generally recognized that manufacturing industry emerged from the 1980s much leaner and fitter, if not actually large enough to satisfy domestic demand. In 1992, United Kingdom manufacturing output was running at 25 per cent above its 1982 level; the country's share of manufactured exports by developed nations rose from 7.5 per cent to 9 per cent from 1987 to 1992, after decades of decline; and industrial disputes were at their lowest for over a century (see page 244).

Some of the sectors of manufacturing industry in which the most successful companies operate are:

Chemicals

The United Kingdom's chemicals industry is the third largest in western Europe and the fifth largest of the OECD member countries. Almost half of its output is exported; in 1990, it had a trade surplus of more than £2.3 billion. One company, ICI, is responsible for half of the industry's production and is the fourth-biggest chemicals company in the world.

Iron and steel

The United Kingdom is the world's tenth-largest steel-producing nation in terms of volume. The country's manufacturers delivered 14 million tonnes of finished steel in 1990, 60 per cent of which was sold on the domestic market and the rest exported. British Steel, privatized in 1988, is the fourth-largest steel company in the western world and accounts for approximately 75 per cent of the country's crude steel production.

Electrical and electronic engineering

This sector of manufacturing industry suffered less than others in the 1980–1 recession, and output has risen steadily since 1982. In fact, sales of electronic data-processing (EDP) equipment increased by more than half between 1985 and 1990, reaching £7.7 billion. Expenditure in the country on EDP as a proportion of GDP is among the highest in western Europe, and leading overseas manufacturers, such as IBM, Wang, Seiko and Unisys, have established manufacturing plants in the United Kingdom.

Mechanical engineering

Much of the output in this sector is capital equipment, and it suffered particularly during the 1980–1 recession. However, from 1984 it began to recover. Over 40 per cent of sales go overseas, and exports of mechanical engineering equipment were responsible for 14 per cent of all visible exports in 1990.

Motor vehicles

The production of cars is dominated by five groups which account for over 95 per cent of the total. They are Rover, in which the government had a majority stake prior to the company's sale to British Aerospace (BAe) in

1988, Ford (including Jaguar), Vauxhall, Peugeot-Talbot and Nissan. Despite falling domestic demand in the 1990–2 recession, the country's car producers were able to maintain manufacturing levels due to substantial exports over the same period.

Aerospace

The United Kingdom's aerospace industry is the third largest in the world. In 1990, its turnover was approximately £11 billion, with exports amounting to $8.1 billion. Almost half of the export effort was provided by BAe. Rolls-Royce, which was privatized in 1987, is one of the three largest manufacturers of aero-engines in the world. The company's RB211-535 engines have been chosen by 75 per cent of airlines using Boeing's new 757airliners.

Leaner and fitter supplier companies account for some of the country's attraction as a target for **direct inward investment**. Direct investment, i.e. setting up or acquiring companies in another country as opposed to portfolio investment, which is the buying of foreign equities or overseas government bonds by financial institutions, reached record levels in the 1980s. In 1986, foreign companies invested £4.8 billion in the United Kingdom; in 1987, £8.1 billion; and in 1988, £7.1 billion in some 320 different projects. Since the beginning of the 1980s, total direct foreign investment in the United Kingdom has been in excess of £29.6 billion.

Much of the direct foreign investment has come from Japan. The first Japanese company to invest in the United Kingdom was YKK zip fasteners at Runcorn in 1972. By February 1987, the number of Japanese firms investing was fifty; by April 1989, the total had risen to 100 when Toyota announced that Burnaston, near Derby, was to be the site of its new European assembly plant, at a cost of £700 million. By 1991, the total was 150 companies. But it is not only the giants of Japanese industry such as Nissan, Toyota and Fujitsu which have invested in the United Kingdom. Citizen wrist watches opened a factory in Scunthorpe. Nikken, an engineering company, has settled in Rotherham. Union Chemicar, a carbon ribbon manufacturer, has opted for Barnsley.

Japanese investment in Europe between 1951 and 1991 reached $59.2 billion. The reasons for this investment have been due in recent years to the EC's single market. The Japanese fear that 'Fortress Europe' might make it more difficult to sell into this market of over 320 million Europeans. While other countries such as the United States would also suffer from a fortress mentality in Europe, most US multinationals already have a substantial presence here. The reasons for the Japanese investment in the United Kingdom in particular, which had attracted 41 per cent of total European investment by 1991, are held to be: the English language, which is compulsory in Japanese schools; low corporation taxes; an efficient distribution system; relative ease of access to mainland Europe; improved labour relations; and competitive labour rates.

The United Kingdom is also the most favoured location for western German investment in Europe, lying second worldwide only to the United States of America. By mid-1990, total western German direct investment, mainly from manufacturing industry, was £7.8 billion. A survey by the German Chamber of Industry and Commerce in 1992 revealed that 82 per cent of western German-owned companies manufacturing in the United Kingdom intended to expand further in the following five years; 19 per cent of German-owned companies not already manufacturing in the country planned to do so within the next five years; 57 per cent of the manufacturing companies claimed good or excellent productivity; 81 per cent of the companies reported good or excellent return on investment; and 92 per cent enjoyed good or excellent labour relations.

A definite cause for concern in terms of its attractiveness for inward investment is the country's **infrastructure**. Government investment in road and rail transport in the 1980s fell behind that in western Germany, France, Italy and Spain, and the transport infrastructure was reported to be the single most worrying issue in 1988 for the thirteen regional chairmen of the CBI. Though the government published a White Paper in 1989, promising a virtual doubling of expenditure on the road-building programme, the most glaring omission was any provision for motorways along the east and south coasts linking the ports there with the industrial heartland.

In 1990, the road network in the United Kingdom totalled some 358,000 km, of which 2993 km were trunk motorways. While motorways and trunk roads account for only 4.5 per cent of road mileage, they bear 32 per cent of all traffic, including almost 60 per cent of heavy goods traffic. In mid-1991, some 80 motorway and trunk road schemes were under construction in England alone, while over 400 schemes were in preparation.

Railways were pioneered in Britain, and the four large railway companies were nationalized in 1947. In 1962 the British Railways Board was established to manage railway affairs. In 1991, the length of the route open for traffic measured 16,584 km, about 25 per cent of which was electrified, including British Rail's busiest InterCity route linking London, the West Midlands, the North West and Glasgow. Government investment in British Rail totalled £858 million in 1990–1 and was expected to rise to over £1 billion in each of the three years from 1991–2. Privatization of parts of British Rail was announced in the Queen's Speech opening the 1992 session of parliament.

Construction work started on the Channel Tunnel in 1988, which entails the provision of twin single-track rail tunnels with a shuttle service for cars, coaches and heavy-goods vehicles. The project, which is being undertaken by Eurotunnel, was estimated to cost some £8.1 billion in 1992. It is the largest civil engineering project in Europe financed by private enterprise.

The country's inland waterways make only a limited contribution to freight carriage. In 1989, an official survey of freight traffic reported that some 68 million tonnes of freight were transported on inland waterways and estuaries, constituting only 1.4 per cent of freight traffic tonne-km.

There are over 300 ports in the United Kingdom, but many are small harbours which do not handle freight on a regular basis. In 1990, traffic through the ports totalled 473 million tonnes. The main ports with total tonnage throughput in 1990 were: London 54.5 million; Tees and Hartlepool 40.2; Grimsby and Immingham 38.9; Milford Haven 32.2; Sullom Voe 30.6; Southampton 28.8; and Forth 25.4.

Total capacity offered by British airlines in 1990 amounted to 20,377 million available tonne-km. Additionally, the airlines transported 38.4 million passengers a year on regular, scheduled services and 21.6 million on charter flights. The main airports are London (Heathrow) with 43.0 million passengers in 1990; London (Gatwick) 21.2; Manchester 10.5; Glasgow 4.4; Birmingham 3.6; Luton 2.7; Edinburgh 2.6; Belfast (Aldegrove) 2.3; Aberdeen 2.0; Newcastle-upon-Tyne 1.63; and East Midlands 1.3.

Services

As the United Kingdom's manufacturing industry has contracted over the decades, an increasing share of GDP has been taken up by services. In 1960, services accounted for approximately 45 per cent of GDP and 48 per cent of persons in employment; in 1987, services contributed about 60 per cent of GDP and employed 68 per cent of those in work; in 1990, these same percentages were 64 and 70 per cent respectively. Foreign trade in services has also grown, particularly in financial services (see page 226), and in 1990 overseas revenue from services totalled approximately 40 per cent of the value of exports of manufacturers. The fastest-growing service sectors, measured by employment, were leisure and personal services, finance, distribution, hotels and catering.

A significant factor in the expansion of services has been the growth of real incomes; personal disposable income has increased since 1948 at an annual rate of approximately 2.8 per cent. As spending power grows, consumers tend to spend a greater proportion of their income on services. For example, increased motorization and expenditure on the running costs of cars are important factors in the rise in expenditure on services. Other changes in the country have also encouraged the growth of services: the increasing number of elderly people in the United Kingdom (see page 234) has expanded the demand for medical services; and the fall in the average number of hours worked has created the need for more leisure services.

Among the major private sector services is tourism, which has become increasingly important and is a large employer especially in London. In 1990, it was estimated that approximately 1.4 million jobs were supported by tourism. Spending by some 18 million overseas visitors amounted to £7.8 billion in 1990. The largest single nationality groups were citizens of the United States, followed by France and western Germany.

A further growth area in the services sector is to be located in the retail trades. Of the largest 25 retailers in western Europe in any of the years from 1988 to 1990, ten were British. According to the 1988 Census of Production, there were 237,832 retail businesses, with 338,248 outlets in the country. Turnover in 1990 was in the region of £114 billion. While the large multiple retailers with ten or more outlets have expanded and diversified in recent years, there has been a decline in the number of small retail businesses and outlets, with independent businesses and retail cooperatives most affected. The largest multiple retailers in the grocery market are the retail cooperatives, Sainsbury, Tesco, Asda, Dee Corporation, Argyll Stores and the Kwik Save discount group. The major mixed retail companies are Marks & Spencer, F.W. Woolworth, Boots, Great Universal Stores, John Lewis Partnership, Burtons, Littlewoods, Sears and the House of Fraser.

In the early 1990s, an expanded services sector had failed as an adequate substitute for a slimmed-down manufacturing base. While manufacturing achieved extraordinary increases in productivity during the 1980s, it also suffered a massive reduction in size. The result was a capacity gap, with domestic suppliers incapable of meeting demand, leading to record trade deficits. In early 1989, the country was consuming more than it produced by the equivalent of 4 per cent of GDP. Most of the excess was in manufactured items. In turn, capacity shortages, and employers taking the opportunity to raise profit margins to international levels, contributed to rises in inflation. It is estimated that investment in capital stock by domestic suppliers would have to increase by 20 per cent above the level in the 1980s to close the gap.

Widespread neglect of the special needs of manufacturing in the United Kingdom remains a disturbing feature of the business culture which looks set to continue well beyond the early 1990s. Though the cultural hostility to manufacturing is slightly weaker in the final decade of the century than it was in the 1980s, it is still sufficiently pronounced to register as a continuing cause for concern.

Business and the law

English law differs fundamentally from the other legal systems to which reference is made in this book. The English common law emerged as a series of devices aimed at settling disputes or controversies; Continental law originated as a system instructing which rights and duties ought to be accepted in society as an ideal of justice. Similarly, the attention of English lawyers was focused for centuries on the types of action which could be claimed from a common law court. Although great changes have taken place over time, a high degree of significance still attaches, under English law, to procedures such as 'due process' and 'fair trial'. Scottish law is different again.

The common law was developed in England by the courts and thus a case law emerged where legal rules and certain procedures are linked with the facts of a particular case; on the Continent, by contrast, legal rules were constructed and laid down by legal scholars and writers. In the fullness of time, these legal rules were then codified.

A further difference is noteworthy which is of significance for the business culture. Legal studies in England are still, for the most part, pursued separately from studies of political science, public administration or management; on the Continent, it is not uncommon to find university courses which embrace all three aspects of scholarship. Thus it is quite rare to meet a business person in England who has studied law in any depth, while on the Continent a legal background is often held to be an ideal preparation for business.

The law in the United Kingdom admits a range of different business organizations. At the one end of the scale are the sole proprietorships; at the other the huge public limited companies. The principal forms of business entities in the United Kingdom are sole traders and partnerships; limited liability companies; and branches of foreign companies. A more comprehensive account can be found in the Price Waterhouse *Guide to Doing Business in the United Kingdom*, but the essential points are as follows:

1 Sole traders

The sole trader is the simplest legal entity within which to conduct business. It consists of one person carrying on business who may employ other persons to work for him or her. The sole trader is entirely responsible for the conduct of the business and has unlimited liability for business debts. Normally, there is no requirement for registration or the independent auditing of accounts.

2 Partnerships

A partnership is defined under the **1890 Partnership Act** as: '... the relationship which subsists between persons carrying on a business in common with a view to profit.' Under English law, a legal personality separate from the partners is not accorded to a partnership. Although the partners may be referred to collectively as a firm, the firm does not have the legal status of a company. Under Scottish law, a partnership does possess a legal status separate from the partners. But the partners in a Scottish firm are ultimately, like those in an English firm, personally responsible to the creditors for the debts and obligations of the firm. One of the few regulatory controls stipulates that a partnership may not consist of more than twenty persons unless they are lawyers, accountants, or members of a recognized stock exchange.

The **1907 Limited Partnership Act** provides for a general partnership with one or more general partners who conduct the firm's business and have unlimited liability, and one or more limited partners with liability limited to their capital contribution to the firm. The limited partners must not partake in the management of the firm otherwise their limited liability status is forfeited. Because of the latter stipulation, limited partnerships have not proved to be popular forms of business entities.

3 Limited liability companies

The most common type of company in the United Kingdom is the limited liability company incorporated by statute, of which the most recent is the **1985 Companies Act**. Limited liability companies are companies limited by guarantee or companies limited by shares. A company limited by guarantee is one where members' liability is limited to such amounts as they pledge to contribute in the event of the company being wound up. Such companies, are, however, rarely encountered. A company limited by shares is one where the members' liability for the company's debts is restricted to the amount paid or unpaid (if any) on their shares. Since companies limited by shares form the vast majority of business entities in the United Kingdom, the remaining remarks under this heading will refer to companies thus limited.

A company may be incorporated either as a public or as a private company. Only a public company may offer shares or debentures to the public, but they need not necessarily be quoted or traded on a stock exchange. Where a company seeks public-company status, it must include a statement to this effect in its memorandum of association. A public company must have an allotted share capital of £50,000, of which at least one-quarter of the shares' par value must be paid up. It must possess a name ending in 'public limited company' which may be abbreviated to 'plc', or their Welsh equivalents. All other companies are regarded as private companies. There is no authorized minimum share capital for a private company, but such a company must include as the last part of its name either the word 'limited' or the abbreviation 'ltd', or their Welsh equivalents.

A public company must have at least two directors; a private company need only have one. Unlike a public company, a private company need not acquire a trading certificate and can do business or borrow as soon as it is registered. There exist other legal requirements from which private companies are exempt, but the requirement to file annual accounts, which are thus made available for public inspection, applies to all limited companies. If the company is only small or medium-sized, it may file modified accounts, though these accounts must contain all the information specified by the 1985 Act.

The document by which a company is incorporated is the memorandum of association. It provides details of the company's name, the country in which its registered office is to be located, the limited liability of its members, its public-company status if appropriate, its authorized share capital, subscribers and objects. The objects clause is normally so widely drafted that it gives the company the powers necessary to conduct any business it may wish. Usually the articles of association are drawn up by lawyers at the same time as the memorandum of association. The articles lay down the internal rules for a company and its members. They set out provisions on voting rights, transfer of shares, the powers of directors and many other items. In fact, Table A in the Companies Regulations 1985 may be adopted as the articles, with or without modification.

A company's authorized share capital and the division of the capital into shares are specified in the memorandum of association. Issued share capital is held to be that part of the authorized share capital which has actually been issued to members. It may not exceed the authorized share capital. Shares may be of any fixed amount, usually £1 or smaller denominations. Shares of no par value are not allowed. They may be of different classes having different voting, dividend, and other rights. Issued shares may be fully or partly paid. Shares may not be issued at a discount in relation to their par value, but may be issued at a premium. Each company is required to keep a register of members, recording details of the shareholders and the quantities of shares they hold. Public companies must also maintain a register of shareholders with an interest of 5 per cent or more of the company's voting shares. Anyone acquiring such a stake is required to notify the company affected. Companies may issue debentures as well as share capital. Debentures are normally issued as security for a loan. They usually bear rights to interest at a specified, often fixed, rate and repayment at some future date.

The conduct of the company's business is the responsibility of the directors. A director need not be a shareholder in the company but sometimes articles of association require of a director a so-called share qualification. The directors often appoint one or more of their number to executive positions in the company, such as managing director. They also appoint one of their number as chairman, who may or may not hold a full-time executive position. The company's articles of association define the powers and duties of directors. Important among the latter is the obligation under company law to ensure that proper information about the company is divulged to the public and to potential and existing investors. In addition, directors must take into consideration the interests of employees as well as shareholders. Every company must appoint a secretary who may also be a director, but a sole director may not also be secretary. The secretary is regarded as an officer of the company and is usually the person responsible for ensuring that the company complies with the requirements of company law.

A company's dividend policy is the responsibility of the directors. The shareholders may either ratify or reject the directors' recommendations or propose that the amount be reduced. No dividend can exceed the amount recommended by the directors.

Every company must hold an Annual General Meeting (AGM) in each calendar year. At least twenty-one days' notice of the meeting must be given in writing to every member entitled to vote at the meeting. Business at the AGM is regulated by the company's articles of association and normally takes in: the accounts of the most recent financial year, including the directors' report; the auditors' report on the accounts; approval of the dividend proposed by the directors; the election or re-election of directors; the appointment of auditors and the fixing of their remuneration. A simple majority of votes will carry an ordinary resolution. Unless the articles of association specify otherwise, a shareholders' meeting may be held anywhere, and not necessarily in the United Kingdom.

4 Branches of foreign companies

Branches of foreign companies, i.e. companies incorporated outside the United Kingdom which set up places of business in the country, must comply with the provisions set forth in Part XXIII of the 1985 Companies Act. Similar legislation is applicable in Northern Ireland. Within one month of establishing a place of business in the country, the company must file with the Registrar of Companies: certified copies of the company's charter, statutes, memorandum and articles; particulars of the directors, such as names and addresses, nationalities and business occupations; a list of one or more British residents authorized to accept notices served on the company's behalf; and a declaration showing the date on which the place of business was established in the United Kingdom. Where the required documents are not in English a translation must be filed. Overseas companies must submit the same accounts as would be required if they were incorporated in the United Kingdom but in most cases it is possible to obtain permission from the Department of Trade and Industry to file the accounts as published in the company's own country, or an English translation of those accounts.

An influential factor in company law in recent years has been the EC. One of the objectives of the EC's industrial policy is: 'The creation of a unified business environment involving the harmonization of company law, and the creation of a community capital market.' The advent of the EC's single market at the end of 1992 lent fresh impetus to such objectives, and existing company law in the United Kingdom could be affected most profoundly by changes currently under discussion.

It is devoutly to be wished that such changes will encompass reforms of the duties of auditors, in the light of the House of Lords judgment in the Caparo case. This judgment held, inter alia, that the purpose of an audit is to provide only guidance to shareholders in discussing the stewardship of the company's directors at an AGM: it is not a statement of fact. Without stricter and independent regulation of the auditing profession, the litany of financial scandals will continue in the United Kingdom which, in the late 1980s and early 1990s, embraced the Bank of Credit and Commerce International (BCCI), the late Robert Maxwell's companies, Barlow Clowes, Polly Peck, and many others.

Business and finance

The United Kingdom is one of the leading financial centres in the world. Concentrated mainly in the City of London, the financial institutions provide services for business in this country and overseas. More international deposit and lending business is done in London than in New York or Tokyo, and more than in the rest of the EC put together. The stock market in the United Kingdom is three times larger than in western Germany; four times larger than in France; seven times larger than in Italy and the Netherlands; and even ten times the size of Spain's. Latterly, the position of London as the pre-eminent market in the European time zone has been reinforced by the rise of the London International Financial Futures Exchange (Liffe), linked to the major exchanges in Tokyo and Chicago to furnish a worldwide futures market. Liffe celebrated by opening a new trading floor costing £31 million in December 1991.

Indeed, the City has recently exerted a profound influence on the United Kingdom's business culture, appearing to enjoy most-favoured status with Conservative politicians, attracting more of the brightest young people that the country produces than ever, and rewarding them most generously. Nevertheless, the Bank of England, the Big Four clearing banks and the stock market are not without their critics.

The Bank of England

Founded in 1694 to furnish money for the government during the War of the Grand Alliance against France, the Bank of England is the central bank in the United Kingdom. Since its establishment, it has undergone several changes in status which have involved modifications to its responsibilities. Perhaps one of the most significant of the changes for the country's business culture occurred when, with the election of the first post-war Labour government, it was nationalized under the **1946 Bank of England Act**.

The Act contained the clearest possible message that the government of the day was henceforth responsible for the country's monetary policy. In fact, Section IV of the Act provides that the Treasury can give such directions to the Bank as it thinks appropriate in the public interest, after consultation with the Governor of the Bank. In its turn, the Bank has the power to issue directives to clearing banks and other financial institutions.

All the banks operating in the United Kingdom, including foreign-based banks, are subject to the supervision and regulation of the Bank of England. In addition to its supervisory and regulatory role, it controls the issue of bank notes (the Scottish banks also enjoying limited rights to issue notes), manages the national debt, acts as a banker to government and the banking system itself, and controls the official reserves.

Notwithstanding the scathing criticism heaped upon the Bank of England for its tardiness in closing down the corrupt Bank of Credit and Commerce International (BCCI) in 1991, it is the Bank's association with the Treasury in their joint failure to keep inflation within tolerable limits that has consistently raised most comment (Table 4.4).

At first glance, it would appear that monetary policy under the Conservatives had succeeded in suppressing inflation. For most of the 1980s, the figures reveal a declining tendency, though they did rise again towards the end of the decade. But if the United Kingdom's record on inflation is compared with, for example, western Germany's (see page 24), the figures appear much less impressive.

One possible solution to the United Kingdom's inflation problems which was widely canvassed in the 1980s was for the country to become a full member of the **European Monetary System** (EMS). Established in 1979, the EMS consists of three elements – the Exchange-Rate Mechanism (ERM), the European Currency Unit (Ecu) and the Monetary Cooperation Fund. By the late 1980s, sterling formed part of the Ecu and contributed to the cooperation fund. Although full membership of the EMS was originally advocated by two of Margaret Thatcher's Chancellors of the Exchequer, Sir Geoffrey Howe and Nigel Lawson, she insisted that the United Kingdom would not join until the time was right. She remained unconvinced over a long period

Table 4.4 *United Kingdom inflation rates (1979–92)*

Year	(%)
1979	13.5
1980	16.3
1981	11.3
1982	8.8
1983	4.8
1984	5.1
1985	5.3
1986	4.2
1987	3.8
1988	5.1
1989	7.8
1990	6.8
1991	6.2
1992	5.4

Source: OECD

of time that significant benefits for the country would flow from full membership.

Her critics pointed out that: the existing full members of the EMS had all achieved low inflation rates; the EMS had furnished a discipline in monetary policy which had been lacking in the United Kingdom; the EMS protected against the possibility of a falling pound bringing with it higher inflation; EMS members had benefited from lower interest rates than the United Kingdom; currency stability encouraged trade; and currency stability led to greater investment because business had the confidence to plan ahead.

Margaret Thatcher's supporters claimed that the year from March 1987 to March 1988, when the pound was informally pegged to the western German DM, was a resounding failure in terms of financial management. Credit ran out of control during this time, preparing the ground for the serious deterioration in the balance of payments from mid-1988 and for a rise in inflation. Among others arguing against full membership of the EMS were the Bruges Group, set up after the Margaret Thatcher's speech in September 1988 which was highly critical of the European Commission. They contended that full EMS membership would require the reinstatement of the country's exchange controls, abolished in 1979, and would jeopardize the City's position as the leading financial centre in Europe. The Bank of England also joined the argument by publishing technical objections to full EMS membership in May 1989.

Despite her misgivings, Margaret Thatcher reluctantly agreed, at the EC's Madrid summit in June 1989, that she could accept stage one of the report by Jacques Delors, French Socialist President of the European Commission, on Economic and Monetary union (EMU). Stage one foresaw the United Kingdom joining the ERM at some unspecified date in the future. Although Robin Leigh-Pemberton, Governor of the Bank of England, together with the governors of the other EC central banks, had sat on the committee which framed the Delors report, Margaret Thatcher refused to recognize any automaticity between stage one and stages two and three which envisaged a European Central Bank and the EC adopting a common currency.

Sterling finally joined the ERM in October 1990, under the chancellorship of John Major, over eleven years after its inception in March 1979. The country thus became a full member of the EMS. 'And about time, too' was business's initial reaction.*

Fundamental to Margaret Thatcher's objections to EMU and all that such involves was a fear of loss of sovereignty in matters of monetary policy. In a paper on *'Europe: Fortress or Freedom?'*, Dr Brian Hindley agrees that the EMS cedes a large degree of control of members' monetary policy to the western German Bundesbank. But he adds: 'I think it very likely … that the British economy would have been better off had its money supply been controlled by the Deutsche Bundesbank over the past two or three decades. And given a choice between the Bank of England and the Deutsche Bundesbank for the next two or three decades, I would be inclined to choose the latter.'

The Big Four

Domestic banking business in the United Kingdom is dominated by the Big Four clearing banks – Barclays, Lloyds, Midland and National Westminster (NatWest). These banks are called clearing banks because they were members of the London Banks' Clearing House which originally administered the cheque-clearing system in the country. There are now seven banks which form the Committee of London and Scottish Bankers (CLSB), and this body has replaced the Committee of London Clearing Banks as the trade association for the major 'high street' banks.

Each of the Big Four, which are among the largest banks in the world, has an extensive network of branches throughout the country and is thus well located to provide financial services to businesses operating anywhere in the United Kingdom. The most frequently encountered service for

* The United Kingdom's membership of the ERM was suspended on Black Wednesday, 16 September 1992.

business offered by the Big Four has been the provision of current accounts, i.e. non-interest-bearing cheque accounts permitting companies to effect payments in a quick and convenient manner. In addition, clearing banks have also lent to their corporate customers, either in the form of flexible overdrafts but with relatively high, floating rates of interest; or in the form of term loans with lower and, usually, fixed rates of interests.

In recent years, the relationship between the clearing banks, whose traditional mode of operation was to borrow short and lend short, and business has changed radically. Business customers have turned increasingly to banks not only for working capital but for capital to expand over medium and longer-term periods. Indeed, the range of financial services offered by all the clearing banks has become so diverse that former clear-cut distinctions between these and other types of banks, such as merchant banks, have become blurred. The clearing banks now offer export finance, factoring, insurance, stockbroking, leasing, investment management advice, and almost any other financial activity.

By the early 1990s, the Big Four had, however, succeeded in alienating shareholders, personal customers, and small corporate clients. Their shareholders felt aggrieved because, by October 1989, Barclays, Lloyds, Midland and NatWest announced that they had written off as irrecoverable debts £1938 million. Moreover, they were committed collectively to provision against further debt of £6.7 billion. These debts arose as the result of loans to the governments of Second and Third World countries. By the autumn of 1989, Midland had already written off £846 million; Lloyds £464 million; NatWest £395 million; and Barclays £235 million. The sheer size of the write-offs had quite naturally affected the banks' trading figures, with the result that the Midland revealed a £531 million loss for the year. In 1992, it was estimated that bad-debt provisions by the Big Four and Abbey National for the previous year, this time mainly as a result of injudicious lending to domestic corporate customers, would total £5.7 billion, a 41 per cent increase on 1990. This means, in fact, that the banks were writing off £650,000 per hour throughout 1991!

In 1989, the clearing banks announced that they were considering a charge for the use of credit cards. The charge was to be levied either for the purchase of the card itself or on those customers who pay their credit card bills promptly, or both. Coming after the banks' practice of refusing to pay interest on current accounts and levying charges on the movements on these accounts under certain conditions, which lasted for many years, this announcement was almost calculated to drive yet more personal customers into the arms of the building societies.

Finally, in the 1990–2 recession, the Big Four came under attack by corporate customers and government for: overcharging small businesses on credit interest; being too willing to put such companies into receivership;

failing to pass on the benefits of the gradual reductions in base rate (see also page 254); gross insensitivity to customer complaints; and running patronizing advertising campaigns. The Bank for International Settlements produced a report in 1991 showing that United Kingdom banks have some of the highest interest margins in the world, exceeded only in Spain and Australia. Although the Big Four were exonerated from accusations of actually running a cartel on interest rates, after an investigation by the Office of Fair Trading in 1991, the study did uphold many of the complaints about high charges and poor service. It backed Chancellor Norman Lamont's call for the banks to introduce codes of practice, which they duly published in 1992.

Stock market

As has been observed, the financial markets appeared to enjoy special treatment under Thatcherism. The tone was set right at the outset when Sir Geoffrey Howe abolished exchange and dividend controls in 1979, thus giving the City the kind of freedom in which it is held that markets work best. Privatizations then furnished the stock markets with excellent business. Nigel Lawson's reforms of corporate taxation also did much to encourage a recovery in company profits, which in turn increased the attraction of the shares of these firms.

Perhaps, however, the most significant single event for the financial markets occurred when Cecil Parkinson, secretary of state for trade and industry at the time, reached an agreement with Sir Nicholas Goodison, chairman of the stock exchange, to break the jobbers' monopoly and the brokers' cartel. The eventual outcome was **Big Bang** on 27 October, 1986. This particular piece of reform appeared appropriate because first it was in line with the government philosophy of deregulation throughout; the economy, or letting market forces hold full sway. Second, it was convenient because the City needed to adapt to new trading systems elsewhere if it was to remain a global player and exploit to the full its position between the time zones of New York and Tokyo.

Although the changes in regulations and trading practices culminated in Big Bang, they were only the last in a series which revolutionized the operations of the stock exchange. The most important changes can be summarized as follows:

- Fixed minimum commissions on the buying and selling of securities were abolished.
- Corporate membership of the stock exchange, with 100 per cent outside ownership, was introduced.

• All firms were allowed to act as broker/dealers or to act as agents for clients and as buyers or sellers in their own right.

One effect of Big Bang was to induce a rush of mergers and acquisitions as banks and other financial institutions bought into traditional jobbing and brokering firms. Another was to create such a demand for staff in the City that recruits were sometimes welcomed not only with inflated salaries but also with 'golden hellos' which assumed the shape of Porsche cars! This state of affairs did not last for long. Within a year, sanity was restored with an even bigger explosion. City firms' combined losses in 1988 totalled approximately £500 million.

The even bigger explosion, which occurred on 19 October 1987, was **The Crash**. After a bull market which had lasted for seven years, 22 per cent of the value of shares was wiped off the London stock exchange within one week. In December 1988, 450 jobs disappeared at Morgan Grenfell, the first big City bloodletting; in January 1989, Chase Manhattan pulled out of equity market-making; in January 1990, Citicorp closed its main broking business; and in May 1990, Kitcat & Aitken shut down. Despite the losses suffered by its shares, manufacturing industry in the country found it difficult to suppress a feeling of *Schadenfreude*. The City was now taking some of the medicine which manufacturing had been obliged to swallow during the 1980–1 recession.

The flood of work associated with takeovers and other deals was good business for City bankers for most of the 1980s. However, the latter years of the decade and the early 1990s saw this flood turn to a trickle. In 1989, there were some 2100 deals worth £45 billion; in 1990, 1500 worth £27.6 billion. Foreign buyers were responsible for breathing life into the corporate market in the first half of 1991. They accounted for over half the £16 billion paid in some 500 deals (Table 4.5).

In the early 1990s, the threat of the arrival in force in the United Kingdom of the highly-leveraged buyout had receded somewhat, with the 1990–2 recession and relatively high interest rates discouraging the large interest payments on the mountains of debt, or junk bonds, which support these companies. In fact, such buyouts are as yet uncommon in the country, only one highly-leveraged bid having succeeded – the £1.1 billion offer by Isosceles for Gateway, the supermarket chain. Hitherto, it had generally been assumed that the giants among the country's companies were safe from corporate raiders: they were too complex in structure to become targets of hostile takeover bidders intent on unbundling, or breaking up, the corporation. Nonetheless, it has been calculated that approximately forty-four of the stocks which constitute part of the FT-SE 100 Index could become targets for leveraged bids.

The highly-leveraged buyout was pioneered in the United States of

Table 4.5 *Top ten British takeover bids 1 July 1990–30 June 1991*

Target	Bidder	Value, £million
STC Plc	Northern Telecom Ltd	1844
Charlotte Plc	Brierley Investments Ltd	649
Yale and Valor Plc	Williams Holdings Plc	319
Fitch Lovell Plc	Booker Plc	315
Foseco Plc	Burmah Castrol Plc	260
Tootal Group Plc	Coats Viyella Plc	250
Rechem Environmental Plc	Shanks & McEwan Plc	177
Thames Television Plc	Thorn EMI Plc	149
Lowe Group Plc	Interpublic Group	138
Bardon Group Plc	Evered Plc	88

Source: The Times 1000, 1992

America by firms such as Kravis Kohlberg Roberts, Bankers Trust and Wasserstein Perella. All three specialist firms now maintain offices in London. Leveraged buyouts may represent good news for institutional fund managers, but their targets are usually large, diversified manufacturing companies with strong cash flows and undervalued assets.

Once interest rates ease sufficiently, there is every sign that such buyout activity could take off rapidly as merchant banks boost their buyout funds. Potential profits are simply too attractive for such buyouts to melt away. Then managers in manufacturing industry in the United Kingdom will have to call upon all their expertise to beat off the challenge from hostile predators. If the political and economic philosophy remains as it has since 1979, cries of 'foul' at yet another attack on the country's manufacturing base will go unheeded. The business culture will continue to be dominated by short-term considerations, such as profit forecasts by stockbrokers' analysts and the interests of institutional fund managers seeking the maximum possible return on investment in the shortest possible time. None of this is conducive to long-term thinking, which is vitally important if manufacturing industry is to plan, invest, equip and train for the future.

Business and the labour market

Business in the United Kingdom in the 1980s and early 1990s had to feed an increasing and, as in most European countries, an ageing population. Moreover, the civilian labour force continued to grow, thus making its own contribution to high levels of unemployment after the 1980–1 recession. However, from 1986 to 1989 unemployment fell by one million, partly due to the fact that the United Kingdom's economy created as many new jobs as the rest of the EC countries combined. Yet it rose again in the 1990–2 recession, with some 9.6 per cent of the workforce employed by June 1992, the highest figure for five years. Moreover, the labour market in the United Kingdom in the future will be affected by certain disturbing demographic developments.

Demographic trends

According to the 1981 census, the population of the United Kingdom numbered 56.4 million in that year. By 1989, it had increased to 57.2 million, comprising 27.9 million males and 29.3 million females. The population is projected to grow steadily to reach 59.0 million by 2001 and just over 61 million by the year 2025.

The age structure of the population has changed perceptibly over recent years. The number of people aged 65 or over (9.0 million in 1989) was above 50 per cent greater than in 1951 (5.5 million). This age group represented 16 per cent of the population in 1989 compared with 11 per cent in 1951. The overall size of this segment of the population is expected to rise to 11.3 million by the year 2025.

At the lower end of the age range, in 1971 there were some 12.4 million children aged under fifteen compared with roughly 10.7 million in 1989, when they formed only 19 per cent of the total population. By the year 2025, this proportion is expected to remain unchanged. The implications for the labour market of the fall in the numbers of children under fifteen will be the subject of subsequent discussion (see page 239).

Over the years from 1985 to 1989, marginally more immigrants (including British citizens) entered the United Kingdom than left. Some 16,000 people applied for refugee status in the country in 1989, three times the average for 1985 and 1988 and ten times more than in 1979. Estimates indicate further substantial rises in the future, but nothing on the scale for western Germany (see page 36). In 1989, 49,000 people subject to immigration control were accepted for settlement in the United Kingdom, 3000 more than in 1987 but 32,000 fewer than in 1976.

Unemployment

The civilian labour force in Great Britain increased at an average rate of 140,000 per year during the 1970s and reached 26.2 million in 1980 and

1981. It fell by over 300,000 between 1981 and 1983, but the upward trend was then resumed, and in 1989 it reached 27.6 million. The net increase in the labour force between 1979 and 1989 of some 1.4 million is, naturally, reflected in the United Kingdom's unemployment rates during the period (Tables 4.6 and 4.7). Between 1990 and the millennium, the number of men in the civilian labour force is projected to remain static, but the number of women to increase by 700,000.

Table 4.6 *Unemployment rates in the United Kingdom*
(1979–92)

Year	(%)
1979	5.1
1980	6.3
1981	10.3
1982	10.6
1983	10.7
1984	11.1
1985	11.3
1986	11.4
1987	10.0
1988	8.0
1989	6.4
1990	5.9
1991	8.7
1992	10.1

Source: OECD

The reason for the discrepancies between Tables 4.6 and 4.7 is that unemployment can be measured in several ways. The OECD unemployment rates up to 1986 were based on the percentage of the total labour force each month without paid jobs who said they were available to start work in the next fortnight and had sought work at some time during the past four weeks or were waiting to start a job already obtained. This definition of unemployment is consistent with the guidelines of the **International Labour Organisation** (ILO). It would appear, however, that since 1987 the OECD has been willing to accept each individual member country's definition of unemployment.

The fundamental measure of unemployment used by the Department of Employment changed at least six times from 1979. Since 1982, the figures have been based directly on the claimant count, i.e. the number of people claiming benefits at Unemployment Benefit Offices. The figures are derived

Table 4.7 *Unemployment rates in the United Kingdom (1979–92)*

Year	(%)
1979	4.0
1980	5.1
1981	8.1
1982	9.5
1983	10.5
1984	10.7
1985	10.9
1986	11.1
1987	10.0
1988	8.0
1989	6.4
1990	5.9
1991	8.7
1992	10.1

Source: *Employment Gazette*

almost entirely from computerized administrative records. They include those people who claim unemployment benefit, supplementary benefits and national insurance credits. They also include some of the severely disabled. However, the figures exclude students claiming benefit during a vacation but intending to return to full-time education when the new term begins, and the temporarily stopped. The latter are held to be people who had a job on the day of the monthly unemployment count (usually the second Thursday of each month) but were temporarily suspended from work on that day and were claiming benefits.

No matter which of the two tables is used, the figures clearly show the unemployment rates rising from 1979 to 1986. In fact, the United Kingdom suffered a deep recession in 1980–1. Unemployment increased to a recorded three million, and industrial production fell further and faster than even in the interwar years. The jump in unemployment in the 1980s was largely the result of a labour shake-out, particularly in the manufacturing sector.

Between 1979 and 1981, manufacturing output dropped by 14.2 per cent; between 1979 and 1982, 385,000 men in manufacturing jobs alone were made redundant. Total redundancies over the same period were well in excess of one million people. Every Friday evening, **Independent Television News** (ITN) broadcast a list of redundancies, with by far the worst of them in the manufacturing sector. In the first four years of the

1980s, some of the most famous names in British industry vanished, either being taken into liquidation or bought up by other companies: Dunlop, Thomas Tilling and Capper Neill, to name but three. The Coats Patons textile group shut down 21 plants in two years; ICI shed 40 per cent of its UK workforce – 41,000 people. Employment in manufacturing in 1979 was approximately eight million; in 1988 it had shrunk to five million.

Unemployment fell by one million from mid-1986 to the end of 1988, by when it was below the EC average and below the national rates in France, Italy, Belgium, the Netherlands, Spain and Ireland. Long-term unemployment decreased by some 450,000 in 1987 and 1988 to 900,000 at the beginning of 1989. Unemployment among workers under the age of twenty-five was then at its lowest level since 1983. Although tougher rules on eligibility to claim unemployment benefits and the expansion of the government's employment measures programmes (see pages 249–250) account for part of this fall, the rapid pace of GDP growth did have a significant impact on the jobs market.

In the 1990–2 recession, it was mainly jobs in the service industries that were being cut back sharply. While manufacturing industries continued to shed jobs, with the total number of workers in this sector below five million by March 1991, over one million positions in the service sector were lost. The South East and South West, with their preponderance of service-based industries, were particularly affected regions (see also page 215).

Ethnic minorities

One of the sectors of the population which was disproportionately affected by unemployment from 1979 to 1989 was that of the ethnic minorities. In the depths of the 1980–1 recession, the Labour Force Survey established that unemployment rates were much higher among non-whites than among whites. Though the high unemployment rates among minority groups were partly related to differences in age distributions, levels of qualifications and proportions of married women in the different ethnic groups, rates were in general significantly greater for non-whites than for whites with similar characteristics. For example, the unemployment rates among West Indian men and Asian women were especially high, at 20.6 per cent and 17.9 per cent respectively, with the corresponding rates among white men and women at 9.7 per cent and 8.7 per cent.

The Labour Force Surveys carried out between 1984 and 1986 found that some 4.6 per cent of the population of working age, or approximately 1.54 million people in Great Britain, were from ethnic groups. Each of the main ethnic groups had a distinctive pattern of involvement in the labour market, and particular ethnic groups tended to be clustered in certain regions, occupations and industries. Once again, in this later study, it was established that the unemployment rates for ethnic minorities were about double those for whites: 20 per cent, compared with 10 per cent, over the three-year period. It was also found that, from 1983 to 1986, as the economy emerged from the 1980–1 recession, unemployment rates reduced by about 0.5 per cent among whites and the rate for ethnic minorities in total was estimated to have reduced by approximately 1 per cent. In view of the higher unemployment rate among ethnic minorities, this fall represented a similar proportionate reduction for whites and ethnic minorities alike.

Combined data from the Labour Force Surveys of 1987 to 1989 show economic activity rates by ethnic origin. According to these studies, economic activity among males was highest in the white population (89 per cent), followed by the West Indian group (85 per cent) and the Indian group (84 per cent). Greater variation in activity rates is to be found among females. The average rate for all groups was 70 per cent, but this varied from only 21 per cent for the Pakistani group to 76 per cent for the West Indian group.

Job creation

Despite the high rates of unemployment which were present among certain sections of the United Kingdom's population during the 1980s, the country did enjoy outstanding success in creating new jobs. From 1983 to 1989, the number of people in employment rose by over two million, surpassing by far the achievements of any other European economy. Even in 1992, despite the recession, the United Kingdom had the second-highest economic activity rate of any country in the EC, after Denmark.

From 1979 to 1989, self-employed companies with five or fewer staff almost doubled to three million. Small businesses employing fewer than 200 persons increased by 60 per cent to 1.6 million. These firms employed a quarter of the workforce and produced a quarter of the nation's wealth. In 1988, new businesses were registering at a rate of over 100,000 per year. In the 1990–2 recession, however, the number of small business failures increased dramatically (see page 254).

But what sort of work was created in the good times? The trend was clearly towards greater employment in the services sector. From 1984 to 1988, employment increased in transport from 897,000 to 927,000; in hotels and catering from 995,000 to 1.6 million; and in banking, finance and insurance from 1.6 million to 2.5 million. Of the fifteen major employment categories, only four registered an employment loss between 1984 and 1988. These were agriculture, forestry and fishing; coal, oil and natural gas extraction; electricity, gas, other energy and water supply; and manufacturing.

Skills shortages

At the beginning of the 1980s, the recession in the United Kingdom was exacerbated because it coincided with the time when the number of young people reaching school-leaving age peaked at more than a million. At the end of the decade, skills shortages which emerged during a period of rapid economic growth since the mid-1980s were aggravated by a decline in the number of young people coming into the job market. By 1995, the proportion of 16 to 24-year-olds will have fallen by 20 per cent compared with 1987.

According to a report published by Hay Management Consultants in 1989, a shortage of graduates had already existed for some time. Most employers from the mid-1980s onwards were finding it increasingly difficult to attract sufficient graduates, and the problems would get worse. For the year 2000, there was a predicted demand for 20 per cent more graduates than in 1986; the supply of graduates would, however, be only 5 per cent greater.

Hardest hit of all in the 1980s and early 1990s were the electrical and electronics industries. Here there had been a shortfall of graduates since 1979, and most large companies had shopping lists for graduates which always exceeded the numbers available. Control and instrument engineers were in particular short supply, and competition for software engineers and computer scientists grew rapidly.

Sponsorship of students through their undergraduate, and sometimes postgraduate, courses was tried as a recruitment tool but produced mixed results. In 1991, one in three undergraduates studying electronics and mechanical engineering was sponsored by companies, but many of them did not join their sponsors once they had completed their studies. Some engineering companies attempted more devious techniques, offering to fund research projects and university chairs in return for introductions to students. Other firms located their research and development centres close to universities. Students were allowed to use company facilities, and the firms spotted the talent.

Faced with these problems, companies were looking increasingly towards Continental Europe to recruit young staff. Western Germany in particular was proving attractive to the United Kingdom's recruiters on account of the graduate surpluses to be found there (see page 35). But how these young Germans would settle in a business culture where engineering is still widely held to be a dirty profession is quite a different issue.

Business and trade unions

The business culture in the United Kingdom has changed radically in so far as it is affected by the relationship between business and the trade unions. The atmosphere of industrial relations in the 1970s was completely different from at the end of the 1980s and early 1990s. Then many employers walked in fear of militant trade-union leaders and intransigent shop stewards; by 1989 at the latest, management had regained the freedom to manage, and the will and incentive to do so.

After the 1978–9 'winter of discontent', newspapers and magazines throughout the world were far from complimentary about the state of relations between business and the trade unions. An Australian newspaper coined the phrase 'British disease' to depict industrial strife. *L'Espresso* even referred to the United Kingdom's trade unions as a 'sovereign power'. Concern about trade unions and their power was also widespread in the United Kingdom itself. In 1978, a **Market & Opinion Research International** (Mori) poll established that 82 per cent of Britons believed the trade unions were 'too powerful'. When asked the identical question in 1989, only 41 per cent of respondents were of the same opinion. In 1989, 58 per cent of Mori respondents thought that bad management was more to blame than the unions for the country's economic problems, while only 19 per cent held the unions to be more culpable.

The transformation in industrial relations in the United Kingdom was brought about by a series of government reforms, aided no doubt by the massive rise in unemployment during the 1980–1 recession. This sea-change encompassed a reduction in trade union power, a decline in trade union membership, fewer days lost through industrial disputes, and a spirit of 'new realism' among certain trade unions. In addition, the **Trades Union Congress** (TUC) has at last embraced the concept of Europeanization, which could lead to far-reaching changes in its relationship with the Labour Party.

Trade union reform

'When Margaret Thatcher declared she would curb the power of the union bosses, we academics scoffed', observed Dr Gavin Mackenzie, senior tutor at Jesus College, Cambridge, and lecturer in industrial relations, in an interview with *The Times* on 11 April 1989. 'If Churchill, at the height of his powers and popularity, could not curb the miners in 1942 . . . how could she?'

The Conservatives under Margaret Thatcher came into government in 1979 convinced that the balance of power between trade unions and employers, and trade unions and their own members, was weighted too heavily in favour of the unions. The restrictions subsequently introduced on the legal immunities of trade unions reflected a fundamental belief among the Conservatives that the long-established tradition of keeping the law out of industrial relations had actually been a contributory factor in the growth of disorder and confrontation.

The clue to the Conservatives' success in reforming the trade unions lies perhaps in the fact that they adopted a step-by-step approach to correcting these imbalances. One huge tranche of what would have been perceived as 'union-bashing legislation', such as was attempted in the early 1970s, might possibly have failed because the unions could have mustered all their opposition to a single piece of legislation. It might not even have been supported by the employers. The unions found it impossible to mobilize, demobilize and remobilize against a series of measures.

The 1980 Employment Act addressed the most obvious manifestations of excessive union power by making secondary picketing illegal.

The 1982 Employment Act narrowed further the scope of the trade unions to take secondary action and defined even more tightly the term 'trade dispute' within which unions can take industrial action without being sued for damages. The Act also reformed the legal liabilities of trade unions so that not only union officials but also the unions themselves can now be held responsible for any unlawful actions undertaken by their officials. Finally, the Act required all existing membership agreements to be confirmed or not by periodic ballots, thus attacking the 'closed shop'.

The 1984 Trade Union Act switched the accent of reform to the internal decision-making processes of the unions themselves. It demanded that elections to the official bodies be conducted through secret ballots and direct election by every member of the union. The Act also requires a union, before pronouncing an official stoppage, to ballot all its members who may be involved, in order to establish whether they wish to take strike action. If a union either fails to ballot its members or ignores the outcome of the ballot, a stoppage which may otherwise be legal loses its immunity from legal action.

The 1988 Employment Act was in many ways a response to experiences of union resistance to earlier legal controls. In particular, the Act enlarged upon the concept of an individual member's rights as a control mechanism over errant union leadership. It gives the trade union member the specific right to prevent his or her union from calling for industrial action without first holding a secret ballot and affords protection against union discipline if he or she decides to work during a strike or return to work before the strike has ended.

The 1990 Employment Act rendered unions legally liable for wildcat strikes called by shop stewards without a proper ballot. All remnants of legal protection for the closed shop are also eliminated. People cannot be refused a job simply because they do not belong to a union.

Although the welter of legislation is often dismissed by committed left-wingers as typical Tory anti-unionism, it is unlikely that a future Labour government would seek to repeal these laws. In 1989, Michael Meacher, former Labour Party employment spokesman, was quoted as saying: 'We will never return to the era of beer and sandwiches', when trade union leaders trooped to 10 Downing Street to give the government the benefit of their opinions, not only on industrial relations but on policy in general.

Trade union membership

One yardstick of the changing influence of trade unions is represented by the level of union membership. Between 1969 and 1979, membership increased by almost 28 per cent to 13.2 million or approximately 53 per cent of the employed labour force. However, from 1979 to 1990, membership of the unions affiliated to the TUC fell by four million members. Although union membership thus measured, at some 8.15 million, still accounted for about 38 per cent of the workforce in employment, the trend since 1979 has been one of unbroken decline.

The reasons for the reduction in membership can be ascribed to: a rise in unemployment during the 1980-1 recession, especially in the sectors of employment where trade union membership was traditionally concentrated, such as manufacturing and public-sector industries; more efficient use of labour by companies throughout the 1980s and early 1990s; and increased use of microchip technology.

Almost all the trade unions lost members during the period from 1979 to 1990. The massive **Transport and General Workers Union** (TGWU), with membership in almost every industry, lost over one-third. The membership of the **National Union of Mineworkers** (NUM) contracted sharply as a result of pit closures and the formation of the breakaway **Union of Democratic Mineworkers** (UDM) following the coal strike 1984–5. Between 1979 and 1987 alone, the NUM forfeited over 43 per cent of its membership. Even the white-collar unions, the **Association of Scientific, Technical and Managerial Staffs** (ASTMS) and the **Association of Professional and Executive Officers** (APEX), sustained heavy losses. By contrast, membership of the **Royal College of Nursing** (RCN) rose by 96,000, an increase of 59 per cent, possibly as a result of its no-strike pledges.

The overall fall in trade union membership has, surprisingly, contributed little to any acceleration in the reduction of the total numbers of unions. Ever since the mid-1960s, when there were 622 different unions, numbers have been declining at the rate of approximately 20 per cent every ten years. In the 1980s, smaller unions appeared to be willing to merge with larger ones for reasons of survival, and larger unions with smaller ones for purposes of diversification. Thus, in 1988, ASTMS and the **Technical Administration Supervisory Section** (TASS) merged to form **Manufacturing, Science and Finance** (MSF) which, with 650,000 members, now forms the fifth-biggest union in the United Kingdom and the largest white-collar union in Europe.

Many unions are still relatively small. In 1986, over half the unions numbered fewer than 1000 members, but these accounted for only 0.4 per cent of total union membership. By contrast, over 80 per cent of union membership was concentrated in just 24 unions with over 100,000 members each. In 1990, the number of trade unions totalled 339. The number affiliated to the TUC dropped from 112 in 1979 to 74 in 1990, mainly as a result of mergers. But this still leaves most large manufacturing plants organized in several, sometimes competing unions. While this situation remains, the danger of demarcation disputes will persist. In fact, the much-discussed model of one union per industry, along the lines of the system developed in western Germany (see pages 37), sometimes seems farther from realization than ever.

Industrial disputes

During the 1970s, an average 13 million working days per year were lost through industrial disputes, with 2631 official stoppages a year. The picture was very different in the 1980s, when there were on average 1129 stoppages per annum. In 1990, the number of official strikes fell to 611. More significantly, the number of days lost through industrial action decreased from over 29 million in 1979, leading up to the 'winter of discontent', to 1.9 million in 1990. In 1991, the record was even better, with 759,000 days lost to industrial disputes, the smallest annual total since records began in 1891 (Table 4.8).

The number of days lost in a particular year is greatly influenced by a few large disputes. In the 1984 figures, approximately 22.5 million days lost out of the grand total of 27.1 million are accounted for by the coal strike. However, the days lost due to smaller stoppages, which form the vast majority of all disputes, dropped dramatically from 7.1 million working days per annum in the 1970s, to 2.8 million in the 1980s. Nonetheless, these figures are still higher than for western Germany, France, Japan or the United States. Moreover, there has been no perceptible improvement in absenteeism. On every working day in 1990, the most recent date on which absenteeism was monitored, 11 per cent of workers were not present at their place of work for one reason or another.

Table 4.8 *Working days in the United Kingdom lost through disputes (1979–91)*

Year	Days lost
1979	29,474,000
1980	11,964,000
1981	4,266,000
1982	5,313,000
1983	3,574,000
1984	27,135,000
1985	6,402,000
1986	1,920,000
1987	3,546,000
1988	3,702,000
1989	4,068,000
1990	1,903,000
1991	759,000

Source: *Employment Gazette*

New realism

In the early 1990s, the trade union movement appeared to be divided between so-called traditionalist, left-of-centre unions, and realist, right-of-centre unions, with the TUC caught in the middle trying to arbitrate between the two factions. Ironically enough, neither the effects of two recessions nor the new legislation, nor even declining memberships, were directly responsible for the split. The movement parted company over the issue of single-union agreements.

These agreements were pioneered by the **Electrical Electronic Telecommunications and Plumbing Union** (EEPTU) in the printing industry and at new Japanese electronics plants. The EETPU's example was followed by the **Amalgamated Engineering Union** (AEU) which, by 1989, had concluded approximately forty single-union deals of which half were with Japanese companies. The bulk of these agreements contain provisions which make strikes improbable, such as binding arbitration. Contrary to popular opinion, the agreements do not render strikes impossible: they merely incorporate substantial anti-strike measures. They cannot, therefore, be classified or dismissed as no-strike agreements.

To date it has not proved possible for the TUC to countenance single-union agreements because, as the umbrella organization for 74 different unions, it cannot give its blessing to a development which advantages one faction and directly disadvantages another. As a result, the EETPU and its 387,000 members were expelled from the TUC in 1988.

By 1992, the AEU and the EEPTU had approved plans for a merger, possibly rendering feasible an historic reconciliation with the TUC. The new, one-million-strong **Amalgamated Engineering and Electrical Union** (AEEU) would also push single-union bargaining further up the industrial agenda. Moreover, Bill Jordan, president elect of the new union, has promised to 'change the face of British trade unionism and forge a new kind of partnership with employers'.

Yet new realism does not begin and end with the promotion of single-union agreements. Nor does it necessarily embrace those unions which have indulged in new-look logos, promotional videos, credit cards, cheap mortgages and cut-price insurance for their members. New realism implies a willingness to accept the new democratic processes which have been forced on the trade unions in the 1980s and early 1990s. Above all, the term signifies an acceptance on the part of the union that it sees nothing wrong in being associated with a profitable company. This is where the AEU and the EETPU stand out from the rest because they actually run training courses for some of their companies. 'Engineers 2000', 'Skills Centres' and 'TAPS' are evidence of the AEU's commitment not only to raising the skill level of its members but also to contributing to firms' profitability.

The way ahead

Gavin H. Laird, general secretary of the AEU at the time, wrote in *The European Business Journal* in February 1989: 'One of the few positive outcomes of the 1988 Trades Union Congress at Bournemouth was the long-overdue embrace of Europe. Trade unionists across a wide variety of unions saw in 1992 and the Presidency of Jacques Delors new opportunities opening up for a productive, cooperative and fair future.'

Shortly before the Bournemouth Congress, the TUC had published a document on the impact of 1992 and the EC's single market. Behind the report lay the conviction that the TUC had virtually no role to play as a lobbying force for legislative change under a right-of-centre Conservative government. Since, however, much of future employment law to affect the United Kingdom's trade unions will be formulated in Brussels, and not in Westminster, it follows that the unions must direct their lobbying powers towards the EC if they are to achieve success.

The TUC commitment to European trade unionism was endorsed at the Blackpool Congress in 1989. The strategy adopted there was to undermine the Conservative government by taking advantage of the increased Socialist Group presence in the European Parliament, in the wake of the

1989 European elections, to ensure that the EC's single market would resemble much closer the 'social dimension' format of Jacques Delors than the free-market model preferred by United Kingdom government. In marked contrast with much of the Conservative legislation, workers would have a right under the Community Charter of Fundamental Social Rights to: a minimum wage; vocational training throughout their working life; information, consultation and participation in their companies; cover from collective agreements; and protection under social legislation.

Though the TUC strategy received a definite setback at the EC's Maastricht summit in late 1991, when alone of the twelve member states, the United Kingdom 'opted out' of the Social Chapter of the Political Union Treaty, the basic thrust of TUC tactics remains as before. In 1989, the TUC voted to establish an office in Brussels, and Norman Willis, general secretary of the TUC, subsequently became general secretary of the European TUC.

But where does such a switch in the focus of lobbying leave the relationship between the United Kingdom's trade unions and the Labour Party? The Labour Party was born out of the trade unions who, with their huge assets, an annual income of tens of millions, vast investments and very large pension funds, still act as paymasters and underwriters of the Labour Party. For this the unions exact a price which is paid annually at each Labour Party Conference, where the trade unions command over 89 per cent of the vote while the constituency representatives share less than 10 per cent. The TGWU alone, for whom Neil Kinnock, the former leader of the Labour Party, is a sponsored Member of Parliament, has one-fifth of the total union block vote at its disposal.

The trade unions will continue their financial support for the Labour Party just as business supports the Conservative Party. Otherwise, the TUC no longer conducts itself like an alternative government and has concentrated on basic issues such as the modernization of the services it offers to members rather than party politics. Although the TUC may well move to a new arm's-length relationship with the Labour Party, there is little likelihood that the unions will revert to their former roles as 'friendly societies' – an idea which has been canvassed in certain quarters of the Labour Party and the press. The days of mass unionism may be numbered but the trade unions are still far too important a force in the land to be confined to running the social security system.

Business, education, training and development

The business culture in the United Kingdom has suffered, to judge from the reports, for over a century and a half from its lack of commitment to the training and development of the country's workforce. As early as 1835,

Richard Cobden stressed the need to remodel the system to match the quality of the Americans. The Royal Commission on Technical Instruction of 1884 drew unfavourable comparisons between Britain and conditions in Germany, France, Italy, the Netherlands, Switzerland and Austria.

In more recent times, business has played a vital role in alerting government to the shortcomings of the United Kingdom's education system. Moreover, complaints that school-leavers were arriving on the factory floor unable to read or write, perform simple arithmetic or express themselves clearly, have finally been heeded. The **1988 Education Reform Act**, fresh initiatives by the Department of Employment, and a heightened awareness among companies of the need to develop their managers mark the beginning of the end, it is hoped, of a long period of comparative neglect of education, training and development for business in the United Kingdom.

Education

Towards the end of the 1980s, a broad consensus emerged that the country's education system bore part of the responsibility for the relatively weak performance of the economy in the post-war period. This resulted in demands for both changes in its structure and an overhaul of its funding process.

The focus of most critical commentaries had been on the low levels of numeracy and literacy of United Kingdom workers compared with those of competitor countries and the low percentage of sixteen to eighteen-year-olds continuing in full-time education. The *Financial Times* of 5 December 1988, pointed out that the average Japanese thirteen-year-old is more adept at mathematics than a British fifteen-year-old. Moreover, in western Germany approximately 30 per cent of age group leave school at sixteen with a certificate for which they are examined in ten subjects embracing compulsory German, a foreign language and mathematics; a comparable level is reached by only 12 per cent of English youngsters leaving school. Over 95 per cent of young people in Japan are in full-time education to the age of eighteen, compared with 32 per cent in England. About 48 per cent of North American and 38 per cent of Japanese eighteen-year-olds enter higher education. A mere 15 per cent of British youngsters continue into tertiary studies.

Although there has been a gradual improvement over the past ten years, it was revealed by **NOW Research** in 1992 that only half of British sixteen-year-olds stay on in full-time or part-time education or training, against 79 per cent in France, 82 per cent in western Germany and 89 per cent in Japan and the United States.

As a consequence, the government targeted improved education as a main priority but relied on policy measures to achieve this end rather than major increases in levels of funding. In 1988, it presented the **Education Reform Act.**, which contained radical reforms for state education. A new national curriculum was adopted throughout England and Wales, designed to provide all pupils with a thorough knowledge of the core subjects, English, science and mathematics. Children's progress through the core subjects is checked by means of tests at the ages of seven, eleven, fourteen and sixteen years. Moreover, the success rate of individual schools in these tests is published. This latter stipulation is aimed at providing parents with more information about the attainment levels of schools within their area so that they are able to choose the best school for their children. In addition, some of the control over schools was taken away from the local authorities which fund them, and given over to governors and head teachers. If a simple majority of parents voting in a secret ballot so wish, a school can opt out altogether of local authority control and take on the status of an independent charitable trust receiving a direct grant from the government. By 1 May 1992, 244 schools in England and Wales had elected for independent, grant-maintained status.

None of the provisions of the Education Reform Act, however, addresses one of the central weaknesses of the system: high-quality education of the type which will be needed to meet the future demands of business is dependent on high-quality teachers. From 1983 to 1987, teachers in the United Kingdom were engaged in a dispute over pay and conditions. It was terminated by a settlement imposed by Act of Parliament which deprived teachers of their pay negotiating rights and laid down a detailed set of contractual terms. In the early 1990s, teachers' pay was modest, their motivation low, and their morale poor. Small wonder there was a severe shortage of teachers in mathematics and science – both core subjects in the national curriculum!

In April 1992, John Patten was appointed secretary of state for education in John Major's new government. His main task will be to ensure that the provisions of the 1988 Act are fully implemented. Vital decisions are still outstanding on the level of sophistication of the promised league tables, schools inspection, and selective schooling. Perhaps, however, his overriding priority should be restoration of teacher morale. Otherwise, a disaffected profession, one which has even gone so far as to form 'escape committees' to assist colleagues to leave teaching, will fail to deliver the reforms on which so many hopes are pinned.

Training

Britain languishes close to the bottom of the international training league although it was estimated that in 1986–7 employers spent some £18 billion per annum on training. Approximately £13.5 billion went on trainees' wages and other labour costs; only £4.7 billion on training materials. Over the same period, the government spent an additional £3 billion, mostly on young people and the unemployed. Yet despite expenditure on this scale, in the period from 1986–7, half of all employees received no training and a third of employees claimed that they had never received any training. A third of companies had no training budget; a fifth of companies provided no training; a further fifth did not evaluate the training they had done.

As was pointed out earlier (see page 46), every year in western Germany approximately 550,000 youngsters start on apprentice training courses which lead to a commercial qualification. Western Germany trains two to three times more qualified building craftsmen, fitters and electricians than Britain and about five times more clerical staff. Similarly, France produces two to three times as many qualified mechanics and electricians as the British, and this is done through vocational schools.

Britain, however, relied for many years on the **Youth Training Scheme** (YTS). Introduced in 1983, over two million young people had been trained in YTS by the end of 1988, over one million since it became a two-year programme in April 1986. In September 1988, there were some 435,500 youngsters in training on YTS – the largest number that Britain had ever seen. Of these trainees, it emerged in August 1989, 26 per cent had numeracy problems and 17 per cent literacy problems ranging from complete illiteracy to relatively minor shortcomings like a persistent inability to spell.

The education service contributed to YTS, with over 40 per cent of trainees attending college as part of their programmes, and the numbers of trainees securing recognized qualification – some 44 per cent of those completing YTS in 1989–90 – rose each year. However, the majority of the young people gaining a vocational qualification attained only the most basic available. 88 per cent of young people leaving YTS went into jobs in 1990 or embarked on further education or training.

With effect from April 1988, every organization applying to participate in YTS had been obliged to secure Approved Training Organisation status. Ten criteria had to be satisfied covering such matters as the training of supervisors, programme design, equal opportunities, health and safety standards. By 1989, over 3000 organizations had achieved the appropriate status, and there was sufficient youth training available for all sixteen and seventeen-year-old school-leavers seeking it.

Since May 1990, YTS has been replaced by a more flexible training package, **Youth Training** (YT), which is administered at local level by **Training** *and* **Enterprise Councils** (TECs) in England and Wales and by the **Local Enterprise Companies** (LECs) in Scotland (see below).

Training for the adult unemployed no longer takes place under the **Job Training Scheme** (JTS). This was replaced in mid-1988 by **Employment**

Training (ET), which succeeded in attracting over 200,000 participants within the first year of its existence. Claimed to be the largest and most ambitious training programme for unemployed people in the world, ET supplies up to twelve months' training. It offers training in the workplace and is available nationwide through over 1000 training managers, with 170 training agents advising potential participants.

Despite the welcome modifications to existing training programmes, the most far-reaching proposals for overcoming Britain's skills deficit were published in *Employment for the 1990s*, a White Paper by the Department of Employment. Here a new framework for training was foreseen at three different levels: the national level, the industry level and the local level. At national level, the main task was seen as developing policies for promoting training through the Training Agency within the Department of Employment. At industry level, the task identified was to set standards and monitor the quality of training provided by employers. At local level, the centrepiece of the new proposals, attention focused on operating the government's training programmes for unemployed people and ensuring that employers' own training endeavours are of the scale and quality required for the local labour market.

Employers have been given a leading role in setting local priorities and deciding how government finance for training should be spent. They do this through employer-led TECs and LECs. Employers in the private sector are in the majority on the governing bodies, occupying at least two-thirds of the seats there. Others on the TECs and LECs are senior figures from local education and the trade unions which support the aims of the Councils or Companies. By no means all trade unions are, however, in favour of cooperation.

By 1991, a network of 82 TECs was in place in England and Wales, and there were 22 LECs in Scotland. The responsibility for delivering the training funded by the tax-payer – £1.7 billion in 1991–2 – had passed to these bodies. Among others, 1200 high-calibre business leaders were playing a leading role in the TECs and LECs.

Employers were also making a significant contribution to designing standards of occupational competence to form the basis of the new **National Vocational Qualifications** (NVQs). Here the National Council for Vocational Qualifications aimed to offer a uniform system of training and awards for 80 per cent of the workforce by the end of 1992.

The government believes that it has placed the ownership of the training and enterprise system where it belongs – with the employers. Improved training should be used, however, not merely to depress the unemployment figures in a locality or to provide workers to fill the vacancies on the job market. It should, ideally, help to move the economy away from the current low-skill level towards a high-skill equilibrium, with companies turning out higher-value-added products to which workers can contribute because they have been appropriately trained.

Development

Past neglect of a thorough educational, training and development ethos in the United Kingdom is evident at all levels in British companies, including management. In 1987, two major studies, the Handy report and the Constable/McCormick report, were published. The first investigated managers' education, training and development in western Germany, France, Japan and the United States, the second British managers'. The reports concluded that approximately 85 per cent of top managers in Japan and the United States, and 62 per cent in western Germany and France, have university degrees (see page 46). Approximately 25 per cent of British top managers were found in a 1985 survey to possess degrees. Similarly, more than 40 per cent of the largest American companies and most big firms in western Germany and Japan provide every manager with at least five days' training, or management development, off-the-job every year. In Britain, the average manager receives just one day's development per annum. However sharp or ambitious they may be, managers who are neither appropriately educated nor developed are unlikely to perform as effectively as their counterparts in competitor countries.

The Handy report recommended that a group of top companies should develop a Charter of good practice and that these companies should form a Charter Group which would set standards for management development and act as its advocate vis-à-vis government and other interested parties. It was suggested that the Charter might comprise such items as: a corporate development plan; a commitment to five days' minimum off-the-job development per annum for every manager; a personal development plan for every manager; reimbursement of tuition fees for approved self-education; foreign language instruction as a routine requirement; and much more.

The **Management Charter Initiative** (MCI) was duly established, and by the end of 1991 over 800 leading companies had pledged their support, in addition to twenty government departments. Unfortunately, some of the impetus from the Handy and Constable/McCormick reports was lost when a misguided attempt was made to introduce the concept of the Chartered Manager. Such had not been recommended in either of the reports because there was no desire to create a 'closed shop for managers' which might have discouraged the entrepreneur from entrepreneuring or the natural manager from managing.

Despite the increased willingness of more companies to train and develop their staff at all levels, one main difficulty remains. Company investment in training and development is risky because staff can change jobs and move to another firm which has perhaps not taken the trouble to train. Of the 51,000 new jobs created in the City of London between 1984 and 1987, 31,000 were filled by poaching from industry and the public sector. In a job-hopping business culture such as that which obtains in the United Kingdom, this means that many companies are still reluctant to provide the right amount of training and development. Not until the vast majority of companies, large, medium-sized and small, subscribe fully to the training ethos will their employees, and with them the companies themselves, benefit from the enhanced levels of skills which will secure both employment and profits in the 1990s and beyond.

Business and enterprise

Ever since the publication of the Bolton report on small firms in 1971, various governments in the United Kingdom have attempted to promote the start-ups of new companies and to encourage the growth of small businesses. But not until the return to power of the Conservatives in 1979 did the term 'enterprise culture' enter popular parlance and begin to exert an influence on the wider business culture in the country. Yet 'enterprise culture' embraces much more than the promotion of small firms: it entails a diminution of the role of the state, which since 1979 has mainly taken the form of privatizations; it involves allowing managers to manage, through reform of the trade unions; it also implies giving greater economic responsibility to the individual through improving incentives to enterprise and efficient working. Though 'enterprise culture' became a slightly tarnished concept during the 1990–2 recession, sufficient vestiges of its former glory still remain to justify its continued existence as an integral part of the overall business culture.

Small firms

From 1979 to 1989, self-employed companies in the United Kingdom with five or fewer staff practically doubled in number to approximately three million. Some of these small companies were helped by government aid packages which, by 1988, had become so numerous and complex that a decision was taken to simplify the sixty-four existing schemes and to place them under the aegis of the Department of Trade and Industry.

As Professor Paul Burns et al. point out in a Cranfield School of Management working paper entitled *Small Business in the United Kingdom*, the schemes introduced since 1979 had addressed four main problem areas for small businesses. First, the financing of new and small firms was facilitated by the Loan Guarantee Scheme, while the Business Expansion Scheme increased the attraction for tax-payers to invest in small companies. Second, the activities of the Small Firms Service were expanded to provide a greater degree of inexpensive, or even free business information. Third, small companies were exempted from certain constraints placed upon them by employment legislation. Fourth, corporate rates of taxation were cut substantially (see page 209).

The **Enterprise Initiative**, embracing much of the substance of the former schemes, was duly launched, in January 1988, by the Department of Trade and Industry. The broad objective was to encourage companies to use their own initiative by spotting business opportunities and seizing them. To this end, it was planned to allocate some £250 million to the Enterprise Initiative by 1991. The money was available to independent businesses in most sectors of the economy employing fewer than 500 people. Grants were forthcoming to subsidize business development consultancy in the fields of design, marketing, quality assurance, manufacturing, export, business planning, financial information systems, research and technology.

By the end of 1988, response to the Enterprise Initiative had exceeded expectations. Moreover, 95 per cent of companies taking part in the scheme reported satisfaction with the aid and advice received. However, even with maximum take-up by 1991, the Enterprise Initiative had reached only 45,000 of the estimated 1,250,000 companies eligible throughout the country.

Enterprise in the form of the establishment of new companies continued to flourish up to the late 1980s: it was calculated in 1989 that business start-ups were well in excess of 100,000 per annum. As Professor Sue Birley of Cranfield School of Management, and Liz Watson, commented in their report on *Successful British Entrepreneurs*: 'It is clear that enterprise has now firmly re-visited the United Kingdom, that starting your own business is a respected and accepted lifestyle more than ever in recent history.'

Nonetheless, many new businesses quickly fail. Analysis of Value Added Tax (VAT) registrations and deregistrations reveals that approximately one-third of new businesses run into serious trouble in the first three years of their existence, and nearly half close by their fifth year. In a survey conducted in September 1989 by the Small Business Research Trust, it was established that certain facets of the country's business culture conspire against small companies. 27 per cent of the directors questioned in the survey had been involved in a business which failed. Half the directors identified management shortcomings as the reason for the close-down, while 37 per cent placed the blame on a shortage of capital. Banks were criticized for their high charges and for demanding excessive security before lending to small firms. 20 per cent of directors found fault with accountants for being too slow and costing too much. Solicitors were sub-jected to reprimands of a similar nature.

High interest rates were foremost among the worries of small companies. 75 per cent of the respondents in the same survey complained that such interest rates had also made some of their customers slower in paying their bills. Among the slowest payers were the United Kingdom's largest com-panies, while only 37 per cent of respondents criticized small firms and the public sector for delays in payment. However, 52 per cent confessed to having experienced trouble with the Post Office, and 33 per cent levelled accusations of poor customer service against British Telecom.

In the 1990–2 recession, collapsing new companies were joined by more established ones. In August 1991, it was reported that one firm in 50 had gone into liquidation; in October 1991, that 130 businesses were disappear-ing every day; in December 1991, that business failures had increased to 200 per day; and in March 1992, that the number had reached a record of 240 a day.

Once again, banks and slow payers came in for particularly severe criti-cism. Banks were accused of having a 'sterile and unimaginative' relation-ship, particularly with small firms. It was alleged that their charges were high, and interest rates at least 2 per cent above base rate. While the gov-ernment refrained from taking any action against the banks and relied upon them to publish, then adhere to, their codes of banking practice, Norman Lamont insisted in his 1992 budget that companies reveal in their annual reports the amount of time they take to settle debts. He also hinted that unless companies were prepared to pay their suppliers and subcon-tractors within thirty days they would find it difficult to secure govern-ment orders. Hitherto, some companies had been taking up to ninety days before settling.

Management buyouts

Enterprise does not exhaust itself in the establishment and running of new small firms. A willingness to seize opportunities and take risks is also evi-denced by **management buyouts** (MBOs). Here a manager or team of man-agers purchase the company or the part of the company for which they are actually working in the conviction that they can run the operation more efficiently than existing management.

Although there is nothing intrinsically novel about MBOs, what is new is the large increase in the number and scale of MBOs in the United Kingdom in the 1980s and early 1990s. As Tom Nash, Assistant Editor of *Director*, pointed out in the February 1989 issue of the journal, the first evidence of increased MBO activity in the country emerged in the late 1970s when the leveraged buyout originally became a legal tool for purchasing a business. This activity gained further momentum in the 1980–1 recession when subsidiaries of some of the United Kingdom's older companies not essential to the core business were bought out by their managements.

MBOs in the United Kingdom became a growing aspect of the business culture throughout the 1980s when the market for such developed into the second largest in the world after the United States of America. The number and size of transactions increased from 205 buyouts with a total value of £315 million in 1983 to 335, accounting for £3250 million, in 1987. Included in the 1987 total is the largest European transaction of this nature to date, the Charterhouse-led buyout of MFI from ASDA MFI plc, which cost £718 million. The average value of individual buyouts also increased over the 1983–7 period from £1,540,000 to £9,700,000. Buyout activity continued to grow in 1988, when there were approximately 350 transactions with an estimated value of £3800 million. It peaked, in terms of value, in 1989, with 374 deals worth £3902 million; and in 1990, in terms of sheer numbers, with 485 deals worth £2526 million. MBOs fell in both number and value in 1991, as a result of the recession, with 444 transactions recorded to the value of £2133 million.

There is every sign that the United Kingdom buyout experience is following that in the United States, with the number and size of the transactions both tending to increase. American trends are also being emulated in terms of the relationship between financial institutions and management. As Norman Murray observed in the December 1988, issue of *The Accountant's Magazine*, a variation on the buyout, namely the **management buyin** (MBI), is being practised. Here underperforming companies are identified by the institutions. External management teams are then put together and financially supported by the institutions in order to undertake a turnaround.

Buyouts in the United Kingdom have also provided an alternative to flotation on the stock exchange for the privatization of parts of the public sector. Two notable examples are the National Freight Consortium, where not only incumbent managers but also employees purchased the company for which they worked, and the break-up of the National Bus Company. The National Freight Consortium was subsequently floated on the stock exchange, with considerable financial gains accruing for managers and employees alike.

Further incentives to enterprise

The large salaries paid to the chief executives of the country's top companies could be regarded as incentives to enterprise, as indeed could the pay of most managers. Unfortunately, many of the salaries paid to company officials in either group are not performance-related, although bonuses as a percentage of salary are on the increase (Table 4.9).

Table 4.9 *The top ten earners (basic salaries 1991)*

	Name	Company	Pay (£)
1	P. Girolami	Glaxo	900,000
2	R. Bauman	SmithKline Beecham	725,400
3	A. Sheppard	Grand Metropolitan	700,000
4	C. Stein	Ladbroke	567,000
5	N. Shaw	Tate & Lyle	555,771
6	P. Sheehy	BAT	529,335
7	A. Tennant	Guinness	510,000
8	B. Corby	Prudential	480,000
9	R. Horton	British Petroleum	441,000
10	D. Henderson	ICI	440,000

Source: Incomes Data Services

Between 1980 and 1990, the average pay of the United Kingdom's executives rose by 281 per cent, from 11 times the pay of a skilled manual worker to 24 times. Moreover, financial rewards of this order of magnitude are almost guaranteed to arouse angry comment. Whenever such lists are published, trade union leaders openly question the need for their members to accept wage restraint since chief executives are rewarded so generously. Conservative politicians, who are not paid anything like so well, have also gone on record as objecting to what look like inflated salaries. In May 1992, even the Archbishop of Canterbury, Dr George Carey, rebuked businessmen who reward themselves large pay increases, especially during a recession.

Nevertheless, the vast majority of the country's executives are still worse off than their counterparts in other European countries. At the end of August 1989, the **European Remuneration Network** (ERN) issued its first report on the pay of some 30,000 managers in France, Switzerland, Italy, western Germany, the Netherlands, United Kingdom, Belgium and Ireland. The report compared the pay of three kinds of manager – managing directors, heads of finance and of production – in companies with no more than 100 employees, and in those with between 250 and 1000. It also took into consideration such factors as personal taxation and cost-of-living indices.

Provided they are subject to broad interpretation, the results offer a rough guide to European differences in the going rates for various managers. After tax and cost-of-living considerations, the United Kingdom's managing directors, aged 45 and employed by manufacturing companies turning over £75 million, were £15,000 per annum worse off than if they had been working in Switzerland, and £9000 down on their western German counterparts. Finance directors in the United Kingdom subject to the same conditions would have been £7500 a year better off working in Italy and almost £3000 richer in France.

Such comparisons on a European scale are also useful because they provide an insight into the remuneration priorities of companies in different countries. Broadly speaking, Italy, France, Switzerland and western Germany all pay their heads of finance less than their heads of production, while in the United Kingdom this is not the case. Similarly, western Germany even pays its research and development director more than its finance directors. In the United Kingdom, the emphasis is reversed. The differences in remuneration priorities act as valuable indicators of the business orientations of companies in the various business cultures.

The response of business to the EC's single market

Business in the United Kingdom, in response to the EC's single market, appears to have taken its cue from the politicians: reaction to date has been hesitant and lacking commitment. Although Europe was responsible for some 50 per cent of the country's exports and even 53 per cent of imports in 1988, a survey in the same year by Ernst & Whinney (subsequently Ernst & Young) found that fewer than 40 per cent of company board directors were aware of plans to create a single market in the EC. In addition, only 30 per cent of British directors at board level stated that their companies had a strategic plan for 1993. Moreover, the vast majority of firms with a strategy were large companies which already had business interests in Continental Europe. The government's own publicity campaign for 1993 was launched on 18 March 1988, with the mailing of an information pack to 125,000 companies.

If business in the United Kingdom has been slow to take up the challenge of Europe, then much of the blame must attach to the attitude of the Conservatives since 1979, and that of Margaret Thatcher in particular. She set the tone at her first EC summit in Dublin by repeatedly demanding, 'I want my money back'; in her first speech on the EC as prime minister in 1979, she emphasized its tendency to 'dwindle its bureaucracy'; in her Bruges speech in 1988, she castigated the European Commission for its plans on economic and monetary union, and the Delors social charter; she also allowed the Conservative party to go into the 1989 elections to the

European Parliament with such xenophobic slogans as 'Stay home on 15 June and you'll live on a diet of Brussels' (and paid the price with the Conservatives polling 6.7 per cent fewer votes than in the 1984 elections as well as forfeiting 13 seats). Finally, she lost her Chancellor of the Exchequer in October 1989, because Nigel Lawson favoured the United Kingdom's full membership of EMS, and she and her advisers did not.

The tone changed perceptibly with John Major's premiership and his insistence that he wished to see the United Kingdom 'at the heart of Europe'. Even the Queen addressed the European Parliament in May 1992, her first visit to a major EC institution in nineteen years of United Kingdom membership of the EC. But the failure of John Major's new government to embrace the Maastricht Treaty wholeheartedly, and its insistence on widening rather than deepening the EC, have served to sustain the mood of anti-Europeanism in the country.

Yet all this high-profile Euro-hostility disguises a deeper commitment to Europe at a different level. In Brussels, the United Kingdom has one of the best reputations of any country for implementing EC directives on time and to the letter. Similarly, the United Kingdom was one of the first in the EC to lift controls on capital entering or leaving the country. In addition, the United Kingdom's road haulage rules are more liberal than all but those in the Netherlands, while the openness of the country's insurance market to outside competitors is rivalled, once again, only by the Netherlands.

Strengths

Indeed, one of the United Kingdom's major strengths lies in its tradition of open trading, which attracts investment from companies outside Europe anxious to gain a foot-hold within the EC. The United States of America and, more recently, Japan and Germany have all taken full advantage of the country's open markets and established considerable business interests. In 1991, the United Kingdom continued to be the target for the largest foreign investment in Europe by non-EC buyers.

A second major strength can be adduced from the fact that, despite two recessions, the United Kingdom's companies have gradually become more competitive during the 1980s and early 1990s as a result of a decade of a free-enterprise climate. Moreover, in 1991 the United Kingdom featured more companies than any other European country in the top 100 in Europe when measured by market capitalization. Of the largest 100 European companies, according to *The FT European Top 500*, 39 were British, 16 French and 14 German. If the first ten companies had been ranked by profits, British or part-British companies would have occupied six of the first seven places.

A third area of strength has already been noted – that of financial services. London's reputation as an international banking centre is pre-eminent in Europe, with over 400 overseas banks operating there at the end of 1991. Moreover, the City's financial markets exceed in size any others in the EC by a long way. Yet British financial institutions were reluctant to forge cross-border collaborations in the run-up to 1992, while Continental European banks indulged in a veritable frenzy of alliances. By March 1992, NatWest had 260 branches throughout Spain; the Royal Bank of Scotland possessed a cross-shareholding with Banco Santander of Spain; and Hambros had also joined several European alliances; but most British institutions had still to make any significant moves across the Channel.

A fourth strength is to be located in the United Kingdom's retailing and distribution companies. The system which has been developed in the country is probably the most efficient in Europe, and British retailers featured in 1992 among the largest in Europe by any measure. Marks & Spencer had 18 stores in France, Spain and the Netherlands, and together with Sainsburys, Tesco and Gateway (pre-reconstruction) ranked in the top six retailers by sales, although Carrefour of France was the largest in this sector.

Weaknesses

It is significant that many more British companies would have appeared in the top 100 companies in Europe if the rankings had been ordered according to profits rather than market capitalization. While the profit-making orientations of the United Kingdom's companies may be regarded as a strength in the short-term, they are responsible at the same time for harmful longer-term weaknesses.

Thus a major weakness of the United Kingdom's economy is to be located in the erosion of the manufacturing base since 1979, due in part to lack of long-term investment in capital equipment and R & D. Even working at near full capacity, manufacturing was incapable, by the end of 1989, of supplying domestic demand by the equivalent of 4 per cent of GDP. Although General Electric took position 40 in the league table of Europe's largest companies as measured by market capitalization, the rest of the United Kingdom's engineering and electrical firms were sadly under-represented.

Similarly, the lack of investment in human capital over the longer term has contributed to a further acknowledged British weakness in response to the single market. Public companies have been too preoccupied with the profit expectations of City analysts to devote enough of their capital and cash flow to the education of their workforces. As a result, the economy as a whole still suffers from a low-level skill equilibrium, and certain future-oriented sectors such as electronics are virtually incapable of expansion on account of skills shortages.

Although the services sector of the country's economy as a whole must be regarded as one of its outstanding strengths, one area in this sector which was giving cause for concern in the early 1990s was that of mail order. With the advent of the single market, home shopping was highlighted as the retail area most easily translated across borders. A Verdict Research survey in 1989 reported: 'The ability for the customer to choose products from all over Europe and for a company to deliver them without cross-border documentation present a major opportunity.' But La Redoute of France held 26 per cent of the British company Empire Stores, and Gecos, the Italian group, had taken its stake in Empire to above 24 per cent. Otto Versand of western Germany, and the largest mail order group in the world, had a 5 per cent stake in Fine Art Development, a small British company.

Opportunities

While the United Kingdom has constantly been the largest target for direct foreign investment in Europe by non-EC countries, British companies since 1980 invested substantially more abroad than foreign companies in the United Kingdom (£73.5 billion compared with £29.6 billion to the end of 1987). However, the focus of much of direct British foreign investment during this time was not the EC but the United States of America, with 65 per cent of such investment in 1987 being placed on the other side of the Atlantic and only 12 per cent in the rest of the EC.

Investment in the United States is not necessarily mistaken, but it has been interpreted as evidence of lack of British commitment in Europe. Yet towards the end of the 1980s things were beginning to change. In 1989, British companies made more acquisitions in mainland Europe than in the United States: they invested a total of £2.6 billion, acquiring some 300 businesses in Continental Europe. This compared with £2.0 billion spent on such acquisitions in 1988. France, western Germany, the Netherlands and Spain proved to be the most popular areas for British companies seeking to expand.

Though the focus of investment shifted back to the United States in 1990, which accounted for 55 per cent of the value of acquisitions and mergers less disposals by United Kingdom companies, compared with 31 per cent for other EC countries, the former imbalance of outward investment is gradually being corrected in favour of the EC.

Threats

Despite such auspicious longer-term trends in British companies' direct foreign investments, there remain substantial grounds for disquiet about their general state of preparedness for the single market. In January, 1989, the CBI surveyed a sample of its members and established that 90 per cent of companies with sales over £20 million were pursuing no market research at all in mainland Europe. 93 per cent were taking no initiatives to train employees in Continental languages. 95 per cent had no sales agents in the rest of the EC, and only one in 100 was opening any manufacturing plants on the Continent. Quoting the CBI survey, Michael Heseltine, comments in his book, *The Challenge of Europe*: 'If that is Britain's corporate response, we are in trouble. I hope that the overwhelming majority of British firms will rise above that attitude; and fear that the rest will not be around long enough to do more than temporary harm.'

In common with most other countries in the EC, the United Kingdom was experiencing problems in interesting smaller companies to explore export opportunities. Although many competitive products from smaller, innovative British companies are incorporated in the goods produced by larger companies, these smaller firms still remain to be convinced that much of their future prosperity depends on servicing all their larger corporate customers throughout Europe, and not just those in the United Kingdom.

A survey in 1992 by Grant Thornton, the chartered accountants, and Business Strategies, the consultants, established that 55 per cent of the United Kingdom's small to medium-sized businesses had done nothing to prepare for the single market. 37 per cent still saw the single market as irrelevant to them; only 5 per cent had carried out market research; and just 3 per cent were training staff in languages.

The British response to the EC's single market may have been diffident and faltering, but companies can still take recourse to the outstanding feature of the business culture in the United Kingdom – its sheer adaptability. Indeed, M Ernest-Antoine Seillère, Vice-President of the Conseil National du Patronat Français, confirmed in an interview with *The Times* on 13 October 1989, that the British enjoyed many advantages in the approach to 1992. Among them figured the fact that English was the language of business in most of Europe. But above all he praised British business people's facility to adapt rapidly to changed economic circumstances and to large international organizations such as those which would prevail in the single market.

The adaptability which permeates the whole of the business culture in the United Kingdom must now be joined by a sense of greater urgency if the country's companies are to take full advantage of a single market of 320 million consumers.

References and suggestions for further reading

Accountant's Magazine, The, various issues between 1979 and 1992.

Acquisitions Monthly, various issues between 1987 and 1992.

Bassett, P. (1987), *Strike Free: New Industrial Relations in Britain*, London: Macmillan.

Bean, C. and Symmons, J. (1989), *Ten Years of Mrs T*, LSE Centre for Labour Economics, working paper no. 1119.

Burns, P. and Dewhurst, J. (1989), *Small Business and Entrepreneurship*, Basingstoke and London: Macmillan.

Cecchini, P. (1988), *The European Challenge, 1992*, Aldershot: Gower.

Channon, D. F. (1977), *British Banking Strategy and the International Challenge*, London: Macmillan.

Clarke, W. M. (1989), *Planning for Europe*, London: Waterflow.

Clutterbuck, D. and Devine, M. (1987), *Management Buyouts*, London: Hutchinson.

Constable, J. and McCormick, R. (1987), *The Making of British Managers*, London: BIM and CBI.

David, R. (1980), *English Law and French Law*, London: Stevens.

Director, various issues between 1979 and 1992.

Economist, The, various issues between 1979 and 1992.

Economist Intelligence Unit (1992), *United Kingdom Country Profile 1991–1992*, London: The Economist Intelligence Unit.

Economist Intelligence Unit (1992), *United Kingdom Country Report*, London: The Economist Intelligence Unit.

Employment Gazette, various issues between 1979 and 1992.

Financial Times, The, various editions between 1979 and 1992.

Fortune, various issues between 1979 and 1992.

Grady, J. and Weale, M. (1986), *British Banking, 1960–85*, Basingstoke: Macmillan.

Handy, C. et al. (1988), *Making Managers*, London: Pitman.

Heseltine, M. (1989), *The Challenge of Europe*, London: Weidenfeld and Nicolson.

Hindley, B. (1989), *Europe: Fortress or Freedom?* London: The Bruges Group.

HMSO (1988), *Employment for the 1990s*, London: HMSO.

James, B. (1989), 'The dam bursts – and the old apathy is swept away', *The Times*, 11 April, © Times Newspapers Ltd 1989.

Lewis, R. (1986), *Labour Law in Britain*, Oxford: Blackwell.

Liston, D. and Reeves, N. (1988), *Invisible Economy: A Profile of Britain's Invisible Exports*, London: Pitman.

Lynch, R. (1990), *European Business Strategies*, London: Kogan Page.

Narbrough, C. (1989), 'French chief sees . . . after 1992', *The Times*, 13 October, © Times Newspapers Ltd 1989.

OECD Economic Surveys, United Kingdom, various years between 1979 and 1992.

Parnaby, J. (1988), 'Creating a competitive manufacturing strategy', in *Production Engineer*, July/August.

Perry, F. E. (1986), *The Elements of Banking*, London: Methuen.

Price Waterhouse (1986), *Doing Business in the United Kingdom*, London: Price Waterhouse.

Sunday Times, The, various issues between 1979 and 1992.

Times, The, various editions between 1979 and 1992.

Wiener, M. J. (1981), *English Culture and the Decline of the Industrial Spirit, 1850–1980*, Cambridge: CUP.

CANTABRIA

BASQUE
COUNTRY

Gijón ●   Santander

La Coruña ●   ASTURIAS

GALICIA   Bilbao

Vigo ●   NAVARRE   Pamplona ●

LA
RIOJA

CASTILE-LEON   CATALONIA

Valladolid ●   Zaragoza ●   Barcelona ●

ARAGON

MADRID   BALEARICS

Madrid ■   Palma ●

Toledo ●

EXTREMADURA   CASTILE-LA MANCHA   Valencia ●

VALENCIA

Badajos ●

Murcia ●

Seville ●   ANDALUCIA   MURCIA

Malaga ●

CANARIES

Las
Palmas ●

5 The business culture in Spain

Kevin Bruton

Introduction

Spanish companies, at the beginning of the 1990s, became caught up in an infectious popular enthusiasm for more contact with Europe and the wider world. Optimism and the desire to compete successfully with companies in other countries which have not had to experience Spain's long recent period of political and economic repression coexist with apprehensiveness and anxiety about the consequences of free, unfettered trading.

It is, however, the dynamism and outward-looking philosophy of the business culture in Spain which most strikes the foreign observer. This is evident in a number of ways which include:

- Continuing steady growth in the Spanish economy following the boom years of 1988 and 1989, with GDP improving from 1985–90 by an average of 4.9 per cent compared with 3.4 per cent for Germany, 3.2 per cent for France and 3 per cent for the United Kingdom.
- Export success, with manufactured exports rising by 11 per cent in 1991, partly the result of government initiatives to raise Spain's export profile through the Chambers of Commerce at home and government offices abroad.
- Very high levels of investment in plant and machinery, often through imported technology, in order to modernize industry.
- An explosion of interest among the business and the wider community in the activities of Spanish and international companies, revealed by the plethora of publications emerging in the 1980s – *Comercio e industria* (circulation up from 34,000 in 1983 to 144,000 in 1987), *Actualidad Económica, Dinero, España Económica* (issued in 1989 as a supplement to the prestigious weekly news journal, *Cambia 16*), etc.

Spain's business culture also has a number of weaknesses which need to be addressed in the 1990s. The principal deficiencies are as follows:

- The very high proportion of small companies, often with a conservative mentality and prone to foreign takeover or collapse through free competition.

266 Business Cultures in Europe

- Inadequate numbers of suitably trained people, at all levels from shopfloor to management.
- Public services and infrastructure, especially roads, railways, health, education, post and telegraph, which are inferior to most of Spain's EC partners and, in some cases, deteriorating.
- The lack (in 1992) of a social compact between government and trade unions, and the threat this causes to economic policy and company planning and profitability.
- Continuing ETA terrorism, which is crippling, economically, the Basque region, the traditional heartland of Spain's heavy industry.

The Spanish government is prioritizing some of these deficiencies by increasing investment in infrastructure and attempting to overcome the terrorism problem. The terms of Spain's EC accession in 1986 meant that Spanish business was preparing for 1992 and the completion of the single market before most other EC countries. The preparation has often been painful but it has also been painstaking so that Spain's business culture, despite its weaknesses, is in a better position than ever to play its part in the opportunities opened by a year, 1992, which has so much symbolic importance for Spaniards.

Business and government

The business world in Spain has had to come to terms with some of the most dramatic changes in the structures of government experienced by any Western European country in the last thirty years. Leaving behind the authoritarian and centralized dictatorship of Franco, which for most of the period between 1939 and 1975 effectively isolated Spain from the rest of Europe, Spanish business has successfully confronted the challenge of transforming itself, over a decade of fragile democratic governments, into a significant competitor in the Western world. The impetus given by EC membership (1 January 1986) has propelled the Spanish economy – and much of business with it – into the forefront of world economies, with booming growth in the late 1980s, which outstripped that of most other countries. (Real GDP growth in Spain in 1988 at nearly 5 per cent was 1.5 percentage points above the EC average.) The inevitable slowdown in economic growth in 1991 and 1992 nonetheless leaves Spain in a much more competitive situation than ever in its history. The problems and successes need to be set within the context of a new framework of democratic central and regional government.

Central government

Since October 1982 Felipe González's Socialist Party, with three general election victories, has pursued a tight monetarist policy based upon containing inflation, promoting greater freedom and flexibility in business, and carrying through a policy of industrial 'reconversion', i.e. a rationalization and modernization of Spain's heavy industry. EC accession in 1986 has assisted the government in its objective of opening Spanish business up to European competition. This 'cold shower' of competition for Spanish industry after years of protection from tariff barriers has met with mixed reaction from the business world. The González government policy in large part though was determined by a number of major economic deficiencies inherited from the Franco era, including:

- The multiplicity of small firms (i.e. employing less than fifty people) in Spain, estimated to constitute some 90 per cent of all companies.
- Technological backwardness vis-à-vis established Western democracies.
- The survival of an inefficient agricultural system, also backward.
- A relatively low level of education and training in the population, with the loss of many skilled workers abroad during the Franco era.
- The Francoist legacy of corporatism, i.e. the large role within the overall economy occupied by a massive infrastructure of State-owned industries, characterized by bureaucratic overmanning and heavy financial losses.

González's incoming 1982 government also faced a decade of rapidly deteriorating macroeconomic indicators, following the first oil price shock. Spain's performance in this period was substantially worse than other European economies, especially in employment. Spain's unemployment rate in 1982 was 16.2 per cent compared with an EC average of 9.3 per cent while inflation at 13.8 per cent was also higher than the EC 9.3 per cent.

Following 1982, the government's implementation of a stabilization programme featuring monetary and budgetary policies which converged on the policies of EC member states, as well as action to moderate wage rises, allowed progress towards reducing inflation, which was moving into single digits by the end of 1986, and towards improving the balance of payments which, after a decade in the red, finally went into the black in 1984.

Despite a manifesto promise in 1982 to create 800,000 new jobs in Spain, González's first period in office actually saw unemployment increase by almost a million to reach 21 per cent in 1986, the highest in the OECD. The increase was in large part the result of the government's industrial 'reconversion' policy, a major restructuring of Spain's overmanned steel mills and shipyards, which awakened trade union militancy at the massive job losses entailed.

González won his second general election in June 1986, a victory founded largely upon his success in achieving EC membership for Spain on 1 January that year and upon the absence of a viable opposition party. The government's economic policies continued much as before, but with Spanish industrialists now trying hard to come to terms with the fierce competition from other EC member states.

In the first two years of EC membership an estimated 150,000 small firms went to the wall as a result of foreign competition, as Spanish business paid the price for moving from a protected economy to a competitive one. Customs barriers and taxes which made it difficult for foreign firms to compete previously have gradually been removed since 1986, allowing a flood of imports into Spain. In fact in the first year of membership, imports to Spain from the EC went up by 32 per cent while trade between Spain and the EC moved from a surplus position of 268,000 million pesetas in 1985 to a deficit for Spain of 139,000 million pesetas in 1986. In other words, the reduction of tariff barriers in 1986 which gave Spanish products an average 25 per cent price advantage over competitors to half that level of 12.5 per cent saw a 400,000 million peseta boom for EC competitors in 1986. Further tariff cuts, with the last (10 per cent) in 1993, have benefited other EC countries and have seen the demise of many thousands of Spanish companies, especially in vulnerable sectors such as light engineering (including manufacturers of bicycles, motorcycles, electrical appliances and machinery), clothing and some food industries.

The initial reaction of some Spanish business people was to affirm that increased imports from Europe merely provided jobs elsewhere in the EC and that the loss of competitiveness of Spanish firms would be disastrous in the long term for Spanish industry.

More enlightened employers, along with the government, reject this view and claim that a significant proportion of the increase in imports has been due to plant and machinery urgently needed to modernize and revitalize industry into more dynamic competitive attitudes. Additionally, the government point to a continuing substantial increase in Spanish exports to the EC over the period 1986–92 as proof of the fact that there are Spanish industries competing successfully in Europe.

While companies like the Valencia-based Tycesa group, which manufactures Western Europe's best selling Lois jeans, demonstrate that Spanish business can be as efficient as any in the world, there is evidence that many Spanish industries still fear competition. The **Confederación Española de Organizaciones Empresariales** (CEOE) (main employers' confederation), has carried out studies which reveal the extent to which the legacy of corporatism persists and claims that at no point in the government's negotiations for EC entry was there any discussion of the private sector's role in the economy. Instead the question was debated in terms of what the government was or was not doing to help business.

1987 and 1988 witnessed a major turnaround in the Spanish economy with unemployment starting to move downwards from a high point of over 21 per cent to stand at 15.9 per cent at the start of 1992. The improvement reflected the government's promotion of special employment programmes and tax incentives to industry to create new jobs as well as a 30 per cent rise in real domestic demand between 1983 and 1989 (compared with an EC average of 18 per cent). Fixed investment and investment in plant and machinery rose by an average 15 per cent in 1987 and 1988 while net capital inflows remained high into 1992, revealing direct investment in Spanish business and real estate by foreign companies and increased foreign participation in Spanish firms.

1991 saw more moderate growth in Spain, partly reflecting policy measures taken in response to the overheating in 1989 and the first half of 1990. After expanding twice as fast as potential output between 1985 and 1990, domestic demand slowed in 1991, led by a decline in car sales and housing starts and a drop in business investment.

Government fiscal policy, in the late 1980s and early 1990s, generated rises in government tax revenues, especially from higher income taxes, and a major campaign was launched to stamp out the widespread tax evasion which has been endemic in Spanish society for decades. Extra tax receipts were used in part to finance additional government expenditure.

Inflation, a major success story for González's government over a six-year period from 1982, which saw a reduction from 13.8 per cent to 5.2 per cent, started to upturn however in 1989, and a 1991 year-end figure of 7 per cent is expected to fall only slowly in 1992 and 1993.

Another problem for the González government, as it faced a general election before October 1993, lay in increasing opposition from the trade union giants, the socialist **Unión General de Trabajadores** (UGT) and the communist Workers' Commissions, to which further reference will be made (see page 295). A general strike on 14 December 1988 was the trade union response to government attempts to force through parliament a Youth Employment Programme to create 800,000 temporary jobs on minimum wage levels. A further half-day strike in May 1992 and a planned general strike in the Autumn of 1992 represented protests at government cutbacks in unemployment benefit. Following a one-off expansionist budget in 1989, which aimed to improve Spain's infrastructure and public services, the government reverted to a more cautious approach, with the 1992 budget more restrictive. Indirect tax increases (with the standard VAT rate rising from 12 per cent to 13 per cent) and higher social security contributions are expected to outweigh a small decrease in income tax and a substantial rise in social spending.

Business Cultures in Europe

After booming growth from 1987–9, GDP slowed to 2.5 per cent in 1991 although this is expected to rise to 3.3 per cent in 1993.

Table 5.1 *Spain's growth rates (1977–92)*

Year	(%)
1977	3.0
1978	1.4
1979	–0.1
1980	1.2
1981	–0.2
1982	1.2
1983	1.8
1984	1.8
1985	2.3
1986	3.3
1987	5.5
1988	5.0
1989	4.8
1990	3.7
1991	2.5
1992	1.4

Source: OECD

As González contemplated the prospect of a fourth general election victory in 1993, his government faced the still unresolved problem of a total breakdown in communication with the trade unions. With consumer demand still buoyant and inflation still rising slowly, an agreement with the trade unions would seem to be the *sine qua non* of future wage moderation and control of inflation. Since the tripartite agreement, between government, employers and trade unions, the Economic and Social Accord, came to an end in 1986, a new consensus has seemed increasingly remote yet still appears crucial if the government is to press ahead with plans to spend more on the infrastructure essential for Spain's businesses to compete successfully. An ambitious programme to raise the share of infrastructure expenditure within GDP to 1.9 per cent in 1992 from 0.9 per cent in 1987 (mainly on roads and railways) is accompanied by plans to give priority to education and training in order to overcome hard evidence of a growing mismatch between employer demand and labour supply. Both aims will need to be realized if Spain's economic boom of the late 1980s is to be translated into long-term stable growth and a healthy business culture within which individual Spanish businesses can flourish.

Regional government

The regional government system ratified by Spain's Democratic Constitution of 1978, which establishes seventeen regional governments, with elected parliaments, represents a totally new framework in Spanish history within which business must operate.

While central government decides overall policy for taxation and income, social security contributions, defence, foreign affairs, internal security and justice, the seventeen autonomous regions have considerable independent powers. Three types of transfer of central government monies are made to the regions:

• Automatic transfers, decided by size of population, *per capita* income, area size, degree of isolation, relative poverty, etc. These types of transfer are not subject to negotiations.
• Transfers via an **Inter-territorial Compensation Fund** (FCI), usually for new investments aimed at correcting regional disparities and therefore distributed according to the infrastructural needs of each region.
• Transfers of central government funds for earmarked purposes.

Regions have the right to levy certain taxes, e.g. wealth taxes, and also to add surcharges on government income tax. Regions have been operating in recent years within the guidelines of a five-year plan, 1987–91, which allocates them wide discretionary powers over expenditure, although the degree of spending autonomy varies across regions with only a few, for example having *full* responsibility for education and health.

Local authorities, i.e. town and provincial councils, also exist with considerable freedom over expenditure but not over raising of revenue. The regions' and local authorities' expenditure has grown since 1978 and accounts, for instance, for half of spending on state education, a fifth on health care, and two-thirds of total fixed investment. The trend throughout the 1980s was toward greater regional expenditure rather than local decentralization. The combined public deficit of all regions in 1991 was 1.1 per cent of GDP and rising fast. As the regions press for greater responsibilities in the next five-year agreement (1992–6), the government seeks tighter financial control. With local elections due in 1992 and 1993, this probably represents wishful thinking.

The two arguably most famous regions, the Basque Country and Catalonia (which includes Barcelona), have each had their major problems in recent years. The Basque Country, historically one of the leading industrial areas of Spain, especially for shipbuilding and iron and steel, has been crippled economically by the long ETA terrorist campaign which has driven many firms to move to safer parts of the country and inhibited foreign investment there. Catalonia, a prosperous area with a powerful regional government, was host, of course, to the 1992 Olympic Games in Barcelona, which took place, however, against a background of complex and bitter disagreements between central government, regional government and the town council over the infrastructural and service arrangements for the Games.

Business and the economy

It is difficult to overstate the tremendous structural changes in the economy with which Spanish business has had to contend in the past thirty years. An industrial revolution which in other European countries happened over a hundred years before, in Spain only really arrived in the 1960s, a decade which witnessed an acceleration of the exodus from countryside to town, the phenomenal growth of mass tourism, and the first stages of an opening-up of the economy to the Western world that was to culminate in Spain's EC accession in 1986. Throughout this entire period, the massive state-owned industries have continued to dominate the Spanish economic scene, even arguably, in the mid-1990s, when the principal challenge for much of Spanish business is to throw off the shackles of recent decades by major capital investment in plant and machinery in order to be able to compete successfully in the modern era against established Western rivals. Thus the advent of a marketing-oriented philosophy has come later to Spanish companies, but the performance of many of these companies, for instance in the new sectors of electronics and telecommunications, shows that the new lessons are being applied.

With consumer demand growing at 7 per cent in 1989, Spanish firms enjoyed fuller order books and company profits mounted in the late 1980s. These profits, helped by a fall in oil prices, led to unprecedented levels of investment in Spain and the creation of new jobs. With the economy growing at 5 per cent in 1988 and 1989 though the difference between what Spain produces and consumes was imported, and, as a result foreign firms in the late 1980s benefited enormously. The response of Spanish firms was dynamic, however, with government estimating that in 1987 and 1988 at least 40 per cent of industrial capacity was updated. Even though growth levels in the early 1990s slowed down to half the previous level, Spanish economists are optimistic that growth will rise again once all of the results of capital investment are seen.

Heavy industry and INI

Long dominated by the state-owned industries of the public holding company, the **National Institute for Industry** (INI), the sheer economic power of heavy industry has set the business agenda in prominent regions of Spain such as the Basque Country.

The government's 'industrial reconversion' policy, launched in 1984, aimed to enhance competitiveness by adjustments to capacity and cuts in the workforce, financial restructuring and technological modernization, supported by public subsidies and credits. By the end of 1987, 85 per cent of envisaged job cuts (approximately 71,000) in shipbuilding, carbon-based steel, specialist steels, etc. had been achieved.

The restructuring has been successful. INI in 1988 registered its first profits since 1975 after record losses in 1983. Thirty firms have gone and of the fifty-eight firms still left in INI, forty-nine improved their financial position by the late 1980s, with the largest profits being made by Endesa, the electricity giant and Inespal, aluminium manufacturers. Government aid bolstered INI's success in the late 1980s but this will no longer be possible, according to EC directives, after 1992. By the 1990s, however, famous INI firms such as Iberia, the Spanish airline and Ensidesa, the steel company, were in trouble again and are now, under 1991 government plans, destined for part or full privatization.

INI is one of the fifty biggest trading groups in the world and in Spain accounts for more than 30 per cent of all production in a wide range of industries – coal, iron and steel, shipyards, electricity, aluminium, air and rail transport, etc. INI's industrial production is 10 per cent of industrial GDP and its internationalization process has gone further than most Spanish firms, with over 30 per cent of its sales (1988) coming via exports as against the average for all Spain of 14 per cent. Its R & D budget is again 23 per cent of the national total.

Tourist industry

It is estimated that one million Spanish families work directly or indirectly in the tourist trade which thus constitutes the largest employer in Spain, providing work for roughly 10 per cent of the active population. Spectacular growth since the 1960s shows little sign of plateauing out, as new tourist resorts continue to spring up and diversification of supply attracts more tourists to the cultural hinterland or away from the high season.

What is astonishing about Spain's revenue from tourism (Table 5.2) is that it is generated by very low levels of expenditure, as revealed by comparative figures for 1986 which show that Spain's income of 12.058 million dollars was matched by only 1.512 million dollars of expenditure, an income/expenditure ratio of 8 to 1. France, the United Kingdom, the United States, and countries such as Switzerland and Austria had virtual

Table 5.2 *Spanish tourism*

Year	Numbers of foreign tourists (millions)	Income (millions $)
1975	30.1	3.404
1980	38.0	6.967
1985	43.2	8.151
1986	47.4	12.058
1987	50.5	14.760
1988	54.2	16.686
1989	54.1	16.174
1990	52.0	18.593
1991	53.5	19.004

Source: *Anuario El País*

parity of income/expenditure in the same year while former West Germany's ratio was 1 to 3.

Construction

The construction industry in Spain, after experiencing sector crises between 1975 and 1985, is now more powerful than ever, with a one million workforce and some of the top companies in Spain, notably Cubiertos and Dragados, which benefited in the late 1980s from a property boom in Madrid and Barcelona and from increased government spending on infrastructure, especially roads.

The new technologies

Whereas firms engaged in the new technologies have been shedding staff throughout the world at the start of the 1990s, in Spain the rapid expansion continues. The number of firms in this sector increased from virtually nil at the start of the 1980s to over one hundred in 1992, with further rises in companies and employment projected, just as other countries in Europe experience contraction.

The Spanish high-tech boom is deliberate government policy, embodied in the National Electronics and Information Technology Plan which, over a three-year period ending in December 1993, allocates an overall budget of

158,000 million pesetas to the sector, 45 per cent from public funds, 38 per cent from the Centre for Technological and Industrial Development, and 17 per cent from the EC.

The telecommunications industry has also grown rapidly, supported by a National Telecommunications Plan for 1989–92 which envisaged continuing government investment in the industry of the level of 500,000 million pesetas annually, equivalent to between 1.1 per cent and 1.5 per cent of GDP. Spain's first communications satellite, *Hispasat*, was placed in orbit in 1991, one of its first tasks being to support transmission of the Olympic Games in Barcelona.

The high-tech sector has always seen Spanish firms linked with foreign multinationals, following the pattern of the 1986 agreement between the Spanish telecommunications company Telefónica and ATT which led to the construction outside Madrid of Western Europe's biggest microchip factory. Foreign multinationals now dominate production in Spain, especially in electronics and information technology. Consumption of personal computers and software is largely through import. Even Telefónica, one of Spain's biggest companies, has lost its telecommunications monopoly (except for the basic telephone service) and foreign participation in the company increased from 3 per cent in 1982 to 30 per cent in 1992.

The major foreign multinationals in Spain include Alcatel-Standard Eléctrica (a subsidiary of the Compagnie Générale d'Electricité de France), ATT Network Systems and LM Ericsson-Intelsa. Another Scandinavian firm, Electrolux, bought out firms in Catalonia in 1988 while a number of electronics industry giants have plants in Spain, e.g. IBM, Olivetti, and Rank Xerox, mostly in the Madrid and Barcelona regions.

Car industry

Spain is the fourth-largest car manufacturer in the EC, a long way behind Germany and France but not far short of Italy and ahead of the United Kingdom. Cars account for a quarter of all Spain's exports and the industry employs nearly one in ten of the working population. All Spain's car producers are now foreign-owned and have been pouring investment into the industry to the tune of 150 billion pesetas a year; VW-Seat maintains a design centre employing 800 people. In terms of exports Spain leads the field in Europe with 800,000 of 1.5 million cars manufactured in 1991 destined for the export market.

Spain also has great potential for continued growth, with labour costs, although rising in the 1990s, still lower than Germany and France, with a workforce surplus and the possibility of further modernization to reduce costs. Thus Ford and General Motors locate their small models in Spain while Renault divides production between Spain and France. The Japanese company Suzuki is also planning to work with VW-Seat to produce a new small car in Spain.

Table 5.3 *Spanish car market (1977 and 1987)*

	1977 share (%)		1987 share (%)
Renault	28	Renault	23
Seat	38	VW-Seat	17
Citroën	12	PSA Group	18
Chrysler	12	G. Motors	14
Ford	10	Ford	16
		Fiat	8
		Others	4

Source: Cambio 16

Car ownership in Spain is low at 296 cars per 1000 inhabitants, the equivalent of the EC twenty years ago and 20 per cent lower than the EC average.

The proliferation of small and medium-sized firms in Spain, known as the PYMES – **Pequeñas y Medianas Empresas** – has determined major shifts in business planning in the last few years. Coinciding with Spain's Presidency of the EC in the first half of 1989, the Industry and Energy Ministry launched a new programme geared to 1992 specifically for PYMES with a triple aim: the promotion of R & D; the strengthening of greater communication at European level with the involvement of PYMES in such schemes as Sprint, BC-NET, Europartenariat, etc.; and the streamlining and simplification of often bureaucratic management structures.

Also in the late 1980s, a movement towards new (for Spain) types of financial corporations, holding companies and consortia was becoming evident, as the PYMES, supported by the government, seek wider markets in Europe. Thus Spanish firms, both large and small, have begun to diversify horizontally, i.e. into areas unconnected with the business of the original firms, and vertically, i.e. in the same sector. Cement and real-estate firms are the leaders in this diversification drive which has attracted private and state-owned concerns. Indeed, the state tobacco company Tabacalera, has pioneered the trend, since it now owns twenty-six firms unconnected with tobacco, which account for 25 per cent of all sales, a figure projected to rise to 50 per cent by 1993.

In terms of exports, Spain's performance over the period 1960–87, an annual improvement of 8.5 per cent, was the highest in the OECD with the exception of Japan, Greece and Turkey and comfortably outstrips the EC average at 5.8 per cent, Germany at 5.7 per cent, the United Kingdom at 4.2 per cent and France at 6.4 per cent. Imports, however, in the same 1960–87 period, were the highest in the OECD at 10.4 per cent, which compares with the EC at 5.8 per cent, Germany at 5.9 per cent, the United Kingdom at 4 per cent and France at 6.5 per cent.

The major trend in exports saw trade with the EC commanding a larger share during the 1980s, while exports to North and South America, perhaps surprisingly, have fallen from 21 per cent of overall exports in 1977 to 8 per cent in 1991 (Table 5.4). Within the EC, Spanish companies were most successful in the 1980s in increasing exports to the United Kingdom, Italy and France.

Table 5.4 *Spain's exports (1977 and 1991)*

	1977 (%)	1991 (%)
France	16	20
Germany	11	16
United Kingdom	6	8
Italy	5	11
Other EC	11	16
North America	11	5
South America	10	3
Other	30	21

Source: OECD

Despite the fact that government economic policy since 1982 has actively welcomed increased foreign investment in Spanish companies, in the early 1990s there was widespread fear in Spain that the process of foreign takeovers was going too far. With Spain's rapid growth, opportunities mushroomed for foreign investors and multinationals, especially in the private sector, where long isolation had left few Spanish firms in a position to withstand competition. State-owned industry and the banks have, to date, been most successful in defending Spanish interests.

Spain's chemical, cement and insurance industries have been the most popular sectors for foreign investors with for, instance the Kuwaiti group, KIO, buying Enfersa, a chemical group, previously part of INI. In a sector where foreign competition accounts for one-third of total consumption, and where Spain's biggest company, Ecros, is only in twentieth place in Europe, it is difficult to resist foreign intervention.

Arab and British companies have been at the forefront of recent wholesale acquisitions of Spanish firms. While the Arabs have bought into food
companies, stationery, finance and real estate, British companies have led
the field with, for example, the acquisition of Alhambra publishing by the
Pearson Group, the olive oil giant José Guiu by Unilever, and the Petromed
refinery by BP.

Most purchases though have been worth less than 50 million pesetas,
perhaps suggesting that foreign companies have been buying into Spain
gradually with one eye on the post-1992 Europe. The Spanish government
has not been averse to selling off state-owned firms to foreigners.
Additionally, foreigners spent approximately 300,000 million pesetas a year
in the late 1980s purchasing property in Spain.

Regional inequalities, which have always existed, have become exacerbated in recent years as Spain's growth has generally benefited already
prosperous areas, notably the area around the two major cities of Madrid
and Barcelona, the Valencia region and the Balearics and Canaries, at the
cost of the traditionally poorer agricultural areas of Extremadura, Castile,
Andalusia and Galicia. The Basque provinces, the heartland of Spain's
heavy industry throughout this century, are in crisis due to the industrial
reconversion programme which has decimated its steel mills and shipyards. Despite specific employment programmes and the establishment of
Zones for Urgent Reindustrialization (ZURs) in areas hit particularly hard
by job losses, there seems little evidence as yet that the nettle of unequal
regional development has been grasped by government or the business
community.

The Socialist government also inherited sudden wage rises which followed Franco's death in 1975 and which saw real labour costs rise more
rapidly in Spain until 1983, admittedly from a very low level, than in any
other Western European economy. The rise occurred when real labour
costs were actually falling in countries like Denmark and the Netherlands.

While Spanish wage levels are generally lower today than in her EC
partners, this advantage is to some extent offset by lower productivity levels and, as a result, with wage costs still continuing to rise faster than production, the maintenance of high levels of employment constitutes an
everpresent challenge.

Although, as was indicated previously, global foreign investment in
Spain is growing yearly, there is a major question mark as to whether it is
growing quickly enough in a country where indigenous sources of capital
are limited and the banks, historically, (though the trend is changing), have
preferred to invest in real estate rather than in industry.

One drawback of the multinational presence is that it does little to stimulate local research. And it is in this area that the structural weakness of
Spanish industry is glaringly apparent. According to the OECD, the only

member countries to spend less on R & D than Spain are Portugal, Greece and Turkey. Without basic research it may be that Spain's commercial future will remain mostly in intermediate industries such as car manufacturing.

Table 5.5 *Spain – the regional picture*

Region	% all GDP (1987)	% total population	Index of level of development (1986) (National average = 100)
Catalonia	19.5	15.4	108.7
Madrid	16.5	12.5	115.5
Andalusia	12.5	18.1	95.6
Valencia	10.4	9.8	105.8
Basque Country	6.0	5.5	103.9
Castile and León	5.9	6.6	92.0
Galicia	5.8	7.4	80.8
Canaries	3.7	3.9	100.3
Aragón	3.5	3.0	97.9
Castile and La Mancha	3.3	4.3	89.2
Balearics	2.7	2.8	110.3
Asturias	2.7	2.8	90.9
Murcia	2.2	2.7	98.7
Extremadura	1.8	2.8	79.0
Navarre	1.5	1.3	101.1
Cantabria	1.3	1.4	92.5
La Rioja	0.7	0.7	99.4

Source: *Banesto* and *The Economist*

Services

A major complaint of the trade unions and opposition parties in Spain is that public services have deteriorated since 1982. Government critics point to the transport system, especially roads, education and health, the postal and telegraph services.

The criticism is not all justifiable. After the first oil shock, investment on the transport infrastructure declined in real terms but the trend has been to a considerable extent reversed since 1982, although there is no doubt that the infrastructure has not been able to cope with the strong demand from an economy in growth.

Between 1975 and 1984 cumulative fixed investment in road transport per tonne-kilometre and passenger-kilometre was more than two-thirds below the OECD average for Europe. In 1984 the ratio of road network per 1000 inhabitants was only 4 km in Spain as against an 11 km Europe average.

In terms of the rail network, Spain was one of the very few countries in Europe where passengers and freight by rail actually declined in the decade up to the 1980s. The González government's plan to improve the transport infrastructure involves a major programme to build 1700 extra motorway kilometres and a further 12 km of trunk roads by 1992. Similarly, railway investment is scheduled to be equivalent to a yearly rise of 1 per cent of GDP (at 1988 prices) up to 1992 and beyond. The major part of this expenditure involves the introduction of high-speed trains, the AVE (Alta Velocidad Española), purchased from France, on the Seville–Madrid route, which commenced operations in April 1992 to coincide with the opening of Expo 92. The extension of the AVE to the Madrid–Barcelona route will be accompanied by a long-term programme which will go well into the next century, to narrow the gauge to that of Spain's EC partners. The wider gauge of 1.668 m compares with 1.435 m in France. The problem of mountainous terrain, however, remains to inhibit the aim of laying more double track in many areas.

One major transport success in the 1980s was the development of domestic air travel, in line with the recommendations of a 1980 plan to strengthen regional airports and facilitate commercial travel. Thus an initial 57,000 million pesetas investment for the period 1981–6 helped to improve facilities at the airports of Madrid, Barcelona, Valencia, Seville, Málaga, Tenerife, Palma de Mallorca and Santiago. Five other airports important to the tourist trade – Alicante, Ibiza, Lanzarote, La Palma and Menorca – also received infrastructural subsidies. The resulting improvements and a consequent increase in domestic air travel have been of enormous benefit to the Spanish business community, faced with lengthy alternative journeys by road or rail.

Business and the law

Although operating openly in a democratic environment, business enterprises in Spain are still largely bound by a legalistic framework established during a Franco era in which the business community was 'given its head'. Most existing legislation governing business practice goes back to before 1975, and in the case of the legal status of limited liability companies dates from the early 1950s. The most glaring anomaly is the failure under Franco to compel firms to carry out independent audits and the consequence has been wide popular mistrust of published accounts. Only in recent years have the majority of firms been persuaded that external auditing is in their own interests, as they learn to take seriously the views of shareholders and employees.

Spain's Democratic Constitution of 1978 recognizes the rights of private enterprise and states that these should be exercised in accordance with the overall requirements of the economy and within the general framework of government economic policy. All types of business, except sole trader, are obliged to register their existence in the Mercantile Register of the provincial capital in which the company's head office is located, a requirement which also extends to foreign companies setting up in Spain. The details are open to public inspection.

The principal types of company permitted by law are briefly summarized below. A more comprehensive account can be found in Donaghy and Newton's *Spain: A Guide to Political and Economic Institutions*.

1 Sociedad anónima – SA (company)

This is the most prestigious type of company in Spain. It can be in the public as well as the private sector and may be a large company quoted on the stock exchange or a smaller family business. No minimum size is stipulated but, hitherto, in accordance with 1951 legislation, any company with capital in excess of 50 million pesetas must register as an SA company. New legislation, however, reduces the minimum capital requirement to 3 million pesetas.

2 Sociedad de responsabilidad limitada – SRL/SL (company)

This type of company has no minimum capital requirement and therefore offers more flexibility. Often found in the retail and service sector, where an SRL company is quoted on the stock exchange, there are legal restrictions on the transfer of shares. There are, however, few other formal legal requirements on this type of company, for example, to provide audits or reliable financial information.

3 Sociedades colectivas (partnerships)

Partnerships are not widely found in Spain although two types exist in law: the **sociedad colectiva**, or general partnership, with unlimited liability; and the **sociedad en comandita/sociedad comanditaria**, or limited partnership, with a minimum of one general unlimited partner and one limited partner.

4 Cooperativas (cooperatives)

The most famous Spanish cooperative, Mondragón, in the Basque region, has attracted worldwide attention since its foundation in 1956 and still welcomes foreign delegations of interested politicians, economists and business people anxious to discover the secret of (arguably) the world's most successful cooperative. Over 100 enterprises, employing almost 20,000 people (and spanning consumer goods, capital goods, agriculture and construction) constitute a cooperative whose international fame undoubtedly derives from its unique supporting organizations: its own bank, with 100 branches in the Basque region; social security system; medical and hospital care; and a technical college.

The Spanish Constitution encourages the development of cooperatives and a separate Cooperative Register exists. The Ministry of Agriculture has pioneered the establishment of cooperatives in recent years, in an attempt to overcome the **minifundio** problem of tiny plots of farming land. Both small cooperatives, involving six or seven plots of land, and very large cooperatives, comprising up to 200 plots, have enjoyed considerable success.

5 Comerciante (sole trader)

Extremely numerous in Spain, comerciantes are found in many sectors especially food and drink, retail, crafts and services and are automatically members of the local **cámara de comercio** (chamber of commerce).

6 Joint ventures

The multiplicity of small firms in Spain has encouraged the government to provide financial incentives to firms to establish joint ventures. Such ventures the government sees as crucial to improving Spain's export performance. 1982 legislation allows two kinds of collaboration: temporary consortia of companies for a maximum ten-year period; and permanent contractual arrangements among groups of companies.

7 Foreign investment

Usually up to 50 per cent of the share capital of a Spanish company can be purchased by foreign investors without prior authorization. Any shareholding in excess of 50 per cent can only be approved by the **Dirección General de Transacciones Exteriores** (Directorate General of Foreign Transactions) where the share capital does not exceed 25 million pesetas. In some sectors, however, the investment percentage requiring authorization is lower, e.g. in shipping, mining, and banking.

Foreign companies therefore have considerable freedom to buy into Spanish companies, with the only exceptions being the defence industry and the mass media, where no foreign investment is allowed. Restrictions operate with regard to banks, but foreign companies are able to set up **sucursales** (branches) in Spain.

Business and finance

The banking system enjoyed a large role under Franco in a country where industry was able to find few alternative sources of finance, although for most of the period up until the early 1970s, the banks found themselves hidebound by a bureaucratic system of rules and regulations, which prevented new initiatives and rapprochement with Western Europe. Legislation in the 1970s though finally relaxed the restrictions to allow new Spanish banks to emerge and also, in 1978, to permit foreign banks to set up in Spain.

The Banco de España

Spain's Central Bank, the Banco de España, was nominally in private hands until 1962 when it was nationalized. In the 1970s, the Banco de España was accorded an important role in managing monetary policy and is now responsible for the monetary system and for supervising the banking system to the government Ministry of Economy and Finance. In this role it performs similar functions to central banks in other countries.

The Banco de España played a crucial interventionist part in the banking crisis which hit the country between 1978 and 1983 and which affected fifty-one of the then 110 banks operating in Spain. The reasons for the crisis were multifarious, including: the oil shocks; the rise in inflation caused by post-Francoist wage settlements; and the tight monetary policy pursued by the first governments of the democratic transition.

The Banco de España was instrumental in establishing a Deposit Guarantee Fund in 1977 to alleviate the crisis for troubled banks or depositors, and itself guaranteed half of the fund, to be matched by compulsory deposits from the Spanish banks. The Fund, run by its own Board of Management, was in fact used to provide help for twenty-six banks in financial crisis between 1978 and 1983 as well as to give some protection and/or compensation to depositors.

As the Banco de España's role has moved closer to that of its EC financial counterparts, so inevitably its role has been crucial in supporting real growth in Spain and in determining interest rates. Above all, the Banco de España has endeavoured to carry through the González government's objective of bringing the rate of inflation into line with that of major trading partners, notably countries participating in the European Monetary System, which Spain itself joined on 19 June 1989, with the peseta located, like the Italian lira, within a 6 per cent margin of fluctuation. The Banco de España's success in assisting the downward trend of inflation from the very high levels experienced up to the mid-1980s can be gauged from Table 5.6.

International comparisons reveal that inflation in Spain has been high through much of this period. As pointed out by the *1988/9 OECD Economic Survey*: 'Starting with a small positive inflation differential at the beginning of the 1970s, the margin relative to the OECD average widened dramatically between the two oil shocks, peaking at almost 16 per cent in 1977. It then diminished equally fast to reach a low of 2.6 per cent in 1980 before attaining a new high of close to 7 per cent in 1983. Since then there has been a rather steady narrowing of the gap to no more than 1 per cent in 1988, only temporarily interrupted in 1986 by the introduction of the VAT which pushed the level of consumer prices up by an estimated two percentage points.'

Table 5.6 *Spanish inflation rates (1977–92)*

Year	(%)
1977	24.5
1978	19.8
1979	15.7
1980	15.5
1981	14.6
1982	14.4
1983	12.2
1984	11.3
1985	8.8
1986	8.8
1987	5.3
1988	4.8
1989	6.9
1990	6.7
1991	5.9
1992	5.9

Source: OECD

Inflation started to upturn again, however, in 1989, finishing the year at almost 7 per cent. With unit labour costs in manufacturing also rising, the Spanish government in the early 1990s is concerned that inflation may disrupt the strength and confidence generated by recent growth. However, further deregulation and trade liberalization have assisted the Banco de España in keeping inflation to manageable proportions. The government plans to reduce inflation to 1 per cent of GDP by 1996 from 4 per cent in 1991.

An interesting footnote is that, according to IMF figures, Spain is fifth in the world league table of countries in terms of foreign currency reserves. The Banco de España's reserves are higher than those of the United Kingdom, France, Canada or Switzerland. Clearly, this is a reflection of international prestige and confidence of foreign investors and another indication of how Spain has become fashionable in international business.

Private banks

According to a 1985 study, there were eighty-five banks in Spain, thirty-seven of national scale, thirteen at regional level, and forty-eight at local level. This classification into national, regional or local banks, is preserved by the **Consejo Superior Bancario** (National Banking Council), which operates as a clearing house for information and statistics on the banks and provides a forum for meetings between representatives of the private and public sector banks.

Since 1985 the number of banks in Spain has increased to approximately 140, an increase due to the high profitability of banks since the mid-1980s.

The trade unions have complained to the government about the excessive profits generated by the banks under a Socialist government and the government itself is unhappy. In fact, in 1988, the government stepped in to demand that the banks allocate a proportion of their profits to the modernization and restructuring of their operations. The banks themselves were not too preoccupied, since they have been sensitive to the charges of excessive profiteering.

Banks' profits must be seen though in the context of profit generated by companies. A survey undertaken by the Banco de España in 1987 of 4000 firms revealed a doubling of profits over 1986 and hence the view of a leading banker in Spain is hardly surprising when he asserts: 'When companies do well, we do well. If firms are doubling profits, then no one should be amazed if we increase ours by 40 per cent!.'

There has, however, been a squeeze on margins in 1990 and 1991 as the Spanish boom calms down. Traditionally Spanish banks have not been internationally minded, but this changed rapidly since 1986, with alliances being formed with foreign banks, as expansion has taken place into foreign markets, and with diversification into a broader range of financial services, leading, for instance to the establishment of investment banking divisions. The main strengths of Spanish banks have been their strong capital and healthy reserves, while their principal weakness is high labour costs through an overcapacity in branches, estimated by some to be as high as 30 per cent.

In 1991 the private banks in Spain reacted in alarm at the creation by central government of a state 'megabank' the Corporación Bancaria de España (CBE). The CBE represents an attempt by government to establish a Spanish bank of European dimensions. In other EC countries the state banks have had greater weight than in Spain (state banking represents only 13 per cent of the system in Spain, compared with 30 per cent in Germany). The private banks fear that the CBE will monopolize finance for the state sector in a country where 40 per cent of GDP is controlled by the government.

Mergermania has taken hold of Spanish banks as the government pressurizes link-ups by offering practical inducements, e.g. a 99 per cent exemption on capital gains tax. The biggest merger to date, between Banco Central and Banco Hispanoamericano in 1991, has created the largest bank in Spain, the Banco Central Hispanoamericano (BCH), which has overtaken the Banco Bilbao Vizcaya (BBV). BBV's profile typifies the leading Spanish banks: it has important stakes in three of Spain's principal electrical companies; it owns a variety of firms in the food industry, including Kas and the Savin wine group; BBV is the biggest client of INI, the state holding company; and in recent years has been buying firms in strategically vital areas of industry.

Foreign banks

The Spanish banks' extensive network of branches is, paradoxically, the reason why foreign banks have been buying up and into Spain. The domestic banks are basically strong, have made large investments in new technology but are still not internationally oriented. Restrictions on foreign banks in Spain have been gradually lifted since the mid-1980s to permit forty banks to operate (twenty from the EC), while ten Spanish banks are foreign controlled.

The top six Spanish banks control approximately 75 per cent of the market and exert continuing pressure on the government and the Banco de España to protect them from foreign competition. Foreign banks account for 16 per cent of total loans in Spain but crucially account for 84 per cent of loans to firms who invoice more than 5000 million pesetas a year. Unsurprisingly, the foreign banks have complained of being unfairly discriminated against in a context where their highest share of the banking market was 10.6 per cent in 1984, stabilizing since at 9 per cent. It appears also that foreign banks did not benefit as much from the consumer boom in the late 1980s as domestic banks although 1988 was a particularly good year for them, with pretax profits rising by 54 per cent over 1987.

A number of foreign banks had already acquired Spanish banks in the early 1980s when the Spanish banking system was in crisis. Citibank and

Barclays bought into Spain at that time, and the Deutsche Bank also took complete control of the ailing Banco Comercial Transatlántico in 1989.

The Barclays story is an interesting one. Beginning with the purchase of thirty-three outlets from the Banco de Valladolid, Barclays then pursued a strategy of opening hundreds of small branches, with a maximum of five staff, across the country, on the basis that more Spaniards are preferring a 'boutique', approach to the traditional Spanish 'department store' approach in banking. Barclays also made headway in the profitable retail market by offering interest on a range of current accounts well ahead of their Spanish rivals. However, the launch in 1990 by the Banco de Santander, Spain's most aggressive and internationally oriented bank, of the 'supercuentas', or interest-bearing current accounts, which was quickly copied by other banks, has led to a highly competitive situation. Greater liberalization of the regulations to allow freer and fairer competition is certain to see foreign banks making further inroads in the mid-1990s.

Cajas de ahorros (savings banks)

The Cajas are an important banking institution and may be compared to the building societies in the United Kingdom, i.e. with no shareholders and designated as non-profit making. Their importance can be gauged from a 1983 Banco de España comparison of the different banking institutions (Table 5.7).

Table 5.7 *Banking institutions in Spain (1983)*

	No. of institutions	No. of offices	% total deposits	% total loans
Banco de España	1	53	0.2	15.1
Banks	135	16,062	61.0	51.8
Cajas	80	11,787	34.7	23.0
Others (e.g. cooperative credit agencies)	155	3,221	4.1	10.1
Total	371	31,123	100.0	100.0

Source: Banco de España

The big two Cajas, La Caixa (from Barcelona), and CajaMadrid are as large as the second and third banks in Spain, and have also been engaged in merger talks which so far have produced only informal agreement to cooperate and plan together in certain areas.

Until recently, the Cajas, almost all of which are regional or local in origin, have been limited by law to a certain geographical area. Although legislation now allows them to operate freely across the country, a new 1989 Law, the LORCA (**Ley de Organos Rectores de Cajas de Ahorro**), was designed by the Socialist government to have the eventual effect of handing over control of the Cajas to the seventeen autonomous regional governments. The ultimate consequence of this would seem to be to reduce the seventy-seven Cajas existing in 1992, to one per region.

Pension funds

An area in which the Cajas are competing openly with the banks is the pension funds market. It was estimated in 1989 that 60 per cent of pension funds business is in the hands of the banks, 22 per cent with the Cajas, and 10 per cent with insurance companies.

The dual appeal of pension funds is that operations involving them do not attract VAT and profits from investments do not attract company tax. The largest holdings are with the main banks especially BBV, Banco Central Hispano-americano, Banco de Santander and Grupo March.

The trade unions have also become involved, with the Socialist UGT establishing an insurance company and the Communist Workers' Commissions also setting up a pension fund company.

Stock markets

In the past few years, Spain's stock exchanges have laboured under an antiquated structure which goes a long way towards explaining why Spanish stock markets have been among the least active and least important in the Western world. Spain has three long-established exchanges in Madrid (1831), Bilbao (1915) and Barcelona (1915), and a newly-opened exchange in Valencia (1980). Madrid accounts for about 80 per cent of all stock market transactions, Barcelona about 15 per cent while Bilbao and Valencia between them represent a paltry 5 per cent.

The traditional recourse of Spanish companies to the banking system for finance to expand meant relatively few transactions on the exchanges until the mid-1980s when a series of reforms transformed the exchanges into modern entities with the latest technology. The process was initiated with a 1978 Commission to examine ways in which to stimulate activity on the exchanges. Reforms followed in the early 1980s, which were successful in persuading more companies to issue new shares as a means of generating more capital for expansion.

The reforms have involved greater decentralization, the establishment of a new body to oversee stock market transactions, and finally in 1989, a Law (the **Ley de Reforma del Mercado de Valores**) to streamline practices and bring them more into line with other Western exchanges. Early signs are that large investors have benefited most from the changes, amid greatly increased stock market activity which has also attracted foreign investors to the Spanish exchanges. Foreign investors are free to invest but are only allowed to acquire up to 50 per cent of a company's stock. Larger stakes need special authorization.

Despite comparatively low levels of exchange activity, more Spaniards appear to be viewing the stock market as a good investment. In 1989, for instance, the average profit increase of firms quoted on the stock market was estimated to be 21 per cent, while a minimum annual rise of 12 per cent was predicted up to 1993. Banks and electrical firms comprise 60 per cent of all firms on the exchanges. A proliferation of real estate companies in the late 1980s reflected the property boom in Spain.

Also in the past few years, six Spanish firms (three state-owned, three private) have taken the revolutionary step of entering Wall Street, with flotation on the US stock exchange. The three state-owned companies – Telefónica, Endesa and Repsol – have met with considerable success to date but the three private banking concerns – Banco Bilbao-Vizcaya, Banco Central and Banco de Santander – have encountered serious problems in appealing to US investors, apparently with long memories of the Latin American Foreign Debt crisis earlier in the 1980s which ruined a number of US banks and which has left investors wary of 'Hispanic' banks ever since. However, the very fact of just 'being on Wall Street' is seen as prestige enough in Spanish quarters and further evidence of Spain's desire to be part of the Western financial scene.

According to the *1988/89 OECD Economic Survey*, the recent Spanish overhaul of the stock exchange, including the abolition of the monopoly position of brokers, has already had a favourable impact on the international community.

Business and the labour market

The principal factors providing the background to the labour market are located in Spain's rapid industrialization since the 1960s, set against the authoritarian isolationism of the Franco dictatorship. Thus a massive exodus of workers from Franco's Spain, which began with the close of the Civil War in 1939 when an estimated half a million left the country as political refugees, was to be supplemented in the decades that followed by a continuing haemorrhage of manpower seeking employment in the more developed countries of Europe, as well as in the USA and Latin America. In 1989 2,800,000 Spaniards still worked in these countries and provide much-needed revenue for their home country.

Alongside emigration, the 1950s, 1960s and 1970s also witnessed wholescale domestic migration from the countryside to the towns and from the agricultural, poorer areas, such as Extremadura and Andalusia, to the more prosperous urban environments of Barcelona, Madrid and Bilbao.

As in other countries, Spanish women began to enter the workforce for the first time in the 1960s and unemployment, in the early post-Franco years of the democratic transition, began to soar, illustrating the human cost of Franco's failure to modernize Spain's economic infrastructure. Spain's business culture is still struggling to come to terms with the impact on the labour market which the sea-changes of the past three decades have generated on a population which in mid-1990 stood at 38,870,000.

Demographic trends – general

The single biggest concern for Spain is a fall in the birth rate more dramatic than that in virtually any other European country. In 1975 live births per 1000 inhabitants stood at nineteen but, by 1986, this had fallen to eleven. Also in 1986, the average number of children per woman in Spain was 1.5 compared with 2.8 in 1975. The figures demonstrate that women in Spain are having fewer children, later, and that more are joining the workforce. In fact, four out of every five new job-seekers are women, although only a third of Spanish women constitute part of the workforce, again one of the lowest levels in Europe.

Social factors are obviously an important contributory factor with fewer marriages in Spain in the 1980s and with the legalization of divorce in 1981, and abortion (under certain legally-defined circumstances) in 1985. While every survey conducted indicates that cohabitation and sex before marriage are now widely accepted, despite being religiously taboo in traditional Spain, it is nonetheless the case that a mere 20,000 marriages a year end in divorce and that illegitimate births constitute only 7 per cent of the total.

Demographic trends – Madrid

The drop in the number of young people in the 15–19 age group in Madrid since 1981 almost certainly is paralleled in other principal urban areas of Spain (for which, however, no information is available) and represents a nationwide problem which threatens business recruitment in the labour market as well as the vitality of Spain's main business centres (Table 5.8).

Table 5.8 *Madrid – fall in numbers of young people (1981–2001)*

	15–29 age (000s)	15–19 age (000s)
1981	741	293
1986	778	269
1991	787	241
1996 (projected)	696	189
2001 (projected)	568	141

Source: Boletín Estadístico de Madrid

From 1981 to 1986, Madrid lost 100,000 inhabitants in total, while the average age increased from 31.6 years to 36.8 years. By the year 2000, Madrid is expected to have half of the total 15–19 year age group that it had in 1986, with a predominance of over-65s. Madrid's birth rate, symptomatic of urban Spain as a whole, has fallen by a third in the last ten years to 1.4 children per couple, the lowest of any capital city in Western Europe.

Madrid's problem has prompted central and local government initiatives to counter the drift away from the major conurbations. The Mayor of Madrid, Juan Barranco, fears the trend could destroy the essential fabric of town centres in Spain and states: 'It could leave us with a centre of offices and shops, heavily depopulated, with only an ageing wealthy residential class.'

One of the main reasons for the population exodus is the spectacular rise in housing prices which has driven young people in particular to live in dormitory towns hours away from the centre or to abandon urban living altogether. The boom in house prices has meant an increase in new-build upmarket housing, inaccessible to most of the labour market, but the virtual disappearance of municipal housebuilding. For those entering the job market or those on low incomes in the first years of employment, the only alternative for the majority of young people is to remain in the family home. 20 per cent of married couples, at the end of 1986, were living with parents. The housing crisis has resulted in severe overcrowding with Madrid's 3.5 persons per dwelling one of the highest levels of any European capital.

A vicious circle has now emerged, with 62 per cent of males in Madrid between the ages of twenty-five and twenty-nine unmarried in 1986 (compared with 48 per cent in 1981). A similar trend for women further accentuates the decline in birth rate.

Labour market trends

In 1960, 39 per cent of the Spanish working population in civilian employment were employed in agriculture. By 1991 this figure had fallen to 14 per
cent, a level equivalent to Spain's Mediterranean EC partners but still
significantly higher than France, with 7 per cent employed in agriculture,
Germany with 5 per cent and the United Kingdom with 2 per cent.

Spain's manufacturing workforce changed very little in this period, from
a much lower base, with 23 per cent employed in manufacturing in 1991, as
in 1960. This figure can be compared with France (22 per cent), Germany
(32 per cent), and the United Kingdom (24 per cent).

Spain, like all of its EC partners, saw a continuing rapid expansion of
employment in services between 1960 and 1991, although the scale of
growth in Spain was even higher than in other countries. Thus, in Spain
between 1960 and 1991 the percentage employed in services increased from
31 per cent to 54 per cent. (In France employment in this sector rose from
40 per cent to 62 per cent, in Germany from 39 per cent to 54 per cent and
in the United Kingdom from 48 per cent to 68 per cent.)

Table 5.9 *Spanish civilian employment (1991)*

By sector	(%)	GDP at factor cost by origin (%)
Agriculture	12	5
Industry	24	30
Construction	10	8
Services	54	57

Source: OECD

Unemployment

Spain's dramatic transition from dictatorship to democracy has been
accompanied by the highest rates of unemployment seen in OECD countries as Spain's economy has undergone the severest adjustments (Tables
5.9 and 5.10).

The very acute employment crisis of the 1980s was caused by many factors including:

• A slowdown in economic growth through the 1970s exacerbated by the
  oil shocks and the uncertain political climate.

- A vigorous surge in wage costs following Franco's death in 1975.
- A marked deterioration in fixed investment in the 1970s.
- Delays in adjusting production structures.

Table 5.10 *Spanish unemployment rates (1977–92)*

Year	(%)
1977	5.2
1978	6.9
1979	8.5
1980	11.2
1981	13.9
1982	15.8
1983	17.2
1984	20.0
1985	21.4
1986	21.0
1987	20.1
1988	19.1
1989	16.9
1990	16.3
1991	15.9
1992	18.0

Source: OECD

From 1974, when employment stood at a record level, to 1982, employment fell by over two million, and a further fall of 1,900,000 was registered between 1983 and 1986. By 1985 also the participation rate (i.e. the ratio of employment to population of working age) had fallen to 43.7 per cent, the lowest level of any industrialized country. As early as 1978, Spain's unemployment rate topped the EC average and in 1985 climbed above 21 per cent, i.e. twice as high as EC member states. In addition, the length of time for which people remained unemployed and the composition of unemployment by age and sex were both unfavourable to Spain. Thus, the proportion of long-term unemployed (i.e. for twelve months or more) at 54.2 per cent in 1986 was higher than all other EC partners, with the exception of the Benelux countries. Youth unemployment (16–24 age group) at 47.5 per cent was also the highest in the OECD in 1987, and compared at the time with the United Kingdom at 33.6 per cent, France at 33 per cent and former West Germany at 22.7 per cent.

294   *Business Cultures in Europe*

A breakdown of the unemployment rate in 1987, compared with an already poor 1981 (Table 5.11), illustrated the severity of the problem facing Spain in the late 1980s.

Table 5.11 *Unemployment breakdown*
(1981 and 1987)

	1981 (%)	1987 (%)
Male	13.0	16.8
Female	17.5	28.0
Under 25 years	34.3	43.0
25–54 years	9.3	15.0
Over 55 years	5.7	9.4

Source: OECD

Due to the economic policies pursued by the government (and outlined earlier), however, the unemployment problem began to turn around in 1987 and especially 1988.

While the agricultural labour force continued to decline, 400,000 new jobs were created in other sectors in the late 1980s, a net increase in the number of employed of 300,000 or 3 per cent. Employment growth in the construction sector in 1988 was running at three times previous levels. In the service sector, female employment grew twice as fast as male employment while the overall female participation rate increased from an average of 29.3 per cent in the 1983–5 period, to 32.5 per cent in 1988. Next to Ireland, though, female participation rates were still the lowest in the OECD.

Also in the early 1990s, greater flexibility in the labour market resulted from a number of Employment Promotion Programmes in firms, sponsored by the government, which initially created many thousands of temporary and part-time jobs. About half of these jobs have, however, since been converted to permanent contracts, with the assistance of tax changes designed to encourage firms to create new permanent forms of employment.

Male unemployment fell by 1.6 percentage points between 1987 and 1988. Youth unemployment, significantly, had the sharpest reduction, mainly due to the special Employment Programmes, although at 40 per cent the 16–24 age group still compared poorly with the 25–54 age group, at 13.5 per cent. Also in 1988 and 1989, further evidence of economic growth in Spain finally influencing the job market was provided by a reversal in the earlier steep upward trend in long-term employment. In 1991 unemployment fell below 16 per cent in Spain for the first time since 1982 although the figure is still intractably high compared with 6.8 per cent for the OECD as a whole.

Unemployment training schemes

Additional to government Employment Programmes outlined earlier, the **National Institute for Employment** (INEM) has been devoting increasing resources (70,000 million pesetas in 1989) to training for the unemployed. Centres have been established throughout Spain but especially in areas affected by industrial 'reconversion'. Emphasis has been upon training in the new technologies and on collaborative ventures with the trade unions. INEM has worked also in close conjunction with regional governments and with the European Commission since it derives half of its budget from the European Social Fund.

Business and trade unions

A crucial element in Spanish business culture has been the development in the last decade of a free trade union structure, from the ruins of an unde-mocratic system of 'vertical syndicates' under Franco in which everyone who worked was obliged to be a member of one of twenty-eight vertical syndicates, arranged by industry, and constructed hierarchically to include all employees from top management to shop-floor worker. There was cen-tral control of the system, with the Minister for Syndical Relations a mem-ber of Franco's nominated government. The essentially undemocratic nature of the system can be gauged by the fact that as late as 1971 only 391 people were eligible to vote directly for the President of the Metal workers' syndicate, although the union had 1,300,000 members.

The collapse of vertical syndicalism, undermined from within by the Communist trade union, the **Comisiones Obreras** (Workers' Commissions) and from without by the unassailable march towards political pluralism, paved the way for a free trade union structure which since the late 1970s has had an increasing influence on the business culture. Led by the Workers' Commissions and the Socialist UGT (General Union of Workers), the trade unions initially, in a period where many companies had to learn how to negotiate with genuine worker representatives, adopted in the early 1980s a policy of conciliation and consensus, exemplified by the signing of a number of social and economic pacts with government and/or employ-ers' confederations.

In the late 1980s, increasing disillusionment with government monetary and fiscal policies, which accepted very high levels of unemployment and appeared to strike at workers' purchasing power, saw the unions turn towards open conflict with government and employers, a process culminating in Spain's first general strike for fifty years on 14 December 1988. Continuing trade union malaise underlay the general election of 29 October 1989 which, with only the narrowest overall majority for Felipe González's Socialist government, left the necessity for early government/employers/trade unions conciliation high on the new government's agenda.

Despite talks, however, trade union disillusionment with government policies remained high in the early 1990s. A further half-day general strike took place in May 1992 as a protest against the government's decision to reduce its budget deficit by cutting unemployment benefit, part of a government strategy to meet the convergence terms set by the EC Maastricht summit of December 1991.

Industrial democracy

Evolution of free trade unions from the vertical syndicates took place in the 1960s and 1970s, with Franco still in power, as employers increasingly began to negotiate with genuine though illegal, workers' representatives rather than through the official vertical organization. Although present-day trade unions have had only a brief modern history, the four decades of Francoism were unable to erase completely from collective memory an earlier period at the start of the last century and up to the 1930s in which Spanish trade unions were among the largest and the most powerful in the Western world. Industrial democracy's recent history has a number of important benchmarks:

Late 1950s/ early 1960s	The birth of the Communist trade unions, Workers' Commissions, as an illegal and clandestine movement, to infiltrate the official vertical syndicates. Quickly spreads throughout Spain to assume national importance.
1962	The first big demonstration of nascent free trade unionism with a Miners' Strike in the North of Spain leading to Franco declaring a state of emergency.
1968	A report of the International Labour Organization acknowledges the primacy of the illegal free trade union movement.
1960s/ 1970s	Internal rebirth of the Socialist trade union, the UGT, helped by the rise of González's Socialist party.
1975	The last Franco government tinkers with vertical syndicalism to allow for emergent trade unions but the attempt fails.

1975–7 Increasing industrial unrest as free trade unions demand full recognition.

1977 Legalization of free trade unions and abolition of vertical syndicates.

1978 First trade union elections to choose workers' delegates in firms.

1980 Workers' Statute becomes law. The Statute lays down workers' rights, representation and collective bargaining procedures. A minimum wage level is to be fixed annually by the government in consultation with unions and employers. The works' committees are established as the effective voice of the workforce in companies, able to negotiate with employers over working conditions and over wages, although local, regional or national wage negotiations will usually determine the parameters.

The tremendous pressure exerted by the workforce on the fragile democracy that was emerging in Spain in the mid-1970s is obvious when one examines the strike record and the number of man-hours lost as a result in the period from 1966 up to 1980. The ten-fold increase in man-hours lost between 1975 and 1976 is the most telling indicator of the Spanish people's reaction to Franco's death, although, as can be seen from Table 5.12, the figure continued to mount to a peak of 171,067,049 hours lost in 1979.

Table 5.12 *Spanish industrial disputes (1966–80)*

Year	No. strikes	Man-hours lost
1966	205	1,785,492
1970	817	6,750,900
1975	855	10,355,120
1976	1,568	110,016,240
1977	994	92,572,050
1978	1,356	128,738,478
1979	1,789	171,067,049
1980	1,669	108,625,662

Source: Spanish Employers' Confederation (Confederación Española de Organizaciones Empresariales)

Social and economic pacts

The fact that strikes in 1980 were still at a high level despite a reduction from 1979 was probably caused by two main factors: works' committees, initially, had insufficient power to represent workers' interests, being restricted to negotiating over health and safety issues; and, also, many Spanish firms were incredibly slow to recognize the reality of the changing situation and instead of engaging in direct dialogue with the workforce, asked government for greater protectionism for their industries. Such dilatoriness merely encouraged workers to join unions and formulate demands.

A developing battle between the Communist Workers' Commissions and the Socialist UGT was exacerbated by a bilateral agreement in 1980 signed between the UGT and the Spanish Employers' Confederation, the **CEOE**, a historic pact (the **AMI**), the first ever in Spain between employers and a national union. The main points of the pact were that wage rises of between 13 per cent and 16 per cent in profit-making companies would be paid and works' committees in each firm were to have access to company balance sheets and to be consulted in any management decision on employment policy, productivity, working methods or conditions.

During 1980, the AMI pact was on the whole a success, with widespread adherence to the wage rise guidelines, and the UGT negotiating successfully to halt potentially major strikes in the car industry and the dockyards. The pact also paved the way for a new agreement, known as the **ANE**, in which the Workers' Commissions joined the UGT, the Employers' Confederation and the government as co-signatories. This pact, which was to last until the end of 1982, kept wage rises to 10.5 per cent maximum (with inflation running at a rate of about 15 per cent), modernized collective bargaining procedures, and secured promises from the government to improve employment and social security provision. A further agreement, (the **AI**), this time between the unions and employers alone, extended cooperation into 1984 when the most far-reaching of the agreements to date was signed, the Economic and Social Accord (**AES**), a tripartite agreement between the UGT, management and the first Socialist government of Felipe González.

The Accord, covering 1985 and 1986, importantly, was the first of the agreements in which the government negotiated public spending plans with both sides of industry. Divided into two parts, the first part of the Accord detailed government commitments, and the second part was a legally-binding agreement between the signatories. The main components of the first part were:

- A government promise to create 190,000 jobs in 1985, via increased public sector funding and extra stimulus for private industry.

- A 'solidarity fund' of £284 million, raised by equal contributions from workers, employers and government, to support training and retraining schemes and innovatory job creation projects, along the same lines as the EC's European Social Fund.
- An increase in personal allowances, the removal of more low income earners from the tax net, and an extension of unemployment benefit from the 25 per cent eligible in 1984 to 48 per cent by the end of 1986.
- A government allocation of £237 million for investment in labour intensive sectors to modernize plant and machinery.

The second part of the Accord applied to around 5 million workers covered by collective agreements in the public and private sectors and comprised:

- A pay increase band of between 5.5 per cent and 7.5 per cent.
- An agreement to increase productivity, lower absenteeism and reduce systematic overtime by eradicating the common practice in Spain of multiple employment or double-jobbing.
- A rationalization programme to reduce the number of collective agreements signed at individual company level (3500 running in 1984) by introducing more national and regional bargaining.
- A new system for resolving disputes through voluntary mediation and arbitration.

Since 31 December 1986, when the Accord terminated, no new pact has been signed in Spain, and there is substantial evidence of growing trade union disenchantment with government economic policies. Whereas the Workers' Commissions refused to sign the Accord, the UGT later came to condemn its sister Socialist party in government for increasing job losses and eroding purchasing power. The Accord can be said, though, to have been successful in maintaining wage moderation, and a symptom of its success, paradoxically, is the mounting social disruption and political uncertainty which followed in the late 1980s and early 1990s when no pact was in place.

Trade unions' power battle in firms

The battle between the Communist Workers' Commissions and the Socialist UGT has centred around trade union elections in which the workforce select delegates on works' committees to negotiate with management. The balance of power between the unions is shown in Table 5.13.

The election results show the rise of the UGT through the 1980s, although the overall picture after 1986 tends to mask a switch in allegiance in large firms of 1000 employees upwards from the UGT to Workers'

Table 5.13 *Spanish trade union elections*

Trade union	Percentage of delegates elected to works' committees		
	1978 (%)	1981 (%)	1986 (%)
Workers' Commissions	34.5	30.7	34.9
UGT	21.6	29.7	41.0
USO (Workers' Syndical Union)	3.7	9.5	4.0
Regional unions	1.0	3.9	4.0
Others/Independents	39.2	26.2	16.1

Source: Cambio 16

Commissions. The Communist union also won twice as many votes as the UGT in the telephone and telecommunications industry and scored major successes in other crucial industries, including gas and energy, the railways and the banks. The UGT performed well in small and medium-sized firms and in the tobacco industry, its only stronghold among large firms. This was surprising, given the fact that in September 1986 the Socialist government had provided its UGT ally with a £21 million subsidy (and over 100 buildings) for its election campaign, representing the return of union assets seized by the Franco régime after the Civil War. The Workers' Commissions, having emerged only in the late 1950s, received practically nothing.

Trade union/government conflict

Increasing industrial unrest in 1987 and 1988, following the breakdown of the AES, the last social compact, reflected growing union anger at the effects of government policy and culminated in a general strike on 14 December 1988.

In the years preceding the strike, the Socialist government, in the view of the unions, had been accommodating the demands of employers, to achieve greater flexibility of labour. For instance, the government introduced six-month, fixed-term contracts in firms as a means of creating new jobs and proposed to abolish the statutory minimum wage for workers aged 18–24, to reduce redundancy payments and to extend part-time labour. At the same time, Spain's low labour costs were being advertised as a national asset as the government attempted to attract multinational enterprises and foreign investment. According to the US business magazine, *Fortune*, in 1987: '. . . labour costs in Spain are mouth-watering'. Some firms expect to pay Spanish workers up to 30 per cent less than workers else-where in Western Europe. Ford's Valencia plant – in which the UGT enjoys a major presence – has the lowest costs of any of the company's eight European factories.

In the absence of a new social pact the UGT has been in bitter conflict with the government since 1987. The UGT opposed González's decision to keep Spain within NATO, UGT MPs voted against the government over pensions legislation and, finally, the UGT leader, Nicolás Redondo, resigned his parliamentary seat in protest at the 1988 Budget.

A 1988 UGT report on Spain's economy from 1977 to 1987 spends 300 pages condemning the government for a 'monetarist and fiscal policy more conservative than Helmut Kohl or Margaret Thatcher'. In contrast to the UGT report, the Spanish Employers' Confederation (CEOE) has been enthusiastic in its support for government policies with José María Cuevas, the Confederation's President, declaring in 1988: '. . . the government should continue to fight inflation, improve firms' competitiveness and bring more flexibility into the labour market'.

1988 general strike

The general strike of 14 December 1988 was monumentally successful, with about six million strikers – two-thirds of the working population – paralysing the country. The trigger for the strike was the government's Youth Employment Plan, which sought to allocate £15,000 million to firms to engage unemployed workers below the age of twenty-five on short-term contracts at the minimum wage level. The UGT condemned the plan as 'the worst attack on workers since the Franco era', arguing that it would not solve the long-term unemployment problem. Redondo complained that 'only 18 per cent of jobs in Spain's expanding textile industry are perma-nent and over 30 per cent of production is in the hidden economy'. The labour market, he argued, has become 'the law of the jungle'.

Young workers in Spain form a reserve army for a huge black economy which some estimates put as high as 15 per cent or 20 per cent of legal GDP. Of every two people unemployed in Spain, one is between the ages of sixteen and twenty-five. There were over 1,400,000 in this category at the start of the 1990s and over 800,000 who have never had a job.

Following the success of the general strike, the UGT and Workers' Commissions agreed to meet Felipe González only if five prior conditions were met: scrapping the Youth Employment plan; compensating employ-ees in state-owned industries and pensioners for their 2 per cent drop in real earnings in 1988; increasing to 48 per cent the number of jobless enti-tled to unemployment pay; recognizing civil servants' right to collective bargaining; and bringing the minimum pension into line with the minimum wage. These demands are only some of a whole battery of social and economic measures the unions are pressing on government to redistribute wealth, protect employees and expand trade union rights and participation in the management of industry. The unions contend that when Spanish companies made low profits in the early 1980s the workforce tightened their belts to boost profitability. Now that profits are higher, they argue, the workforce deserve their share.

Throughout 1989 and 1990 there was an impasse between the unions and government, with the Socialist party even threatening to set up its own trade union in competition with its long-time ally, the UGT. Most importantly the general strike saw the greatest cooperation yet between Spain's two main trade unions, determined to increase the union movement's power to the level of some of her neighbouring countries. The task is a difficult one in an economy based mainly on hundreds of thousands of small firms and where trade union membership is between 20 per cent and 25 per cent of the working population (see below). As one UGT leader commented: 'With such low membership the unions are left out of the major economic decisions made in Spain. Most of the government's plans for the economy we learn about through the newspapers!'

A further half-day general strike in May 1992 and a threatened full-day strike for the Autumn of 1992 clearly indicated mounting trade union anger at government economic measures, announced shortly after the Maastricht summit, to reduce Spain's budget deficit by capping health spending, ending public sector bale-outs, and reducing unemployment provision.

Trade union membership

The unreliable figures provided by the unions themselves make membership levels difficult to estimate, although independent observers believe that membership in recent years has fallen away from the late 1970s when it may have reached a maximum of 30 per cent of the working population. The current level is unlikely to be much higher than 20 per cent, the level attained in 1981, and the lowest in Western Europe.

A May 1989 article in the Spanish magazine *Cambio 16* estimated membership at 17 per cent, but what is certain is that existing trade unions are poorly organized and inefficient. Poor collection procedures mean that between 50 per cent and 70 per cent of total membership dues are probably not collected. Strike funds are minimal so that extended strikes are only possible in small companies or those areas where the local population identify closely with the demands of the workforce.

Table 5.14 *Spanish trade union membership (20 per cent) (mid-1980s)*

Trade union	No. of members	% total membership
Workers' Commissions	730,000	42.0
UGT	692,000	39.9
Workers' Syndical Union (USO)	205,000	11.8
Basque TU (ELA/STV)	58,000	3.4
Others/Regional TUs	53,000	2.9

Source: Cambio 16

New initiatives

The UGT estimates that within a few years half of their funds will derive from the profits of a new holding company it is establishing, **UGTSA**. The holding company will be led by a new Trade Union Bank; by a house-building corporation, **PSV**, which will promote cooperative ventures; and by an insurance company, **UNIAL**.

These three companies will form the basis of a holding company, as UGT attempts to achieve financial autonomy and distancing from the Socialist party, and sets out to become a huge service trade union like its counterparts elsewhere in Western Europe. UNIAL, with forty-six offices projected throughout Spain, and with the use of UGT offices, has ambitions to attract business beyond the UGT membership itself. UGT points out that in Sweden, for instance, one person in two invests in a trade union insurance company, while in Austria a union company is market leader in the sector.

Employers' organizations

The main Employers' Confederation, CEOE, formed in 1977 from 165 employers' organizations, claims to represent 1.3 million companies controlling 75 per cent of all jobs in Spain in the private sector. 90 per cent of firms employ fewer than fifty workers. An organization for small and medium-sized firms, **CEPYME**, was integrated into CEOE in 1980 but still preserved special autonomous status and has appeared as a separate signatory in the social and economic pacts made with government and the unions. CEOE, increasingly combative and assertive since 1980, has assumed an important public profile in the 1980s and early 1990s, taking advantage of the unions' weakness through lack of funds, lack of unity (until recently) and the employment situation.

Business, education, training and development

In evaluating the contribution made to the Spanish business culture by education, training and development, it must be realized that Spain is starting in this area from a very low base. The decades of Francoism held back educational reforms and it was only in 1970 that an Education Reform Act introduced the present-day educational structure. The Act, however, in revolutionizing schooling, did not solve many of its attendant problems. Hence, a major plank of the first Socialist government's legislative programme in the 1980s was further educational reform, to be effected by two new Laws, the 1983 **University Reform Law** (LRU) and the *1985* **Organic Law on the Right to Education** (LODE), designed to democratize and modernize the school and university system. In 1990, the most far-reaching of all Spanish educational reforms was introduced, the **Organic Law on the General Organisation of the Education System** (LOGSE). This Law seeks to widen nursery provision, to make secondary schooling 'comprehensive', and to improve technical education.

The democratic transition inherited from Franco one of the least-educated or trained workforces in the Western world. The impact of 1970 education legislation was felt however as the percentage of unskilled workers fell from 46 per cent in 1963 to 33 per cent in 1976. The increase in skilled workers was particularly noticeable in administrative jobs, which constituted 12 per cent of wage earners in 1963 but increased to 19 per cent by 1976. The overall standard of education changed also so that in the 1970s education among workers to secondary school level became common for the first time, whereas previously the majority of workers had only reached primary level, if that. In 1964, only 5 per cent of the active population had secondary education. By 1980 it was almost 25 per cent.

Primary and secondary education

Divided between state and private schools, all pupils between the ages of six and fourteen study the compulsory **Basic General Education** course (the EGB). At the age of fourteen, the more academically able go on to study for a two-year **Bachillerato** while for others a course of vocational training known as **Formación Profesional** (FP) is available. The separation at fourteen has caused innumerable problems since parents have tended to keep their children in the academic lane by having them repeat years rather than allowing them to proceed along the less prestigious FP route. FP diplomas have also been slow to gain acceptance from Spanish employers.

The new 1990 LOGSE Law will eventually extend the period of obligatory education to the age of sixteen, thus avoiding premature specialization in a particular area of the curriculum.

Access to the universities is generally via the **University Orientation Course** (COU), a one-year pre-university course which involves compulsory subjects (Spanish language and literature, a foreign language and mathematics) and three optional subjects. In recent years other 'selectivity' exams have provided a route to higher education, which saw a rapid expansion in the 1970s and 1980s to the present level of 960,000 university students in the academic year 1991–2 (compared with 383,000 in 1975).

Universities

The spectacular rise in student numbers has caused chaos in a university system originally designed to accommodate only a tenth of the current student population. It has added to the problem of 'massification', i.e. the anonymous, impersonal, distant and bureaucratic treatment of students by institutions living, until recently, in the last century. The González government has, in the University Reform Law, attempted to update the universities, by placing tighter limits on the numbers admitted, in order to improve academic standards, by reorganizing university departments along Anglo-Saxon lines, and by reducing the bureaucracy which was strangling the system. (For instance, the Law reduced the forty-five categories of university teachers to four!) Naturally, the restrictions on numbers generated the most vociferous public protests and demonstrations.

Currently, there are thirty-four universities in Spain, thirty state-run and four private church-owned universities, the consequence of the 1953 Concordat between the state and the Catholic Church. These four universities suffer the least from 'massification'. The biggest universities in Spain are the Complutense in Madrid, Barcelona Central, Santiago de Compostela and Valencia. In all of them there is a space crisis, with Salamanca's half a square metre per student not untypical. The top universities, in terms of research expertise, are Complutense and Barcelona Central, but, overall, the universities suffer from a lack of teaching staff with expertise in business and management studies, and in technology.

Spain also has its **National University for Distance learning** (UNED) – the equivalent of the United Kingdom's Open University – which was inaugurated in 1972 but has been consistently underfunded ever since so that numbers have scarcely increased beyond the 60,000 students registered in 1980–1.

Government plans for universities

In 1989–90 the Spanish government, looking beyond 1992, announced a further overhaul of the university system. The main components of the new plan are as follows:

- The criteria of productivity is to be applied in determining the salaries of university lecturers, with top rates for academic high-fliers.
- Students, for the first time in Spain, will be able to study at any university, rather than at the nearest.
- A ranking list of universities is to be drawn up to encourage more competition in the sector.
- New, more relevant, and shorter degree courses are to be phased in e.g. eighty new (mostly three-year) degrees were introduced in 1989–90.
- Spain's first non-religious private university is to be established, specializing in Law and Economics (the **Escuela Libre de Derecho y Economía**).
- New university campuses are to be founded in Madrid and Barcelona.
- The Ministry of Education is to create a new system of university grants. Until now grants have been few and difficult to obtain.

Opposition from staff trade unions to some of these measures is not expected to prevent full implementation from a government widely predicted to win a fourth term in office.

New private universities

A Bill presented in the Spanish parliament in 1990 has facilitated the creation of new private universities in Spain. A number of projects have been under examination, including two in Madrid and one each in Barcelona and Valencia. The Catholic Church, owners of private schools and a number of major companies, have all expressed interest in the idea.

While the Private University of Madrid, run by private school proprietors, is expected to be first to commence operations, with 12,000 students on two campuses, the most innovative aspect of the venture is the interest being shown by Spanish companies. The banks, BNP and Banco Central Hispano-americano, Repsol (the petrol giant), and El Aguila (brewers) all want to be involved, but perhaps the most unusual application is that of the oil company Petromed which is pursuing its interest in a private university jointly with Mercedes-Benz under the aegis of the EC ERASMUS initiative.

While university student numbers have grown in recent years, so also have pupils studying vocational training under the FP banner. Numbers have doubled between 1975 and 1985. In the same decade, the enrolment rate in education overall increased by two-thirds while the number of students in higher education as a share of the total population rose by 50 per cent.

A growing mismatch between employer demand and supply of labour at all levels has been increasingly noticeable since the 1980s. Industry has experienced longer delays in filling vacancies. A recent survey by the Ministry of Labour demonstrated that Formación Profesional is not providing the skills and qualifications which firms need. Hence, with government support, new Professional Training Programmes have been initiated in order to improve the quality of labour supply, especially in sectors with a skilled labour shortage.

Table 5.15 *Spanish education: input and output indicators (1975 and 1985)*

	1975	1985
Pre-university education		
Number of pupils (thousands)	7517	8696
State schools	4340	5593
Pre-primary	920	1127
Compulsory	5473	5594
Post-Compulsory (FP)	305	737
Post-Compulsory (General)	818	1238
Numbers of teachers in state schools (thousands)	156	271
Higher education		
Students (thousands)	557	822

Source: OECD

Management training

The Ministry of Labour estimates that Spanish firms require a minimum of 30,000 executives per year trained in business and management studies. Spanish business schools in fact are only producing 11,000 per year and not all of these are trained to a sufficiently high level.

The first MBAs appeared in Spanish business schools in the mid-1960s and the schools themselves are flourishing, but the failure to apply strict criteria on the qualifications awarded has meant that any educational institution can appropriate the title 'Masters' and apply it to virtually any course of any standard or duration. Thus, many business schools and even the in-house training agencies of the Cajas de ahorros have been attaching the 'Masters' label to courses on an indiscriminate and arbitrary basis. Another problem is that in Spain, unlike the USA for example, no ranking list of business schools is produced.

Despite the problems, demand in the marketplace is very high indeed, with Spain's top business school **IESI**, in Navarra (**Instituto de Estudios Superiores de Empresa**), regularly attracting in excess of 2000 applications for its 200 MBA places, and with even the less prestigious schools receiving at least four or five applications per place. One of Spain's leading business magazines, *España Económica*, suggested recently that the market could probably absorb ten times the number of places currently available.

By general consent, the top business schools in Spain, of a standard comparable with other EC countries are IESI, **ESADE** in Barcelona (**Escuela Superior de Administración y Dirección de Empresas**), and the **Instituto de Empresas** in Madrid. New schools are opening up though to supply market demand, e.g. the new Madrid Business School. IESI estimates that each student graduating with a qualification receives an average of three job offers, while other schools claim this can rise to eight per student. The business schools of Madrid and Barcelona account for about 80 per cent of student intake amid ferocious competition for the best students.

An indication of rising standards and the growing esteem in which the top Spanish business schools are held is the increase in US, Canadian and other European students on MBA courses in Spain. The US magazine, *Fortune*, in its ranking of the top five business schools in Europe put IESI (which incidentally introduced the oldest MBA in Europe, in 1964, in conjunction with Harvard) in fifth place behind INSEAD (Fontainebleau), London Business School, IMEDE (Lausanne) and IMI (Geneva). IESI's ranking is undoubtedly due to its rigorous training programme for would-be lecturers who spend three or four years in a top US school such as Harvard before returning to lecture in Spain.

Research and development

In February 1988, the government approved a National Plan for Scientific Research and Technological Development. The Plan, which came into operation in the Autumn of 1988, aims to raise the scientific and technological base, especially in terms of research, in higher education and in companies. The base, historically, has been very low, with research grants, which were first awarded in 1968, having little or no relevance to the world of business.

For many years R & D has constituted only about 0.4 per cent of GDP, although this level doubled in the second half of the 1980s, increasing from 0.48 per cent GDP in 1984 to 0.85 per cent GDP in 1990 (equivalent to 300,000 million pesetas). The Plan aims to raise the level further to 1.2 per cent GDP by 1992, a substantial increase, although this must be set against the 3 per cent GDP devoted to R & D in western Germany (see page 1).

A prime aim of the Plan is to train greater numbers of personnel up to Masters' and Doctorate level in order better to face the challenge of post-

1992 Europe. A massive investment in training in priority areas includes the provision of sending more Spaniards abroad for training. Over 20 per cent of the National Plan's budget is allocated to the training of researchers in a bid to elevate the total of 25,000 trained researchers estimated to be working currently in Spain.

Considerable progress has already been made under the auspices of the Plan. Thus, the number of research grants awarded went up from 3002 in 1986 to 5210 in 1988, with further increases planned. In 1988, 7000 scientists were receiving training and this figure rose to 9000 in 1989, as the government improved its funding by 60 per cent over the previous year. In addition, a number of regional governments are now beginning to budget for research grants. This has helped to raise the international profile of Spanish researchers, as evidenced in the *Science Citation Index* which recorded a 13 per cent growth in Spanish publications in the world's top scientific journals between 1987 and 1988. Initial results are therefore encouraging, but the 1988 experience also indicated that demand for research grants to study abroad in certain vital areas is woefully inferior to the country's requirements. Less than twenty applications apiece were received in the areas of agrarian research, marine research, and information technology, while some areas such as robotics attracted no applicants at all.

The National Plan also aspires to establishing some kind of research base in industry, which has hitherto virtually ignored R & D. The Plan envisages the establishment of structures to improve the integration of scientific research with technological knowhow and industrial experience, i.e. the Plan proposes to link the universities, government research councils and Spanish companies. A crucial element in this is the creation of a national network, the **Office for Relay of Research Results** (OTRI), which will coordinate research projects and findings in all of Spain's universities and will eventually access these to Spanish industry. The Plan also seeks to boost the participation of Spanish firms and universities in the various EC programmes such as EUREKA.

Javier Solana, the Education Minister, also committed, in early 1990, an additional 11,000 million pesetas to scholarships and funding for training research students. This is an enormous boost to the Ministry's recent campaign to increase the number and quality of researchers and scientists. In 1982, the Ministry was spending just 1000 million pesetas on funding research training; in 1987 the figure had only risen to 3150 million pesetas.

Business and the environment

The business culture in Spain is only just beginning to be aware of environmental issues, which are relatively new on the political and business agenda and which occupy the nation's attention far less than in most other EC countries. Thus, while ecology groups and 'green' parties have emerged in Spain in the 1980s, they have not hitherto achieved the public profile or the electoral support seen elsewhere. In the general election of October 1989, the environment was one of the lesser campaign issues and only one party, the opposition Popular Party, advocated the creation of a government Ministry of the Environment to bring Spain into line with her European partners.

The rapid changes of the past thirty years, however, have created in Spain a massive environmental problem, the scale of which Spaniards are finally appreciating when, for instance, the air pollution in towns like Madrid makes it virtually impossible to breathe on occasions or when the polluted nature of Spain's Mediterranean beaches and coastal towns attracts the unwelcome attention of the foreign media (as happened in the summer of 1989 when the resort of Salou, south of Barcelona, was condemned by the British popular press). The results of an industrialization process which brought a massive exodus from the countryside to the towns in the 1960s, and the uncontrolled development of manufacturing industry, were accompanied by all the depredations which mass tourism and its service industries brought to Spain's coastlines. The 1980s perceived the problem; the 1990s have barely begun to address it.

Responsibility for the environment

Central government promulgates environmental legislation while the regions may pass supplementary regulations. Only in 1972 did Spain approve its first legislation on the environment and establish a public body to coordinate environmental policy, known as the **Comisión Interministerial del Medio Ambiente** (Inter-ministerial Committee for the Environment), responsible to the **Ministerio de Obras Públicas y Urbanismo** (Ministry for Public Works and Town-planning). CIMA's decisions, however, are not legally binding and its limited scope prevents it from achieving many objectives. Environmental issues emerge under different government ministries – Industry, Agriculture, Health, Transport, etc. – but the lack of a single government department responsible for environmental affairs is an obvious impediment to rapid address of the problem. At regional level, notably in Andalusia and Asturias, some attempts have been made to establish **Agencias de Medio Ambiente** (Environmental Agencies) but these have not so far met with conspicuous success.

Only in 1992 did Spain finally appoint an Environment Minister, José Borell, but the fact that he is also Minister for Transport and Public Works, a department which is the worst offender against EC green laws, justifies criticism that he is both 'gamekeeper and poacher'!

Since the scale of Spain's environmental problem far outweighs the remedial measures taken hitherto, the major environmental issues which the political and the business community must face in the 1990s are summarized below. Where appropriate, the response to date of government and business is outlined.

Air pollution

1972 legislation governs the prevention, monitoring and correction of air pollution, and establishes acceptable emission levels. Special provisions were made for the worst-affected areas, mainly the areas with the highest concentration of heavy industry – Bilbao, Madrid, Avilés, Huelva, Cartagena – and the first anti-air pollution campaigns were launched with government grants. The worst offenders in terms of industrial air pollution are power stations, oil refineries, iron and steel works and cement works.

Table 5.16 *Spanish emissions of atmospheric pollutants by industry (1980)*

Sector	Particulates (1000 tonnes)	Sulphur dioxide (1000 tonnes)	Nitrogen oxides (1000 tonnes)
Power stations	341	1,610	186
Oil refineries	–	130	17
Iron and steel works	214	178	–
Cement works	268	50	11
Sulphuric acid plants	–	38	6
Paper mills	21	44	8

Source: European Commission

In the late 1980s, government and industry began to work together to counter air pollution. As well as grants and tax concessions to firms, government has also made available to firms in high-pollution areas special subsidies for up to 30 per cent of the total cost of installing anti-pollution equipment. Also in 1985 the first legislation was passed to improve vehicular air pollution, when the lead content of petrol was reduced from 0.6 g/l to 0.44 g/l, in line with EC regulations.

Waste pollution

In 1985 Spain's 39 million population generated 10.6 million tons, or 265 kg per person per year, of urban solid waste. A high proportion of urban waste disposal is accounted for by uncontrolled dumping, an estimated

46.5 per cent of the total in 1985. Spain's forty composting plants make 700,000 tons of compost each year from 1.5 million tons of waste. Although it is government policy to support schemes for the recovery of raw materials from urban waste, the high cost and energy consumption of reclamation plants are becoming prohibitive. Few towns, and few industries, have equipment for selective material recovery. Despite this, government has drafted guidelines to encourage local authorities to rationalize urban waste management. More and more recycling – of glass, paper, board, etc. – is taking place yearly. In 1982 for instance only five towns in Spain had bottle banks, which recovered 837 tons of glass but, by 1986, 179 towns recovered 13,318 tons of glass.

Over 10 million tons of industrial waste are generated yearly of which 1.5 million tons is considered hazardous. Several centres for the treatment of hazardous waste have been established, notably the acid neutralization plant in the Basque region and three oil regeneration plants run by the oil company, CAMPSA. Even though 1986 legislation makes contraventions punishable by fines and banning, there are insufficient waste treatment centres to deal with industrial waste.

Water and sea pollution

A new Water Law was passed in 1986 which established a single body to manage surface and ground waters. Serious river pollution increased in the 1980s and the government responded by allocating grants to the regions to install water purification plants. Firms have also been awarded subsidies to introduce recycling plants. The proportion of the population served by water treatment plants went up from 18 per cent in 1980 to 40 per cent in 1986.

Mass tourism and its attendant industries have helped to create a major threat to Spain's 6121 km of coastline, 63 per cent of which is rocky terrain, 23 per cent sand, 8 per cent man-made and 4 per cent mud flats. 20 per cent of Spain's 3090 beaches are estimated to be in danger of disappearing from a combination of all factors, including increasing urbanization along coastal areas which now accommodate 12 million of Spain's population and 65 per cent of industry. Government has sponsored schemes to clean up the coastline and monitor sea pollution. Thus, of the 190 towns on the Mediterranean coast, approximately two-thirds had sewage treatment plants by the end of 1989, with more under construction.

Forestry

Spain has more natural forest land than any other EC country (the ratio is twice as great as France and four times as great as former West Germany and Italy). Concern now focuses on the gradual depletion of natural forests as farmers clear and cultivate woodland sites and on the poor condition of trees that remain. With 73.8 per cent of the territory in private hands, the government's 1984 legislation to replant land has affected only a small proportion of the total area and even this has met with criticism from ecology groups unhappy with the methods or species used.

The greatest threat to Spain's natural environment comes from forest fires and their contribution to soil erosion. The 1980s saw a sharp increase in the incidence of forest fires which in 1985 damaged an area four times greater than the reforestation of 1984. Soil erosion now is a bigger problem in Spain than any other EC country. In 1986 alone, 64.2 per cent of Spanish land surface was affected by high or moderate levels of soil erosion. The situation has undoubtedly worsened since then.

Parks and nature reserves

Although Spain was the first EC country to introduce the concept of National Parks in 1916, little was done until 1975 to protect the huge areas of countryside which 10 million people now visit each year. In recent years the creation of 250 special nature recreation areas for picnicking, camping, bathing, etc. has been accompanied by a national campaign to elevate the status of nature studies.

Flora and fauna

1980 legislation created protected areas and game reserves for 300 threatened species and, yet, forty-three species are currently in danger of extinction due to uncontrolled hunting, urbanization, new agricultural methods, etc. These include the Spanish imperial eagle, the black vulture, osprey, brown bear and ibex. Similarly, national legislation (1984) and supplementary regional regulations have done little to protect an estimated 1277 endangered species of endemic plants.

A 1988 directive from the EC to Spain to spend 300,000 million pesetas in industry and technology to improve the environment is only one indication of the tremendous strides Spain needs to make in order to catch up with EC partners. Failure to prioritize the environment on the part of government and a virtually non-existent environmental industry does not suggest that this task is likely to be undertaken in the near future. It is to be hoped that increasing public concern and EC pressure will cause government and business to devote more attention and resources to Spain's environmental problems.

The response of business to the EC's single market

The Spanish business community's attitude to the EC's single market has been characterized by guarded apprehension alongside keen anticipation. The apprehension is based upon the painful adjustments already made since the demise of Franco and entry into the EC in 1986. Accompanying the apprehension, however, is a realistic acceptance of the price Spanish industry must pay if it is to be a serious major international competitor. Investment in modern plant and machinery has been rapid, as the business community reflects the near-unanimous enthusiasm for Spain's full participation in the EC among the general population. Such enthusiasm has meant that, within the institutions of the EC, Spaniards have quickly acquired a reputation as whole-hearted Europeans.

The Spanish media have appeared to be obsessed with the implications of 1992, not least of course because the completion of the single market coincided happily with the Barcelona Olympics, Expo 92 in Seville, and the fifth centenary of Columbus' discovery of America. While there is little evidence to suggest that Spanish industry as a whole has examined its own response to 1992 with the same thoroughness, nonetheless a new breed of younger, business-school trained, European-minded executives is emerging in enough Spanish companies to encourage longer-term optimism. Symbols are potent in Spain and the new captains of industry look to the successful example of Spain's 'Lois' jeans in the 1980s where, against the odds, a Spanish product took on French and Italian fashions in one case and the jeans market in the other. In both cases, hard-and-fast rules of reinvesting were observed by a single shareholder company that put a high premium on advertising and kept growing.

Strengths

Spanish manufacturing labour costs in the late 1980s were only half the level of former West Germany's and Spain's wage levels were the lowest in the EC, after Greece and Portugal. Spanish business, therefore, had a headstart over competitors. Even though labour costs rose in line with inflation in 1989, 1990 and 1991, as long as real wage rises do not exceed productivity growth, Spanish business can hope to continue expanding in the 1990s. New planned legislation on restrictive business practices will further enhance competition, already galvanized by the lifting of import quotas and the halving of tariffs since EC accession. Spain's historical links with Latin America and her friendly relations with the Arab world are other factors which give Spanish business a distinct trading advantage over EC partners, a fact acknowledged by some foreign companies which bought into Spain precisely to gain a foothold in markets notoriously difficult to penetrate.

No one should underestimate the positive motivational influences on the business community which the worldwide fashionableness of Spain in the past few years has generated. Spanish fashion (**diseño**) and the complex sociocultural phenomenon of the **movida** – an explosion of the plastic and fine arts combined with a youth pop-cult – have been exported successfully to other EC countries. A proliferation of fashion shows and exhibitions in the major cities of Europe (e.g. Harrod's one-month 'made in Spain' exhibition in 1988) has been accompanied by renewed enthusiasm for Spanish artists. In 1988, for instance, plays by Lorca were staged to great acclaim in Paris and London; Italy fêted some of Spain's best-known writers; and the film director, Pedro Almodóvar, became a cult figure. *Newsweek*'s issue of 23 May 1988, a special devoted to Spain, captured the mood succinctly with its front cover picture of Felipe González and a caption which read: 'Spain. Racing into the Future. Europe's Tortoise turns into a Hare.'

Some commentators believe that the conglomeration of events in 1992 – the Olympics, Expo 92, Madrid's stint as cultural centre of Europe, etc. – has already helped to forge a unity of national purpose in Spain as the country fights to meet a deadline of the kind which Spaniards, well known for their improvisation rather than their planning, excel at fulfilling. Sponsorship on a massive scale has been secured from Spanish and foreign companies for the events of 1992.

Coca-Cola was the biggest sponsor of the Barcelona Olympics, and also sponsored the Spanish team. Expo 92's main sponsors were the Spanish banks – Banco de Bilbao y Vizcaya, Español Central de Créditos, Banco Central Hispanoamericano and the Banco Exterior de España. Even before 1992, Spain was the second most-successful country in the world – behind the US – in terms of sponsorship income. Clearly, the entrepreneurial spirit is thriving and looking forward eagerly to all the various opportunities afforded post-1992.

Weaknesses

The legacy of underinvestment, overmanning, and poor training has been outlined in previous sections, as have the tremendous efforts made by the business community and by government to overcome these deficiencies. Infrastructural weakness – the roads, railways, etc. – is, as we have seen, also being addressed. Spanish industry will have to wait well beyond 1992 to reap the full rewards of such labours, despite individual company successes. It remains to be seen, though, how the essential framework of a business culture founded upon a proliferation of small and medium-sized firms will withstand the growing intensity of competition from Europe (and the world's) multinationals.

The traditional weakness, however, of Spain's agricultural system, based upon the equally inefficient **latifundios** or large tracts of land in the South and the **minifundios** or tiny plots in the North West, continues to underlie Spanish economic growth and to undermine the efforts of the business community. Spanish agricultural products are moving gradually towards parity of price with other EC countries and although they enjoyed a competitive price advantage in 1989, this disappeared in 1993. Under the terms of Spain's EC accession, restrictions will continue until the end of 1995 on the export of certain products, including oils, fruit and vegetables, which the Spaniards produce too cheaply for the comfort of the French and Italians. Spain would like to see these restrictions removed on completion of the single market.

In November 1988, the European Commission sanctioned a new system of aid to small farmers in Spain which parallels existing schemes in other countries and which has benefited half a million Spanish farmers to the tune of 20,000 million pesetas yearly up to 1992. The aid, half funded by the EC and half by central government, is intended to put Spanish agriculture on a more competitive basis with its Northern neighbours. New machinery and modernization to reduce the costs of harvesting will mostly go to farmers under the age of thirty-five in an endeavour to rejuvenate the agrarian workforce. The new subsidies, strictly awarded on the investment potential of small farmholdings, supplement youth programmes previously initiated by the government to assist 30,000 young farmers. If the reforms are successful, Spain will become more efficient in its agriculture and the subsidizing of surplus produce by the EC. In addition, the Spanish government produced a Rural Employment Plan in 1992 designed to halt the decline in agricultural employment by allocating 114 billion pesetas to rural areas, with Andalucia receiving 70 per cent of total funds.

Opportunities

Many Spanish businesses are opting for joint ventures with counterparts in other EC countries as a means of seizing the opportunities afforded by the single market. Spain's fourth-biggest bank, the Banco de Santander, was a pioneer in this field by linking in 1989 with the Royal Bank of Scotland. The Banco de Santander's youthful chief executive, Juan Inciarte, typifies the new entrepreneurial breed of Spanish executive who dismisses any suggestion of Spanish inferiority, by asserting in July 1989 that: 'In Spain, we have a combination of people and products second to none.

That gives us a competitive advantage that foreigners cannot provide easily.'

The tie-up between the two banks justifies the Spanish bank's belief that there are other ways of growing, apart from takeovers, and that flexibility is needed to cope with the wide variations between what *pace* 1992 are still separate and hugely different markets. The link between Banco de Santander and the Royal Bank of Scotland will elbow them into each other's home markets at a fraction of the cost of building up a branch network from scratch. Juan Inciarte insists that the move towards a single financial services market is not going to happen overnight adding that: 'Many corporate institutions are looking at Europe as a single country, but if a bank does not have the ability to differentiate Scotland from Italy, it will lose in the battle for the future.' The most profitable area for collaboration looks like being between Banco de Santander's merchant bank and the Royal Bank's subsidiary, Charterhouse. The Spanish bank is keen to import expertise in financial engineering into a country where techniques such as leveraged buyouts are still in their infancy.

Other Spanish companies are looking at networking arrangements such as the Banco Bilbao-Vizcaya, which has joined a fee-sharing network of banks across Europe that includes Bayerische Vereinsbank in Germany, Instituto Bancario San Paolo di Torino in Italy and the Hambros group in the UK.

Spain's textile industry is another example of an industry which is now starting to look at joint ventures with foreign firms to gain access to new markets. With 315,000 legal workers and tens of thousands of undeclared ones, the textile industry is a major employer and the pillar of the economy of Catalonia. Better equipped and capitalized than ever before after a state-aided investment blitz from 1982–6, productivity has increased by 40 per cent since 1982. The recent slump in European textiles and clothing generally, plus undercutting by cheap imports, however, put the industry into deficit in 1987 and 1988. Spain's textile industry, with low wages and high levels of skill and design but, with poor marketing abroad hitherto, exemplifies the kind of business which ought to excel in the single market context. An appreciation of the problems and the application of new marketing techniques should place this industry in an excellent position to expand in the 1990s.

The Spanish IT industry is the fastest growing in the world, at 1.5 per cent GDP in 1988, and 23 per cent growth in 1989. Predictions are that the industry will grow at four times the rate of the economy overall up to 1993 but of the 1988 sales of 758,439 million pesetas only 11 per cent is accounted for by exports, suggesting again that potential for growth overseas is enormous. The single market represents an outstanding opportunity for IT, textiles, the banks and many other business sectors to implant themselves firmly in foreign markets. Early indications are that the Spanish business community is gearing itself up to do exactly that.

Threats

In an important sense, 1993 merely meant 'more of the same' to Spanish industry. In other words, more imports from abroad at increasingly competitive prices and more interest from foreign firms in buying into or buying out Spanish firms.

The market for electrical household goods best exemplifies the problem. Already in the years since EC entry, Spain has experienced an invasion of imported goods – Italian washing machines, German television sets, French refrigerators and Dutch hi-fi equipment. The gradual reduction of tariff barriers and import taxes since 1986 has continued with a further 12.5 per cent reduction on 1 January 1990, followed by 12.5 per cent in 1991, 12.5 per cent in 1992 and a final 10 per cent in 1993. Any product carrying a 100 pesetas tariff before 1986 paid only 35 pesetas in 1989 but nothing in 1993.

The retail chain-store giant El Corte Inglés, in 1989, signed an agreement with an Italian producer of electrical goods to supply its stores. Previously El Corte Inglés had always used Spanish manufacturers. The majority of Spain's supermarkets have foreign capital behind them, with French interests predominant, and with the gradual removal of tariff barriers, are retailing more imported goods.

Spain's traditionally strong electrical sector illustrates the threat to Spanish ownership of companies. 1000 companies make up the sector, with 70 per cent privately owned and 30 per cent in state hands. Twenty-one firms, however, produce 98 per cent of the total, in which 1.5 million small shareholders have a stake. The market is vulnerable to rationalization and foreign intervention, with the German company RWE leading the way.

Although global foreign investment in Spain has increased yearly since 1982, the country seeks more, to compensate for limited sources of indigenous capital and the historic tendency of Spanish banks (though this is changing) to prefer to invest in real estate rather than in industry. Many small and medium-sized Spanish companies, especially family firms, are ripe for purchase: they are relatively cheap and do not have the finance necessary for technological updating. Opportunities have been available in every sector, as can be seen from a sample selection of foreign investment initiatives in recent years. State-owned car manufacturers Seat and Enasa have passed into German hands. Banks have changed ownership with, for example, a 75 per cent stake in Banco Atlántico taken by the Arab Aresbank. In construction, the Arabs and Italians have been to the fore, with Gianni Agnelli now owning one third of Huarte. In food and drink, the brewers El Aguila now have Heineken as major shareholder, while Benedetti from Italy own 27 per cent of the food manufacturer Pascual Hermanos. The British firm, Wiggins Teape, bought up Ceasa, a leading wood pulp manufacturer. Household names in Spain, therefore, have gone 'foreign' and, with foreign investment increasing 600 per cent since 1982, the trend is accelerating.

Strategies

The Spanish business community is understandably wary about the implications of the single market and yet has been prepared to undertake the necessary readjustments, often painful, of capital modernization and manpower training which full European integration involves.

A new breed of business executives genuinely aspires to establish Spanish business in European markets, while defending domestic interests against foreign incursions. A recent study published by the business consultants SRU gives hope that the aspiration can become a reality. According to the study, the ideal executive to lead companies into the post-1992 Europe will be from a small country, multilingual, of flexible mind and social brilliance, will come from a multicultural family, will be a male graduate of a business school, and will almost certainly not be British.

This identikit picture could describe the new executive breed in Spain, usually from the wealthy classes, often with an MBA from a US university. José Barroso, thirty-one-year-old head of the multimillion peseta enterprise, Don Algodón, with over 100 fashion shops in Spain, fits the picture exactly. Barroso, from a comfortable upper middle-class Madrid family, borrowed £350 from a bank when he was seventeen years old, started selling T-shirts to schoolfriends, and, at twenty, travelled to Italy to bid successfully for the Benetton franchise in Spain. In the 1990s, with plans to extend the Don Algodón operation across Europe, Barroso's company – with the successful example of Lois jeans to follow – seems certain to be one of the first of a whole succession of Spanish companies to take full advantage of the opportunities afforded by the single market.

References and suggestions for further reading

Anuario El País, published yearly, Madrid: Altamira.
Cambia 16, published weekly, Madrid.
Donaghy, P. J. and Newton, M. T. (1987), *Spain: A Guide to Political and Economic Institutions*, Cambridge: CUP.
Economist Surveys on Spain.

European Commission Statistics.

European Information Development (1983), *Problems of Enlargement – Taking Stock and Proposals*, London.

Gillespie, R. (1989), *The Spanish Socialist Party*, Oxford: Clarendon Press.

Gilmour, D. (1985), *The Transformation of Spain*, London: Quartet.

Graham, R. (1984), *Spain. Change of a Nation*, London: Michael Joseph.

Harrison, J. (1978), *An Economic History of Modern Spain*, Manchester: Manchester University Press.

Hooper, J. (1986), *The Spaniards*, London: Penguin.

OECD Economic Surveys, Spain, Paris, 1989.

OECD Statistics, OECD Publications, Paris.

Preston, P. (1986), *The Triumph of Democracy in Spain*, London: Methuen.

Preston, P. and Smith, D. (1984), *Spain, the EEC and NATO*, London: RKP.

Sagardoy Bengoechea, J. A. and León Blanco, D. (1982), *El Poder Sindical en España*, Barcelona: Planeta.

Salmon, K. (1991), *The Modern Spanish Economy*, London: Pinter Publishers.

Sampedro, J. L. and Payno, M. A. (19893), *The Enlargement of the European Community – Case Studies of Greece, Portugal and Spain*, London: Macmillan.

Shlaim, A. and Yannopoulous, G. N. (eds) (1976), *The EEC and the Mediterranean Countries*, Cambridge; CUP.

6 The business culture in the Netherlands
Peter King

Introduction

Business culture in the Netherlands, more even than in Scandinavia, has pre-eminently the advantage of a basic education in three or more foreign languages. The business personnel's ready access to other European languages not only facilitates communication, but also means that technical literature in other languages is immediately available to them in their training and research. The Dutch, it is often said, are always thinking across frontiers. Dutch business culture is very definitely export-minded, and in their market resourcefulness they are willing to go abroad, work abroad and engage in novel forms of trade and technical experimentation.

Moreover, enforced inactivity during the Occupation in the Second World War provided an opportunity for visionary planning for peacetime, and the loss of 30 per cent of its capital assets and 96 per cent of its stocks meant that, like former West Germany, it could replace with modern equipment and introduce automation rather earlier than the United Kingdom.

Since the 1960s rationalization has advanced rapidly, and a consequent ·rise in wage costs led to an intensification in capitalization at a rate comparable with West Germany's and the United Kingdom's, but ten years ahead of West Germany and fifteen years ahead of the United Kingdom in 1960. It is the success of the resultant growth in productivity that is a major factor in the present high-unemployment situation in the Netherlands.

Another common post-industrial development is cartel formation. This is almost unrestricted in the Netherlands, so that there are about 600 registered cartels, the majority of which are price cartels.

Although it was American models that were followed in the rationalization of industry and commerce, the Dutch still regard the Germans as their trading partners and (like it or not, for there is still a marked love–hate relationship with that country) they admire their business efficiency. They respect knowledgeable authority, they like the idea that someone 'really knows' or 'is an expert', and they are certainly not flamboyant speculators. On the other hand, their trading and colonial traditions show through in their explicit commercial instincts, and there is in their business culture a recognition of the importance of a mix of social graces and general aptitudes in higher posts.

Despite its impressive history of trading and agriculture, the Netherlands has, since the war, become an important industrial producer. It is internationalist and anti-protectionist in outlook, which accounts for its early promotion of the Benelux Union; it is politically stable, has a well-educated workforce and a high standard of living.

Business and government

The post-war cabinets from 1945 to 1958 were dominated by the Socialist principles of Willem Drees, who had earlier been a co-author of the radical **Plan van de Arbeid** (Labour Scheme). So it was consistent with this that the first cabinet in 1945 announced that the reconstruction of the country's economy could only succeed on the basis of a social as well as an economic and financial programme. One outcome of this was the introduction in 1950 of the **Publiekrechtelijke Bedrijfsorganisatie** (PBO), (the Statutory Industrial Organization), and the **Central Planbureau** (CPB), (Central Planning Office), both of which still exist. The PBO ensures that every trading organization has an elected council of equal numbers of employers and employees, with a central advisory board, the **Social-economische Raad** (SER) (Social and Economic Council) representing on equal terms management, shop floor and **kroonleden**, (crown appointees), i.e. independent advisers to the government. The SER took over many of the functions of an earlier **Stichting van de Arbeid** (Labour Council), at one time providing a three-cornered board to maintain a balance between wages and prices, agreed by an equal representation of kroonleden, management and labour.

The government, with its free-market policy in recent years, has withdrawn from its intervention in private business, though the SER has remained to advise the government on particular matters. The CPB provides economic forecasts, in cooperation with the **CBS** (Central Bureau of Statistics).

With the help of some Dfl 80,000 million of Marshall Aid and a remarkable discipline in wage and price restraints, the economy in the 1950s expanded very rapidly, assisted by the establishment in 1948 of the Benelux Union. It was largely to Drees's personal credit that his policies achieved a reasonable distribution of income. His own frugality was widely known by the fact that he frequently preferred the tram to his car to take him to his office!

The mainly centre-right cabinets of the 1960s and 1970s introduced budgets that increased public spending (including national insurance) from

38.7 per cent of GNP in 1960 to 70.2 per cent in 1983. This was largely due to considerable revenues from the gas (and more recently oil) discovered in 1959 at Slochteren, which in 1985 were still worth Dfls 23,100 million. But the 1973 oil crisis that increased the value of this revenue had a far greater adverse effect, raising import prices by 35 per cent and consumer prices by 10 per cent. Moreover the gas revenues had overheated the economy by boosting the GNP and allowing wage increases that compounded the recession in 1973 by making the Netherlands less competitive and hence introducing an alarming increase in unemployment.

In the 1960s growth in GNP had been sustained at about 5 per cent per annum and, because of investment in technology and concentration into larger concerns, productivity continued to rise. But the unionized work-force, no longer content with full employment alone as it had been in the 1950s, began to demand higher and higher wages in a market where labour was in such demand that foreign workers were being brought in by the thousand. The subsequent rise in nominal wage rates set up a spiral of cost inflation. At the same time, with inflation running up to 10 per cent before the oil crisis, successive centre-right cabinets (and one centre-left) launched welfare programmes introducing widows' and orphans' pensions, child allowances, supplementary benefits and disability pensions, as well as an increase in the minimum wage.

To counter this, the government under Den Uyl's premiership (1973–7) adopted a Keynesian policy of allowing a budget deficit to rise to 3.5 per cent of GNP in 1977. This, with the subsequent increase to 8 per cent of GNP under Van Agt's administration (1977–82), accounts for the serious balance of payments crisis which Lubbers as prime minister inherited in 1982. As Den Uyl's finance minister Lubbers had already introduced the **Wet op de Investeringsregeling** (WIR), (Investment Act), a truly labyrinthine piece of legislation intended to replace existing subsidies by selective incentives for particular (regional, energy-saving, milieu-friendly,etc.) investments. It was abandoned in 1988 and replaced by reductions in employers' insurance contributions and in corporation tax.

This was in keeping with the policies of Lubbers' first (centre-right) cabi-net, 1982–6, soon popularly recognized as the 'no-nonsense-cabinet', with a VVD (Volkspartij voor Vrijheid en Democratie – free market, conservative) minister of economic affairs and CDA (Christian Democratic Appeal, a fusion of the Protestant and Catholic parties) ministers in the posts of Finance and Social Services. His three-point programme of deregulation and privatization was aimed at restoring investment and economic growth, reducing unemployment, redistributing labour, and maintaining price lev-els. To achieve this, drastic steps were needed to cut back on government spending and lower the budget deficit by reducing the wage base and employment in the public services sector. A reduction of 4.4 per cent in the former and cutbacks of some 75,000 jobs in the latter achieved a decrease in the deficit of almost Dfl 29,000 million by 1986.

The election in 1986 showed the general approval of Lubbers' deflationary policy by giving his CDA party nine additional seats (to a total of fifty-four out of 150 members). The new government's policy statement began: 'The situation facing the new cabinet differs considerably from the crisis situation confronting the previous cabinet in 1982. Then there was an almost hopeless unemployment situation rising by over 10,000 per month . . . The financial deficit was approaching 11 per cent of the national income: the purchasing power of workers and recipients of social benefits plunged as a result of constantly rising taxes and national insurance contributions.'

However, an unemployment rate of 14 per cent gave no grounds for relaxation. The new programme envisaged a reduction to half a million unemployed by 1990, a further cut in the financial deficit to 5.25 per cent of GNP by 1990 with a stabilization of public expenditure. Further measures aimed at reducing the gap between gross wage costs and net income and continued promotion of (re)training, the redistribution of labour, and part-time working. The similarities with Thatcherism are obvious.

The new cabinet had scarcely held its first meeting when disaster struck. Oil prices slumped. As a consequence Ruding, the finance minister, announced that natural gas revenues would drop by at least Dfls 12,000 million, i.e. 3 per cent of GNP. To meet a shortfall in total income of about 8 per cent, Ruding budgeted to save a further Dfl 5,500 million on public expenditure and to raise an additional Dfl 7,000 million from income and corporation taxes, withdrawing depreciation and wealth tax relief, and raising VAT and the duty on oil products.

The stock market crash in 1987 proved less serious than expected. 1988 indeed showed an encouraging improvement in production (3.5 per cent) and exports rose by 8 per cent (both excluding gas and oil). Unemployment, however, remained persistently indifferent to all the reforms. In 1987 and 1988 unemployment stagnated at around 685,000. A further complication was the shortage in 1988 of highly-qualified personnel in, for instance, financial management and information technology. The Social and Economic Council and the Central Planning Office advised a reduction of 15 per cent in the minimum wage, estimated to reduce the unemployment of unskilled workers by 150,000 and produce savings of Dfl 2000 million in unemployment benefit. The Socialist and CDA parties in Parliament and the trade unions successfully resisted repeated efforts of the government to act on this advice.

Otherwise Ruding's measures were entirely successful. The budget deficit responded as planned, and in 1988 income tax was reduced, followed in 1989 by a reduction in VAT. The **Investment Act** (WIR) was also modified to cut employers' national insurance contributions and corporation tax. A more important change is envisaged in a radical reform of the taxation system. If the policy of the last government is followed after the September 1989 elections – Lubbers' second government fell in June 1989 when the VVD refused to support his proposal to cut tax relief on travelling to and from work – the present nine taxation rates will be reduced to three, at 35, 50 and 60 per cent, with a uniform base-line for direct taxation and national insurance contributions.

Nevertheless, the outward signs of prosperity in the Netherlands conceal the fact that the austerity measures of the Lubbers government's terms of office have, despite their successes, failed to master the two major problems: a huge budget deficit and high unemployment. The national debt is running at 80 per cent of GNP, unemployment has been at 14 per cent or more throughout the 1980s, and in spite of Dfl 900 million allocated to job-training schemes in the public sector, the original goal of reducing unemployment by 200,000 was put back from 1990 to 1992. The CPB forecast 585,000 jobless in 1989, though this was optimistic, and their forecast of wage increases of 2.25 per cent was threatened by union warnings of demands for 5 per cent. This must be set against the CPB's assumption of a 2 per cent growth in GNP, and a central government financing deficit of Dfl 23.5 billion, 5 per cent of GNP. The CBS predicted a growth of 2 per cent in 1989 (3 per cent in 1988), though the OECD was less sanguine about Dutch recovery, assuming a growth of 1.75 per cent.

Taxation (at 72 per cent in the top range) and national insurance premiums are among the highest in the world and will remain so even if and when taxation is restructured. Government receipts take a higher percentage of GDP than any country outside Scandinavia.

The largest opposition party, the **Partij van de Arbeid** (PvdA) (Socialist) accuses the government of underinvesting in the country's infrastructure, (and it was a related issue that brought Lubbers' second cabinet down). Despite the vast budget deficit, the (recent) government earmarked Dfls 400 million for infrastructural improvements from 1990. The PvdA also contests the cut in VAT from 20 per cent to 18.5 per cent and the reduction in corporation tax from 42 per cent to 35 per cent. It also deplores the widening gap in income distribution (echoes of Westminster!) and calls for an end to the government's eight-year freeze on minimum wage and unemployment benefit levels. The IMF will doubtlessly be following the results of the recent elections in Holland with interest!

The considerable fluctuations in the economy can be seen from the figures in Table 6.1.

Table 6.1 *Percentage changes, volume (1980 prices)*

	1989	1990	1991	1992
Private consumption	3.9	3.9	3.1	1.6
Government consumption	0.2	0.1	−1.0	−1.1
Gross fixed capital formation	4.5	5.1	0.8	−1.4
Final domestic demand	2.8	3.5	1.9	0.4
Change in stockbuilding*	1.4	0.3	0	0.1
Total domestic demand	4.3	3.9	1.9	0.6
Exports of goods and services	6.3	4.7	4.1	4.9
Imports of goods and services	5.8	5.4	3.6	3.3
Change of foreign balance*	0.5	-0.3	0.4	1.2
GDP at market prices	4.0	3.9	2.2	1.8
GDP implicit price deflator	1.5	2.9	3.1	3.2
Memorandum items				
Consumer prices1.6	1.6	2.3	3.4	3.4
Industrial production	4.4	3.5	1.7	1.1
Unemployment rate	7.4	6.5	6.1	6.4
Current balance ($ billion)	8.0	10.3	10.5	13.1

* As a percentage of GDP in the previous period.
Source: OECD

Business and the economy

Government departments rely heavily on medium- and long-term planning forecasts. This means that econometrics is a serious business in financial planning, and the primary function of the CPB is to provide the government with a macroeconomic forecast in September each year, at the time of the budget.

The economy of the Netherlands has many similarities with that of the United Kingdom. Both countries depend largely on their trade – with their colonies before the war and with Europe since, and both have industries that process raw materials into finished and semi-finished goods. Like the United Kingdom, the Netherlands is an important producer of gas and oil, though revenue from these sources is now declining because earlier revenues were boosted by substantial exports which have seriously depleted the supply.

In the 1960s and up to the middle of the 1970s the economy expanded more rapidly than the other major industrialized countries. In general, however, the economic performance in the Netherlands since 1965 bears most similarity with former West Germany's. The annual shifts in GDP are not dissimilar in both countries, the value of the Dfl (since 1971) has risen at about the same rate as the DM, and inflation rates settled down from their higher level in 1980 to the same as West Germany's in 1985 (2.6 per cent) achieving some deflation (–0.7) in 1987 against West Germany's 0.3 per cent (see also page 24). The economies of the two countries are closely related by more than their membership of the EMS since they are tradition-ally trading partners exchanging some 30 per cent of their output.

Real GDP growth increased from 1.5 per cent in 1987 to 2.75 per cent in 1988. With moderate wage increases and lower import prices, inflation 'was virtually the lowest in the OECD area'. There was an external trade surplus increase from Dfl 6 billion in 1987 to Dfl 10.5 billion (2.25 per cent of GDP) in 1988. Factory wages, which increased in the United Kingdom by 8.4 per cent in 1988, increased in the Netherlands by 1.3 per cent. Wholesale price increases of 5.2 per cent in the six months to March 1989 in the United Kingdom compare with an increase of 1.8 per cent in the Netherlands, with consumer price increases of 3.6 per cent in the same period comparing with a decrease in the Netherlands of 0.2 per cent. Unit labour costs were 7.75 per cent up in the United Kingdom in 1988 and down 0.75 per cent in the Netherlands. On the other hand, at the end of 1988 the index of West German industrial production stood at 109.2 (1985 = 100) and United Kingdom production at 111.7, whereas the Dutch achieve-ment was only 102.8 (seasonally adjusted).

The striking differences between the Netherlands and former West Germany, as we should expect from previous comments, are in govern-ment spending, with the Dutch state spending some 14 per cent more of its GNP than the West Germans in the peak year, 1983, and in 1986 still spend-ing 59.1 per cent as against 46.6 per cent of GNP in West Germany. This inevitably results in higher taxation and social security payments in the Netherlands, and it may also account for the far higher rate of unemploy-ment – in 1986 12.5 per cent as against 9 per cent in West Germany, and in 1990 running at 14 per cent with only a modest reduction to 13.8 per cent forecast (see also page 32).

With its unparalleled advantages of port facilities and an extensive rail, road, pipeline and waterway infrastructure over a flat terrain (not to men-tion a highly-integrated and efficient airport at Schiphol) transport makes a relatively important contribution to the tertiary sector, which is a major fac-tor in the Dutch economy, accounting for about 46 per cent of net domestic product at factor cost. Industry, including manufacturing, construction and the energy industries, accounts for 35 per cent. Agriculture, forestry and fishing account for just 4.5 per cent and the government sector claims the remainder. About the same number of people are employed in trade, catering, hotels and transport as are employed in industry and construction.

Services

With the vast increase in population mobility and the fact that Holland offers a modern hotel network and an attractive coastline to tourists (who know that they will hear their own (West-European) language spoken almost universally), the hotel, catering and transport sectors maintain a high employment rate. Rotterdam, handling twice as much cargo as New York and more than Antwerp, Hamburg, Le Havre and London combined, has over 300 shipping lines offering scheduled freight services to well over 1000 ports.

Schiphol, Amsterdam's airport, has sixty airlines with scheduled services to 180 cities in seventy-five countries and a freight centre handling half a million tons of goods each year. The Rhine has an inland fleet of 6000 vessels with a carrying capacity of 5 million tons. A highly developed road network carries over 40 per cent of the goods crossing European frontiers.

An extremely reliable public transport network brings most towns to within $1\frac{1}{2}$ hour's travelling time of each other, but the ubiquitous **snelweg** (motorway) entices the motorist away from the railways, producing notorious congestions at major intersections even far outside the conurbations. Without the relief provided by 4350 miles of waterways and efficient freight distribution by rail, the density of 1126 people to the square mile would throw up almost insuperable problems.

Industry

Manufacturing industry (excluding construction and public works), with some 27,000 companies, accounts for 27 per cent of net domestic product, and employs 29 per cent of the total labour in the economy. Business output rose by 2.75 per cent in 1986, although gas and oil actually declined. Its rate of growth fell to 1.5 per cent in 1986 due to shorter working hours, but recovered to 4.25 per cent in 1988, with wage levels rising by 2.5 per cent and production prices by only 0.5 per cent, so that the labour share of business income was down to 81 per cent. The league table of turnover is headed by the food, beverage and tobacco sector (dominated by Heineken's brewery and a tobacco consortium controlling 90 per cent of the market), followed by the petroleum and chemical industries, centred in the extensive refinery and storage complexes at Europoort (with a turnover of more than Dfl 10 billion), and electrical and mechanical engineering, printing, publishing and allied industries, metal products, basic metal industries, transport equipment, building materials (including earthenware, glass and glass products), and paper and paper products in descending order in the Dfl 2–10 billion range. Textiles, leather goods, rubber and plastics and wood products continue to be minor contributors, despite government attempts to stimulate growth in regional development areas (the North and East).

In 1982, however, the government transferred its programme of subsidies from the weaker sectors (notably shipbuilding) to high-technology and innovative ventures, though this new **WIR** (Investment Act) has since been abandoned. It remains to be seen whether the proposed tax reforms will do more to revitalize industry than the complex system of allowances and subsidies ever did in the past, and the reduction in 1986 of the corporation tax from 48 per cent to 43 per cent, together with the lower cost of energy, will certainly compensate for the loss of Dfl 1.8 billion in subsidies.

Dutch industry is dominated by the four multinationals – Philips, Unilever, Royal Dutch Shell and Akzo, of which Unilever is 50 per cent British owned and Shell 40 per cent. In 1980 about half of the industrial labour force was employed by these and other multinationals, 30 per cent of them in Dutch-owned concerns and 20 per cent in foreign-based firms. While the considerable growth in exports (from 32 per cent of GNP in 1950 to 51 per cent in 1986) is largely attributable to the activities of the largest companies, they must also be held responsible for the dramatic decline in internal investment. The 1970s and 1980s saw a steady increase in the flow of capital abroad: an increase of Dfl 16,500 million in investment abroad between 1974 and 1984 and in the same period a decrease of Dfl 9000 million in direct investment in the home industry – a net capital outflow of Dfl 25,000 million. So that whereas up to 1973 investments in the Netherlands from abroad roughly equalled Dutch investments abroad, the adverse ratio since then has been at least two to one. A university economist's report on this export of capital concludes: 'If we then compare domestic and foreign investment in the expansion of Dutch firms over an extended period, we discover a sorry development for domestic employment. Whereas expansion investment abroad between 1969 and 1971 only represented 16 per cent of expansion investment at home, in the period 1980 to 1983 that increased to 57 per cent. In other words there has been a landslide affecting the geographical location where Dutch concerns decided to expand.'

More than half of these investments were in EC countries, and there was also a strong flow of capital to the USA. Indeed, for some years the Netherlands was a leading foreign investor in the United States. Apart from the environmental attraction of such investment (labour supply and cost, available markets, raw materials, infrastructure, etc.), tax havens are particularly seductive for businesses paying high corporation taxes. It is estimated that of the 114 largest Dutch concerns, no less than seventy-six have a finance company in one or more tax havens. The Dutch Antilles alone list fifty such offices belonging to Dutch multinationals.

The business culture of the Netherlands also has a good track record in attracting foreign investment. The USA, for instance, has invested in the Netherlands twice the average investment in Europe as a whole. This is in no small measure due to the activities of the **Commissariaat voor de Buitenlandse Investeringen** (CBIN), (Commissariat for Foreign Investment), a department of the Ministry of Economic Affairs. It was this commissariat that took immediate advantage of the relaxation in the Taiwan law on foreign investment, attracting three Taiwan firms to the Netherlands in 1987.

Between 1979 and 1984 the turnover of foreign businesses in the Netherlands increased from Dfl 80,410 million to Dfl 125,170 million. The leading sectors for this investment are foodstuffs, chemicals and electrical engineering. More recently mergers and share-swopping deals have increased with 1992 in mind. Instances of this are the Leyland-DAF merger in 1987 and the share swop in 1988 between the Pearson publishing, banking and industrial group and the Elsevier publishing house.

Since the 1960s some 2 per cent of GNP has been spent annually on research, most of it generated by industry, and in particular by the largest concerns, the four leaders and DSM (Dutch State Mines) accounting for two thirds of R & D expenditure. The rationalization of the last three decades has often followed Taylor's theory of scientific management. As a result the organizational structure has tended more and more towards a production bureaucracy in which:

- The production line is 'scientifically' analysed by outside experts.
- The work is rationalized and more tightly structured, leaving less room for decision-making margins and flexibility on the factory floor.
- There is increased centralization of the control of the timing and sequence of operations.
- Routines and work units are the order of the day.
- The increased standardization and adherence to routines tend to accrue manpower which in turn increases labour costs.

Mining and energy

With the discovery in 1959 of a natural gas field in the northern province of Groningen (the largest proven reserves in Western Europe), the anthracite mines in Limburg (in the south east) were phased out, with consequent problems of re-employment of a large workforce. There is also some oil, providing about 23 million barrels a year, but this is dwarfed by the 75 mil-

lion cubic metres of natural gas annually produced from a source confi-
dently estimated at 1,900,000 million cubic metres in 1987, and expected to
last for some thirty years.

In the 1960s and 1970s the industrialization of the country was greatly
helped by this windfall, half of which could be exported as excessive to the
country's needs. In the early 1980s gas production accounted for about 7
per cent of GDP and contributed about 15 per cent to government tax revenue. The resultant bonanza in the development of energy-intensive production lines, and heavy government investment in welfare provision and
education, resulted in what has subsequently been recognized as the **Dutch
disease**. The symptoms were seen in the rising value of the guilder, forced
up by an increasing surplus in the balance of trade, and hence loss of competitiveness in the international market on which the Netherlands with its
small home market has to depend.

Second, as a result of higher labour productivity in the high-energy
industries, a spiral in demands for wage increases followed, labour-intensive industries saw their labour costs outstripping the economies of cheap
energy, and redundancies ensued. Since the public services were simultaneously expanding, a resultant rise in unemployment was delayed until
the more recent cutbacks in government expenditure were needed to
reduce the financial deficit.

Dutch disease was further exacerbated by the decline, and sometimes
slump, in oil and hence gas prices since the 1970s, and too late the economists realized that the gas revenues had been spent in private and public
consumption rather than on modernizing the manufacturing base of the
country. As *The Economist* stated, vast quantities of cheap energy 'became a
mixed blessing for a trading nation'.

A policy of energy conservation now means that new industrial plants
may use gas only as feedstock, not as a fuel for firing purposes. Spare storage capacity in Europoort (the area south of the Maas estuary) is being
used to build up large stocks of imported coal, and there are plans for the
extraction of coal gas. Two nuclear plants currently operate in the
Netherlands, and nuclear capacity will only be increased if safety and environmental safeguards can be guaranteed. Energy research is directed
towards providing new industrial development in specialized equipment,
measurement and control systems, transport and storage and all forms of
insulation, and energy investment as a percentage of total investment is
expected to increase considerably.

Agriculture

The agricultural sector (with fishing) employs 268,000 person-years, that
is 5.7 per cent of the total workforce. The value added to the domestic

product is 4.5 per cent of the total, and this indicates that Dutch farming is very intensive, highly capitalized, and employs a high degree of modern technology.

More than half of the agricultural product is exported. Dutch horticulture is internationally recognized for its marketing techniques and auctions, and the Dutch dominate the world export markets in cut flowers and potted plants. They are also the world's largest exporter of dairy products, yielding annually 12.5 million tonnes of milk, 270,000 tonnes of butter and 560 tonnes of cheese. It is the glasshouse growers' boast that orchids cut in the morning will regularly grace the tables of the New York Waldorf Astoria the same evening. The chitted seeds of new strains raised in their highly-developed research programmes are constantly improving the standards of greenhouse products in other countries.

Such intensive farming, sustained with the help of huge imports of feedstuffs and fertilizers, is not without its costs. A country partly below sea-level cannot afford water pollution, and the overproduction of manure and high levels of fertilizer application are testing the ingenuity of the biochemists in their efforts to deal with this. The problem is compounded by the contamination of so-called sweet-water rivers by industrial effluent produced outside the country, and by the constant struggle against salination, seepage under the dunes into the coastal lands below sea level.

Distribution of labour

With almost half of the total population of nearly 15 million living in the **Randstad**, the urban arc consisting of Amsterdam, Utrecht, Rotterdam, The Hague and the intermediate towns in the west of the country, it is obvious that serious congestion has to be remedied by government attempts to disperse industry to the less-populated regions in the north, east and southeast. This has been little more successful than similar initiatives in the United Kingdom, though there is not the same employment and cost-of-living differential in the Netherlands as there is between North and South in the United Kingdom (see page 214).

Where there is a marked difference is in the distribution of males and females in the labour market. The proportion of employed women in the Netherlands is smaller than in the surrounding countries, and is similar to that in Greece, Italy and Ireland. This suggests that religious tradition imposes some restraint, and this may have an influence. But it is also true that although the trend is now towards house purchase, the large majority of dwellings are still rented. This, even in a country with mortgage rates a fraction of those in the United Kingdom, means that there is less economic necessity for married women to contribute to the household budget.

In 1987, 36 per cent of women and 64 per cent of men were in employment, respectively 53 per cent and 9 per cent of whom were in part-time work. Women are also concentrated in a small range of occupations, almost entirely within the service sector. The divide between men and women in occupations is referred to as **beroepssegregatie** (job segregation), and this appeared to be lessening in the 1970s. But this did not in fact mean much of an improvement in the status of women, since it was brought about by the increased number of men in traditionally female occupations.

Women are paid less than men. The average wage of women was 24 per cent less than of men in 1984. This is not so much due to a lower rate for the same job as to the fact that many more women than men are doing work below the levels justified by their training and experience. A survey conducted in 1985 concluded: 'although the Act introducing equal pay for men and women has been in force for a decade, there is no mention of a reduction in the inequality between the pay of men and women on the labour market.'

Business and the law

Foreign investment is welcomed in the Netherlands, which is proud of its principle of non-discrimination. The status of a foreign-owned company is normally the same as that of a purely Dutch enterprise, apart from a few exchange control formalities. Moreover, some of the rules restricting the powers of shareholders in large enterprises have been specifically relaxed for foreign-owned firms.

Every new business entity must register with the local offices of direct taxation, indirect taxation and social security, and must be entered in the **Handelsregister** (Trade Register) of the district in which its registered address or legal domicile is located. This rule also applies to the appointment of trade agents who are authorized to conclude agreements on behalf of foreign principals. The Trade Register is kept at the municipal or regional office of the **Kamer van Koophandel** (Chamber of Commerce), of which all companies must be members and to which they pay a mandatory annual fee.

The **Hinderwet**, or Public Nuisance Act, requires that any enterprise that is likely to cause danger, damage or nuisance to its surroundings must apply for a licence from the municipal authorities. Other provisions concerning water or air pollution, as set out in the **Wet Verontreiniging Oppervlaktewateren** (Pollution of Surface Waters Act) and the **Wet Inzake de Luchtverontreiniging** (Air Pollution Act), must also be complied with if applicable.

Until 1971 the Netherlands did not have a special form of enterprise

available to a small group of associates wishing to operate with limited liability, such as the GmbH in Germany or the Sarl in France (see pages 20
and 112). The plc form had to be used by enterprises with only two or three
shareholders. As a result of company law harmonization throughout the
EC, the Netherlands introduced a private corporate form, the **Besloten
Vennootschap met beperkte aansprakelijkheid** or BV, a private company
with limited liability. Now, most small or closely held businesses, including subsidiaries of many foreign parents that do not need to raise funds
from the public, are formed as BVs. The liability of shareholders (**aandeel-
houders**) is limited to their capital subscriptions; the company is an independent legal entity that can enter into contracts and sue and be sued;
shares can be transferred (subject to certain restrictions) without affecting
the continued existence of the company, although they may not be offered
for public subscription or trading.

A BV must be organized by at least two individuals, who sign the **Akte van
oprichting,** (articles of association, usually referred to as *statuten*) before a
public notary. A **notaris** is a public official appointed by royal decree, whose
legally prescribed functions include drawing up articles of incorporation. A
founder need not be a Dutch resident or citizen. As a group, the founders
must pay in a minimum capital of Dfl 40,000 in cash or other assets. The public notary must submit a draft of the articles to the Minister of Justice to
obtain a 'declaration of no objection' (**geen bezwaar**). Since the formalities
take some time, a company is allowed to start trading on a provisional basis
before the declaration geen bezwaar is obtained, but it must signify this by
adding IO (**In Oprichting** – in formation) to the initials BV. Until completion
of the formalities and the company's registration in the Trade Register, its
directors are personally liable for its acts and obligations.

The articles, which must be in the Dutch language, set out not only the
aims and objects of the company but also its internal regulations. No separate document containing bye-laws is required.

The shareholders in a BV may be either corporate bodies or individuals,
and in general all shares may be held by foreigners. Types of share issued
are mostly similar to their counterparts in other countries. **Gewone aandelen**, ordinary shares are usual, but **preferente aandelen**, preference shares,
which may or may not have cumulative rights, may also be issued. Shares
may be divided into fractional or subshares (**onderaandelen**).

A small company need only have one **directeur** or director and no **commissaris** or supervisory director. The **raad van bestuur**, or board of directors of a larger company, is advised by the commissaris who is not an
executive, and his appointment is only compulsory for larger companies.
The **Wet op de Naamloze Vennootschappen**, the 1971 Structure of
Corporations Act, requires companies with consolidated assets of at least
Dfl 12 million and 100 or more employees to establish a **raad van commis-**

sarissen, a supervisory board, consisting of at least three supervisory directors. Its members are elected by the general meeting of shareholders to oversee the management and allow employees to have some influence in the company's affairs. Unlike smaller BVs, these large BVs must file their annual accounts and audit report in the Trade Register.,

The **Naamloze Vennootschap** or NV, the public company, is the form adopted by entities that wish to raise capital publicly, whether listed on the stock exchange or not. It corresponds to the public company or corporation form in most other countries. There is normally no restriction on the issue or transfer of an NV's shares. The regulations applicable to NVs are mostly identical to those applicable to BVs. Such difference as there is between the two was widened by the EC's second directive on company law which became effective in the Netherlands in 1981. This meant that the minimum for paid-up capital was raised from Dfl 35,000 to Dfl 100,000, that shares issued for cash must be at least 25 per cent paid up on subscription, and those issued for other consideration must be 100 per cent paid up, and the company may not purchase more than 10 per cent of its own shares.

An NV may issue both **aandelen op naam**, registered shares and **aandelen aan toonder**, bearer shares, except that shares cannot be in bearer form until fully paid up. A 1947 decree, **Beschikking Beursverkeer** (stock exchange trading order), stipulated that shares may be bought and sold only through certain banks or stockbrokers. A proposal by the board to apply for a stock exchange listing for any of its company's securities must be approved by the supervisory board, and the company's share capital must be at least Dfl 2.5 million for a listing on the stock exchange itself, or Dfl 250,000 for the over-the-counter market.

In 1971 some 35,000 NVs became BVs. Since then more than 100,000 new BVs have been established. In 1988 there were about 130,000 BVs and 1815 NVs in the Netherlands.

A **Vennootschap onder firma** (FOV, normally referred to simply as 'firma') is the usual form of commercial partnership, in which all partners are jointly and severally liable for all its debts and obligations. Partnerships are not legal entities separate from the individuals who compose them. The word **maatschappij**, literally meaning a partnership, is often adopted by professional firms, but it denotes a civil and not a commercial law entity.

A **Commanditaire Vennootschap** (CV) is a limited partnership in which the general partners are fully liable for the debts of the partnership, but there are also one or more limited partners liable only to the extent of the contributions they have made to the partnership capital. The limited partners (**commanditaire** or **stille vennoten**) can take no part in the management of the business.

All partnerships must be registered in the Trade Register. For a general partnership, a **firma-akte**, a written partnership agreement is required, but not a notarial deed. Partnership accounts do not have to be published, but partnerships with thirty-five or more employees must set up a works' council (see below).

Bijkantoren or **filialen** are branches or establishments of a parent body, in whatever form that body carries on its business, and as such, like the partnerships, have no separate legal entity.

The **coöperatieve vereniging** or cooperative is a popular institution in the Netherlands. It is legally defined as an association to promote the material interests of its members. It is a legal entity and the liability for its exploitation is borne corporately by its members. Its function falls into one of the following categories:

- Production cooperatives, e.g. building firms.
- Credit cooperatives, accumulating a reserve fund for capital expenditure as required, e.g. farmers and horticulturists.
- Purchasing cooperatives, buying in bulk for distribution to members, e.g. farming and horticulture, retail traders, consumers.
- Processing cooperatives, processing and marketing raw materials provided by their members, e.g. dairies, sugar factories.
- Marketing cooperatives, e.g. auctioneers, dairy, potato and corn farmers.
- Service cooperatives, supplying goods and services for specific needs, e.g. machinery for farmers, staff for offices.
- Housing cooperatives, e.g. housing associations.
- Mutual insurance cooperatives, large general offices and smaller specialized insurers.

Every cooperative must give some indication of its objectives, and its name must include certain initials to indicate the liability of its members: WA (unlimited liability), BA (limited liability) or UJA (no liability).

Eenmanszaak (sole trader), although a business carried out by a single individual whose liability for the settlement of debts is unlimited, may employ a large number of people (for example Ford in the United States and previously Verolme in the Netherlands).

Overheidsbedrijven (state-controlled enterprises) are increasingly acquiring the legal form of NV, in which the government is the sole shareholder, as in the Staatsdrukkerij (cf. HM Stationery Office) and PTT (Post Office), the Dutch Railways, the Nederlandsche Bank and DSM (Dutch State Mines). There are also a number of companies in which the state is a principal shareholder, such as KLM, and the Royal Dutch Foundries and Steel Mills.

Similarly, provincial and city councils own their own enterprises (e.g. Amsterdam has its own insurance office, gas and electricity boards, port industry and giro bank). The national and regional industries seem to avoid criticism by operating efficiently and cost-effectively.

Cartels and monopolies have in principle been allowed if not actually encouraged. Only abuses are controlled by the **Wet Economische Mededingen** (Economic Competition Act), resulting in hundreds of cartels in the Netherlands, and this despite the EC treaty of 1956, whose article 85 specifically forbids formations that limit competition.

Business and finance

The Nederlandsche Bank

Monetary policy is controlled by the Nederlandsche Bank, whose head office is in Amsterdam, and the Minister of Finance. The **1948 Bank Act** entrusted three tasks to the Nederlandsche Bank: 'The Bank shall regulate the value of the Dutch currency so as to further the country's prosperity and at the same time to stabilize that value as far as possible.' Second, the Bank controls the cashflow between the trading banks as well as issuing banknotes and releasing foreign currencies. Third, the bank controls credit facilities by its instructions to the trading banks.

Though since 1948 the Bank has been entirely state-owned, it still retains a considerable measure of autonomy. Its policy is to maintain as closely as possible the link between the values of the guilder and the Deutschmark. In this it has been largely successful, although the Dutch rate of inflation has been fairly consistently rather higher than the West German rate. The **Wet Toezicht Kredietwezen** (Credit Control Act) empowers the Bank to exercise considerable control over almost all the banks in the country by setting levels for their capital reserves and liquidity. It can also introduce any of three measures to control the economy: by fixing the bank rate, by purchasing or selling treasury bills or bonds, and by regulating the reserves to be held by banks against credit, or limiting the credit facilities of the banks.

In 1977 the Bank introduced credit controls, lasting until 1981, as a result of a surge in liquidity in the previous year. In the 1980s, however, the Bank recommended the minister to moderate the monetary policy, which was not controlling public spending and was indirectly adversely affecting unemployment, and this policy has since been abandoned.

The Bank is the licensing authority for foreign exchange transactions, but authorizes the commercial banks and other institutions to act as intermediaries in handling international payments. It also supervises the issue of securities on the international market through a gentleman's agreement with the other banks. In accordance with this agreement, each domestic public issue of securities of Dfl 16 million and over requires a 'declaration of no objection' from the Bank. The Bank itself does not engage in commercial business.

General banks

Banks in the Netherlands have an excellent reputation for the range and quality of their services. The four general banks, the Rabobank, ABN (Algemene Bank Nederland), Amrobank and NMB (Nederlandsche Middenstandsbank) are 'universal' in their scope, like the German banks (trading in stocks and new issues). Many have joined consortia operating from London or elsewhere. Exceptionally, the ABN has established its own branches – 249 in 44 countries throughout Europe and the world. Future trends may be marked by negotiations between the AMRO (Amsterdam–Rotterdam) Bank and the Belgian bank Société Générale for a fusion with a 10 per cent participation in each other's capital. This would make the new institution the largest Benelux bank and the sixth largest in Western Europe, even without the proposed further extension to include the French Banque de Suez.

The four leading Dutch banks rank seventh among the world's 100 largest banks, according to their assets, capital reserves and profits. They have gained from the very high level of foreign investment in the Netherlands, particularly from the USA, due to a higher rate of return on capital than in other Western European countries, with no restrictions on the repatriation of capital, profits, royalties or loan interest. Most of the $8 million of US direct investment in the Netherlands in 1984 was in the petroleum and chemicals sector, and foreign investment in the Netherlands has continued to strengthen. Investment abroad has also been high – Dfl 10,000 million in 1985 and Dfl 8000 million in 1986, much of it in the form of direct investment by the Dutch multinationals in the USA and Third World.

Forty foreign banks have established offices in the Netherlands, among them the leading institutions from North America, Europe and Japan.

Although the commercial banks have broadened their range in recent years, there is still a certain amount of specialization in that they tend to concentrate on short-term lending. However, several of them have set up their own medium-term credit subsidiaries, and have diversified into such areas as merchant banking, housing finance, leasing and factoring. Moreover, deregulation measures introduced by the government in the late 1980s will encourage penetration of the Dutch security markets from abroad. Indeed, there is already some foreign ownership of Dutch banks, such as the former Slavenburg's Bank, taken over by the French Crédit Lyonnais in 1983 as the Crédit Lyonnais Bank Nederland, which later also took over the Nederlandsche Gredietbank in 1988. Short-term bank finance is usually provided through overdraft facilities rather than by setting up bank loans or discounting bills.

Interest at very low rates is usually allowed on current accounts, although small charges are made for any special services provided. Cheques are, however, seldom used in settlement of debts because of the efficient giro system in the Netherlands.

For personal accounts, the **Postbank** (national giro) is undoubtedly the most important banking institution in the Netherlands. It has seven million account holders (almost half the population!), served by over 3000 post offices and 724 cash points. Originally a state-owned subsidiary of the postal and telegraph service, the post office savings bank, as it then was, handled 45 per cent of all transactions after the Second World War. The commercial banks, complaining of unfair competition, succeeded in pressing for legislation to cede a large part of its business accounts to them. In 1977 a fusion of the savings bank and giro service resulted in the establishment of the independent Postbank. The high street banks again objected, this time to the state control of the bank. They were supported in this by the right-wing parties, so that in 1984 legislation was passed to privatize the bank, which started operations in 1986 as a limited company, with the state as sole shareholder. The Postbank, with assets of Dfl 48 billion, is now strictly limited to the retail trade with only marginal credit facilities.

In the postal giro transfer system, or PCGD, each depositor has a numbered account and receives a book of preprinted transfer forms. Since a transfer form is not a negotiable instrument, security risks are reduced as the only consequence of loss is the non-execution of the transfer. Whenever the balance in a giro account changes, the depositor receives a new statement. No postage is required for any transaction and no charges are imposed. Accounts may be overdrawn by no more than Dfl 500. Since the depositor is also issued with non-negotiable orders, **betaalkaarten**, which can be used universally for payment or withdrawals, the flexibility and efficiency of the system have reduced the need for personal cheques and credit cards. The advantages of economies, achieved by minimizing its overheads in using post office staff at its outlets, outweigh the disadvantages of a relatively impersonal service offered by staff who are not trained bankers and cannot handle complex transactions.

Hypotheekbanken are banks dealing in long-term mortgage loans, for the construction of industrial or commercial buildings and private houses. The slide in property prices in the mid-1980s left these banks in a weaker state, with truncated assets.

Spaarbanken are savings banks whose funds are normally invested in government or similar bonds, and can provide finance for private house purchase.

The **Nationale Investeringsbank** in The Hague is an investment bank jointly owned by the state and a number of large banks, granting long-term interest-bearing loans. The **Nederlandse Participatie Maatschappij** is an offshoot of the National Investment Bank, and it provides equity capital.

Long-term loans granted by the Investment Bank are generally of Dfl 100,000 or more, for terms of about ten years. Government guarantees may be available, and regional institutions have also been set up to provide finance in special cases. Where investment in promising enterprises is stimulated by loans of Dfl 250,000 to Dfl 50 million, these may offer conversion rights into share capital.

The **Maatschappij Industriële Projecten** (the Company for Industrial Projects) is a venture capital fund with Dfl 500,000 million paid-up capital supplied by the government, major banks and institutional investors. It works independently (only two of its nine members are representatives of the government), and it can be compared to similar funds in other countries. Its principal aim is to set up high-technology companies in the Netherlands, employing the talents of local as well as foreign entrepreneurs. Its participation, which may not exceed 49 per cent of the total investment, usually amounts to more than Dfl 4 million.

There are also some twenty Private Participation Companies with a minimum capital of Dfl 1 million licensed by the Netherlands Bank to invest in small businesses.

Onderhandse leningen (debt contracts) are provided by institutions (e.g. insurance companies and pension funds) and private investors, offering loans for ten to twenty-five years. They are far more widely used than bonds or notes through the stock exchange, and the market for them (**onderhandse markt**) is used by institutional investors. They are a major source of finance in the Netherlands, and have several advantages for the borrower: quick access to funds, low issue costs and tailormade terms.

Share capital, as distinct from retained reserves, does not form as high a proportion of capital employed in the Netherlands as it does in some other countries. Loan capital is much more important. Banks rarely take up share capital as principals.

The **Wet op de Investeringsregeling**, the Investment Act of 1978, popularly known as the WIR is used to provide tax-free bonuses to encourage investment in fixed or capital assets. The bonuses are offset against tax assessments. Since 1984 the bonus rate has been set at 12.5 per cent.

Grants under the **Investment Premium Regulations** (IPR), or investment subsidies, are given to encourage investment in 'assisted areas', in addition to WIR bonuses. The assisted areas comprise the north-eastern provinces of Groningen, Friesland and Drenthe, the northern part of Overijsel, the south of the south-eastern province of Limburg and some towns and cities in the province of North Brabant.

There are also regional development corporations offering up to 49 per cent of equity holdings with one seat on the supervisory board. They are generally also able to offer a subordinate loan, guaranteed by the government at the interest rate of the capital market.

Stock markets

The official stock exchange is in Amsterdam. As the world's oldest stock exchange, it can trace its history back to the beginning of the seventeenth century. It lists about 230 Dutch companies' stocks and 320 foreign ones as well as government and other bonds. Private investors are estimated to hold nearly one-half of all listed equities, and institutional investors are less influential than in some other countries. The new-issue functions of the stock exchange are at present relatively small. Amsterdam is also the home of the first European options exchange, which began operations in 1978.

The exchange is governed by the Association of the Stock Exchange, a group of banks and other share brokers who, by law, must have their head-quarters in Amsterdam. They are the only persons who may buy or sell securities in the exchange. The Association is supervised by the Ministry of Finance.

Business and the labour market

The population of the Netherlands steadily increased during the 1980s from nearly 14 million to nearly 15 million. This increase was due to net immigration and longer life expectancy, rather than to a rise in the birth rate. Between 1980 and 1990 the age group 20–64 years will have increased by 1.1 million, while the 0–19 year age group will have decreased by 800,000 and the 65+ group will have grown by 200,00.

Immigration rose throughout the 1980s from about 8000 per annum to about 40,000 per annum. About one-third of this number came from European countries outside the EC and about one-half came from the Third World.

Although the proportion of employed women is increasing relative to males, the traditional belief that a woman's place is in the home (and there was no war industry to bring women into the factories) still affects a situation in which only just over one-third of the workforce is female. The gradual increase in the percentage of women seeking employment, together with the half million increase in the employable population in the past decade, accounts for a substantial part of the 1990 figure of 670,000 unemployed, so that the reduction in the labour demand is in real terms about 150,000. In other words, without these demographic increases, the unemployment rate would be only 2.8 per cent. It is ironic, therefore, that the population growth – a classic indicator of economic prosperity – dictates a need not just to combat the decline in the labour demand, but to create a higher level of labour intensity in order to increase the labour market. The alternative is, of course, to increase the labour market by job-sharing or by curtailing the working life/hours of those in employment. This problem is by no means confined to the Netherlands where, as we have seen, it is compounded by government overspending.

The unemployment curve (see Table 6.2) broadly follows that of most OECD countries, and is attributable to the same factors, but the high rate of immigration, and the very favourable unemployment benefits available until very recently, may have aggravated the situation. While there was no obligation on people seeking employment to accept a wage lower than that for which they were professionally qualified, with a guaranteed unemployment benefit initially of 80 per cent (now 70 per cent) of the last wage, there was no great incentive to find work, particularly when income could be supplemented by 'black' labour.

Unemployment in the Netherlands, as in other countries, hits the migrant 'guest workers' the hardest, as Table 6.3 shows.

The explanation for the discrepancies between autochthonous and immigrant unemployment lies largely in educational levels. Whereas 73 per cent of the Dutch unemployed had only some secondary education, the same applied to 87–99 per cent of the ethnic minority groups (with the exception of 'others', at 69 per cent).

Table 6.2 *Dutch unemployment rates (1989–92)*

Year	(%)
1989	7.4
1990	6.5
1991	6.1
1992	6.4

Source: OECD

The high labour costs in the 1970s had a knock-on effect in the rising unemployment in the 1980s. With wage costs per unit at twice the level of net earnings, labour costs in the Netherlands were higher than all its competitors in Japan, the USA and Europe apart from West Germany. This was exacerbated by the appreciation of the guilder, and it was only by reducing the levels of social security contributions and, until 1983, imposing wage controls, that the situation could be rectified in the 1980s, when, in 1984, Dutch labour costs were for the first time lower than its competitors.

Table 6.3 *Unemployment of ethnic minorities in absolute numbers and as percentages of the labour force as at June 1990*

	Absolute	As percentage
Indigenous Dutch people	418,925	14
Surinamese	18,319	ca. 25
Antilleans	6,787	ca. 30
Turks	28,585	ca. 38
Moroccans	19,947	ca. 45
Others (refugees, etc.)	23,163	ca. 14

Source: Ministry of Employment and Social Security

Trends in employment

With the exception of the primary sector (agriculture and fisheries), which has declined steadily since 1950, increasing its productivity with a reducing labour force, there was a steady growth in employment in the 1950s and 1960s, levelling off in the 1970s and thereafter declining, except in the government sector. In the first of three phases in the secondary sector (manufacturing), expansion (horizontal investment) was encouraged by low wages under a policy of wage control. In the 1960s a labour shortage and resultant wage demands, together with growing competition, necessitated modernization of the production process and consequent vertical investment. Investment, however, was concentrated mainly in chemicals and mining, and where output failed to match productivity, manufacturing (as for instance in textiles) ran into serious problems. In the 1970s growth in output slackened off further, investment dropped, productivity grew – more slowly – and employment levels dropped rapidly.

The service sector fared rather better. Commercial services (advertising, transport) benefited from the increase in industrial output and increasing prosperity raised the demand for recreational provision and insurance. But the retail trade was doubly hit in the 1980s, by the reduced domestic demand as a result of government economy measures and the knock-on effect of price-cutting and discount trading. In 1970 chain stores with eighty or more branches had a 35 per cent share of the market and the 'corner shop' retailer 65 per cent. Fifteen years later the situation was reversed, with multiples taking 60 per cent of the market. In the six years prior to 1984 some 170,000 jobs were lost in retailing – an annual decline of about 2.8 per cent in employment as compared with about 1 per cent in manufacturing.

The social services obviously benefited from the new social security legislation, until in the 1980s the government cut back on public spending.

The increase in the labour force from 3.9 million in 1947 to about 6 million in 1985 was mainly due to the natural increase in the population. As mentioned earlier, the relative increase in the employment of women shows in the rise in the percentage of women in employment from 27 per cent in 1947 to 34 per cent in 1985 as against a drop in male employment from 85 per cent in 1947 to 66 per cent in 1985. The particular decline since 1975 in the male employment of under-24-year-olds and over-50s is due to prolonged education in the former and early retirement in the latter (under a state scheme with compensation as part of its work-sharing legislation).

The external factors contributing to the decline in employment are well known: the oil crises, the expansion of production from the developing countries (undercutting, for instance, the clothing trade) and the massive rise in Japanese exports. But variations in the exchange value of the guilder have also affected the problem. Between 1970 and 1983 the guilder appreciated by about 40 per cent. It has been estimated that a $0.1 rise in the value of the guilder costs the Dutch economy Dfl 2 billion a year, and the appreciation of the guilder in the 1970s cost the Netherlands 10 per cent of its export total.

By 1983 the Dutch economy was clearly in crisis. There was no longer any question of economic growth, and real national output was declining. Between 1979 and 1983 more than 300,000 jobs were lost. Within five years unemployment rose to more than 800,000. Production began to recover in 1983 and in 1985 employment again showed a modest expansion.

In one respect, the Netherlands may be moving in a direction shared in the EC only by the United Kingdom. In 1980 the **Wetenschappelijke Raad voor het Regeringsbeleid** (WRR), a prestigious government advisory body or 'think tank', published a report stating that the Netherlands was in a process of 'deindustrialization'. Their reasons for this were:

- The Netherlands since the war has specialized in intermediate products (e.g. petrochemicals and steel), electrotechnical apparatus, foodstuffs and luxury goods. Capital goods scarcely figure in Dutch output.
- Dutch industry is very energy-intensive and its export is mainly EC-oriented.
- World trade is now growing in those sectors in which the Netherlands is weak.
- The output of intermediary products in the Netherlands has now levelled off.
- The 'sensitive' sectors (textiles, leather, clothing, wood, furniture) have suffered a far greater decline in the Netherlands than elsewhere.

In the event, this report has proved too pessimistic. Nevertheless, the huge foreign investments of the multinationals probably cost the Dutch labour market some 16,000 to 30,000 jobs in the decade up to 1984.

Business and trade unions

Labour relations in the Netherlands have a reasonably good record (Table 6.4).

Table 6.4 *Working days in the Netherlands lost through disputes (1987–90)*

Year	Days lost
1987	58,276
1988	8,922
1989	23,820
1990	206,717

Source: Central Statistics Office of the Netherlands, 1992

A number of factors favour stability. Coalition governments resulting from an electoral system with proportional representation reduce the polarity between right and left-wing interests, and the trade union movement broke its association with the Dutch Labour Party after the Second World War. The unions themselves are organized according to branches of industry and commerce and not by individual craft, so that there are far fewer unions than in some other countries and few demarcation disputes. Moreover, the unions historically owe their origins to confessional or ideological loyalties arising out of a vertical pluralism across social boundaries. Although this typically Dutch phenomenon of **verzuiling** (literally, pillarization) is now rapidly dissipating, its effects, as we shall see, still provide an enviable stability in legislation and hence in labour relations and social reform.

It has been said that the fragmentation of political and social organization because of the triple structures of Catholic, Calvinist and non-confessional partisanship in all aspects of Dutch life must result in frustration or ineffectual compromise. Arend Lijphart has, however, demonstrated in his *The Politics of Accommodation* that the necessity to legislate within clearly defined pluralist parameters has produced a remarkably consistent and stable form of democracy. The shift in the balance of power between one coalition government and the next will always be minimal and transitional, and there will thus be no economic or social U-turns. If this minimizes confrontation in politics, it also reduces the risk of confrontation in labour relations.

As a result of the **'ontzuiling'** ('depillarization') in recent years, the basically socialist NVV joined with the **Nederlandse Katholieke Vakvereniging** (NKV) in 1976 to form the **Federatie Nederlandsche Vakbeweging** (Federation of Dutch Trade Unions) with almost 900,000 members in 1985 (58 per cent of organized labour). Since its inauguration the FNV has provided an effective bargaining power for the shop floor. Labour is, however, far less organized in the Netherlands than in other countries. Since the closed shop is virtually unknown in the Netherlands, only 30 per cent of the labour force are in fact union members.

It is interesting to note that whereas a recent political alignment brought the two Christian parties together in the CDU, the trade union movement brought the Socialists and Catholics together, leaving the Protestant **Christelijk Nationaal Vakverbond** (CNV) on its own. In 1970 it reaffirmed its specifically confessional approach to social reforms, retaining the independence of its twelve trade unions in a federation with 300,000 members in 1985. On the other hand, the Protestant Public Servants Union did merge with the Catholic Civil Servants Union to form the **Algemeen Christelijke Federatie van Overheidspersoneel** (CFO) which has joined the CNV.

Finally two Official and Management unions merged to form the **Vakcentrale voor Middelbaar en Hoger Personeel** (MHP).

An Association of Employers, the **Verbond van Nederlandse Ondernemingen** (VNO), was formed from the fusion of two associations, one emphasizing the social and the other the economic aspects of management–worker cooperation. It has about ninety branch associations with 10,000 members or firms. A smaller association was created by the fusion of the Protestant and Catholic Employers Associations into the **Nederlands Christelijk Werkgeversverbond** (NCW) with under eighty branches, of which some 70 per cent are also members of the VNO.

Medium and small firms are represented in two federations, the **Koninklijk Nederlands Ondernemers Verbond** (KNOV) and the small splinter-group, **Nederlands Christelijk Ondenemersverbond** (NCOV), an evangelical Protestant association.

The farmers and market gardeners have (predictably) retained their separate Protestant and Catholic unions, and have a high membership of 75 per cent. Though they are thus well organized, much of their power has now fallen to the EC, whose restructuring policy is largely responsible for reducing the number of businesses by 49 per cent, with a consequent loss of 48,600 jobs.

In the last sixty years the system of negotiating wages has turned full circle. In the 1930s wage agreements made by individual firms were replaced by *Collectieve Arbeidsovereenkomsten* (CAO) (collective labour agreements) applied to the whole branch of an industry. After the Second World War, wage control became a matter of national policy in order to level upwards the wages of depressed industries and to strengthen the country's economic position by controlling labour costs. In recent years, when it was believed that wage-fixing stifled incentives in expanding employment, CAO have been replaced by local wage negotiations.

The **Stichting van de Arbeid** (Labour Council), and the **Sociaal-economische Raad** (SER, Social and Economic Council) that took over many of its functions, at one time provided a three-cornered council to maintain a balance between wages and prices, agreed by an equal representation of **kroonleden**, management and labour. Deregulation has reduced the powers of the Labour Council and the Social and Economic Council to negotiate wage agreements but they are still retained as advisory boards to the Minister of Social Affairs. They take part in the preparation of the budget, discussing such matters as unemployment, retraining and supplementary pension schemes. Since 1982 industry and government have concurred in the decentralization of wage negotiations, and the Labour Council's central plan of 1983 agreed to strive towards wage restraint, shorter working hours and increased productivity.

Ondernemingsraden (works' councils), which are a legal requirement for all firms employing thirty-five or more employees, have the right to advise on decisions that must be reported to them. In enterprises with 100 or more employees, the works' councils must be consulted on all important matters such as mergers, closures, changes of location and major reorganizations, and they have a right of veto in decisions regarding personnel.

The maximum working week is forty-eight hours, though forty hours is now normal, decreasing from an average of 40.6 in 1980 to 40.3 in 1986. Firms are now encouraged to introduce work-sharing by government subsidies offered to employers with at least 10 per cent of their workforce working part time.

Since the SER has to be consulted by the government on all important matters affecting social or economic policy, and since the central organizations of management and labour are represented on the SER, those engaged in producing the nation's income still have, despite deregulation, some influence in its management. In much of the social and labour legislation, the advice of the SER has been taken by the government.

The employers' associations stimulate scientific research in business management, provide specialist information, and run courses through their **Nederlands Instituut voor Efficiency**.

Wages, benefits and pensions

There is a statutory minimum wage for employees between twenty-three and sixty-five years, with a stepped decrease for those under twenty-three. Recent legislation (1987) provides for disability pensions, child allowances (paid to men or women) for all children under the age of eighteen (and thereafter if they are in full-time education), old-age and widow(er)'s pensions. Health insurance is provided for those below the **welstandsgrens** (income limit), and contributions are levied equally from the employer and employee. There is a mandatory holiday allowance of 8 per cent in addition to normal pay (for a minimum of twenty working days, normally extended), and a 'thirteenth month's pay' is often paid to clerical and managerial staff as a bonus at Christmas. These provisions claimed 10.8 per cent of net national income in 1963 and 22.2 per cent in 1986. The seriousness of this financial burden can be gauged from a comparison with the lower increase in taxation: from 24.8 per cent of net national income in 1963 to 29.0 per cent in 1986. It was for this reason that the severe cutbacks were introduced in 1985 to reduce the state's contribution to social security to just over 3 per cent.

The combination of social security contributions and taxation creates a 'wedge' between labour costs for the employer and net income for the employee. This means that on average a worker costs his employer twice to two-and-a-half times the take-home pay of the worker, which is a far higher ratio than among almost all foreign competitors.

Business, education, training and development

Dutch management is very well educated. The majority of managers are qualified with university or higher technical degrees and relatively few of them have 'worked their way up' on native ability. Managers are also vocationally educated, with qualifications (as in most Continental countries) in engineering, law, economics, or applied technical and business specialisms.

The orientation towards technical grounding is less marked than in former West Germany, but in the words of the Finniston report (1980), 'the engineering dimension is stronger and more readily definable in management in the Netherlands than in Britain.' Their qualifications are more substantial and technical functions (as elsewhere abroad) have a higher standing than in the United Kingdom. The technical universities in the Netherlands are more securely established and their role vis-à-vis industry is more universally recognized than are the former polytechnics in the United Kingdom. Engineers may well spill over into non-technical functions in general management.

Dutch attitudes to management fall somewhere between the American or British preference for the 'good all-rounder' eschewing tight professional labels, and the German emphasis on specialization in qualifications, recruitment and promotion.

An enquiry among Dutch managers of the qualities they sought in applicants indicated their ideal of the well-rounded man/woman. They tended to strike a balance between knowledge and analytical grasp on the one hand and social and personality factors on the other. As one manager put it: 'There is a well-trained explicit behaviour in attaining your own targets. One is always in a bargaining situation. The successful manager is always a good bargainer. A sound integrator. We say, **hij is handig**, he makes good manoeuvres, not Machiavellian, not just social integration, and certainly not just task-oriented, but handig.' So the qualities of bargaining and reconciling implicit in this word handig, suggest that management work involves judgemental rather than dogmatic qualities.

A survey carried out by the Nederlands Centrum van Directeuren and Hay Management Consultants in 1985 shows a significant rise in the number of respondents attaching importance to product innovation compared with responses in the 1982 survey. But the stolidness often attributed to the Dutch does often consist in an overconcern with details, and the business person attempting to innovate may be confronted with proceduralism and factual nit-picking. Their **degelijkheid** (solidity and reliability) also makes them very security-minded, and hence concerned with tenure and pension provisions. The Dutch have a reputation for being absolutely honourable in business. (There is no more truth in the adage 'the fault with the Dutch is giving too little and asking too much' than there is in the saying that the Scots are mean.) And if their business culture is honest, this is certainly reflected in the generosity of Dutch politics where international agencies and Third World development are supported with very substantial aid, little of which is tied.

Dutch business people are even less careerist than the Germans, and career planning or management development are almost dirty words. A top personnel executive of a Dutch multinational considers that consensus strategies for the graduate trainee are more important than leadership qualities. The danger is, of course, that the promising graduates are not moved out of a post that they are content to do well in, because they do not themselves take the necessary initiative.

Despite their pride in their egalitarianism, the Dutch do tend to recruit from the top echelons, so that the Netherlands is really not much less meritocratic than the United Kingdom is believed to be. On the other hand, Dutch business people are still surprised at the unpredictability of some of their English colleagues, and they retain an apocryphal belief that all British business deals are settled at the lunch table or on the golf course. It is, however, striking how the older generation also clings to the conviction that Churchill's spirit must survive in the British at large.

There is an unusually low mobility between companies in the Netherlands. Regionalism and confessional differences tend to discourage geographical relocation, and it is 'not done', since it implies disloyalty to the firm. In any case, the specialist nature of management qualifications makes sideways movement difficult. Finally, pension rights are not transferable and recent attempts to remedy this have so far failed. With the importance placed on pension rights, this is certainly a disincentive. Clearly this does not affect multinationals, which move personnel at will and also attract personnel from smaller companies. This means that all but the largest companies promote internally, with senior executives normally ending up on the board.

Legislation traditionally aimed at limiting the disparity in wage and salary levels has resulted in a situation in which net salaries in the Netherlands are lower than in all West-European countries, and directors are particularly hard hit by taxation and insurance premiums, though this will be ameliorated by the tax changes soon to be introduced. As a result (or cause?) there appears to be little material motivation, i.e. crudely put, it is very un-Dutch to ask for a rise. On the other hand, companies are very reluctant to fire poor performers, and who can blame them when it costs about Dfl 700,000 in severance pay to fire a manager earning Dfl 100–120,000?

Because of the resistance to inter-company mobility, the 'brain drain' has not been conspicuous in the Netherlands (except at certain times among academics), and yet there was in 1989 a shortage of professionally qualified people, particularly of engineers and marketing and computer specialists. This is entirely due to the lack of enrolment in the relevant courses in the 1970s, just before the upturn in the economy.

In the recruitment of personnel, the Dutch often use psychological and aptitude tests, not just for government posts and industry, but also for educational streaming.

Lifelong learning

The state educational and training structure is extremely diverse and comprehensive and there is practically no private education – or rather, education at the primary and secondary level is all private in the sense that it is independent, but entirely financed by the state.

There are seven universities in the Netherlands, two more in formation (at Tilburg and Maastricht) and three technical universities. They admit all students qualifying by passing the grammar school final examination, they have longer courses, larger taught lecture classes and higher drop-out rates than in the United Kingdom. The oldest technical university is at Delft and specializes in engineering and architecture. Electrical engineering and electronics are the specialisms in the foundation (1948) at Eindhoven (the home and world headquarters of Philips), and more recently a third technical university has been established at Twente. There is no 'Oxbridge' or Ivy League discrimination in Holland, though Leiden likes to remember that it is the oldest university, founded in 1574 by William the Silent as a reward for the town's heroic resistance in the Spanish Revolt. There are two further institutions with university status and awarding their own degrees: the Landbouwhogeschool at Wageningen, a university specializing in agriculture, and Nijenrode, exclusively offering management education.

Hoger Beroepsonderwijs (HBO, higher vocational training) provides an education at a slightly lower level than the universities to some 10–15 per cent of school-leavers. They can be compared with technical colleges in the United Kingdom, awarding diplomas similar to HNCs and HNDs. They specialize in one of a large number of branches, such as engineering (**Hogere Technische Scholen**, HTS), teacher training, social work and personnel management (**Sociale Akademies**), economics and commerce (**Hoger Economisch en Administratief Onderwijs**), police training, administration for civil servants (**Bestuurs Akademie**) and so on.

With the need for retraining and for 'topping up' courses for those in employment, part-time vocational courses are on the increase alongside the full-time courses, but entry qualification is a six-subject examination taken at school at seventeen. The present trend towards high unemployment rates among university graduates is causing a growing number of school-leavers qualified for university entrance to opt for vocational courses, where life is more structured and disciplined than at the universities, and where the choice is more varied; (there are thirty-four HTSs but only three technical universities, and the HTSs are sometimes more progressive than the universities).

HBO lecturers normally have practical experience as well as formal qualifications (university or HBO), though this is not a legal requirement. Practical training is included in the HBO course, with placements of about six months in the third year.

The HBO Act of 1986 put the financing of HBOs on a par with the universities, and encouraged them to engage in research. This, together with the amalgamation of colleges in the same geographical area, will enable them to compete better with the universities in their contacts with the business world.

The structure of research in the Netherlands has changed considerably since the mid-1970s. This reflects government policy, but at the same time changes in government policy reflect developments that have taken place in the world of research. Recent developments have had six policy objectives:

- Research should be geared towards the wishes of the market.
- 'Horizontal' technologies should be stimulated and developed. Examples are biotechnology and microelectronics, which can influence virtually every branch of science and many sectors of society.
- The link between fundamental and applied research should be strengthened through 'strategic' research and in other ways.
- The quality of research should be improved, and it should be given new stimulation.
- Science and technology should be better integrated into society.
- International cooperation should be increased.

The 1979 White Paper on innovation, published by the Ministry for Science Policy, played a major role in achieving this for industrial users.

Progress in this direction has also been made in the fields of energy, space, health research and the social sciences. This marked the start of an era of specifically-directed stimulation of science and technology. A research programme in biotechnology was launched in 1981 in response to the White Paper. Dutch research is now in a relatively strong international position in terms of its quality, organization, concentration on promising topics and broad industrial applicability.

In 1984 Dfl 1700 million was allocated by the government to stimulate information technology in education, research and the market sector, and to inform the public on the subject. The activities proposed in a five-year plan under this scheme are extensive, and include a project to stimulate IT research in the Netherlands, known as SPIN, which is one of several activities that will help to bridge the gap between fundamental and applied research. Allocations will be made to publicity, education, research, the private sector and the public sector in roughly the following percentages respectively: 1 per cent, 21 per cent, 13 per cent, 59 per cent, 4 per cent, so that education and the private sector will benefit most. Much of the educational allocation is being used on hardware and course programmes throughout secondary and tertiary educational establishments.

In the private sector small and medium-sized firms are the major target, where information, advice and education are particularly necessary. The further promotion of telecommunication is working towards an integrated network of a broadband system of glass fibres for the transfer of speech, data and pictures. In the country having the world's third largest output of integrated circuits (at Philips), microelectronic development is obviously also important, and part of the government's R & D budget will support research into the development of a new generation of megabit chips, now being developed jointly by Philips and Siemens.

In energy research, a joint project with France has been running since 1982. Lievense, a hydraulic engineer, has published a scheme using wind turbines and energy storage in high water reservoirs which could provide 20 per cent of Dutch electricity requirements. Feasibility studies have shown that the scheme is viable. Future programmes envisage further research in the deep-sea production of oil and gas, further development of durable energy resources (sun and wind) and new conversion techniques, such as fuel cells.

Business and the environment

No one could be more aware of their environment than the Dutch. They know that many of the windmills romantically associated with the flat countryside were built to keep the water out – with good reason, since 48 per cent of the country lies below sea level, much of this in the most highly populated areas. It is, after all, a delta country, of alluvial deposits, polder clay and sand. This accounts for the intensive dairy production on the high-yielding grasslands, but it also explains the high costs of civil engineering in the building and maintenance of opening bridges and dykes, and in pile-driving, not only for buildings but for roads and railways in the west of the country.

This also raises environmental problems of its own, since new building in the areas where it is most needed involves transporting (often by pipeline) vast quantities of sand from the Veluwe regions in the east, to provide a blanket overlay before piling and building. This affects the landscape of the rare wooded areas in the centre of the country. More spectacular, and hence better known, are the reclamation schemes and sea-defence works in the IJsselemeer or Zuiderzee and the delta of the great rivers (Scheldt, Maas and Rhine) which have produced substantial increases in agricultural land, urban development areas, and recreational facilities.

But though these works have now been completed, relieving the huge public finances needed for them, the 'overheads' of sustaining an economy in such a geographical location will always remain high.

Problems of environmental pollution have been with the Dutch since long before green became a political colour. A perennial and age-long problem in the coastal areas below sea level has been the salination of farmlands due to seepage from the sea under the dunes. The universal problems of irrigation and drainage in a low-lying country whose freshwater supply comes largely from other countries, are not alleviated by the massive industrial pollution of the major rivers, specifically the Rhine and Maas. And as, for instance, in such matters as the debatable use of nuclear power stations, international claims can lead to acrimonious counterclaims and procrastination.

As far back as the early 1960s, a movement among Amsterdam students, the **provos**, conducted a jocular campaign against air pollution (by painting the tops of factory chimneys white) and against traffic congestion (by leaving unlocked white bicycles all over the city for anyone's use). Unfortunately the burgomaster's sense of humour did not rise to the occasion and the police were deployed in force. Later, when there was some pressure on the movement to enter politics, it voluntarily disbanded itself. But it certainly laid the foundation for the established political lobbying of the greens and ecologists.

The origins of the problem

Of the 41,160 square km of land mass, 7300 square km are waterways, lakes and inland seas, so that nearly 15 million Dutch people live within an area of 33,860 square km – a population density of 440 persons per square km. About 6.5 million people live in the conurbation known as the **Randstad**, a horseshoe-shaped crescent in the west of the country including Amsterdam, The Hague, Rotterdam and Utrecht. The concentration of petrochemical refineries to the west of Rotterdam has, of course, provided particularly serious problems in a highly-populated region, and the planners' well-meaning intention of placing people in high-rise flats near to their place of work proved to be a disastrous mistake when they could not open their windows in hot weather because of the fumes. But more generally the overpopulation of the western area causes, as we have seen, serious infrastructural and social congestion, resulting in a widespread claustrophobia. This is relieved by those that can afford it by the purchase of second homes in the rural provinces of the north or in the French Dordogne, and by the less affluent in the phenomenon of **bermtoerisme**, the week-end exodus of families picnicking on the grass verges of the roads leading out of the towns.

The numerous canals make traffic dispersal more difficult, and the high water table makes tunnelling for underground railway systems very costly, though Amsterdam and Rotterdam now have metro networks. Probably the most efficient and relatively extensive motorway network in Europe has offered an apparently irresistible alternative to the equally efficient electric train service and the slower, but also environmentally preferable, waterway freight service. In 1987, 234 million tons of freight were carried by road, 195.5 million tons by barge and only 5 million tons by rail.

The political response

In 1971, for the first time, political action was taken in the establishment of environmental protection within the new ministry of Public Health and the Environment, and in 1973 the Minister of Science Policy initiated a National Research Programme. Various studies were carried out which proved valuable later on: for instance, risk-perception, industrial safety and the environment, and carbon dioxide discharge. When the national programme drew to a close in 1980, the group's activities were taken over by a newly created **Council for Environmental Research and the Physical Sciences**. Although this new group received no funding, a number of projects were set up with a systems approach. In the last few years, projects have been replaced by programmes. In all this, the example of former West Germany has undoubtedly provided a model for the Dutch, and if the West German experience can be relied on, there will be an increase in employment in the environmental projects of some 70,000 to 78,000 person-years in the next decade.

The first legislation was the passing of the *1979* **Waste Substances Act** to deal with the 28 million tons of waste generated annually in the Netherlands. An amendment to this bill was passed, establishing an Indicative Multiyear Programme for Waste Substances which forms a basis for ministerial directives under the Act. This was followed in the same year by the *Chemical Waste Act*, and both were designed to replace dumping as far as possible by recycling. A comparison with other countries throughout the world shows that the Netherlands is relatively successful in the separation and reuse of waste, taking one of the two top places in the charts. No one familiar with Amsterdam would take comfort from this. In the capital of a country once renowned for its cleanliness, the canals can look like open drains.

In 1985 the three Ministries of Physical Planning and Environment, Agriculture and Fisheries and Transport and Water Management published an integrated **Environmental Programme of the Netherlands**, *1986–90*. It incorporates the programmes on waste disposal referred to above, together with subsequent policy statements on air, noise, radiation and water. This report inaugurates an 'environmental renovation' plan involving the government, firms and households over a five-year period, implemented by proposed legislation. The plan envisages three phases. In the first of these the government will target specific areas for attention, and the source causes of the pollution there. The second phase will involve the Finance Ministry in determining the financial support necessary to carry through the programme and in the third phase the target groups responsible for harming the environment will be made responsible for carrying out the renovation required in the legislation.

The total costs to be borne by central and local government, the water boards (**waterschappen**), firms and households rose from Dfl 4.3 billion in 1985 to Dfl 5.3 billion in 1990. The government's share of this cost will reduce from 30 per cent to 21 per cent, households' will remain constant at 20 per cent, traffic's contribution will increase from 3 per cent to 6 per cent, industry's will increase from 44 per cent to 45 per cent and agriculture's from 3 per cent to 6 per cent. The costs of controlling acid deposits, for instance, will rise from Dfl 210 million to Dfl 680 million, and of fertilizer discharge from Dfl 170 million to Dfl 325 million. A proposed reduction in fertilizer deposits by 75 per cent within ten years will necessitate a revolution in the means of production. Attempts are being made to develop a completely closed production for horticulture under glass, from which there would be no more emissions whatsoever. The agricultural sector is paying at least half the financial cost of staff and equipment for research. The capital cost per individual undertaking will be in the order of Dfl 100,000–200,000.

High on the list of priorities in the environmental programme are water-shortage, underwater soil pollution, carbon dioxide emissions, environmental conditions in the Third World and the quality of the indoor environment.

The problem of water shortage is in fact rather one of dehydration due to heavy demands on groundwater for agriculture and domestic use in the conurbations. This is causing an extensive reduction in the native flora and fauna in certain areas.

Pollution of the soil under the rivers means that sludge brought up during dredging operations has to be treated to avoid spreading the pollution. The surface water of the Rhine and Maas contains heavy metals, chromium, copper, cadmium, lead, arsenic and mercury, and organic compounds such as polychlorinated biphenyls, polycyclic aromatics and pesticides, and these collect in high concentrations in the bottom where the current is sluggish. It is hoped that the **Surface Waters Pollution Act** will be supported by the International Rhine Commission.

Carbon dioxide emissions and Third World environmental problems are on the Dutch agenda for government cooperation in the EC, OECD and international agencies concerned with these issues.

Air pollution in the Netherlands is attributable mainly to refineries, power stations and traffic. Oil refineries are responsible for 30 per cent of the sulphur dioxide emission (101,000 tonnes), and electricity generation for a further 29 per cent, and these will be reduced to 13 per cent and 5.3 per cent by the year 2000.

The 5,300,000 private cars travel some 140 billion passenger-kilometres per annum, emitting 1000 tonnes of lead, 175,000 tonnes of hydrocarbons and 250,000 tonnes of nitric oxide into the atmosphere every year. It is assumed that lead emissions will be eradicated by the year 2000 and that hydrocarbon and nitric oxide discharges will be reduced to 50,000 and 185,000 tonnes respectively. This is on the assumption that automobility will increase at the rate of 1 per cent per annum. EC standards of controls in new car engines came into force in 1988, but will only have a cumulative effect.

It is in conclusion worth noting that the cabinet crisis in the summer of 1989 arose over the government's policy on road usage, and even before the government fell, the Minister for Transport and Waterways resigned on the principle of environmental protection.

The response of business to the EC's single market

It is perhaps not surprising that the Dutch appear to be 'taking the single market in their stride', since it is only an extension of what has been the practice in the Benelux Union since 1948, and their export policies have been Europe-oriented since the Second World War.

The strong support for the Lubbers administration in the 1989 European elections was confirmed in the national election in September, when Lubbers' CDA party was returned with an increased majority. The other major parties lost some ground, but the two progressive parties D66 (Democracy 1966) and Groen links (an amalgamation of radicals) made some gains. The present coalition cabinet of CDA and the Socialists led by Lubbers contains many experienced ministers, and this means that the Netherlands may be expected to cope well initially with the coming challenges.

Strengths

A comparison between the exchange rates of the guilder and the Deutschmark in the ERM, shows a remarkable parity in the performance of both currencies since 1985, and a strong economy has been sustained with a low inflation rate – at 2.5 per cent in 1990 (the lowest in all the OECD countries), and 3.5 per cent in 1991.

The Netherlands Institute for Banking and Stock-trading has issued a report forecasting that since the Netherlands, the United Kingdom and Luxembourg have the most competitive tariff rates, they will be least affected by the anticipated drop in prices in the financial sector of the 1993 internal market. The exception here is the stock market, where the powerful competition and efficiency of the Dutch financial sector is believed to be

Business Cultures in Europe

able to withstand foreign competition, as it does at the moment, and even to expand its share of the market.

Although some smaller insurance companies and banks are combining operations (notably in the recent agreement between AMEV – the General Society for the Exploitation of Insurance Companies – and the Verenigde Spaarbank – the United Savings Bank), the indications are that the larger insurance companies will remain independent of the commercial banks.

Regulations preventing mergers between banks and insurance companies are indeed being reviewed, and although such a merger between a large bank and a large insurance office would command a powerful strategic position in a small country, short-term gains might be offset by losses since at present the larger banks and insurance houses do a great deal of business with each other.

One of the conclusions of this report states: '. . . the relatively advanced international activity of the Dutch banks stands them in good stead for further expansion in the EC. Their size is also relatively favourable in terms of the size of the Dutch economy. They are, however, somewhat vulnerable in their market value which is lower than their visible intrinsic value. As national fiscal authorities have to yield their controls over bank mergers to a European fiscal authority in the future, a new situation will arise involving the possible statutory protection of banks. An answer to this problem may lie in cross-holdings, such as the recent arrangement between the AMRO bank and the Belgian Société Générale.'

After making the economic forecasts for the government in October 1989, international political events radically affected the world economy. The sudden unification of Germany and the abrupt end to the Gulf crisis were followed by the decision by the United States administration to phase in more gradually a reduction in the Federal budget deficit.

This has resulted in higher interest rates and an intensification in economic trends, but also a slight improvement in growth prospects in the medium term and less uncertainty in the balance of payments forecast.

In the OECD countries a reduction of GNP to 1–1½ per cent in 1991 was expected to be followed by a growth to about 3 per cent annually in the period 1993–4. Annual inflation would marginally come down to 4–4½ per cent, while unemployment after rising slightly in 1991 would gradually fall to about 6 per cent of the workforce.

Overall trends in the world economy indicate a growth in world trade from 6 per cent in 1992 to 6–7 per cent in 1993–4. But the contrary trends in the German economy, on which Dutch export trade is so dependent, will result in a more modest growth in the Netherlands of 6–6½ per cent in 1993–4. With this growth, Dutch trade should be able to follow world trends without further price concessions or reductions in profit margins.

Reduction on the pressure on profit margins will mean that inflation will rise to 4 per cent in 1993–4 thereby anulling the previous Dutch trading advantage. Increased trading and the slightly improved employment situation will cause a rise in wage levels of 4¾ per cent in 1993–4, ½–¾ per cent above the cost of living index.

The sombre outlook represented in Table 6.5 reflects an international economic outlook that may or may not improve. Other factors, such as oil prices and the exchange rate of the dollar, could of course have positive and negative effects. The assumption in the forecast is that crude oil prices will rise from $20 in 1992 to $22 in 1994 and that the dollar rate will gradually rise to $1.75 in 1974.

Table 6.5 *Economic forecast 1993–94*

	(%)
Wage per employee in the company sector	5.25
Private consumption (volume)	2.5
Corporate investment	4.5
Merchandise exports (volume)	6.0
Merchandise exports excluding energy	6.5
Merchandise imports	6.0
GNP (volume)	2.5
Prices private consumption	4.0
Export prices	3.5
Export prices excluding energy	3.0
Real disposable income	0.5

Source: Central Planning Office

Weaknesses

The assumption written into the forecasts that oil prices will remain stable is challenged by the OECD which expects a drop in oil (and hence North Sea gas) prices. A loss of revenue in this area will have serious repercussions on the administration which will have to slash public expenditure further in order to reduce the budget deficit while maintaining tax cuts. The further measures promised to combat the 'black economy', due to what is taken to be widespread tax fraud, may not be simple to implement, and the further (re)training programmes that are needed will certainly require a substantial revenue.

Threats

It seems highly likely that the **1956 Economic Competition Act** will have to be reviewed in the light of the EC's own ruling, unless the Dutch can satisfy the European Court that their numerous cartels do not limit competition, at any rate outside the Netherlands.

A comment in *The Independent* in 1991, that Schiphol Airport constitutes 'a threat to Heathrow' refers to the energetic measures taken at Schiphol to survive as one of the five international airports retained in the new Europe, and to fend off the threat of foreign competition.

Opportunities

Against the threat to small and middle-sized firms of takeovers can be set the growing awareness in the Netherlands that 'work is the best means of self-fulfilment' should replace the old dictum 'work is a duty'. This means that individual enterprise and self-employment are on the increase (an increase of 45 per cent is forecast in the decade up to 1992), and the leisure and hotel industries will certainly benefit from increased tourism without necessarily being exposed to takeovers. Where large concerns in surrounding countries will certainly continue to establish themselves on Dutch soil, this will bring with it welcome investment, and will presumably continue to be part of economic planning in the Netherlands, in which Dutch companies will also themselves continue to reach out abroad. Moreover, such a high foreign investment in the Netherlands (slightly above even that in the United Kingdom and five times that in France) will shield it from additional excessive foreign competition.

The 1991 OECD report notes a marked reduction in economic growth in 1991 to about 2 per cent, due to sluggish domestic demand, though this reduced the growth of imports and encouraged a surge in exports to Germany. A modest economic growth is forecast in 1992–93, in which exports could increase substantially, due to an improvement in the share of the international market and to weak domestic demand. But GDP growth could fall to less than 2 per cent in 1992, less than half the rate of growth in 1989–90.

The Netherlands will certainly benefit from relaxed border controls in its trading of perishable goods. AHOLD is a Dutch conglomerate owning Albert Heyn, a high street supermarket and corner-shop chain throughout the country, with supermarket chains also in the USA and the United Kingdom. It has, with its further investments in the leisure industry, good reason to look forward to 1992.

The Dutch may give the impression of self-effacement in their internationalism and lack of respect for their own language and culture, but let no one be deceived by this. They secretly believe the saying, 'God made the world, but the Dutch made Holland', and if they can tame the elements, they are survivors!

References and suggestions for further reading

Blume S. S. (1985), *The Development of Dutch Science Policy in International Perspective 1965–85*, (Raad van Advies voor het Wetenschapsbeleid), The Hague: Distributiecentrum Overheidspublicaties.

Buunk, H. (1986), *De Economie in Nederland*, Groningen: Wolters-Noordhoff.

Cock Burning, A. de and Verheijen, L. (1987), *The Netherlands in Brief*, The Hague: Ministry of Foreign Affairs.

Commission of the EC (1988), *Panorama of EC Industry*, Luxembourg: Commission of the EC.

Department of Trade and Industry (1986), *Country Profile, Netherlands: Export Europe*, London: Department of Trade and Industry.

Dunnen, E. den (1985), *Instruments of Money Market and Foreign Exchange Market Policy in the Netherlands*, Dordrecht: Nijhoff.

Hartof, F. (ed) (1988), *De Sociaal-economische Besturing van Nederland*, Groningen: Wolters-Noordhoff.

Knoester, A. (1989), *Economische Politiek in Nederland*, Leiden: Stenfert Kroese.

Lawrence, P. (1991), *Management in the Netherlands*, Oxford: Clarendon Press.

Lijphart, A. (1975), *The Politics of Accommodation: Pluralism and Democracy in the Netherlands*, 2nd edn, London: University of California Press.

Ministerie van Economische Zaken (1986), *Nederlandse Industries 1985: Plaats en Ontwikkeling*, The Hague: Ministerie van Economische Zaken.

Ministry of Economic Affairs (1984), *An Investment Guide to the Netherlands*, The Hague: Ministry of Economic Affairs.

Ministry of Housing, Physical Planning and Environment/Ministry of Agriculture and Fisheries/Ministry of Transport and Water Management (1985), *Environmental Program of the Netherlands 1986–90*, The Hague: Ministry of Housing, Physical Planning and Environment/Ministry of Agriculture and Fisheries/Ministry of Transport and Water Management.

Penninx, M. J. A. (1988), *Minderheidsvorming en Emancipatie: Balans van Kennisverwerving ten aanzien van Immigranten en Woonwagenbewoners*, Alphen a. d. Rijn: Samson.

Tempel, W. J. and Dam, J. E. van (1986), *Trends in Research and Development in the Netherlands – the Influence of National Science Policy between 1973 and 1986*, The Hague: Distributiecentrum Overheidspublicaties.

Vries, J. de (1983), *De Nederlandse Economie tijdens de Twintigste Eeuw: Een Verkenning van het meest Kenmerkende*, Bussum: Fibula van Dishoeck.

Wensveen, B. M. N. van (1989), *Het Europese Bankwezen op weg naar 1992*, Amsterdam: Nederlands Instituut voor het Bank-Effectenbedrijf.

Wintle, M. J. (1988), 'The Netherlands Economy', in *Western Europe 1989*, pp. 356–65.

Wintle, M. J. (1991), 'Profile: The Netherlands' and 'Perspectives on European Integration from the Netherlands', in *European Research*, 2, part 6, pp. 6–13.

Conclusion

So, what do we conclude from reading the foregoing chapters? Perhaps the first lesson that should be learnt is that there is no such thing as a common European business culture: the six largest economies in the EC reflect as many different business cultures as they do countries. It is also more than likely that if one were to study the other six economies in the EC in the same detail, or the seven currently in the European Free Trade Association (EFTA), or even the others in central and eastern Europe, one would arrive at the same conclusion. Europe from the Atlantic to the Urals embraces a whole mosaic of different business cultures.

The EC itself will continue to enjoy a rich variety of business cultures long after 1992. Anyone who seriously thought that, with the completion of the single market at the end of 1992, business cultures would be the same throughout the EC must now be thoroughly disabused of the notion. Although convergence of economic performance among EC countries features as one of the Commission's most treasured aims for the rest of this century, convergence of business cultures is even more remote, if at all desirable. Perhaps the Commission should in fact be aiming at unification without damaging diversity because diversity can be perceived as a merit, or even a competitive advantage over the Americans or Japanese, who cannot access these cultures so readily.

Indeed, any convergence of business cultures in the EC will remain in the realms of the fanciful so long as agreement is lacking on perhaps the most fundamental question in any business culture: why are companies in business?

In just two EC countries, we see dramatically contrasting answers to this apparently simple question. In western Germany, companies are mostly in business to make surpluses and plough these back into the company in order to stay in business. Indeed, according to a former management board chairman of one of the large western German chemical companies: 'Shareholders are dumb and arrogant: they are dumb because they give me their hard-earned money with which to run my company; they are arrogant because they turn up at my AGM and try to tell me how to run my company.' In the United Kingdom, by contrast, the prevailing philosophy is that shareholders' interests should be paramount, and that as large a portion of the profits as prudent should be disbursed to them.

The repercussions of the different responses to the very question of a company's *raison d'être* are obvious: long-termism on the one hand; short-termism on the other, with all that the different approaches imply.

A further basic consideration which prevents the convergence of business cultures in the EC is the one relating to the attitude of governments to business. Here, perhaps, a three-way comparison is appropriate. In western Germany, the government attitude is encapsulated in the social market economy – as much market as possible: as much state as necessary. In France, the policy of national champions continues to be pursued, though perhaps not so overtly as in the 1970s, with the government still involved in economic planning, despite certain protestations to the contrary. In the United Kingdom, the virtues of the free market economy are extolled by Conservative governments, with even the Labour Party increasingly espousing such values.

The business culture in any country grows out of the business environment past and present, and interacts constantly with that business environment. It would, however, be idle at this stage to list all the determinants of business culture contained in the various business environments, as these have been portrayed in each of the chapters for each of the countries covered.

Perhaps the best way forward at this stage is to encourage the reader to take a step backward. He or she should now re-read the chapters on Germany, France, Italy, the United Kingdom, Spain and the Netherlands and make up his or her own mind as to what constitute the salient features of the business culture in any one of these countries and what comparisons can be made across the six.

- Do the large companies in all these countries enjoy equal opportunities for success in the EC's single market?
- Are small and medium-sized enterprises in these countries facing the same problems?
- Do manufacturing businesses obtain a similar degree of support from governmental and non-governmental institutions?
- Will service firms continue to flourish in all the countries?
- How soon will environmental consciousness begin to predominate in the other countries as it does already in Germany and the Netherlands.

By thinking about such issues, the reader will move further along the road towards cultural fluency, which is as vital for business success in Europe as fluency in European languages.

Collin Randlesome

Index